Handbook of Bioinformatics

Handbook of Bioinformatics

Edited by **Christina Marshall**

New York

Published by Callisto Reference,
106 Park Avenue, Suite 200,
New York, NY 10016, USA
www.callistoreference.com

Handbook of Bioinformatics
Edited by Christina Marshall

International Standard Book Number: 978-1-63239-373-9 (Hardback)

Printed in the United States of America.

Contents

Preface

Bioinformatics is a multidisciplinary scientific field that is focused on developing software methods and tools for storing, organizing, retrieving and analysing biological data. It is an interdisciplinary field and as such combines under its aegis statistics, computer science, engineering and mathematics to study and analyse biological data and processes. In simpler words it is the application and use of computer technology towards the management of biological information. Bioinformatics has slowly come to be an essential part of biology. In the field of genetics, genomics and even experimental molecular biology, bioinformatics techniques such as image and signal processing as well as sequencing and annotating genomes and their mutations play a large role. Even fields such as the textual mining of biological literature and the development of biological and gene ontologies utilize bioinformatics. Thus one sees that that the advancement of the scientific field of bioinformatics will aid in a lot of scientific research, especially in learning more about our own genetic heritage. The science of bioinformatics is also crucial to the use of genetic information in understanding even human diseases and in the classification of new molecular targets for drug discovery. Thus the need for skilled scientists and researchers has never been greater.

This book is an attempt to compile and collate all available research on bioinformatics under one aegis. I am grateful to those who put their hard work, effort and expertise into these researches as well as those who were supportive in this endeavour.

Editor

TOPPER: Topology Prediction of Transmembrane Protein Based on Evidential Reasoning

Xinyang Deng,[1] Qi Liu,[2,3] Yong Hu,[4] and Yong Deng[1,5]

[1] School of Computer and Information Science, Southwest University, Chongqing 400715, China
[2] School of Life Sciences and Biotechnology, Shanghai Jiao Tong University, Shanghai 200240, China
[3] Department of Biomedical Informatics, Medical Center, Vanderbilt University, Nashville, TN 37235, USA
[4] Institute of Business Intelligence and Knowledge Discovery, Guangdong University of Foreign Studies,
   Sun Yat-sen University, Guangzhou 510006, China
[5] School of Engineering, Vanderbilt University, Nashville, TN 37235, USA

Correspondence should be addressed to Yong Deng; ydeng@swu.edu.cn

Academic Editors: S. Jahandideh and M. Liu

The topology prediction of transmembrane protein is a hot research field in bioinformatics and molecular biology. It is a typical pattern recognition problem. Various prediction algorithms are developed to predict the transmembrane protein topology since the experimental techniques have been restricted by many stringent conditions. Usually, these individual prediction algorithms depend on various principles such as the hydrophobicity or charges of residues. In this paper, an evidential topology prediction method for transmembrane protein is proposed based on evidential reasoning, which is called TOPPER (topology prediction of transmembrane protein based on evidential reasoning). In the proposed method, the prediction results of multiple individual prediction algorithms can be transformed into BPAs (basic probability assignments) according to the confusion matrix. Then, the final prediction result can be obtained by the combination of each individual prediction base on Dempster's rule of combination. The experimental results show that the proposed method is superior to the individual prediction algorithms, which illustrates the effectiveness of the proposed method.

1. Introduction

According to the present genome data, roughly 20–30% of the genes in a typical organism code for α-helical transmembrane (TM) protein [1–3]. Transmembrane protein is the principal executives of the biomembrane's functions and plays many important roles in cell such as substance transportation, and energy conversion. In order to explore the structure, function, and transmembrane mechanism of transmembrane protein, the topology prediction of transmembrane protein has been a hot field in bioinformatics and molecular biology [1, 2, 4].

The topology of transmembrane protein [5], that is, the number and position of the transmembrane helixes and the in/out location of the N and C terminal of the protein sequence, is an important issue for the research of transmembrane proteins. For a protein sequence, if both transmembrane helixes and location of the N and C terminal have been predicted correctly, the topology of the protein sequence is said to be predicted correctly. Recently, information science and technology are widely used in the biology and medicine [6–8]. In essence, the topology prediction of transmembrane protein is a typical pattern recognition problem. As shown in Figure 1, given a protein sequence, the task is to determine the class label for each residue among these three classes of "i" (intracellular), "M" (transmembrane), and "o" (extracellular). At present, the most accurate methods to determine the topology of transmembrane protein are some experimental techniques, such as nuclear magnetic resonance (NMR) and X-ray crystal diffraction. However, these experimental techniques usually require strict conditions so that they cannot be applied on a large scale. They cannot meet the needs of the increasing protein sequences. Therefore, various computational methods have been developed to predict the topology of transmembrane protein [9–11].

Generally speaking, in a previous study there mainly exist three primary kinds of algorithms to predict the topology of transmembrane protein. The first kind of algorithms is on the basis of the chemical or physical properties of amino acids, for example, the hydrophobicity of residues or the charges of residues in different location. Some classical prediction algorithms are TopPred [2], and so on [12, 13]. The second kind of algorithms for the topology prediction is based on the statistical analysis on a huge amount of structure known as transmembrane proteins, such as MEMSAT [14], TMAP [10], and PRED-TMR [15]. In the third kind of algorithms, various machine learning technologies such as hidden Markov model (HMM) and support vector machine (SVM) have been introduced to the prediction of transmembrane protein topology. A series of algorithms have been developed, for example, HMMTOP [11], PHDhtm [16, 17], and so forth [18–21].

According to the mentioned above, even though there exists many algorithms for the prediction of transmembrane protein topology, however, different algorithms depend on different principles, and their applicable scopes are different. To a prediction system, if more information have been taken into consideration, the prediction ability of the system must be much more stronger. Essentially, it is a viewpoint of ensemble learning [22–25]. Using this idea to the topology prediction of transmembrane protein, various prediction algorithms have been treat as basic predictors; the task is the combination of multiple predictors to obtain a combination predictor which has a better performance than basic predictors. Within this process, there are two critical problems, that is, the representation of each predictor's prediction results and the combination method of combining multiple predictors. In regard to the representation of predictor's prediction results, as Xu et al. [23] pointed three types of output information can be utilized for different prediction algorithms, namely, the information in the abstract level, rank level, and measurement level, respectively. As to the combination method, traditional methodologies are usually on the basis of the framework of probability theory. To some degree, it is very effective, especially for the randomness. However, in the real world there are various uncertainties, not only the randomness but also the fuzziness and incompleteness, and so forth [26, 27].

As a theory of evidential reasoning under the uncertain environment, the Dempster-Shafer theory of evidence [28, 29] has an advantage of directly expressing various uncertainties and has been widely used in many fields [30–37]. It provides a general and effective framework for the representation and combination of multiple individual algorithms. In this paper, a new topology prediction method of transmembrane protein based on evidential reasoning approach, called TOPPER, has been proposed. In the proposed TOPPER method, the prediction results of basic predictor are represented by basic probability assignment (BPA) which has been constructed in terms of the confusion matrix of the predictor. Then, various basic predictors are combined by using the

Dempster's rule of combination. Finally, the topology of a transmembrane protein sequence are determined according to the combination prediction results. In this paper, an experiment demonstrates the effectiveness of the propose prediction method.

The rest of this paper is organized as follows. Section 2 introduces some basic concepts about the Dempster-Shafer theory of evidence. In Section 3 the proposed method is presented. Section 4 gives experimental verification to demonstrate the effectiveness of the proposed method. Conclusions are given in Section 5.

2. Preliminaries

In this section, a few concepts commonly in the Dempster-Shafer theory of evidence will be introduced.

The Dempster-Shafer theory of evidence [28, 29], also called the Dempster-Shafer theory or evidence theory, is used to deal with uncertain information. As an effective theory of evidential reasoning, the Dempster-Shafer theory has an advantage of directly expressing various uncertainties. This theory needs weaker conditions than the Bayesian theory of probability, so it is often regarded as an extension of the bayesian theory. For completeness of the explanation, a few basic concepts are introduced as follows.

Definition 1. Let Ω be a set of mutually exclusive and collectively exhaustive, indicted by

$$\Omega = \{E_1, E_2, \ldots, E_i, \ldots, E_N\}. \tag{1}$$

The set Ω is called frame of discernment. The power set of Ω is indicated by 2^Ω, where

$$2^\Omega = \{\varnothing, \{E_1\}, \ldots, \{E_N\}, \{E_1, E_2\}, \ldots, \{E_1, E_2, \ldots, E_i\}, \ldots, \Omega\}. \tag{2}$$

If $A \in 2^\Omega$, A is called a proposition.

Definition 2. For a frame of discernment Ω, a mass function is a mapping m from 2^Ω to $[0, 1]$, formally defined by

$$m : 2^\Omega \longrightarrow [0, 1], \tag{3}$$

which satisfies the following condition:

$$m(\varnothing) = 0, \qquad \sum_{A \in 2^\Omega} m(A) = 1. \tag{4}$$

In the Dempster-Shafer theory, a mass function is also called a basic probability assignment (BPA). If $m(A) > 0$, A is called a focal element, the union of all focal elements is called the core of the mass function.

Definition 3. For a proposition $A \subseteq \Omega$, the belief function Bel : $2^\Omega \to [0, 1]$ is defined as

$$\text{Bel}(A) = \sum_{B \subseteq A} m(B). \tag{5}$$

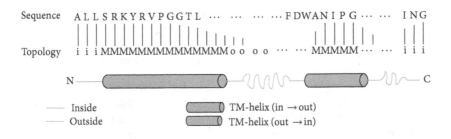

FIGURE 1: Topology prediction of transmembrane protein.

The plausibility function Pl : $2^\Omega \rightarrow [0, 1]$ is defined as

$$Pl(A) = 1 - Bel(\overline{A}) = \sum_{B \cap A \neq \varnothing} m(B), \qquad (6)$$

where $\overline{A} = \Omega - A$.

Obviously, $Pl(A) \geq Bel(A)$; these functions Bel and Pl are the lower limit function and upper limit function of proposition A, respectively.

Consider two pieces of evidence indicated by two BPAs m_1 and m_2 on the frame of discernment Ω; the Dempster's rule of combination is used to combine them. This rule assumes that these BPAs are independent.

Definition 4. The Dempster's rule of combination, also called orthogonal sum, denoted by $m = m_1 \oplus m_2$, is defined as follows:

$$m(A) = \begin{cases} \dfrac{1}{1-K} \sum_{B \cap C = A} m_1(B) m_2(C), & A \neq \varnothing; \\ 0, & A = \varnothing, \end{cases} \qquad (7)$$

with

$$K = \sum_{B \cap C = \varnothing} m_1(B) m_2(C). \qquad (8)$$

Note that the Dempster's rule of combination is only applicable to such two BPAs which satisfy the condition $K < 1$.

3. Proposed Method

In this section, a new transmembrane protein topology prediction method is proposed based on evidential reasoning. For the sake of convenience, it is briefly written down as TOPPER (Topology prediction of transmembrane protein based on evidential reasoning). The proposed prediction method TOPPER is on the basis of the combination of multiple individual prediction algorithms. In order to obtain the combination predictor, the process is presented step by step as follows.

3.1. The Selection of Basic Predictor. Because the proposed topology prediction method is the combination of multiple individual prediction methods, the basic predictors should be constructed first. Here, five individual prediction algorithms, OCTOPUS [3], PRO-TMHMM and PRODIV-TMHMM [38], SCAMPI-msa, and SCAMPI-seq [13], have been selected to construct these basic predictors. In pattern recognition, the prediction performance of each predictor is expressed by confusion matrix. In the topology prediction of transmembrane protein, since there are only three classes "i" (intracellular), "M" (transmembrane), and "o" (extracellular), the confusion matrix is formulated by

$$C_\varphi = \begin{bmatrix} n_{ii} & n_{iM} & n_{io} \\ n_{Mi} & n_{MM} & n_{Mo} \\ n_{oi} & n_{oM} & n_{oo} \end{bmatrix}, \qquad (9)$$

where each item n_{pq} is the number of residues belonging to the class p but predicted as the class q according to the basic predictor φ.

3.2. The Representation of the Basic Predictor's Prediction Results. In the combination of multiple predictors, the representation of the basic predictor's prediction results is a critical problem. In this paper, BPA is used to represent these prediction results. But the next is how to construct BPAs. For example, a residue in a protein sequence has been predicted that it belongs to transmembrane helix (i.e., class "M") by a basic predictor. However, due to that the prediction is not 100% correct, how can we represent this uncertainty. Here, a classical and effective method proposed by Xu et al. [23] has been adopted to construct BPAs. In Xu et al.'s method, the output was treated as single class labels, and the source of evidence for the propositions of interest was defined on the basis of the performance of predictors in terms of recognition, substitution, and rejection rates which are generated from confusion matrix. Briefly speaking, it is a BPA construction method based on confusion matrix.

To a predictor of transmembrane protein topology φ with confusion matrix C_φ, according to Xu et al.'s method [23], a BPA can be constructed for each class p by

$$m_P^\varphi(\{p\}) = R_c^\varphi, \quad \forall p \in \Omega,$$

$$m_P^\varphi\left(\overline{\{p\}}\right) = 1 - R_c^\varphi, \quad \forall p \in \Omega, \ \overline{\{p\}} = \dfrac{\Omega}{\{p\}}, \qquad (10)$$

with

$$R_c^\varphi = \frac{\sum_{p\in\Omega, p=q} n_{pq}}{\sum_{p\in\Omega}\sum_{q\in\Omega} n_{pq}}, \tag{11}$$

where $\Omega = \{i, M, o\}$.

For a residue in a protein sequence, the constructed BPA is m_i^φ if the prediction result shows that the residue belongs to class i. In two other situations of M and o, the constructed BPAs are m_M^φ and m_o^φ, respectively.

3.3. The Combination of Multiple Predictors.

Once all BPAs of each predictor have been constructed, the prediction results of multiple predictors can be combined. In this paper, these prediction results of basic predictors have been treated as various evidences coming from different sources. The various prediction results can be combined by using the Dempster's rule of combination, as shown in Figure 2.

Assume there are N basic predictors in the evidential prediction system, S^φ is the set of constructed BPAs for all classes from basic predictor φ, and $S^\varphi = \{m_i^\varphi, m_M^\varphi, m_o^\varphi\}$. $g(S^\varphi)$ is an operation used to obtain the matched BPA for a residue predicted by φ. The combination of multiple predictors to predict the class of residue r can be expressed by

$$m_r = g\left(S^{\varphi_1}\right) \bigoplus g\left(S^{\varphi_2}\right) \bigoplus \cdots \bigoplus g\left(S^{\varphi_N}\right). \tag{12}$$

3.4. The Determination of Topology.

Through the above steps, the combination prediction result has been derived for each residue in a transmembrane protein sequence. It is indicated by a BPA m_r. In order to get the final class that the residue belongs to, the BPA will be translated into a probability distribution by using the so-called pignistic probability transformation (PPT) function, proposed by Smets and Kennes in the transferable belief model (TBM) [39]. The PPT function [39] is defined as follow.

Let m be a BPA on a frame of discernment Ω, a pignistic probability transformation function $BetP_m : \Omega \rightarrow [0, 1]$ corresponding to m is

$$BetP_m(x) = \sum_{A\subseteq\Omega, x\in A} \frac{1}{|A|}\frac{m(A)}{1-m(\varnothing)}, \quad m(\varnothing) \neq 1, \tag{13}$$

where $|A|$ is the cardinality of proposition A.

By using PPT function, the BPA m_r can be translated into a probability distribution p_r. Then the class of the residue r can be determined according to the maximum value of the probability distribution p_r. At last, the topology of a transmembrane protein can be determined when the classes of all residues in the protein sequence have been determined. For each protein, the transmembrane orientation is determined by the location of the first residue, and each transmembrane region whose length exceeds a threshold consists of these residues labelled as class "M." According to the topology, all transmembrane helixes and the orientation of each transmembrane helix can be derived.

TABLE 1: Confusion matrices of residue prediction for various algorithms.

Truth	Algorithm	Prediction		
		i	M	o
i	OCTOPUS	7655	389	839
	PRO	7574	450	859
	PRODIV	7323	442	1118
	SCAMPI-msa	7655	389	839
	SCAMPI-seq	7359	455	1069
	TOPPER	7636	358	889
M	OCTOPUS	1877	9785	1458
	PRO	1922	9588	1610
	PRODIV	1819	9884	1417
	SCAMPI-msa	1877	9785	1458
	SCAMPI-seq	1907	9628	1585
	TOPPER	1799	9817	1504
o	OCTOPUS	1230	578	6091
	PRO	1051	714	6134
	PRODIV	1117	775	6007
	SCAMPI-msa	1230	578	6091
	SCAMPI-seq	1101	564	6234
	TOPPER	916	518	6465

4. Experimental Verification

In this paper, a data set of 125 transmembrane protein sequences with known topology is collected from the data set of MPtopo [40] to verify the effectiveness of the proposed method TOPPER.

In order to reflect the performance of combination predictor faithfully and to avoid overfitting, the experiment is performed using tenfold cross-validation. For each fold, it roughly contains 12-13 transmembrane proteins and their homology has been reduced to 30% below by using cd-hit program [41].

In order to assess the prediction performance of transmembrane regions (i.e., transmembrane helixes without considering orientation) of different algorithms, an evaluation method developed by Tusnády and Simon [11] is adopted in this paper. To a transmembrane region, the prediction is considered successful when the overlapping region of predicted and observed transmembrane region contains at least 9 amino acids. The total numbers of predicted and real observed transmembrane regions are indicated by N_{prd} and N_{obs}, respectively. The overlapping predicted and real observed transmembrane regions are indicated by N_{cor}. The efficiency of the transmembrane regions prediction is measured by $M = N_{cor}/N_{obs}$ and $C = N_{cor}/N_{prd}$. The overall prediction power is defined by

$$Q = \sqrt{M \cdot C} \times 100\%. \tag{14}$$

Besides, if all transmembrane regions and orientation of a transmembrane protein sequence have been predicted correctly, the topology of the transmembrane protein is said to be predicted correctly.

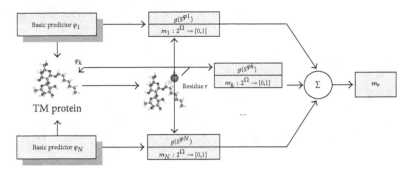

FIGURE 2: The combination of multiple predictors.

TABLE 2: Prediction performance of various algorithms in residue level.

Algorithm	Class	Recall (%)	Precision (%)	F score	Accuracy (%)
OCTOPUS	i	86.18	71.13	0.7793	
	M	74.58	91.01	0.8198	78.69
	o	77.11	72.62	0.7480	
PRO	i	85.26	71.81	0.7796	
	M	73.08	89.17	0.8033	77.91
	o	77.66	71.30	0.7434	
PRODIV	i	82.44	71.38	0.7651	
	M	75.34	89.04	0.8162	77.63
	o	76.05	70.32	0.7307	
SCAMPI-msa	i	86.18	71.13	0.7793	
	M	74.58	91.01	0.8198	78.69
	o	77.11	72.62	0.7480	
SCAMPI-seq	i	82.84	70.98	0.7646	
	M	73.38	90.43	0.8102	77.66
	o	78.92	70.14	0.7427	
TOPPER	i	85.96	73.77	0.7940	
	M	74.82	91.81	0.8245	80.00
	o	81.85	72.98	0.7716	

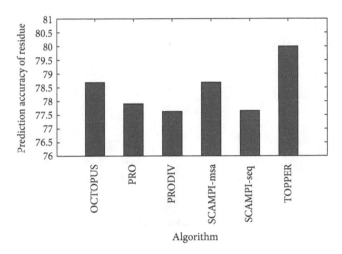

FIGURE 3: The comparison of residue's prediction accuracy between the proposed method and other algorithms.

TABLE 3: Prediction performance of various algorithms in transmembrane region level.

Algorithm	N_{obs}	N_{prd}	N_{cor}	M (%)	C (%)	Q (%)
OCTOPUS	515	512	500	97.09	97.66	97.37
PRO	515	512	498	96.70	97.27	96.98
PRODIV	515	524	503	97.67	95.99	96.83
SCAMPI-msa	515	512	500	97.09	97.66	97.37
SCAMPI-seq	515	507	494	95.92	97.44	96.68
TOPPER	515	507	500	97.09	98.62	97.85

In the rest of this section, various prediction algorithms will be compared from three aspects, namely, the prediction performance of residue level, transmembrane region level, and topology level, respectively.

In the level of residue prediction, the confusion matrix of residue prediction for each algorithm is shown in Table 1. According to these confusion matrices, Table 2 shows some indexes to measure the performance of residue prediction, including the recall rate, precision rate, F score of each class, and the prediction accuracy of residues. In TOPPER, the prediction accuracy of residue is 80.00%, while in other algorithms they are 78.69%, 77.91%, 77.63%, 78.69%, and 77.66%, respectively. The proposed method has the highest prediction accuracy of residue, shown in Figure 3. In addition, investigate the F score of each class in these algorithms. The TOPPER also has the highest value of F score no matter to class "i", "M", and "o", shown in Figure 4. Hence, it is quite clear that the proposed TOPPER outperforms other algorithms.

In the level of transmembrane region prediction, Table 3 shows the prediction performance of various algorithms to the prediction of transmembrane region. According to the overall prediction power defined in [11], the Q value of TOPPER is 97.85%, while the Q values of other algorithms are 97.37%, 96.98%, 96.83%, 97.37%, and 96.68%, respectively. The Q value of TOPPER is the highest, shown in Figure 5. So TOPPER is superior to other algorithms.

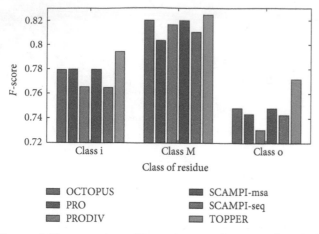

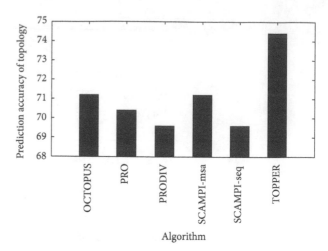

FIGURE 4: The comparison of F score between the proposed method and other algorithms.

FIGURE 6: The comparison of topology's prediction accuracy between the proposed method and other algorithms.

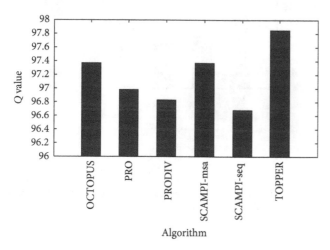

TABLE 4: Prediction performance of various algorithms in topology level.

Algorithm	Prediction accuracy of topology (%)
OCTOPUS	71.2
PRO	70.4
PRODIV	69.6
SCAMPI-msa	71.2
SCAMPI-seq	69.6
TOPPER	74.4

FIGURE 5: The comparison of transmembrane region's prediction performance between the proposed method and other algorithms.

individual prediction algorithms. In the proposed method, the Dempster-Shafer theory has been used to represent and combine the results of basic predictors. Experimental results show that the proposed method is superior to the individual prediction algorithms and demonstrates the effectiveness of the proposed method.

In the level of topology prediction, Table 4 shows the prediction accuracy of topology for each algorithm. The topology's prediction accuracy of TOPPER is 74.4%, which is the highest among these algorithms, shown in Figure 6. Therefore, the proposed TOPPER is superior to other algorithms.

According to the mentioned above, the proposed TOPPER outperforms other algorithms no matter in the level of residue prediction, transmembrane region prediction, and topology prediction. Hence, the effectiveness of the proposed method has been demonstrated.

Acknowledgments

The work is partially supported by the National Natural Science Foundation of China, Grant nos. 30400067, 61174022 and 71271061, the Chongqing Natural Science Foundation, Grant no. CSCT, 2010BA2003, the Fundamental Research Funds for the Central Universities Grant no. XDJK2010C030, and the Doctor Funding of Southwest University Grant no. SWU110021.

5. Conclusions

Transmembrane proteins are some special and important proteins in cells. The topology prediction of transmembrane protein is a foundation of the research of transmembrane proteins. In this paper, a new topology prediction method of transmembrane protein is proposed based on evidential reasoning. The proposed method is the combination of multiple

References

[1] A. Krogh, B. Larsson, G. Von Heijne, and E. L. L. Sonnhammer, "Predicting transmembrane protein topology with a hidden Markov model: application to complete genomes," *Journal of Molecular Biology*, vol. 305, no. 3, pp. 567–580, 2001.

[2] G. Von Heijne, "Membrane protein structure prediction. Hydrophobicity analysis and the positive-inside rule," *Journal of Molecular Biology*, vol. 225, no. 2, pp. 487–494, 1992.

[3] H. Viklund and A. Elofsson, "OCTOPUS: improving topology prediction by two-track ANN-based preference scores and an

extended topological grammar," *Bioinformatics*, vol. 24, no. 15, pp. 1662–1668, 2008.

[4] B. Honig, "Combining bioinformatics and biophysics to understand protein-protein and protein-ligand interactions," *The Scientific World Journal*, vol. 2, pp. 43–44, 2002.

[5] G. Von Heijne, "Membrane-protein topology," *Nature Reviews Molecular Cell Biology*, vol. 7, no. 12, pp. 909–918, 2006.

[6] L.-P. Tian, L.-Z. Liu, Q.-W. Zhang, and F.-X. Wu, "Nonlinear model-based method for clustering periodically expressed genes," *The Scientific World Journal*, vol. 11, pp. 2051–2061, 2011.

[7] A. J. Lightfoot, H. M. Rosevear, and M. A. O'Donnell, "Recognition and treatment of BCG failure in bladder cancer," *The Scientific World Journal*, vol. 11, pp. 602–613, 2011.

[8] B. Ercole and D. J. Parekh, "Methods to predict and lower the risk of prostate cancer," *The Scientific World Journal*, vol. 11, pp. 742–748, 2011.

[9] K. Melén, A. Krogh, and G. Von Heijne, "Reliability measures for membrane protein topology prediction algorithms," *Journal of Molecular Biology*, vol. 327, no. 3, pp. 735–744, 2003.

[10] B. Persson and P. Argos, "Topology prediction of membrane proteins," *Protein Science*, vol. 5, no. 2, pp. 363–371, 1996.

[11] G. E. Tusnády and I. Simon, "Principles governing amino acid composition of integral membrane proteins: application to topology prediction," *Journal of Molecular Biology*, vol. 283, no. 2, pp. 489–506, 1998.

[12] J. Kyte and R. F. Doolittle, "A simple method for displaying the hydropathic character of a protein," *Journal of Molecular Biology*, vol. 157, no. 1, pp. 105–132, 1982.

[13] A. Bernsel, H. Viklund, J. Falk, E. Lindahl, G. Von Heijne, and A. Elofsson, "Prediction of membrane-protein topology from first principles," *Proceedings of the National Academy of Sciences of the United States of America*, vol. 105, no. 20, pp. 7177–7181, 2008.

[14] D. T. Jones, W. Taylor, and J. Thornton, "A model recognition approach to the prediction of all-helical membrane protein structure and topology," *Biochemistry*, vol. 33, no. 10, pp. 3038–3049, 1994.

[15] C. Pasquier, V. J. Promponas, G. A. Palaios, J. S. Hamodrakas, and S. J. Hamodrakas, "A novel method for predicting transmembrane segments in proteins based on a statistical analysis of the SwissProt database: the PRED-TMR algorithm," *Protein Engineering*, vol. 12, no. 5, pp. 381–385, 1999.

[16] B. Rost, R. Casadio, P. Fariselli, and C. Sander, "Transmembrane helices predicted at 95% accuracy," *Protein Science*, vol. 4, no. 3, pp. 521–533, 1995.

[17] B. Rost, R. Casadio, and P. Fariselli, "Refining neural network predictions for helical transmembrane proteins by dynamic programming," *Proceedings of the International Conference on Intelligent Systems for Molecular Biology*, vol. 4, pp. 192–200, 1996.

[18] Q. Liu, Y. S. Zhu, B. H. Wang, and Y. X. Li, "A HMM-based method to predict the transmembrane regions of β-barrel membrane proteins," *Computational Biology and Chemistry*, vol. 27, no. 1, pp. 69–76, 2003.

[19] Y. Deng, Q. Liu, and Y. X. Li, "Scoring hidden Markov models to discriminate β-barrel membrane proteins," *Computational Biology and Chemistry*, vol. 28, no. 3, pp. 189–194, 2004.

[20] T. Nugent and D. T. Jones, "Transmembrane protein topology prediction using support vector machines," *BMC Bioinformatics*, vol. 26, no. 10, article 159, 2009.

[21] J. Wang, Y. Li, Q. Wang et al., "Pro- ClusEnsem: predicting membrane protein types by fusing different modes of pseudo amino acid composition," *Computers in Biology and Medicine*, vol. 42, no. 5, pp. 564–574, 2012.

[22] J. Kittler, M. Hatef, R. P. W. Duin, and J. Matas, "On combining classifiers," *IEEE Transactions on Pattern Analysis and Machine Intelligence*, vol. 20, no. 3, pp. 226–239, 1998.

[23] L. Xu, A. Krzyzak, and C. Y. Suen, "Methods of combining multiple classifiers and their applications to handwriting recognition," *IEEE Transactions on Systems, Man and Cybernetics*, vol. 22, no. 3, pp. 418–435, 1992.

[24] W. Wong, P. J. Fos, and F. E. Petry, "Combining the performance strengths of the logistic regression and neural network models: a medical outcomes approach," *The Scientific World Journal*, vol. 3, pp. 455–476, 2003.

[25] K. Kusonmano, M. Netzer, C. Baumgartner, M. Dehmer, K. R. Liedl, and A. Graber, "Effects of pooling samples on the performance of classification algorithms: a comparative study," *The Scientific World Journal*, vol. 2012, Article ID 278352, 10 pages, 2012.

[26] A. M. Barbosa and R. Real, " Applying fuzzy logic to comparative distri- bution modelling: a case study with two sympatric amphibians," *The Scientific World Journal*, vol. 2012, Article ID 428206, 10 pages, 2012.

[27] H. Al-Mubaid and S. Gungu, "A learning-based approach for biomedical word sense disambiguation," *The Scientific World Journal*, vol. 2012, Article ID 949247, 8 pages, 2012.

[28] A. P. Dempster, "Upper and lower probabilities induced by a multivalued mapping," *Annals of Mathematics and Statistics*, vol. 38, no. 2, pp. 325–339, 1967.

[29] G. Shafer, *A Mathematical Theory of Evidence*, Princeton University Press, Princeton, NJ, USA, 1976.

[30] Y. Deng, R. Sadiq, W. Jiang, and S. Tesfamariam, "Risk analysis in a linguistic environment: a fuzzy evidential reasoning-based approach," *Expert Systems with Applications*, vol. 38, no. 12, pp. 15438–15446, 2011.

[31] D. Yong, S. WenKang, Z. ZhenFu, and L. Qi, "Combining belief functions based on distance of evidence," *Decision Support Systems*, vol. 38, no. 3, pp. 489–493, 2004.

[32] Y. Deng and F. T. S. Chan, "A new fuzzy dempster MCDM method and its application in supplier selection," *Expert Systems with Applications*, vol. 38, no. 8, pp. 9854–9861, 2011.

[33] Y. Deng, F. T. S. Chan, Y. Wu, and D. Wang, "A new linguistic MCDM method based on multiple-criterion data fusion," *Expert Systems with Applications*, vol. 38, no. 6, pp. 6985–6993, 2011.

[34] Y. Deng, W. Jiang, and R. Sadiq, "Modeling contaminant intrusion in water distribution networks: a new similarity-based DST method," *Expert Systems with Applications*, vol. 38, no. 1, pp. 571–578, 2011.

[35] Y. Deng, Y. Chen, Y. Zhang, and S. Mahadevan, "Fuzzy Dijkstra algorithm for shortest path problem under uncertain environment," *Applied Soft Computing*, vol. 12, no. 3, pp. 1231–1237, 2012.

[36] Y. Zhang, X. Deng, D. Wei, and Y. Deng, "Assessment of E-Commerce security using AHP and evidential reasoning," *Expert Systems with Applications*, vol. 39, no. 3, pp. 3611–3623, 2012.

[37] B. Kang, Y. Deng, R. Sadiq, and S. Mahadevan, "Evidential cognitive maps," *Knowledge-Based Systems*, vol. 35, pp. 77–86, 2012.

[38] H. Viklund and A. Elofsson, "Best α-helical transmembrane protein topology predictions are achieved using hidden Markov models and evolutionary information," *Protein Science*, vol. 13, no. 7, pp. 1908–1917, 2004.

[39] P. Smets and R. Kennes, "The transferable belief model," *Artificial Intelligence*, vol. 66, no. 2, pp. 191–234, 1994.

[40] S. Jayasinghe, K. Hristova, and S. H. White, "MPtopo: a database of membrane protein topology," *Protein Science*, vol. 10, no. 2, pp. 455–458, 2001.

[41] W. Li and A. Godzik, "Cd-hit: a fast program for clustering and comparing large sets of protein or nucleotide sequences," *Bioinformatics*, vol. 22, no. 13, pp. 1658–1659, 2006.

Mortality Predicted Accuracy for Hepatocellular Carcinoma Patients with Hepatic Resection Using Artificial Neural Network

Herng-Chia Chiu,[1] Te-Wei Ho,[2] King-Teh Lee,[1,3] Hong-Yaw Chen,[4] and Wen-Hsien Ho[1]

[1] *Department of Healthcare Administration and Medical Informatics, Kaohsiung Medical University, 100 Shi-Chuan 1st Road, Kaohsiung 807, Taiwan*

[2] *Bureau of Health Promotion, Department of Health, No. 2 Changqing St., Xinzhuang, New Taipei City 242, Taiwan*

[3] *Department of Surgery, Kaohsiung Medical University Hospital, 100 Shi-Chuan 1st Road, Kaohsiung 807, Kaohsiung, Taiwan*

[4] *Yuan's Hospital, No. 162 Cheng Kung 1st Road, Kaohsiung 802, Kaohsiung, Taiwan*

Correspondence should be addressed to Wen-Hsien Ho; whho@kmu.edu.tw

Academic Editors: H.-W. Chang, Y.-H. Cheng, Y. Liu, and C.-H. Yang

The aim of this present study is firstly to compare significant predictors of mortality for hepatocellular carcinoma (HCC) patients undergoing resection between artificial neural network (ANN) and logistic regression (LR) models and secondly to evaluate the predictive accuracy of ANN and LR in different survival year estimation models. We constructed a prognostic model for 434 patients with 21 potential input variables by Cox regression model. Model performance was measured by numbers of significant predictors and predictive accuracy. The results indicated that ANN had double to triple numbers of significant predictors at 1-, 3-, and 5-year survival models as compared with LR models. Scores of accuracy, sensitivity, specificity, and area under the receiver operating characteristic curve (AUROC) of 1-, 3-, and 5-year survival estimation models using ANN were superior to those of LR in all the training sets and most of the validation sets. The study demonstrated that ANN not only had a great number of predictors of mortality variables but also provided accurate prediction, as compared with conventional methods. It is suggested that physicians consider using data mining methods as supplemental tools for clinical decision-making and prognostic evaluation.

1. Introduction

Hepatocellular carcinoma (HCC) is the fifth common cancer and the third leading cause of death worldwide. According to the World Health Organization (WHO) statistics in 2000, it has been estimated that there are at least 564,000 new cases of HCC per year around the world [1]. Though Asia and Africa have accounted for 80% of incidence cases of HCC for years, the incidence rates have been found to be significantly increasing in the United States [2] and some European nations [3].

Hepatic resection is one of the most effective treatments and the standard modality to achieve a long-term survival for HCC [4, 5]. However, even with progress in diagnosis and treatment, the overall mortality in HCC patients is still higher than in other types of cancer patients. The factors associated with mortality have been explored by traditional statistical methods, such as logistic regression (LR) and Cox regression [6]. Logistic analysis models hypothesize that as mean values of a given predictor variable increase, the predicted risk of the outcome increases. Despite its recognized limitations [7], LR is still widely used in clinical outcome studies.

Recently, artificial neural networks (ANNs) have proven effective for nonlinear mapping based on human knowledge [8]. Like a network of brain neurons, an ANN containing multiple layers of simple computing nodes can accurately approximate continuous nonlinear functions and can reveal previously unknown relationships between given input and output variables [8–10]. The unique structure of ANNs is well suited for machine learning methods such as back-propagation [11] and evolutionary algorithms [8, 12, 13]. Because of their universal approximation capability, potential applications of ANNs have attracted interest in some fields [14–18]. The novel application of ANN in this study was in predicting postresection prognosis in HCC patients in order to enhance their clinical management by quantifying expected risks.

To our knowledge, no study has applied ANN in predicting the prognosis of HCC patients after resection. Additionally, despite the numerous comparisons of ANN and LR in the literature, no study has convincingly demonstrated which is superior in terms of predictive accuracy [19]. The objectives of the study are accordingly, firstly, to construct an ANN model and predict the input variables associated with the mortality of HCC patients undergoing resection and examine the differences in significant predictors between the ANN and LR models, and secondly, to compare the predictive accuracy of ANN and LR in different survival year estimation models.

2. Patients and Methods

The inclusion and characteristics of the study population are the same as those described in the previous report [6]. Briefly, the study population consisted of 608 consecutive patients with HCC who underwent liver resection at Kaohsiung Medical University Hospital and Yuan's Hospital in Taiwan. In this study, we first excluded patients who received or underwent the following treatments or conditions: (i) received liver resection before ($n = 20$); (ii) treatments with radiofrequency ablation ($n = 24$) and microwave ablation ($n = 15$); (iii) histopathological reports indicated benign tumor and/or nonprimary liver cancer ($n = 27$); (iv) had case history missing and/or was incomplete ($n = 34$); (v) expired within thirty days after surgery ($n = 5$); and (vi) tumor remained after resection ($n = 1$). Further, to enhance data completeness, we excluded patients with missing values in key explained variables ($n = 30$) and patient follow-up days of less than one year ($n = 18$). Finally, 434, 341, and 264 were included in 1-, 3-, and 5-year survival groups, respectively.

There were two sources of data examined and used in our study: patient clinical information and death registry data. Patients' clinical information was derived from medical charts and review by attending physician from both hospitals using a constructed questionnaire. The information included patients' demographics and hepatic biochemical parameters. The mortality data bank is established and maintained by the Statistics Office, Department of Health, Taiwan. Two datasets were merged by unique identifier. All patients were followed until death or December 31, 2008, whichever came first.

2.1. Development of the Artificial Neural Network Models.
Waikato Environment for Knowledge Analysis (WEKA) software V3.6.0 (with backpropagation algorithm) was used to construct the ANN model. This user-friendly software is compatible with Microsoft Windows and has been validated for use in developing new machine learning schemes [20].

The outcome variables in this study were death during the study period (event) and survival (no event), which were coded as 1 and 0, respectively. To minimize the effects of extreme values and to enhance the computing efficiency of the ANN model, all continuous explanatory variables were first transformed into categorical variables. The cut-off points

for these variables were based on those used in previous clinical studies [6, 21–25]. Low and high risk were coded as 0 and 1, respectively. The variables included BUN AST, α-fetoprotein, ALT, total bilirubin, and others. Other recoded items included TNM stage, a common prognostic index of cancer risk or severity, and ASA, a risk score for surgical procedures, were also recoded. The TNM stage ranges from 1 to 6, and ASA score ranges from 1 to 4. Two variables were recoded as 0 for low risk, 1 for medium risk, and 2 for high risk (Table 1). High risk was assumed to increase the probability of death (event).

Model development in this study was performed in two stages. Firstly, to enhance the calculation efficiency and prediction performance of the ANN model construct, a univariate Cox proportional hazard model was used to test variables for potential associations with survival or death. Variables with statistically significant (log-rank test) associations with survival were retained to construct the ANN model (Table 1). Of the 33 input variables, the following 21 statistically significant variables were retained for constructing ANN models: age, comorbidity, liver cirrhosis, α-Fetoprotein, AST, total bilirubin, albumin, BUN, platelet, ASA classification, Child-Pugh classification, TNM stage, tumor number, tumor size, portal vein invasion, biliary invasion, surgical procedure, postoperative complication, recurrence, and postoperative treatment. Additionally, gender was included as a control variable.

Secondly, Figure 1 shows the numbers of neurons in the input, hidden, and output layers of the ANN models of 1-, 3-, and 5-year survival. In all three models, the input layers contained 21 neurons. In the hidden layers, the numbers of neurons were optimized using training and validation data in a trial-and-error process to maximize predictive accuracy [26], which resulted in 13, 28, and 17 neurons in the 1-, 3-, and 5-year models, respectively. The output layer in all models contained only one neuron, which represented survival status.

Studies suggest that an ROC plot should present the trade-off between sensitivity and specificity for all possible cut-offs [27]. The SPSS Windows version 6.1 software used for model building in this study automatically generated 110 possible cut-offs for each of the 1-, 3-, and 5-year models. For each of the three models, the authors then selected the best cut-off in terms of accuracy, sensitivity, and specificity.

2.2. Training Groups and Validation Groups.
The 1-, 3-, and 5-year survival data were randomly divided into training sets and validation sets. The training data set was used to develop the model whereas the validation data set was used to assess its predictive accuracy [28]. In accordance with the literature, 80% of the data were used for training, and the remaining 20% were used for validation [29, 30]. In the 1-year survival group, for example, data for 347 and 87 patients were used for training and for validation, respectively. Data validation is needed to avoid overtraining an ANN to recognize specific subjects in the training data rather than learning general predictive values. Additionally, χ^2 and Fisher's exact test analysis were performed to compare the effects of each

TABLE 1: Potential input variables and output variable for prognostic models.

Variables	Value	P value
Input variable:		
Demographic		
Age (years)*	0: ≦65, 1: >65 (mean = 57.7)	0.04
Gender	0: male, 1: female	0.37
Clinical features		
Comorbidity*	0: no, 1: yes	0.04
Liver cirrhosis*	0: no, 1: yes	<0.001
Chronic hepatitis	0: no, 1: HBV, 2: HCV, 3: HBCV	0.68, 0.12, 0.48
α-Fetoprotein (ng/mL)*	0: ≦100, 1: >100	<0.001
AST (U/L)*	0: ≦80, 1: >80	<0.001
ALT (U/L)	0: ≦80, 1: >80	0.07
Total bilirubin (mg/dL)*	0: ≦1.0, 1: >1.0	0.01
Albumin (g/dL)*	0: >3.5, 1: ≦3.5	<0.001
BUN (mg/dL)*	0: ≦21, 1: >21	0.01
Creatinine (mg/dL)	0: ≦1.4, 1: >1.4	0.24
Platelet ($10^3/\mu L$)*	0: >150, 1: ≦150	0.02
Prothrombin time (%)	0: ≦80, 1: >80	0.43
$ICGR_{15}$ (%)	0: ≦15, 1: >15	0.30
ASA classification*	0: ASA = 1, 1: ASA = 2, 2: ASA = 3	0.01, 0.94
Child-Pugh classification*	0: A, 1: B, C	<0.001
TNM Stage*	0: I, 1: II, 2: IIIa, IIIb, IIIc, IV	<0.001, <0.001
Tumor number*	0: single, 1: multiple	<0.001
Tumor size (cm)*	0: ≦5, 1: >5	<0.001
Portal vein invasion*	0: no, 1: yes	<0.001
Biliary invasion*	0: no, 1: yes	0.01
Surgical process and outcome		
Surgical procedure*	0: laparoscopic, 1: open surgery	0.02
Extent of resection	0: minor, 1: major	0.12
Resection margin (mm)	0: >10, 1: ≦10	0.08
Surgical time (minutes)	0: ≦180, 1: >180	0.75
Blood loss (mL)	0: ≦1000, 1: >1000	0.29
Blood transfusion	0: no, 1: yes	0.55
Blood transfusion (mL)	0: ≦1000, 1: >1000	0.07
Postoperative complication*	0: no, 1: yes	<0.001
Prognostic		
Recurrence*	0: no, 1: yes	<0.001
Preoperative treatment	0: no, 1: yes	0.08
Postoperative treatment*	0: no, 1: yes	<0.001
Output variable:		
Status	0: survival, 1: dead	

*Significant input variables.

input variable in terms of training and validation. Table 2 shows that the effects of all input variables in all three survival models did not significantly differ between training and validation, which confirmed the reliability of the data selection.

In accordance with the criteria used for performance comparisons reported in the literature, the ANN and LR models were compared in terms of overall accuracy (sum of correct predictions divided by total predictions), sensitivity, specificity, and area under the receiver operating characteristic curve (AUROC) [9, 14]. Higher scores were considered

better for validation. In the WEKA program, ANN model parameters for learning rate, momentum, and training time were set to 0.3, 0.2, and 500, respectively.

3. Results

In this section, the significant predictors were selected according to predictive error ratio (greater than one) for 1-, 3-, and 5-year survival models using ANN and LR in the order of features of demographic, clinical, surgical outcome, and

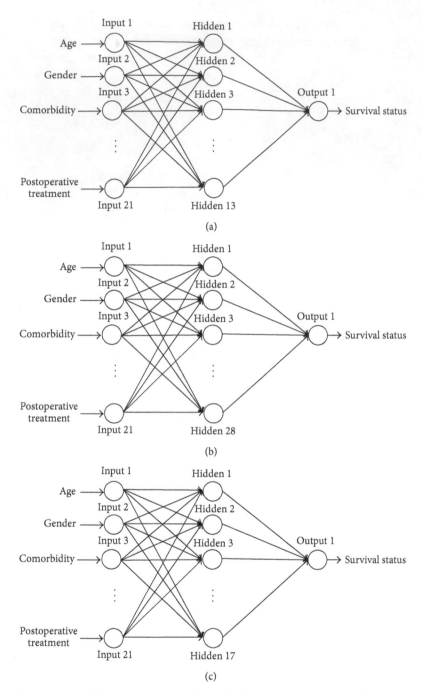

FIGURE 1: (a) Artificial neural network model for 1-year survival. (b) Artificial neural network model for 3-year survival. (c) Artificial neural network model for 5-year survival.

prognosis. Overall, ANN models had more significant input variables at 1-, 3-, and 5-year survival models than that of LR models. More specially, ANN had 15, 13, and 9 significant predictors at 1-, 3-, and 5-year survival models, whereas LR only had 8, 4, and 4 variables accordingly.

Notably, six variables in the clinical features dimension were significant predictors in all three survival models constructed by ANN: comorbidity, liver cirrhosis, α-Fetoprotein, platelet, ASA classification, and TNM stage. Among these variables, liver cirrhosis, α-Fetoprotein, and TNM stage were

significant predictors for the LR model at 1-year survival model but were consistently significant for ANN at 1-, 3-, and 5-year models.

Table 4 shows the accuracy, sensitivity, and specificity of the 1-, 3-, and 5-year survival estimation models using ANN and LR of the training groups. All three performance criteria were superior in the models using ANN to those using LR in any survival estimation models. For the 1-year survival ANN model, the accuracy was 99.1% in contrast with the 1-year survival model using LR, whose accuracy was 89.0%.

TABLE 2: Comparison of clinical features between training data and validation data.

Variables	Definitions	1-year (N = 434) Training (N = 347) N	%	Validation (N = 87) N	%	P	3-year (N = 341) Training (N = 273) N	%	Validation (N = 68) N	%	P	5-year (N = 264) Training (N = 211) N	%	Validation (N = 53) N	%	P
Age	≤65	251	72.3	62	71.3	0.842	197	72.2	53	77.9	0.335	157	74.4	37	69.8	0.498
	>65	96	27.7	25	28.7		76	27.8	15	22.1		54	25.6	16	30.2	
Gender	Male	262	75.5	68	78.2	0.604	209	76.6	54	79.4	0.616	162	76.8	38	71.7	0.440
	Female	85	24.5	19	21.8		64	23.4	14	20.6		49	23.2	15	28.3	
Comorbidity	No	170	49.0	39	44.8	0.487	144	52.7	35	51.5	0.850	112	53.1	31	58.5	0.480
	Yes	177	51.0	48	55.2		129	47.3	33	48.5		99	46.9	22	41.5	
Liver cirrhosis	No	118	34.0	30	34.5	0.933	91	33.3	19	27.9	0.395	63	29.9	11	20.8	0.187
	Yes	229	66.0	57	65.5		182	66.7	49	72.1		148	70.1	42	79.2	
α-Fetoprotein (ng/mL)	≤100	243	70.0	62	71.3	0.822	192	70.3	43	63.2	0.258	135	64.0	38	71.7	0.291
	>100	104	30.0	25	28.7		81	29.7	25	36.8		76	36.0	15	28.3	
AST	≤80	283	81.6	72	82.8	0.795	222	81.3	53	77.9	0.528	169	80.1	40	75.5	0.459
	>80	64	18.4	15	17.2		51	18.7	15	22.1		42	19.9	13	24.5	
Total bilirubin	≤1.0	255	73.5	57	65.5	0.139	200	73.3	52	76.5	0.590	152	72.0	41	77.4	0.435
	>1.0	92	26.5	30	34.5		73	26.7	16	23.5		59	28.0	12	22.6	
Albumin	>3.5	270	77.8	68	78.2	0.944	210	76.9	52	76.5	0.937	153	72.5	39	73.6	0.875
	≤3.5	77	22.2	19	21.8		63	23.1	16	23.5		58	27.5	14	26.4	
BUN	≤21	293	84.4	75	86.2	0.681	231	84.6	57	83.8	0.872	174	82.5	46	86.8	0.450
	>21	54	15.6	12	13.8		42	15.4	11	16.2		37	17.5	7	13.2	
Platelet	>150	170	49.0	48	55.2	0.303	133	48.7	36	52.9	0.533	99	46.9	23	43.4	0.646
	≤150	177	51.0	39	44.8		140	51.3	32	47.1		112	53.1	30	56.6	
ASA classification	1	87	25.1	19	21.8	0.616	75	27.5	21	30.9	0.599	63	29.9	23	43.4	0.149
	2	179	51.6	50	57.5		147	53.8	32	47.1		106	50.2	23	43.4	
	3, 4	81	23.3	18	20.7		51	18.7	15	22.1		42	19.9	7	13.2	
Child-Pugh classification	A	335	96.5	85	97.7	0.584	263	96.3	67	98.5	0.360	201	95.3	52	98.1	0.353
	B, C	12	3.5	2	2.3		10	3.7	1	1.5		10	4.7	1	1.9	
TNM stage	I	190	54.8	49	56.3	0.444	142	52.0	29	42.6	0.374	93	44.1	26	49.1	0.095
	II	119	34.3	25	28.7		95	34.8	29	42.6		86	40.8	14	26.4	
	IIIa, IIIb, IIIc, IV	38	11.0	13	14.9		36	13.2	10	14.7		32	15.2	13	24.5	
Tumor no.	Single	238	68.6	63	72.4	0.489	190	69.6	39	57.4	0.054	127	60.2	38	71.7	0.122
	Multiple	109	31.4	24	27.6		83	30.4	29	42.6		84	39.8	15	28.3	
Tumor size (cm)	≤5	268	77.2	67	77.0	0.965	204	74.7	50	73.5	0.840	154	73.0	37	69.8	0.644
	>5	79	22.8	20	23.0		69	25.3	18	26.5		57	27.0	16	30.2	
Vascular invasion	No	275	79.3	65	74.7	0.358	206	75.5	54	79.4	0.493	156	73.9	40	75.5	0.819
	Yes	72	20.7	22	25.3		67	24.5	14	20.6		55	26.1	13	24.5	
Portal vein invasion	No	335	96.5	87	100	0.079	265	97.1	66	97.1	0.996	203	96.2	51	96.2	0.995
	Yes	12	3.5	0	0.0		8	2.9	2	2.9		8	3.8	2	3.8	
Surgical procedure	Laparoscopic	69	19.9	15	17.2	0.577	51	18.7	16	23.5	0.368	51	24.2	10	18.9	0.413
	Open surgery	278	80.1	72	82.8		222	81.3	52	76.5		160	75.8	43	81.1	
Postoperative complication	No	310	89.3	78	89.7	0.931	240	87.9	59	86.8	0.797	182	86.3	45	84.9	0.800
	Yes	37	10.7	9	10.3		33	12.1	9	13.2		29	13.7	8	15.1	
Recurrence	No	158	45.5	37	42.5	0.614	115	42.1	23	33.8	0.212	71	33.6	17	32.1	0.828
	Yes	189	54.5	50	57.5		158	57.9	45	66.2		140	66.4	36	67.9	
Postoperative treatment	No	156	45.0	35	40.2	0.427	104	38.1	27	39.7	0.807	67	31.8	19	35.8	0.570
	yes	191	55.0	52	59.8		169	61.9	41	60.3		144	68.2	34	64.2	
Status	Survived	295	85	79	90.8	0.162	165	60.4	37	54.4	0.365	80	37.9	14	26.4	0.118
	Expired	52	15	8	9.2		108	39.6	31	45.6		131	62.1	39	73.6	

Sensitivity for ANN was 100% at the 5-year survival model compared to 67.5% for LR. Specificity for ANN was 96.2% at the 1-year model whereas it was 34.6% for LR.

Table 5 shows the accuracy, sensitivity, and specificity of the 1-, 3-, and 5-year survival estimation models using ANN and LR for validation groups. Although the results were mixed in scores of accuracy, sensitivity, and specificity between ANN and LR, most performance criteria were superior in the models by using ANN to those using LR in any survival models. Take the 5-year survival model, for example, the accuracy was 79.2% for ANN, whereas LR was 70.6%. LR had a relatively higher score (94.9%) in specificity measure at 1-year survival model, but poor value in specificity (25.0%). In contrast, ANN had relatively higher values at both scores in sensitivity (88.6%) and specificity (50.0%).

AUROCs for training data and validation data (Figures 2 and 3, resp.) were significantly higher in ANN models than in LR models. For training data, 1-, 3-, and 5-year survival AUROCs were 0.980, 0.989, and 0.993 in ANN models and 0.845, 0.844, and 0.847 in LR models, respectively. For validation data, the 1-, 3-, and 5-year survival AUROCs were 0.875, 0.798, and 0.810 in ANN models and 0.799, 0.783, and 0.743 in LR models, respectively.

4. Discussion

We have created models for prediction of outcome of HCC patients undergoing resection using ANN with input variables which were found to be significantly associated at univariate analysis. Clinical factors such as comorbidity, liver cirrhosis, α-Fetoprotein, platelet, ASA classification, and TNM stage were significant for 1-, 3-, and 5-year survival in ANN models as shown in Table 3. Among those, only liver cirrhosis, α-fetoprotein, and TNM stage were also found significant for LR at the 1-year prediction model. The consistently significant variables in mortality are suggested to be reviewed by clinicians to examine both short- and long-term clinical outcomes for HCC patients.

The appropriate selection of input variables is vital to the success of ANN construction. The process improves efficiency of the ANN model's appropriate complexity (by using the most predictive variables) and low redundancy. We first employed traditional statistics to select those variables statistically significant as input variables to make equal comparative analysis. The crude hazard ratio has been widely used by biostatisticians and clinicians to explore the difference between crude and adjusted hazard ratio.

Our study found that ANN had double to triple numbers of significant predictors at 1-, 3-, and 5-year survival models as compared with LR models. A previous study also found such a gap between models derived from ANN and traditional statistical methods [17]. The reason for the difference might be owing to the fact that models derived from logistic regression usually employ variables that are statistically significant predictors of the outcome, and ANN utilizes all possible interactions between all input variables and the outcome, regardless of their statistical significance. ANN can be developed using a number of different training

TABLE 3: Comparison of predictors for 1-, 3-, and 5-year survival using ANN and LR.

Predictive variables	1-year survival		3-year survival		5-year survival	
	ANN	LR	ANN	LR	ANN	LR
Age	◎					
Gender	◎		◎			
Comorbidity	◎		◎		◎	◎
Liver cirrhosis	◎	◎	◎		◎	
α-Fetoprotein	◎	◎	◎		◎	
AST	◎					
Total bilirubin	◎		◎			◎
Albumin		◎	◎	◎		
BUN						
Platelet	◎		◎		◎	
ASA classification	◎		◎		◎	
Child-Pugh classification	◎	◎	◎			
TNM stage	◎	◎	◎		◎	
Tumor number				◎	◎	
Tumor size			◎			
Portal vein invasion	◎			◎		◎
Biliary invasion	◎	◎				
Surgical procedure			◎		◎	
Postoperative complication	◎	◎			◎	
Recurrence	◎		◎	◎		◎
Postoperative treatment	◎					
Total	15	8	13	4	9	4

TABLE 4: Comparison of predictive models for 1-, 3-, and 5-year survival using ANN and LR: training data.

	1-year survival ($N = 347$)		3-year survival ($N = 273$)		5-year survival ($N = 211$)	
	ANN	LR	ANN	LR	ANN	LR
Accuracy	0.991	0.890	0.985	0.791	0.995	0.801
Sensitivity	0.997	0.986	0.988	0.879	1.000	0.675
Specificity	0.962	0.346	0.981	0.657	0.992	0.878

algorithms, many of which are continually being developed and may offer improved prediction accuracy. On the other hand, ANN cannot provide detailed information such as the hazard ratio, which generally provides direction and magnitude of individual variables on outcome variables.

As compared with the 1-year mortality model, numbers of predictors at both ANN and LR models decreased at 3- and 5-year survival models, though the ANN model appeared to have lower decreased rates. This suggested that relationship between input variables and survival status may be correlated

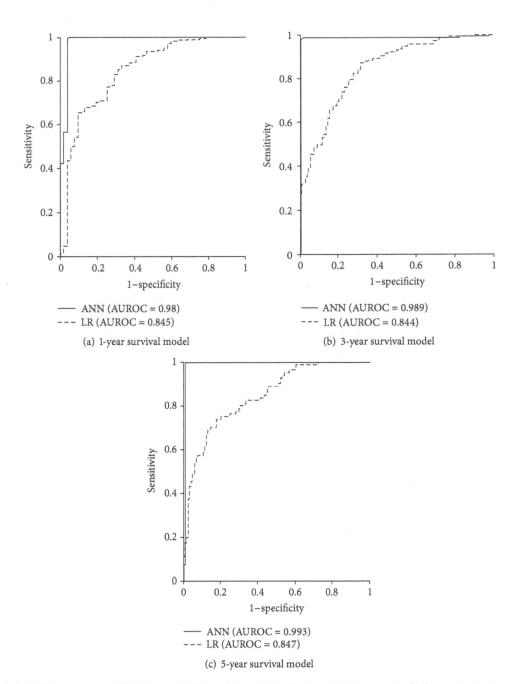

FIGURE 2: ROC curves and AUROCs for ANN and LR models of 1-, 3-, and 5-year survival when using training data.

rather than simply for the prediction of short-term outcome, and that 3- and 5-year survival status may be confounded by factors that are more complex. The change in health status over time should be examined to have better knowledge on long-term survival estimation.

In all training sets and in most validation sets, accuracy, sensitivity, specificity, and AUROC were higher in the 1-, 3-, and 5-year survival models constructed by ANN than in those constructed by LR, which is consistent with other reports that ANN outperforms LR in both training [15, 31–35] and validation [14, 36, 37].

Although the ANN models in the current study generally had higher sensitivity and specificity compared to LR models when using both training data and validation data, a notable exception was specificity when using validation data in the 1-year LR model (Table 5). Compared to the 1-year ANN model, the 1-year LR model had higher sensitivity (94.9%), higher accuracy (88.5%) but lower specificity (25.0%) when using validation data. The literature [38] suggests that specificity and sensitivity values lower than 40% should be considered poor. Sensitivity and specificity are important when testing the capability of a model to recognize positive and negative outcomes. Sensitivity and specificity must also be measured to determine the proportion of false negatives or false positives produced by a model [39]. Comparing false positive and false negative rates explains the tendency of a model

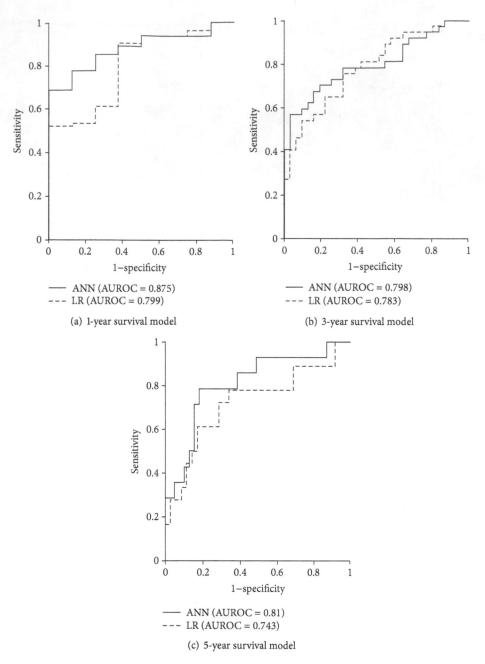

FIGURE 3: ROC curves and AUROCs for ANN and LR models of 1-, 3-, and 5-year survival when using validation data.

to misclassify positive patients as negative patients and vice versa [40]. Ideally, both sensitivity and specificity should be high [40]. According to comparisons of ANN and LR models reported in the literature as well as the experimental results in this study, ANN models have fewer prediction errors.

Although the proposed ANN-based models generally outperformed LR models in this study, the findings of this study should be interpreted cautiously. First, the WEKA program cannot be used if the ANN is constructed with numerous input variables, which can cause "insufficient computer memory" error messages. However, the number of input variables used in the present study was 21 suitable for the program used. Second, an ROC plot should be

constructed for all possible cut-offs for a clear representation of the trade-off between specificity and sensitivity. Since the cut-offs used for each of the 1-, 3-, and 5-year survival models in this study were selected by the authors from possible cut-offs generated by a statistical software package, bias could not be ruled out. Third, although previous works adopted a 20% validation group [29, 30], this study adopted 25% and 30% validation groups to detect the sample difference. Therefore, the potential treat from the sample should be noted. Fourth, since the HCC patient sample in the current study was derived from only two hospitals, the ability to generalize the findings is limited. For a stronger methodological conclusion, future studies should test external validity such

TABLE 5: Comparison of predictive models for 1-, 3- and 5-year survival using ANN and LR: validation data.

	1-year survival (N = 87)		3-year survival (N = 68)		5-year survival (N = 53)	
	ANN	LR	ANN	LR	ANN	LR
Accuracy	0.851	0.885	0.721	0.706	0.792	0.706
Sensitivity	0.886	0.949	0.730	0.757	0.714	0.613
Specificity	0.500	0.250	0.710	0.645	0.821	0.763

as by analyzing hepatic resection outcomes in HCC patients treated in different medical institutions.

5. Conclusions

In conclusion, survival estimation models at 1-, 3-, and 5-year intervals for HCC patients undergoing hepatic resection could be constructed by ANN, a data mining method as compared with conventional logistic regression. Arguably more significant predictors of mortality were identified by ANN at 1-, 3-, and 5-year models as compared with LR. The values in accuracy, sensitivity, specificity, and AUROC of ANN models were generally higher than those of LR models.

The study supported previous studies that ANN had better performance in prediction as compared with LR. The study suggested that ANN could become one tool for predicting clinical short- and long-term outcomes. It is suggested that physicians consider using data mining methods as a supplemental tool to make clinical decision-making and prognostic evaluation.

Acknowledgment

This work was in part supported by the National Science Council, Taiwan, under Grant nos. NSC 99-2320-B-037-026-MY2, NSC 95-2314-B-037-079-MY3 and NSC 101-2320-B-037-022.

References

[1] World Health Organization, Mortality Database, WHO Statistical Information System, December 2008, http://www.who.int/whosis.

[2] Centers for Disease Control and Prevention, "Hepatocellular carcinoma—United States, 2001–2006," Morbidity and Mortality Weekly Report, vol. 59, pp. 517–520, 2010.

[3] R. Capocaccia, M. Sant, and F. Berrino, "Hepatocellular carcinoma: trends of incidence and survival in Europe and the United States at the end of the 20th century," The American Journal of Gastroenterology, vol. 102, pp. 1661–1670, 2007.

[4] X. D. Lin and L. W. Lin, "Local injection therapy for hepatocellular carcinoma," Hepatobiliary and Pancreatic Diseases International, vol. 5, no. 1, pp. 16–21, 2006.

[5] K. Hanazaki, S. Kajikawa, N. Shimozawa et al., "Survival and recurrence after hepatic resection of 386 consecutive patients with hepatocellular carcinoma," Journal of the American College of Surgeons, vol. 191, no. 4, pp. 381–388, 2000.

[6] K. T. Lee, Y. W. Lu, S. N. Wang et al., "The effect of preoperative transarterial chemoembolization of resectable hepatocellular carcinoma on clinical and economic outcomes," Journal of Surgical Oncology, vol. 99, no. 6, pp. 343–350, 2009.

[7] I. H. Witten and E. Frank, Data Mining: Practical Machine Learning Tools and Techniques, Elsevier San Francisco, Calif, USA, 2005.

[8] J. T. Tsai, J. H. Chou, and T. K. Liu, "Tuning the structure and parameters of a neural network by using hybrid Taguchi-genetic algorithm," IEEE Transactions on Neural Networks, vol. 17, no. 1, pp. 69–80, 2006.

[9] A. Das, T. Ben-Menachem, F. T. Farooq et al., "Artificial neural network as a predictive instrument in patients with acute non-variceal upper gastrointestinal hemorrhage," Gastroenterology, vol. 134, no. 1, pp. 65–74, 2008.

[10] W. H. Ho and C. S. Chang, "Genetic-algorithm-based artificial neural network modeling for platelet transfusion requirements on acute myeloblastic leukemia patients," Expert Systems with Applications, vol. 38, no. 5, pp. 6319–6323, 2011.

[11] T. Nguyen, R. Malley, S. H. Inkelis, and N. Kuppermann, "Comparison of prediction models for adverse outcome in pediatric meningococcal disease using artificial neural network and logistic regression analyses," Journal of Clinical Epidemiology, vol. 55, no. 7, pp. 687–695, 2002.

[12] W. H. Ho, J. H. Chou, and C. Y. Guo, "Parameter identification of chaotic systems using improved differential evolution algorithm," Nonlinear Dynamics, vol. 61, no. 1-2, pp. 29–41, 2010.

[13] W. H. Ho, J. X. Chen, I. N. Lee, and H. C. Su, "An ANFIS-based model for predicting adequacy of vancomycin regimen using improved genetic algorithm," Expert Systems with Applications, vol. 38, no. 10, pp. 13050–13056, 2011.

[14] N. Tangri, D. Ansell, and D. Naimark, "Predicting technique survival in peritoneal dialysis patients: comparing artificial neural networks and logistic regression," Nephrology Dialysis Transplantation, vol. 23, no. 9, pp. 2972–2981, 2008.

[15] S. Y. Peng and S. K. Peng, "Predicting adverse outcomes of cardiac surgery with the application of artificial neural networks," Anaesthesia, vol. 63, no. 7, pp. 705–713, 2008.

[16] J. M. Luk, B. Y. Lam, N. P. Y. Lee et al., "Artificial neural networks and decision tree model analysis of liver cancer proteomes," Biochemical and Biophysical Research Communications, vol. 361, no. 1, pp. 68–73, 2007.

[17] T. Hanai, Y. Yatabe, Y. Nakayama et al., "Prognostic models in patients with non-small-cell lung cancer using artificial neural networks in comparison with logistic regression," Cancer Science, vol. 94, no. 5, pp. 473–477, 2003.

[18] P. Bassi, E. Sacco, V. De Marco, M. Aragona, and A. Volpe, "Prognostic accuracy of an artificial neural network in patients undergoing radical cystectomy for bladder cancer: a comparison with logistic regression analysis," BJU International, vol. 99, no. 5, pp. 1007–1012, 2007.

[19] D. J. Sargent, "Comparison of artificial neural networks with other statistical approaches: results from medical data sets," Cancer, vol. 91, no. 8, pp. 1636–1642, 2001.

[20] M. Hall, E. Frank, G. Holmes, B. Pfahringer, P. Reutemann, and I. H. Witten, "The WEKA data mining software: an update," SIGKDD Explorations, vol. 11, pp. 10–18, 2009.

[21] C. N. Yeh, M. F. Chen, W. C. Lee, and L. B. Jeng, "Prognostic factors of hepatic resection for hepatocellular carcinoma with cirrhosis: univariate and multivariate analysis," Journal of Surgical Oncology, vol. 81, no. 4, pp. 195–202, 2002.

[22] G. Ercolani, G. L. Grazi, M. Ravaioli et al., "Liver resection for hepatocellular carcinoma on cirrhosis: univariate and multivariate analysis of risk factors for intrahepatic recurrence," *Annals of Surgery*, vol. 237, no. 4, pp. 536–543, 2003.

[23] N. Shimozawa and K. Hanazaki, "Longterm prognosis after hepatic resection for small hepatocellular carcinoma," *Journal of the American College of Surgeons*, vol. 198, no. 3, pp. 356–365, 2004.

[24] K. H. Liau, L. Ruo, J. Shia et al., "Outcome of partial hepatectomy for large (>10 cm) hepatocellular carcinoma," *Cancer*, vol. 104, pp. 1948–1955, 2005.

[25] A. Sasaki, Y. Iwashita, K. Shibata, M. Ohta, S. Kitano, and M. Mori, "Preoperative transcatheter arterial chemoembolization reduces long-term survival rate after hepatic resection for resectable hepatocellular carcinoma," *European Journal of Surgical Oncology*, vol. 32, no. 7, pp. 773–779, 2006.

[26] C. J. Robinson, S. Swift, D. D. Johnson, and J. S. Almeida, "Prediction of pelvic organ prolapse using an artificial neural network," *American Journal of Obstetrics and Gynecology*, vol. 199, no. 2, pp. 193.e1–193.e6, 2008.

[27] P. Royston and D. G. Altman, "Visualizing and assessing discrimination in the logistic regression model," *Statistics in Medicine*, vol. 29, no. 24, pp. 2508–2520, 2010.

[28] D. G. Altman, Y. Vergouwe, P. Royston, and K. G. M. Moons, "Prognosis and prognostic research: validating a prognostic model," *BMJ*, vol. 338, no. 7708, pp. 1432–1435, 2009.

[29] A. Lo, Y. Y. Chiu, E. A. Rødland, P. C. Lyu, T. Y. Sung, and W. L. Hsu, "Predicting helix-helix interactions from residue contacts in membrane proteins," *Bioinformatics*, vol. 25, no. 8, pp. 996–1003, 2009.

[30] J. Tilmanne, J. Urbain, M. V. Kothare, A. V. Wouwer, and S. V. Kothare, "Algorithms for sleep-wake identification using actigraphy: a comparative study and new results," *Journal of Sleep Research*, vol. 18, no. 1, pp. 85–98, 2009.

[31] M. Green, J. Björk, J. Forberg, U. Ekelund, L. Edenbrandt, and M. Ohlsson, "Comparison between neural networks and multiple logistic regression to predict acute coronary syndrome in the emergency room," *Artificial Intelligence in Medicine*, vol. 38, no. 3, pp. 305–318, 2006.

[32] S. P. Lin, C. H. Lee, Y. S. Lu, and L. N. Hsu, "A comparison of MICU survival prediction using the logistic regression model and artificial neural network model," *The Journal of Nursing Research*, vol. 14, no. 4, pp. 306–314, 2006.

[33] S. Sakai, K. Kobayashi, S. I. Toyabe, N. Mandai, T. Kanda, and K. Akazawa, "Comparison of the levels of accuracy of an artificial neural network model and a logistic regression model for the diagnosis of acute appendicitis," *Journal of Medical Systems*, vol. 31, no. 5, pp. 357–364, 2007.

[34] C. H. Wang, L. R. Mo, R. C. Lin, J. J. Kuo, K. K. Chang, and J. J. Wu, "Artificial neural network model is superior to logistic regression model in predicting treatment outcomes of interferon-based combination therapy in patients with chronic hepatitis C," *Intervirology*, vol. 51, no. 1, pp. 14–20, 2008.

[35] M. Hannula, K. Huttunen, J. Koskelo, T. Laitinen, and T. Leino, "Comparison between artificial neural network and multilinear regression models in an evaluation of cognitive workload in a flight simulator," *Computers in Biology and Medicine*, vol. 38, no. 11-12, pp. 1163–1170, 2008.

[36] A. Alkan, E. Koklukaya, and A. Subasi, "Automatic seizure detection in EEG using logistic regression and artificial neural network," *Journal of Neuroscience Methods*, vol. 148, no. 2, pp. 167–176, 2005.

[37] B. Eftekhar, K. Mohammad, H. E. Ardebili, M. Ghodsi, and E. Ketabchi, "Comparison of artificial neural network and logistic regression models for prediction of mortality in head trauma based on initial clinical data," *BMC Medical Informatics and Decision Making*, vol. 5, article 3, 2005.

[38] A. Das, T. Ben-Menachem, F. T. Farooq et al., "Artificial neural network as a predictive instrument in patients with acute nonvariceal upper gastrointestinal hemorrhage," *Gastroenterology*, vol. 134, no. 1, pp. 65–74, 2008.

[39] L. Trtica-Majnaric, M. Zekic-Susac, N. Sarlija, and B. Vitale, "Prediction of influenza vaccination outcome by neural networks and logistic regression," *Journal of Biomedical Informatics*, vol. 43, no. 5, pp. 774–781, 2010.

[40] D. Simon and J. R. Boring III, *Clinical Methods: The History, Physical, and Laboratory Examinations*, Butterworth, Boston, Mass, USA, 1990.

3

Prediction of Associations between OMIM Diseases and MicroRNAs by Random Walk on OMIM Disease Similarity Network

Hailin Chen[1,2] and Zuping Zhang[1]

[1] School of Information Science and Engineering, Central South University, Changsha 410083, China
[2] Department of Computer Science and Technology, Hunan University of Humanities, Science and Technology, Loudi 417000, China

Correspondence should be addressed to Zuping Zhang; zpzhang@mail.csu.edu.cn

Academic Editors: K. Abdelmohsen and Y. Xi

Increasing evidence has revealed that microRNAs (miRNAs) play important roles in the development and progression of human diseases. However, efforts made to uncover OMIM disease-miRNA associations are lacking and the majority of diseases in the OMIM database are not associated with any miRNA. Therefore, there is a strong incentive to develop computational methods to detect potential OMIM disease-miRNA associations. In this paper, random walk on OMIM disease similarity network is applied to predict potential OMIM disease-miRNA associations under the assumption that functionally related miRNAs are often associated with phenotypically similar diseases. Our method makes full use of global disease similarity values. We tested our method on 1226 known OMIM disease-miRNA associations in the framework of leave-one-out cross-validation and achieved an area under the ROC curve of 71.42%. Excellent performance enables us to predict a number of new potential OMIM disease-miRNA associations and the newly predicted associations are publicly released to facilitate future studies. Some predicted associations with high ranks were manually checked and were confirmed from the publicly available databases, which was a strong evidence for the practical relevance of our method.

1. Introduction

MicroRNAs (miRNAs) are a class of small noncoding RNAs typically about 22 nucleotides in length. They have been identified in eukaryotic organisms ranging from nematodes to humans [1–3]. *Caenorhabditis elegans* (*C. elegans*) lin-4 and let-7 are the first two discovered miRNAs [4, 5]. Over the past decade, thousands of miRNAs have been discovered. miRNAs normally function as negative regulators of gene expression [6–8]. Research also reports that miRNAs may act as positive regulators in some cases [9, 10].

Many investigators have reported that miRNAs are critical in tissue development [11], cell growth [12], cellular signalling [13], and so on. As such, the mutation of miRNAs, the dysfunction of miRNA biogenesis, and the dysregulation of miRNAs and their targets may result in various diseases, such as lung cancer [14], lymphoma [15], and breast cancer [16]. Therefore, research on the relationship between miRNAs and diseases has become an important biomedical goal.

The Online Mendelian Inheritance in Man database (OMIM, http://www.ncbi.nlm.nih.gov/omim/) is a comprehensive knowledgebase of human genetic disorders. It contains information about genes and genetic phenotypes. As of December 2012, OMIM comprised 5442 Mendelian diseases (which are prefixed using "#" ($n = 3676$) if the responsible gene is known and with "%" otherwise ($n = 1766$)). However, efforts made to reveal OMIM disease-miRNA associations are lacking and the majority of diseases in the OMIM database are not associated with any miRNA. To provide testable hypotheses to guide future experiments, it is of great importance to devise computational models to infer potential OMIM disease-miRNA associations.

Recently, some important conclusions and computational methods about the relationship between diseases and miR-NAs have been presented. Lu et al. [17] performed a comprehensive analysis to the human miRNA-disease association data and disclosed that miRNAs tend to show similar or different dysfunctional evidences for the similar or different disease clusters, respectively. Jiang et al. [18] proposed a computational model based on the hypergeometric distribution to infer potential miRNA-OMIM disease associations by prioritizing the entire human microRNAome for diseases of interest. The notation that functionally related miRNAs tend to be associated with phenotypically similar diseases was reconfirmed in their manuscript. Although miRNAs functional network, disease similarity network, and known miRNA-disease associations were integrated in their work, only the neighbor information of each miRNA was used in their scoring system. Prediction accuracy would be increased by taking advantage of the global network similarity information. Another limitation is that *in silico* predicted associations were used as data sources in this method. It is known that these predicted associations used as data sources have some false-positive and false-negative results, thus influencing the final prediction accuracy. To test the hypothesis that some miRNAs could be potentially responsible for a number of "orphan" OMIM diseases, Rossi et al. [19] developed a novel approach OMiR to calculate the significance of the overlap between miRNA loci and OMIM disease loci. Results suggested that "orphan" genetic disease loci were proximal to miRNA loci more frequently than to loci for which the responsible protein coding gene is known.

In this paper, we propose a computational approach to infer potential human OMIM disease-miRNA associations by random walk to prioritize the candidate diseases for miRNAs of interest. We first constructed an OMIM disease similarity network and an OMIM disease-miRNA association network. We subsequently implement random walk on the OMIM disease similarity network to prioritize candidate diseases for an miRNA of interest. Cross-validation has illustrated the excellent performance of our method. The comprehensively predicted OMIM disease-miRNA associations also enable us to suggest many potential OMIM disease-miRNA associations, which can offer help in further experiments and hence increase research productivity. We further manually checked some strongly predicted associations and encouraging confirmation results were found from the publicly available databases.

2. Materials and Methods

2.1. Data Preparation. The benchmark dataset (see Supplementary material S1 available at http://dx.doi.org/10.1155/2013/204658) used in this manuscript is downloaded from [20, 21]. Here below we provide a brief description.

2.1.1. The OMIM Disease Similarity Data. We download the disease phenotype similarity scores from the MimMiner [21],

developed by van Driel et al. who computed a phenotype similarity score for each phenotype pair by the text mining analysis of their phenotype descriptions in the Online Mendelian Inheritance in Man (OMIM) database [22]. The phenotypic similarity scores have been successfully used to predict or prioritize disease-related protein-coding genes [23, 24].

OMIM disease similarity matrix is defined as O, where the entity $O(i, j)$ in row i column j is the similarity score between OMIM disease i and j. Based on the similarity matrix, OMIM disease similarity network (ODSN) is constructed, where vertex set $D = \{d_1, d_2, \ldots, d_n\}$ denotes the set of n OMIM diseases. Vertices d_i and d_j are linked by an edge in the network if the similarity between diseases i and j is more than zero. The similarity score between diseases i and j is used as the weight of this edge.

2.1.2. The OMIM Disease-miRNA Association Data. Previous studies have produced a large number of miRNA-disease associations. Lu et al. [17] and Jiang et al. [20] manually retrieved the associations of miRNA and disease from literatures and constructed two curated databases, human miRNA-associated disease database (HMDD) and miR2Disease, respectively. They aim to offer comprehensive resources of experimentally confirmed miRNA-disease associations. Yang et al. [25] also created a publicly available database of Differentially Expressed miRNAs in human Cancers (dbDEMC) with the goal to provide potential cancer-related miRNAs by *in silico* computing.

The OMIM disease-miRNA association data used in our paper was downloaded from miR2Disease [20]. After mapping these downloaded diseases into OMIM disease IDs, we finally received 1226 OMIM disease-miRNA associations consisting of 61 OMIM diseases and 365 miRNAs. These associations were used for performance evaluation, and the latest versions of the HMDD [17] and dbDEMC [25] data were applied for prediction confirmation.

OMIM disease-miRNA association network (ODMAN) was constructed based on the 1226 verified associations, where vertex set $D = \{d_1, d_2, \ldots, d_n\}$ denotes the set of n OMIM diseases and $M = \{m_1, m_2, \ldots, m_k\}$ denotes the set of $k$miRNAs. Vertices m_i and d_j are linked by an edge in the ODMAN if disease j is associated with miRNA i in our datasets. The weights of all edges are set to be 1.

2.2. Method Description. Random walk is a ranking algorithm. It simulates a random walker who starts on some given seed nodes and moves to their immediate neighbors randomly at each step. Finally, all the nodes in the network are ranked by the probability of the random walker reaching this node. Let p_0 be the initial probability vector and p_s a vector in which the ith element holds the probability of finding the random walker at node i at step s. The probability vector at step $s + 1$ can be given by

$$p_{s+1} = rp_0 + (1 - r) D_{\text{norm}} p_s, \tag{1}$$

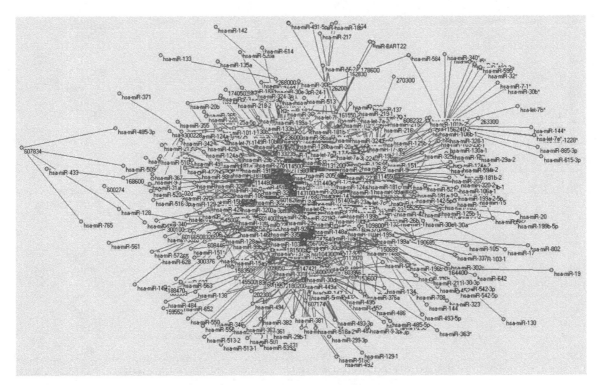

FIGURE 1: OMIM disease-miRNA association network (ODMAN). The network is generated by using 1226 experimentally verified associations between OMIM diseases and miRNAs. The network is prepared by Pajek (http://vlado.fmf.uni-lj.si/pub/networks/pajek/).

where r is the restart probability of random walk in every time step at source nodes and D_{norm} is the normalized similarity network.

After some steps, the probability will reach a steady state. This is obtained by performing the iteration until the difference between p_s and p_{s+1} (measured by the $L1$ norm) falls below 10^{-10}. The steady-state probability p_∞ gives a measure of proximity to seed nodes. If $p_\infty(i) > p_\infty(j)$, then node i is more proximate to seed nodes than node j.

In this paper, based on the observation that functionally related miRNAs are often associated with phenotypically similar diseases [17], random walk was proposed to uncover the potential associations between OMIM diseases and miR-NAs. The source code in Matlab can be downloaded from Supplementary Material S2. As we want to predict potential OMIM diseases for a given miRNA m of interest, all the OMIM diseases which have already been confirmed to be associated with this miRNA will be considered as seed nodes. Other nonseed OMIM diseases will be considered as candidate diseases. The initial probability p_0 is formed such that equal probabilities are assigned to the seed nodes, with the sum equal to 1, while the initial probabilities of nonseed miRNAs are 0. Here we allow the restart of random walk in every time step at source nodes with probability r ($0 < r < 1$). After some iteration, the random walk is stable. The stable probability is defined as p_∞. Candidate OMIM diseases are ranked according to p_∞. The high-scored OMIM diseases can be expected to have a high probability to be associated with the given miRNA.

3. Results

3.1. OMIM Disease-miRNA Association Network (ODMAN) Analysis. In this study, we first focus on the verified OMIM disease-miRNA associations. The set of 1226 known OMIM disease-miRNA associations is regarded as the "gold standard" data and is used for evaluating the performance of our proposed method in the cross-validation experiments as well as training data in the comprehensive prediction. We constructed the OMIM disease-miRNA association network using a bipartite graph representation (see Figure 1) and analyzed some statistics for the OMIM disease-miRNA association network. In the bipartite graph, the heterogeneous nodes correspond to either miRNAs or diseases, and edges correspond to associations between them. An edge is placed between a miRNA node and a disease node if the disease is known to associate with the miRNA.

Figure 2 shows the degree distributions for miRNAs and diseases in the OMIM disease-miRNA association network. The degree of the miRNA (respective disease) node is the number of diseases that the miRNA has associations with (resp., the number of miRNAs targeting the disease).

Table 1 details some statistics for the OMIM disease-miRNA association network, such as the average degree of miRNAs and the average degree of diseases.

Inspection of the OMIM disease-miRNA association network shows that most edges in the network are connected and form a large connecting subnetwork.

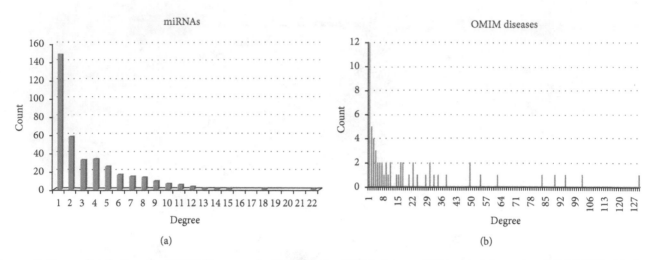

FIGURE 2: Degree distributions for OMIM diseases and miRNAs in the OMIM disease-miRNA association network (ODMAN). (a) shows the histograms of the degree of miRNAs. (b) shows the histograms of the degree of OMIM diseases.

TABLE 1: Statistics for the OMIM disease-miRNA association network.

No. of OMIM diseases	No. of miRNAs	No. of OMIM disease-miRNA associations	Average degree of OMIM diseases	Average degree of miRNAs
61	365	1226	20.10	3.36

TABLE 2: The effect of restart probability value on the cross-validation results.

Restart probability	0.1	0.2	0.3	0.4	0.5	0.6	0.7	0.8	0.9
AUC	0.6703	0.6903	0.7011	0.7082	0.7126	0.7135	0.7138	0.7142	0.7138

3.2. Performance Evaluation of the Proposed Method. In order to assess the power of our method to predict OMIM disease-miRNA associations by prioritizing the entire candidate OMIM diseases, we performed a leave-one-out cross-validation on the 1226 known OMIM disease-miRNA associations. For a given miRNA m, each known related OMIM disease was left out in turn as test disease and other known OMIM diseases were taken as seed nodes. The candidate disease set consisted of all the OMIM diseases which have no evidence to show their association with miRNA m.

We calculated the sensitivity and specificity for each threshold. Sensitivity refers to the percentage of the associations whose ranking is higher than a given threshold, namely, the ratio of the successfully predicted experimentally verified OMIM disease-miRNA associations to the total experimentally verified OMIM disease-miRNA associations. Specificity refers to the percentage of associations that are below the threshold. The value of area under receiver-operating characteristics (ROC) curve (AUC) was calculated and an AUC value of 71.42% was achieved, suggesting that our method can recover the known experimentally verified OMIM disease-miRNA associations and therefore has the potential to infer new OMIM disease-miRNA associations.

3.3. Effects of Parameter in the Proposed Method. Restart probability r is one parameter in our method. To investigate the selection of the parameter for the performance of our method, we set various values for it and calculated the AUC values in the framework of leave-one-out cross-validation. Table 2 details the effect of the parameter on the cross-validation results in the benchmark dataset. After a comprehensive searching, the parameter ($r = 0.8$) which led to best AUC result is selected for further association prediction. It could also be observed that the predictive result is robust to the restart probability.

3.4. Comparison with Other Methods. Until recently, efforts made to discover potential OMIM disease-miRNA associations are lacking. Meanwhile models have been constructed based on different data features, which makes direct performance comparison difficult. The most recent study related with our work is the computational model proposed by Jiang et al. [18], which was based on the hypergeometric distribution to infer potential miRNA-OMIM disease associations by prioritizing the entire human microRNAome for diseases of interest. Only the neighbor information of each miRNA was used in their scoring system. Another limitation is that *in silico* predicted associations were used as data sources in this method. It is known that these predicted associations have some false-positive and false-negative results, which may bring noises to the experiments. Our method is based on the experimentally verified OMIM disease-miRNA associations.

TABLE 3: The newly confirmed OMIM disease-miRNA associations in the top 10 predicted results of *hsa-let-7g*.

miRNA	OMIM ID	Rank	Source
hsa-let-7g	114480	1	HMDD
hsa-let-7g	155720	2	HMDD
hsa-let-7g	180200	3	HMDD
hsa-let-7g	256700	4	
hsa-let-7g	188470	5	
hsa-let-7g	109800	6	
hsa-let-7g	133239	7	dbDEMC
hsa-let-7g	603956	8	HMDD
hsa-let-7g	155255	9	dbDEMC
hsa-let-7g	607174	10	

3.5. Comprehensive Prediction for Unknown OMIM Disease-miRNA Associations. After confirming the usefulness of our method, we conduct a comprehensive prediction of unknown associations between all possible OMIM diseases and miRNAs. In the inference process, we trained our method with all the known associations. We ranked the nonassociating pairs with respect to their probability scores and extracted the top 20 predicted associations for each of the 365 OMIM diseases. The full list of the prediction results can be obtained from Supplementary Material S3.

Furthermore, we manually checked some strongly predicted associations. Take the top 10 predicted associations of *hsa-let-7g* as an example. We confirmed that 6 associations (Table 3) are now annotated in at least one of the two latest online versions of HMDD [17] and dbDEMC [25] databases. We take these as a strong evidence to support the practical application of our method. Note that the predicted associations that are not reported yet may also exist in reality.

4. Discussion

We have applied random walk on OMIM disease similarity network to predict potential OMIM disease-miRNA associations. Differing from using local network similarity measures, like the method proposed by Jiang et al. [18], we adopted global network similarity measures. Excellent performance based on leave-one-out cross-validation suggested that our method has the potential to infer new OMIM disease-miRNA associations. The newly predicted associations are publicly released to facilitate future studies. Further confirmation of some strongly predicted associations in publicly accessible databases indicates the realistic application of our method.

Despite the encouraging results of our method, there are also limitations. The known experimentally verified OMIM disease-miRNA associations were rare. Therefore, integrating other bioinformatics sources, such as Gene Ontology, might improve model performance. Our method cannot be applied for miRNAs which do not have any known associated OMIM diseases. Thus miRNA similarity information should be taken into consideration. From a technical viewpoint, the performance of our method could be improved by using more accurate similarity information designed for OMIM diseases.

Acknowledgments

The authors are grateful to Dr. Yixiong Liang at the Central South University for useful discussions. They thank Dr. Qinghua Cui from Peking University Health Science Center and Professor Yadong Wang of Harbin Institute of Technology for their help. This research was supported by the National Natural Science Foundation of China (Grants 60970095, 61003124, and M1121008), Research Fund for the Doctoral Program of Higher Education of China (Grant no. 20120162110077) and the National High Technology Research and Development Program of China (863 Program, no. 2012AA011205).

References

[1] M. Lagos-Quintana, R. Rauhut, A. Yalcin, J. Meyer, W. Lendeckel, and T. Tuschl, "Identification of tissue-specific microRNAs from mouse," *Current Biology*, vol. 12, no. 9, pp. 735–739, 2002.

[2] N. C. Lau, L. P. Lim, E. G. Weinstein, and D. P. Bartel, "An abundant class of tiny RNAs with probable regulatory roles in Caenorhabditis elegans," *Science*, vol. 294, no. 5543, pp. 858–862, 2001.

[3] R. C. Lee and V. Ambros, "An extensive class of small RNAs in Caenorhabditis elegans," *Science*, vol. 294, no. 5543, pp. 862–864, 2001.

[4] R. C. Lee, R. L. Feinbaum, and V. Ambros, "The C. elegans heterochronic gene lin-4 encodes small RNAs with antisense complementarity to lin-14," *Cell*, vol. 75, no. 5, pp. 843–854, 1993.

[5] B. J. Reinhart, F. J. Slack, M. Basson et al., "The 21-nucleotide let-7 RNA regulates developmental timing in Caenorhabditis elegans," *Nature*, vol. 403, no. 6772, pp. 901–906, 2000.

[6] V. Ambros, "The functions of animal microRNAs," *Nature*, vol. 431, no. 7006, pp. 350–355, 2004.

[7] D. P. Bartel, "MicroRNAs: genomics, biogenesis, mechanism, and function," *Cell*, vol. 116, no. 2, pp. 281–297, 2004.

[8] G. Meister and T. Tuschl, "Mechanisms of gene silencing by double-stranded RNA," *Nature*, vol. 431, no. 7006, pp. 343–349, 2004.

[9] C. L. Jopling, M. Yi, A. M. Lancaster, S. M. Lemon, and P. Sarnow, "Modulation of hepatitis C virus RNA abundance by a liver-specific MicroRNA," *Science*, vol. 309, no. 5740, pp. 1577–1581, 2005.

[10] S. Vasudevan, Y. Tong, and J. A. Steitz, "Switching from repression to activation: microRNAs can up-regulate translation," *Science*, vol. 318, no. 5858, pp. 1931–1934, 2007.

[11] A. M. Krichevsky, K. S. King, C. P. Donahue, K. Khrapk, and K. Kosik, "A microRNA array reveals extensive regulation of microRNAs during brain development," *RNA*, vol. 9, no. 10, pp. 1274–1281, 2003.

[12] A. Esquela-Kerscher and F. J. Slack, "Oncomirs—microRNAs with a role in cancer," *Nature Reviews Cancer*, vol. 6, no. 4, pp. 259–269, 2006.

[13] Q. Cui, Z. Yu, E. O. Purisima, and E. Wang, "Principles of microRNA regulation of a human cellular signaling network," *Molecular Systems Biology*, vol. 2, article 46, 2006.

[14] A. Esquela-Kerscher, P. Trang, J. F. Wiggins et al., "The let-7 microRNA reduces tumor growth in mouse models of lung cancer," *Cell Cycle*, vol. 7, no. 6, pp. 759–764, 2008.

[15] R. W. Chen, L. T. Bemis, C. M. Amato et al., "Truncation in CCND1 mRNA alters miR-16-1 regulation in mantle cell lymphoma," *Blood*, vol. 112, no. 3, pp. 822–829, 2008.

[16] T. E. Miller, K. Ghoshal, B. Ramaswamy et al., "MicroRNA-221/222 confers tamoxifen resistance in breast cancer by targeting p27Kip1," *Journal of Biological Chemistry*, vol. 283, no. 44, pp. 29897–29903, 2008.

[17] M. Lu, Q. Zhang, M. Deng et al., "An analysis of human microRNA and disease associations," *PLoS ONE*, vol. 3, no. 10, Article ID e3420, 2008.

[18] Q. Jiang, Y. Hao, G. Wang et al., "Prioritization of disease microRNAs through a human phenome-microRNAome network," *BMC Systems Biology*, vol. 4, no. 1, article S2, 2010.

[19] S. Rossi, A. Tsirigos, A. Amoroso et al., "OMiR: identification of associations between OMIM diseases and microRNAs," *Genomics*, vol. 97, no. 2, pp. 71–76, 2011.

[20] Q. Jiang, Y. Wang, Y. Hao et al., "miR2Disease: a manually curated database for microRNA deregulation in human disease," *Nucleic Acids Research*, vol. 37, no. 1, pp. D98–D104, 2009.

[21] M. A. van Driel, J. Bruggeman, G. Vriend, H. G. Brunner, and J. A. M. Leunissen, "A text-mining analysis of the human phenome," *European Journal of Human Genetics*, vol. 14, no. 5, pp. 535–542, 2006.

[22] A. Hamosh, A. F. Scott, J. S. Amberger, C. A. Bocchini, and V. A. McKusick, "Online Mendelian Inheritance in Man (OMIM), a knowledgebase of human genes and genetic disorders," *Nucleic Acids Research*, vol. 33, pp. D514–D517, 2005.

[23] U. Ala, R. M. Piro, E. Grassi et al., "Prediction of human disease genes by human-mouse conserved coexpression analysis," *PLoS Computational Biology*, vol. 4, no. 3, Article ID e1000043, 2008.

[24] X. Wu, R. Jiang, M. Q. Zhang, and S. Li, "Network-based global inference of human disease genes," *Molecular Systems Biology*, vol. 4, article 9, 2008.

[25] Z. Yang, F. Ren, C. Liu et al., "dbDEMC: a database of differentially expressed miRNAs in human cancers," *BMC Genomics*, vol. 11, no. 4, article S5, 2010.

4

Discovering Weighted Patterns in Intron Sequences Using Self-Adaptive Harmony Search and Back-Propagation Algorithms

Yin-Fu Huang,[1] Chia-Ming Wang,[2] and Sing-Wu Liou[3]

[1] *Department of Computer Science and Information Engineering, National Yunlin University of Science and Technology,*
123 University Road, Section 3, Douliu, Yunlin 640, Taiwan
[2] *Graduate School of Engineering Science and Technology, National Yunlin University of Science and Technology,*
123 University Road, Section 3, Douliu, Yunlin 640, Taiwan
[3] *Supercomputing Research Center, National Chen Kung University, 1 University Road, Tainan, 70101, Taiwan*

Correspondence should be addressed to Yin-Fu Huang; huangyf@yuntech.edu.tw

Academic Editors: H.-W. Chang, Y.-H. Cheng, Y. Liu, and C.-H. Yang

A hybrid self-adaptive harmony search and back-propagation mining system was proposed to discover weighted patterns in human intron sequences. By testing the weights under a lazy nearest neighbor classifier, the numerical results revealed the significance of these weighted patterns. Comparing these weighted patterns with the popular intron consensus model, it is clear that the discovered weighted patterns make originally the ambiguous 5SS and 3SS header patterns more specific and concrete.

1. Introduction

Pre-mRNA splicing was a critical event in gene-expression pathways and mainly involved in intron removing [1]. Introns were noncoding segments in gene sequences conjoined with the protein-coding exons at splicing sites (see Figure 1). Identifying introns was the foundations for predicting the gene's structures and functions; therefore, predicting introns effectively and precisely would provide great helps in uncovering the secrets of genes [2]. Intron splicing accomplished by the spliceosome is closely related with four *cis-acting* elements, that is, the 5' splicing sites (5SS), the 3' splicing sites (3SS), the poly-pyrimidine tract (PPT), and the branch point (BP) [3]. Intron identification and qualification heavily depend on the four splicing signals, and, consequently, intronic sequence patterns are crucial in intron-related researches, especially in predicting the 5SS and 3SS.

Some efforts have been devoted to specifying sequence features of introns, and conceptual information such as bimodal GC% distribution [4], statistical features [5], and motifs [6] were found, but these patterns lacked concrete and specific descriptions, thereby making them hard to be used as basis of computational predictions and analyses. One more thing should be noticed is that the above-discovered patterns were all *statistically* significant only, and prejudging weights without testing the effectiveness might take a lot of risks in biased decisions. If going one step further to make the patterns *biologically* significant, it would be very inspiring.

The essentials comprising patterns were seriously explored and termed computational concerns. Three computational concerns were firstly identified as expressions, locations, and ranges. Expressions are the representations of patterns such as consensus, locations are start positions in sequences, and ranges are their possible lengths. Furthermore, for discovering biologically meaningful patterns, the *weight* concern was proposed for specifying the biological significance.

In this paper, patterns with four concerns were termed the weighted patterns. A postjudged weights discovering the methodology using hybrid self-adaptive harmony search (SAHS) and back-propagation (BP) algorithms were devised and implemented to fulfill the idea of weighted patterns. The entire processes of discovering weighted patterns were fulfilled through a frame-relayed search method [7] together

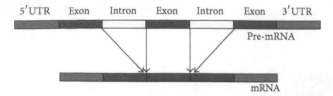

FIGURE 1: An illustration of pre-mRNA to mature mRNA.

with a hybrid SAHS-BP and sensitivity analysis as depicted in Figure 2.

2. SAHS-BP and Sensitive Analysis

In [8], Liou and Huang divided the intronic sequence features (ISF) into two categories: the uniframe pattern (UFP) and the multiframe pattern (MFP), where UFPs are the intraframe patterns and MFPs are the interframe patterns. Based on their frequencies and distributions, the significant UFPs focus on vertical distributions of tandem repeats, and the significant MFPs focus on horizontal ones, as shown in Figure 3. For detailed discussions on intronic sequence features and frame-relayed search method, see [7, 8].

After obtaining the patterns by frame-relayed search method [7], their relative importance could be derived from a new hybrid SAHS-BP mining system. The basic idea is to extract the instinct relationships between the input attributes and the output responses from the trained network by means of a postsensitivity analysis. Subsequently, the relative importance of input attributes could be determined according to these relationships. Thus, the quality of the relative importance is highly dependent on the network.

2.1. Hybrid SAHS-BP. Artificial neural networks (ANN) are robust and general methods for function approximation, prediction, and classification tasks. The superior performance and generalization capabilities of ANN have attracted much attention in the past thirty years. Back-propagation (BP) algorithm [9] (i.e., the most famous learning algorithm of MLP) has been successfully applied in many practical problems. However, the random initialization mechanism of ANN might cause the optimum search process (the learning problem can be though as search through hypotheses for the one best fit the training instances [10]) to fail and return an unsatisfied solution, since the back-propagation is a local search learning algorithm [11]. For example, once the random initialization of the synaptic weights led to the search process start from hillside 1 as shown in Figure 4, BP algorithm would update the synaptic weights and go along the gradient direction. Consequently, it seems hopeless to reach a better solution near the global optimum in valley 2. Therefore, lots of trials and errors were the general guideline in most practical usage.

On the other hand, a new metaheuristic optimization algorithm-harmony search (HS) with continuous design

variables was proposed recently [12]. This algorithm is conceptualized using the musical improvisation process of searching for a perfect state of harmony. Harmony search exhibits a nice global search property and seldom falls into a trap. Moreover, the HS has been successfully applied to several real-world optimization problems [13]. A recently developed variant of HS, called the self-adaptive harmony search (SAHS) [14], used the consciousness (i.e., harmony memory) to automatically adjust its parameter values. The self-adaptive mechanism not only alleviates difficulties of parameter setting but also enhances precision of solutions.

According to these observations, we are motivated to combine the advantages of SAHS and BP together and complement their own weaknesses. SAHS is used as an initializer of the neural network, that is, the generator of initial synaptic weights of BP. In other words, the lowest valley in Figure 4 is first found by SAHS; then a gradient descent-based ANN would go down carefully to obtain a precise solution. Finally, a sensitivity analysis was conducted on the well-trained network to estimate the relative importance of input attributes.

2.2. Sensitivity Analysis. Sensitivity analysis is a common technique to realize the relationships between input variables and output variables. It could be used to check the quality of a hypothesis model as well. The basic idea behind sensitivity analysis is to slightly alter the input variables, and then the corresponding responses with respect to the original ones would reveal the significance of the variables. Therefore, the most important part of sensitivity analysis is to determine the adequate measurements as disturbance of input variables. Although applying sensitivity analysis to neural networks had been studied in some works [15, 16], their purposes were usually identifying important factors only, while we go one step further, in this work, not only significant input attributes will be recognized but also the relative important of them will be estimated. We proposed a new measurement, disturbance, for the relative sensitivity.

Definition 1. The elements of disturbance instances used in the sensitivity analysis are defined as follows:

$$xm = \begin{cases} (1 \otimes d) \times xm, & \text{if } m = j, \\ xm, & \text{otherwise,} \end{cases} \quad \forall xm \in x^i_{j\uparrow}, \quad (1)$$

where $x^i_{j\uparrow}$ is the ith instance in the training set, with the jth attribute *increased* according to the disturbance ratio d; that is, the symbol $\otimes$ denotes a plus sign. In other words, except the jth attribute, all other attributes of the ith instance are fixed. Similarly, $x^i_{j\downarrow}$ is with the jth attribute *decreased*; that is, the symbol $\otimes$ denotes a minus sign.

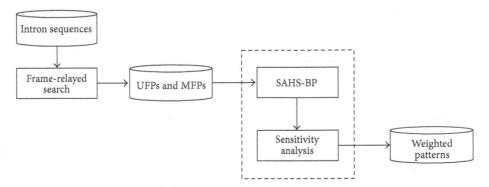

FIGURE 2: Procedure for discovering weighted patterns.

Definition 2. The relative sensitivity of *j*th attribute is defined as follows:

$$
rsj = \left(\sum_{i=1}^{p} \left(\left| \mathrm{net}\left(x_{j\uparrow}^i\right) - \mathrm{net}\left(x_j^i\right) \right| + \left| \mathrm{net}\left(x_{j\downarrow}^i\right) - \mathrm{net}\left(x_j^i\right) \right| \right) \right)
$$

$$
\times \left(\min_j \left\{ \sum_{i=1}^{p} \left(\left| \mathrm{net}\left(x_{j\uparrow}^i\right) - \mathrm{net}\left(x_j^i\right) \right| \right. \right. \right.
$$

$$
\left. \left. \left. + \left| \mathrm{net}\left(x_{j\downarrow}^i\right) - \mathrm{net}\left(x_j^i\right) \right| \right) \right\} \right)^{-1},
$$

$$(2)$$

where function net is the trained network, and the relative sensitivity is normalized by the minimal sensitivity attribute among all attributes.

3. Experiments

3.1. Data Sets. Since the lengths of introns are varied violently, for determining an adequate sequence length for pattern discovery, a pilot study on sequence compositions of introns is performed (data not shown here). As a result, we found that introns are very different from random sequences around 97 bps in the flanking regions of 5SS and 3SS. Therefore, we defined position 97 as the start position of the last frame, and then the final sequence length in the data sets would be 101 bps. For the completeness of analysis, all introns in human chromosome 1 (NCBI human genome build 36.2) were extracted, and the final data set comprised 22,448 sequences.

3.2. Weighted UFPs and MFPs. The weighted UFPs and MFPs discovered by the proposed SAHS-BP mining system and sensitivity analysis are listed in Tables 1 and 2, respectively. To verify the effectiveness of these weighted codons for qualifying human introns, a two-layer classifier was constructed to test the significance of these weights.

3.3. Two-Layered Classifier. In order to reveal the strength of discovered weighted patterns, a simple two-layered lazy classifier was constructed. The well-known nearest neighbor classifier was adopted as the based classifier due to its

Sequences					
CAT	TAG				
CAT	TAG				
CAT	TAG	GAT	GAT	GAT	GAT
CAT	TAG	GAT	GAT	GAT	GAT
CAT	TAG	GAT	GAT	GAT	
CAT	TAG				
CAT	TAG				
UFPs		MFPs			

FIGURE 3: Tandem repeats of condons from the UFPs and MFPs.

simplicity and efficiency. In contrast to an eager classifier, the lazy nearest neighbor classifier only memorizes the entire training instances in the training phase and then classifies the testing instances based on the class labels of their neighbors in the testing phase. In other words, the basic idea behind the nearest neighbor classifier is well explained by the famous idiom "Birds of a feather flock together."

The Euclidean distance is the original proximity measure between a test instance and a training instance used in the nearest neighbor classifier. A weighted Euclidean distance could be extended as $d(x, x') = sqrt(\sum_{i=1}^{n} wi(xi - x'_i)^2)$, where n is the number of dimensions and w_i, x_i, and x'_i are the ith attribute of weight vector w, training instance x, and test instance x', respectively.

The experiment was carried out with the 10-fold cross-validation for each specific k (i.e., the k closest neighbor). First, the whole sequence was randomly divided into 10 divisions with the equal size. The class in each division was represented in nearly the same proportion as that in the whole data set. Then, each division was held out in turn and the remaining nine-tenths were directly fed into the two-layered nearest neighbor classifier as the training instances. Since every sequence could be expressed as two parts (i.e., uniframe patterns and multiframe patterns), the first layered nearest neighbor classifier filtered out those non-intron candidates based on the weighted uniframe patterns. Finally, the prediction was made by the second layered nearest neighbor based on the weighted multiframe patterns.

TABLE 1: UFPs of 5SS and 3SS.

ID	Weight	Expression	Location	Range
		5SS		
1	5.30	AAG	1	5
2	2.01	GAG	1	5
3	3.98	GTA	1	5
4	2.02	TAA	1	5
5	2.32	TGA	1	5
6	4.54	AGT	4	5
		3SS		
7	3.12	ACA	1	5
8	6.26	CAG	1	5
9	1.00	CCA	1	5
10	1.09	GCA	1	5
11	2.69	TAG	1	5
12	2.33	TCA	1	5

TABLE 2: MFPs of 5SS and 3SS.

ID	Weight	Expression	Location	Range
		5SS		
1	2.15	TTT	7	5
2	1.23	TGG	7	5
3	3.13	GGG	7	5
4	1.00	CTG	7	5
5	6.49	TTT	10	17
6	2.25	TGG	10	17
7	3.42	TCT	10	17
8	8.45	GGG	10	17
9	4.52	CTG	10	17
10	23.76	TTT	25	68
11	5.90	TGG	25	68
12	9.66	TCT	25	68
13	34.39	GGG	25	68
14	11.63	CTG	25	68
15	17.72	AAA	25	68
16	7.11	TTT	91	11
17	2.02	TCT	91	11
18	4.18	GGG	91	11
19	3.23	CTG	91	11
20	3.65	AAA	91	11
		3SS		
21	7.63	TTT	4	5
22	5.08	TCT	5	5
23	33.13	TTT	7	17
24	11.63	TGT	7	17
25	25.46	TCT	7	17
25	3.80	CTG	7	17
27	3.20	ATT	7	17
28	20.08	TTT	22	47
29	7.39	TGT	22	47
30	12.52	TCT	22	47
31	9.78	CTG	22	47
32	7.07	ATT	22	47
33	17.48	AAA	22	47
34	2.11	TTT	67	8
35	1.76	TCT	67	8
36	2.28	CTG	67	8
37	1.89	ATT	67	8
38	2.25	AAA	67	8
39	1.51	TTT	75	5
40	1.27	CTG	75	5
41	1.02	ATT	75	5
42	1.23	AAA	75	5
43	8.31	TTT	76	26
44	3.41	ATT	76	26
45	9.53	AAA	76	26

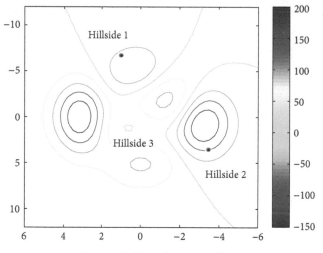

FIGURE 4: Optimization surface.

The flowchart of two-layered nearest neighbor classifier is shown in Figure 5.

3.4. Numerical Results. In this subsection, the performance comparisons between the weighted k-NN classifier and the conventional one are presented. Although no explicit weight vectors were used in the conventional k-NN classifier, the Euclidean distance indirectly implied the same importance of all input attributes. Here, we used identity vectors (i.e., all elements in the vector are one) as its weight vectors and conducted the experiment in the same process as shown in Figure 5 for the performance comparisons. The reported values of performance evaluation measures here are the averages from the 10-fold cross-validation.

As shown in Figures 6, 7, 8, and 9, the numerical results clearly indicate that the weighted k-NN classifier performs much better than the conventional one in terms of error, F-measure, and the recall on different k, except precision. In addition to error decreased from 25.21% to 16.88% on average, F-measure (or recall) is also increased 12.73% (or 14.21%),

respectively. From the perspective of k value used in k-NN, slightly better numeric results could be obtained from both weighted and conventional nearest neighbor classifiers for

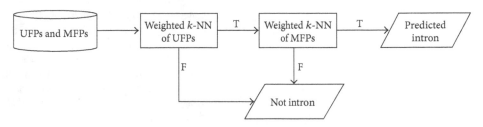

FIGURE 5: Two-layered nearest neighbor classifier.

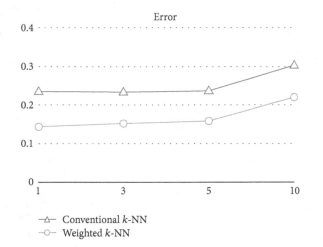

FIGURE 6: Error of the conventional k-NN classifier and the weighted k-NN classifier on different k.

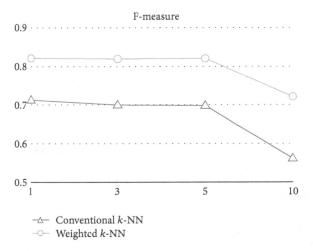

FIGURE 7: F-measure of the conventional k-NN classifier and the weighted k-NN classifier on different k.

TABLE 3: The P values of the t-test on the weighted and conventional k-NN classifiers.

#k	Measure			
	Error	F-measure	Precision	Recall
1	$2.35E-09$	$4.58E-09$	$1.23E-05$	$2.13E-09$
3	$7.64E-08$	$5.67E-09$	$1.89E-05$	$4.23E-07$
5	$1.87E-09$	$3.56E-08$	0.09	$3.87E-08$
10	$6.43E-08$	$2.33E-10$	0.87	$7.56E-09$

$k = 3$. Furthermore, one might argue that both weighted and conventional k-NN achieve such high scores in precision and relatively low scores in recall; that is, there are few predicted false positives and lots of predicted false negatives in both models. However, we believe that the reason for this circumstance is due to the inherent model bias and lazy characteristics of the nearest neighbor method. It lacks the ability to well describe the learning concept because the basic idea is merely distance comparisons. Nevertheless, such a simple weak classifier is appropriate to demonstrate the effectiveness of the weighted patterns.

Besides, since a limited number of samples were used to compare the performances of two models, we want to know whether the better performance of the weighted k-NN classifier is just as a result of the chance effects in the estimation process (i.e., the 10-fold cross-validation). More precisely, we should determine whether the observed difference of performance measures between two classifiers

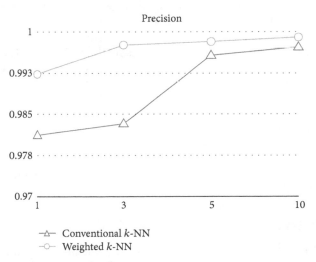

FIGURE 8: Precision of the conventional k-NN classifier and the weighted k-NN classifier on different k.

is really statistically significant (i.e., significantly better). Therefore, we used a paired t-test [17] on the weighted k-NN classifier and the conventional one with a 95% confidence coefficient. Table 3 reveals that the weight vectors not only significantly reduce the classification error of simple nearest neighbor classifiers but also significantly improve recall and F-measure. In other words, the predicted true positives are

30   Handbook of Bioinformatics

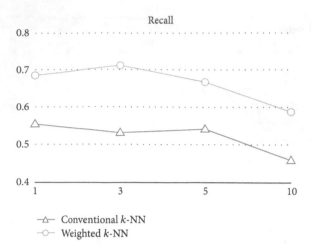

Figure 9: Recall of the conventional k-NN classifier and the weighted k-NN classifier on different k.

enhanced, and the false negatives are reduced as well. Thus, we could claim that some meaningful characteristics for intron identification are really enclosed in the weighted patterns.

4. Discussions

Intron identification played a key role in gene-expression researches, and pattern recognition was the basis for computationally predicting exon-intron junction sites. For discovering biologically meaningful patterns in introns, three computational concerns (pattern representation, position in sequences, and the spread range of patterns) were firstly identified by frame-relayed search method [7]. After that, a hybrid self-adaptive harmony search (SAHS) and back-propagation (BP) mining system was devised and implemented to fulfill the idea of mining weighted patterns. The weighted patterns clearly provide more specific and concrete information about introns. Thus, they should be of potentials in promoting the progress of gene analyses, providing great helps in discriminating authentic splicing sites from fictitious ones and revealing the visions of *in silico* validation of intron candidates.

References

[1] M. L. Hastings and A. R. Krainer, "Pre-mRNA splicing in the new millennium," *Current Opinion in Cell Biology*, vol. 13, no. 3, pp. 302–309, 2001.

[2] P. A. Sharp, "The discovery of split genes and RNA splicing," *Trends in Biochemical Sciences*, vol. 30, no. 6, pp. 279–281, 2005.

[3] P. A. Sharp, "Splicing of messenger RNA precursors," *Science*, vol. 235, no. 4790, pp. 766–771, 1987.

[4] X. H. F. Zhang, C. S. Leslie, and L. A. Chasin, "Dichotomous splicing signals in exon flanks," *Genome Research*, vol. 15, no. 6, pp. 768–779, 2005.

[5] M. Q. Zhang, "Statistical features of human exons and their flanking regions," *Human Molecular Genetics*, vol. 7, no. 5, pp. 919–932, 1998.

[6] X. H. F. Zhang, K. A. Heller, I. Hefter, C. S. Leslie, and L. A. Chasin, "Sequence information for the splicing of human pre-mRNA identified by support vector machine classification," *Genome Research*, vol. 13, no. 12, pp. 2637–2650, 2003.

[7] S. W. Liou, C. M. Wang, and Y. F. Huang, "Integrative discovery of multifaceted sequence patterns by frame-relayed search and hybrid PSO-ANN," *Journal of Universal Computer Science*, vol. 15, no. 4, pp. 742–764, 2009.

[8] S. W. Liou and Y. F. Huang, "Mining intronic sequence features of splice sites with depth-breadth fused codon analyses," in *Proceedings of International Conference on Bioinformatics and Computational Biology (BIOCOMP '08)*, pp. 203–209, July 2008.

[9] P. Werbos, *Beyond regression: new tools for prediction and analysis in the behavioral sciences [Ph.D. thesis]*, Harvard University, Cambridge, Mass, USA, 1974.

[10] T. M. Mitchell, *Machine Learning*, McGraw-Hill, New York, NY, USA, 1997.

[11] D. E. Rumelhart, G. E. Hinton, and R. J. Williams, "Learning representations by back-propagating errors," *Nature*, vol. 323, no. 6088, pp. 533–536, 1986.

[12] Z. W. Geem, K. S. Lee, and C. L. Tseng, "Harmony search for structural design," in *Proceedings of Conference on Genetic and Evolutionary Computation (GECCO '05)*, pp. 651–652, ACM, 2005.

[13] Z. W. Geem, "Harmony search applications in industry," *Studies in Fuzziness and Soft Computing*, vol. 226, pp. 117–134, 2008.

[14] C. M. Wang and Y. F. Huang, "Self-adaptive harmony search algorithm for optimization," *Expert Systems with Applications*, vol. 37, no. 4, pp. 2826–2837, 2010.

[15] Y. Yoon, T. Guimaraes, and G. Swales, "Integrating artificial neural networks with rule-based expert systems," *Decision Support Systems*, vol. 11, no. 5, pp. 497–507, 1994.

[16] D. M. Steiger and R. Sharda, "Analyzing mathematical models with inductive learning networks," *European Journal of Operational Research*, vol. 93, no. 2, pp. 387–401, 1996.

[17] D. C. Montgomery and G. C. Runger, *Applied Statistics and Probability for Engineers*, John Wiley & Sons, New York, NY, USA, 2006.

5

Effects of Pooling Samples on the Performance of Classification Algorithms: A Comparative Study

Kanthida Kusonmano,[1,2] Michael Netzer,[3] Christian Baumgartner,[3]
Matthias Dehmer,[1] Klaus R. Liedl,[2] and Armin Graber[1,4]

[1] Institute for Bioinformatics and Translational Research, UMIT, 6060 Hall in Tyrol, Austria
[2] Faculty of Chemistry and Pharmacy, Leopold-Franzens-University Innsbruck, 6020 Innsbruck, Austria
[3] Institute of Electrical and Biomedical Engineering, UMIT, 6060 Hall in Tyrol, Austria
[4] Novartis Pharmaceuticals Corporation, Oncology Biomarkers and Imaging, One Health Plaza, East Hanover, NJ 07936, USA

Correspondence should be addressed to Armin Graber, armin.graber@novartis.com

Academic Editor: Zhenqiang Su

A pooling design can be used as a powerful strategy to compensate for limited amounts of samples or high biological variation. In this paper, we perform a comparative study to model and quantify the effects of virtual pooling on the performance of the widely applied classifiers, support vector machines (SVMs), random forest (RF), k-nearest neighbors (k-NN), penalized logistic regression (PLR), and prediction analysis for microarrays (PAMs). We evaluate a variety of experimental designs using mock omics datasets with varying levels of pool sizes and considering effects from feature selection. Our results show that feature selection significantly improves classifier performance for non-pooled and pooled data. All investigated classifiers yield lower misclassification rates with smaller pool sizes. RF mainly outperforms other investigated algorithms, while accuracy levels are comparable among all the remaining ones. Guidelines are derived to identify an optimal pooling scheme for obtaining adequate predictive power and, hence, to motivate a study design that meets best experimental objectives and budgetary conditions, including time constraints.

1. Introduction

High-throughput technologies generate large amounts of data, which allow analysis of a broad range of biomolecules in living organisms [1, 2]. For example, the transcriptome, proteome, and metabolome can be studied by exploiting high-dimensional datasets that comprise RNAs, proteins, and metabolites, respectively. One of the most useful techniques, that have been applied to high-dimensional biological data, is sample pooling. It is a technique where subsets of samples are randomly selected and pooled within each group, and the cardinality of the samples subset is termed pool size. Pooling helps to cut experimental costs and reduces analytical run times; furthermore, it can compensate for limited amounts of samples or can mitigate effects of biological sample variation. Many biological experiments have been performed by pooling individual biological specimens (e.g., [3, 4]). For instance, messenger RNA (mRNA) samples are pooled

together before hybridization in a microarray experiment. Instead of employing as many array chips as number of samples n, actually required chips are reduced by a factor $1/p$, where p is the pool size.

The effects and efficiency of pooling samples have been statistically investigated in many studies [5–9], which showed that appropriate pooling can provide equivalent power as obtained in comparable studies, where samples of individual subjects are not pooled (i.e., pool size is equal to 1). Thus, it becomes very interesting to study the effects of virtual pooling on high-dimensional classification problems. Recently, this very active research area in bioinformatics has received widespread attention in the biomedical scientific community; primarily, as a result of the recent medical paradigm shift towards personalized medicine. This new strategy reflects an early and ongoing focus on targeted medicines, driven by a rigorous pathways approach to drug and biomarker discovery, which incorporates the qualification of biomarkers and their translation into companion diagnostics in the codevelopment process. The discovery and qualification of biomarkers as well as assay development, validation, and commercialization are empowered by an unprecedented evolution and emergence of exciting new molecular technologies including high-throughput "omics" microarrays, next-generation sequencing, functional imaging, and evolving nanotechnologies. Classification methods have been commonly employed to discover and validate sets of biomarkers in system-wide biomedical studies that fulfil predefined performance metrics, demonstrate clinical utility, and meet technical, practical clinical, and business-related expectations, which permit pursuing the development and commercialization of a clinical assay. Those studies frequently aid the prognostic and diagnostic assessment, and the predictive comparison of treatments of diseases such as cancer [10, 11], liver [12], or neurodegenerative diseases [13].

Recently, a study has been published investigating effects induced by pooling data [14]; however, this analysis did not explicitly include feature selection, which is a frequently used analysis step in high-dimensional classification problems. Feature selection is applied prior to the classification process for reducing noise features and selecting key features, which in general leads to a better discrimination by classification methods.

In the current work, we investigate the impact of pooling biological samples on classification algorithms in combination with feature selection. The data employed in our study are systematically synthesized with various numbers of markers and different human and animal (e.g., mice or rats) data scenarios. The data of human scenario mimick real-life experiments with larger sample size and higher biological variance comparing to animal scenario. A comparative study on the performance of commonly used classifiers in non-pooled and pooled data is performed. We apply supervised machine learning where predictive functions are deduced from training data. We focus on five important classifiers, support vector machines (SVMs) using linear and radial kernels, random forest (RF), k-nearest neighbors (k-NNs), penalized logistic regression (PLR), and prediction analysis for microarrays (PAMs).

Technical preliminaries of pooling samples, investigated classification algorithms, and feature selection are described in the next section. The materials and methods of data simulation and analysis framework are then explained. As results of this study, first we report the benefits of feature selection on both non-pooled and pooled datasets. Then, the effects of pooling data are presented. This comparative evaluation depicts the performance of classifiers on datasets of individual and pooled samples with several pool sizes. We also provide a comparison of human and animal scenarios, denoting the simulation of datasets that exemplify data characteristics typically observed in human studies and animal experiments. These results are discussed according to properties of data and classification algorithms. We conclude the work by deducing guidelines for the selection of classification algorithms and pool sizes that allow researchers to identify a study design that meets best their experimental objectives and budgetary conditions, including time constraints.

The main contribution of our paper is as follows: a thoroughly chosen experimental design, which combines an applicable pool size with a proper classification algorithm, allows constructing predictive models with performance characteristics comparable to models resulting from regular non-pooled strategies. These pooling designs can be primarily applied in biomarker discovery studies to build classification models to predict the class of future non-pooled subjects. Depending on the application and clinical utility of respective classifiers, such predictions might relate to the diagnosis and prognosis of disease, or the prediction of treatment success for individual patients.

2. Technical Preliminaries

2.1. Pooling Samples. For a general high-throughput experimental setup, let n denote the number of samples, and m represent the number of pooled samples or performed experiments (e.g., microarray chip or mass spectrometry runs). Thus, m is equal to n in non-pooled experiments. The observed value of a feature f in sample i is denoted by z_i. We assume for each feature f (e.g., gene expression or metabolite concentration) that $z_1, \ldots, z_n$ are independent and identically distributed random variables with mean μ_f and biological variance σ^2. By considering the technical variance $\varepsilon_k \sim N(0, \sigma_\varepsilon^2)$ to account for experimental variability, the experimental measurements can be represented as

$$y_i = z_i + \varepsilon_i. \tag{1}$$

The biological and technical variations are independent. Assuming that each individual contributes equally to the pool, the pooled value z' is the average of p individuals

$$z' = \frac{1}{p} \sum_{i=1}^{p} z_i, \tag{2}$$

where p refers to the pool size. In this study, we consider designs where $n = pm$ and m is the number of pooled samples. The measured values of pooled samples $y'_1, \ldots, y'_m$ can be represented as

$$y'_k = z'_k + \varepsilon_k, \tag{3}$$

where $\varepsilon_k \sim N(0, \sigma_\varepsilon^2)$ as in (1). The biological variance of pooled sample is then reduced to σ^2/p [14, 15].

2.2. Classification Algorithms. The general procedure in classification is to train a classifier on labeled training samples and to classify future unlabeled samples employing the trained model [16, 17]. Let x be a data set of a variables $\{f_1, \ldots, f_a\}$, called features and c_i be a class variable. Then a classifier is a function $f : f_1 \times \cdots \times f_a \to c_i$.

SVMs can be explained by four basic concepts: (i) the separating hyperplane, (ii) the maximum margin hyperplane, (iii) the soft margin, and (iv) the kernel function [18, 19]. SVMs construct a separating hyperplane which gives the largest separation margin between two classes. Soft margin allows some errors occur between the separation and a kernel function maps data into higher dimensional data space allowing the linear separation in nonlinear classification problems [12, 20].

RF is an ensemble-based machine learning method, which relies on the aggregation of results from several individual decision trees [21]. Each tree in the procedure is constructed by bagging data from the original dataset. A number of features are randomly selected to build a tree. The predicted class for each sample is then assumed to be the class that obtained the majority vote based on all trees.

k-NN is an instance-based learning method [16]. Giving a new query point (i.e., sample) x, k-NN finds k points in a training set, which are closest in distance to x. The class of x is determined by majority voting of k nearest neighbors using, for example, the Euclidean distance as metric.

PLR combines the logistic regression criterion with a penalization of the L_2-norm of the coefficients which enables a stable fit, even with a large number of features [22]. It performs similarly to SVMs, but in addition provides an estimate of the underlying probability [23].

PAM classifies samples based on the method of *nearest shrunken centroids*. The method assigns an unknown sample to the class whose centroid is closest (i.e., smallest squared distance). The centroids are *shrunken* by moving class centroids toward the overall centroids after standardizing by the within-class standard deviation for each feature. If the difference between the centroids of all classes and the overall centroid is smaller than a user-defined threshold for a feature, the feature is eliminated [24].

2.3. Feature Selection. The performance of classifiers strongly depends on properties of the feature set, such as which information is irrelevant or redundant. Feature selection uses different measures to select relevant features and is an important first step in building diagnostic, prognostic and predictive models [25]. Methods for feature selection can be classified into filter, wrapper, and embedded methods [26]. Wrappers use estimates of discriminatory performance (e.g., accuracy) provided by machine learning approaches to evaluate feature subsets. Similar to wrappers, embedded methods integrate with classifiers but take into account search strategies that require less computational power. Filter methods rank features based on their ability to distinguish between predefined classes and are independent of the classification algorithm and easier to interpret. In this paper, we apply statistical hypothesis testing, the Student's t-test, which is commonly used in bioinformatics.

3. Materials and Methods

3.1. Datasets. The mock datasets have been generated by simplicity mimicking various biological scenarios. Let n be the number of samples and a denote the number of features. A sample consists of features $\{f_1, \ldots, f_a\}$, which represent, for example, gene expressions or metabolite concentrations in a biological context. The dataset can be described as a set of samples $D = \{(x_i, c_i) \mid x_i \in X, c_i \in C\}$, where X is a set of samples, $x_1, \ldots, x_n$, and C is a set of class labels. The

data are balanced and dichotomous with a set of class labels $C = \{control, case\}$. For each feature, samples among each class are assumed to follow a Gaussian distribution, which is denoted as follows:

$$X_{control} \sim N(0, \sigma^2),$$
$$X_{case} \sim N(\gamma, \sigma^2). \tag{4}$$

σ^2 is considered as biological variance. γ denotes the relative mean difference between two groups. We define a discriminator (i.e., biomarker in biological context) as a feature with $\gamma \neq 0$. In this study, γ is randomly chosen from uniform distribution $U(0.3, 0.4)$ [27]. Thus, the value of γ in the case group of a nonmarker is 0, otherwise it is greater than 0. In addition, the technical variance is taken into account as $\varepsilon_i \sim N(0, \sigma_\varepsilon^2 = 0.2^2)$ according to (1). The numbers of markers are varied from 1 to 10.

From the data properties described above, we consider two simplified scenarios of data set characteristics. Scenario 1 is defined with $a = 1000$ and $n = 90$ per class. The biological variance σ^2 has the value of 0.2. These assumptions are used to simulate human data set characteristics. Scenario 2 is defined with $a = 1000$, $n = 30$ per class, and $\sigma^2 = 0.1$. The later assumptions are used to imitate animal (e.g., mice and rats) data set characteristics. Human biomarker discovery studies are generally designed and executed with a higher number of samples than animal experiments. On the other hand, the variability in animal experiment is smaller than in human settings according to in-bred and genetic homogeneity of study subject populations as well as better means to standardize and control experimental conditions [28].

3.2. Pooling Data Simulation. Let p be the number of samples that are pooled. In this study, we set $p = 2$, 3, and 5, that $n = pm$, where m is the number of pooled samples. Most measurements of pools were reported to be similar to averages of individuals comprising the pool [8, 15]. Thus, in this study, each pooled sample was obtained by averaging p samples. For $p = 2$, 3, and 5, the pooling datasets are in sizes of 90, 60, and 36 instances in the human scenario of total 180 samples and in size of 30, 20, and 12 instances in the animal scenario of total 60 samples, respectively. In order to mimic a real-life experiment, in which the pooling is done before the samples are analyzed, the simulated data were transformed by performing exponential function to the basis e prior to pooling [29]. Then the pooled data were transformed back into the natural log scale. The new value of derived pooled samples y' can be represented as

$$y' = \log_e \left(\frac{1}{p} \sum_{i=1}^{p} e^{z_i} \right) + \varepsilon_k, \tag{5}$$

where z_i denotes the value of each individual sample and ε_k denotes technical errors, $\varepsilon_k \sim N(0, \sigma_\varepsilon^2 = 0.2^2)$ of a pooled experiment as applied from (2) and (3). Note that each value y' is calculated for each feature.

3.3. Classification, Feature Selection, and Model Evaluation. The discriminatory ability of popular classifiers, which are

SVMs using both linear and radial kernels, RF, k-NN, PLR, and PAM are compared based on synthetic data. Feature selection by using statistical t-test is included. The features are ranked according to the t-statistics and the top 10, 100, and 1000 features are selected for classification. The implementation of the R package classification for microarrays (CMAs) [30] was used for feature selection, classification and model evaluation. In this work, for model evaluation, we did not perform common-applied k-fold cross-validation (CV), which subdivides data into k partitions and each turn uses one partition as test set and the remainder as training set. This is specific to the pooling problem since in real life the constructed classifier only utilize future individual sample for class prediction. The training sets can be pooled since the classes of subjects are already known. However, new subjects cannot be pooled for testing as they might belong to different classes. Thus, the CV or even other model evaluation method, for example, bootstrap cannot be applied in the pooling approach as the test set cannot consist of pooled samples in real use. Consequently, we used separate training and test sets for model evaluation. Classifier construction utilizes a training set and then model validation is performed by using a test set. The test set comprised 450 individual samples and the average misclassification rates from each test sample was obtained. The pipeline from data simulation to model evaluation was repeated 300 times. The selected number of test samples and the number of replications were found to give a small variance and stable results in our setting, respectively.

Feature selection was performed for each training set. A number of top ranked features (10, 100, and 1000) were selected based on a training data. The selected ranked features were then utilized in the test set for model estimation.

Parameter tuning for every classifier was performed using internal 3-fold CV with customized grids [30] on the training set. The number of folds was found to have no significant effect on classifier performance. By applying a 3-fold CV strategy, the training set was subdivided into three equal partitions where each one took turns and consecutively was used for model validation, and the remainder for training. Finally, the optimal parameters were derived from the CV. By performing CV, soft margin values (c = 0.1, 1, 5, 10, 50, 100, 500) were tuned for SVMs both linear and radial kernel. The gamma values (0.25, 0.50, 1.00, 2.00, and 4.00) were determined for radial kernel. For RF, numbers of randomly sampled features (4, 8, 16, 32, and 64 considered based on squared root of total features which is 1000) were adjusted and the number of trees was set to 1000. A k value (1 to number of top ranked features) was selected for k-NN. The lambda values (0.0625, 0.1250, 0.2500, 0.50, 1.00, 2.00, 4.00, 8.00, and 16.00) were tuned for PLR. The thresholds for deltas were searched among (0.1, 0.25, 0.5, 1, 2, and 5) in PAM.

4. Results and Discussion

Five well-known classifiers, comprising SVMs using both linear and radial kernels, RF, k-NN, PLR, and PAM, were

TABLE 1: Comparison of classification performance with different numbers of top-ranked features.

Classifiers	Misclassification rate		
	Top 10	Top 100	Top 1000
Individual			
SVM with linear kernel	0.2191**	0.3479**	0.3757
SVM with radial kernel	0.2178**	0.3211**	0.3712
RF	0.2436**	0.2926**	0.2975
k-NN	0.2515**	0.3270**	0.4354
PLR	0.2160**	0.3329**	0.3761
PAM	0.2096**	0.3185**	0.2310
Pool size = 5			
SVM with linear kernel	0.3229**	0.3817**	0.4131
SVM with radial kernel	0.3167**	0.3771**	0.4571
RF	0.3272**	0.3568**	0.3841
k-NN	0.3133**	0.3779**	0.4720
PLR	0.3113**	0.3772**	0.3983
PAM	0.3005**	0.3799*	0.3681

Classification performance is presented for different number of top-ranked features. The dataset contains a total of 1000 features and 90 samples per class with 10 markers. Top 1000 features denote no feature selection. The table shows results using individual samples and illustrates results derived by means of a pooled dataset when pool size is 5, respectively. Significance levels $*P < 0.05$ and $**P \ll 0.05$ indicate comparisons where no feature selection is performed by using the Wilcoxon rank sum test.

selected to investigate discriminatory performance for (i) different number of top ranked features, (ii) different pooling sizes including different numbers of virtual discriminators (i.e., biomarkers in biological context), and (iii) human and animal (e.g., mice or rats) scenarios.

4.1. Effects of Feature Selection. In this study, we used the Student's t-test, the most popular statistical test to filter genes [31], for feature selection. Filter methods have the advantages of classifier independence, lower computational complexity, and they provide ranking and prioritization of features which are important for biological contextualization and interpretation [26].

Results (based on the human scenario) demonstrate that the examined classifiers generally show significantly smaller misclassification rates (using the Wilcoxon rank sum test) when employing feature selection in both individual and pooled data, compared to runs without feature selection (Table 1). This observation can be explained by the ability of feature selection to reduce noise and to avoid model overfitting. The findings are in concordance with several other studies showing that feature selection methods yield better discriminatory power of classification algorithms (e.g., [12, 27]). However, PAM performs better without feature selection when compared with the parameter setting where the 100 top-ranked features are selected in our datasets. This may be an effect of internal feature selection and the optimal parameter delta from parameter tuning, which shrinks the standardized centroid for each class in this particular algorithm [24].

4.2. Effects of Pooling Samples. In order to investigate the effects of pooling samples on classification algorithms, datasets of different numbers of pooled samples were mimicked (see Section 3). The evaluation was based on human scenario and 100 top-ranked features using the *t*-test for feature selection.

Misclassification rates obtained by the six classifiers were investigated for individual subjects and pooled samples (pool sizes of 2, 3, and 5). The results show that the misclassification rates increase with larger pool sizes (Figure 1), which is in accordance with the study of Telaar et al. [14]. This characteristic can be observed with both small and larger numbers of markers in datasets. Although pooling helps to decrease variances of biological samples, the sample size is reduced when samples are pooled [15] which can degrade the discriminatory ability of classifiers. In addition, the increase of misclassification rates with raising pool sizes follows a linear pattern. The difference among the performance of classifiers is larger for higher numbers of markers than for small numbers of markers in the data.

Significant differences in the performance of classifiers between individual subjects and various pool sizes become apparent from the Wilcoxon rank sum test (Figure 2). In datasets with large number of markers, the performances of classifiers show significant differences in every pair of pool size (Figure 2(b)). On the other hand, in the datasets with small numbers of markers, there is no statistical significant difference ($P > 0.05$) between some pairs of pool sizes (Figure 2(a)). For example, there is no statistically difference between individual sample and pool size = 2 and between pool size = 3 and pool size = 5 in PLR. For SVMs with both linear and radial kernels, performances of classifiers do not show statistical differences at pool sizes of 2 and 3, respectively. These results could motivate the use of classifiers with different pool sizes in cases where the data is noisy and only a small number of markers are expected.

In order to gain further insight on the performance of different classifiers, the misclassification rate of classifiers with different number of markers from 1 to 10 was investigated (Figure 3). RF outperforms other classifiers for every pool size (2, 3, and 5) in our settings (with 100 top-ranked features). For other classifiers, the performance-ranked order slightly differs, depending on the pool size. SVM with linear kernel does not perform as well as SVM with radial kernel in our settings. The kernel function helps to map data into higher dimension space. This could allow the linear hyperplane providing better separation between data points of two classes. The performance variation of classifiers is greater for individual and small pool sizes than for larger pool sizes.

The RF classifier demonstrates a good predictive performance even when most predictive features are noisy and turns out to be robust against overfitting. In earlier studies, it was also reported to produce favorable results [32, 33]. In addition, ensemble methods like RF are generally well-suited for reducing the total expected error [34].

Also performance trends of classifiers with increasing numbers of markers are demonstrated in Figure 3. The higher the number of markers, the better the classification

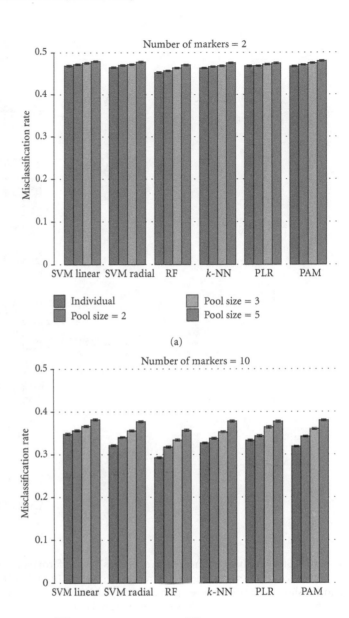

(a)

(b)

FIGURE 1: Performance of classifiers on individual samples and various pool sizes. A comparison of classifiers performances for datasets of individual samples and pool sizes of 2, 3, and 5 are shown. Misclassification rates rise with larger pool sizes. (a) and (b) show the comparison when numbers of markers are 2 and 10, respectively. The height of bars indicates 95% confidence interval from 300 replications.

performance [20]. This trend is apparent with any number of pooled data.

4.3. Results of the Mimicked Animal Scenario. To provide a real-life scenario, we mimicked datasets of human studies and animal (in this case mice or rats) experiments. The animal datasets were simulated with a smaller sample size

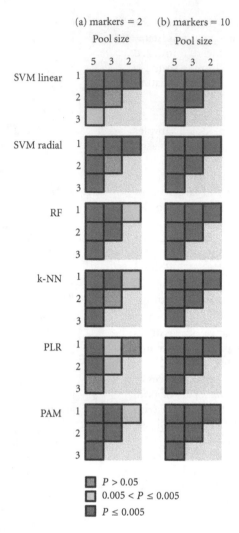

FIGURE 2: Statistically significant matrices of classifiers performances among various pool sizes datasets. Statistically significant differences of performances of classifiers among different pool sizes of 1 (individual), 2, 3, and 5 are shown using Wilcoxon rank sum test, respectively. (a) and (b) show the matrices when numbers of synthesized markers are 2 and 10, respectively. Each square represents a comparison between two pool sizes datasets. The colors indicate the level of significance.

and smaller variance compared to the human scenario (see Section 3), reflecting properties of real-world data [28, 35]. For instance, mice experiments are generally conducted with smaller sample sizes. The variability in mice is smaller than in human settings due to in-bred and genetic homogeneity of populations as well as means to standardize and control experimental conditions (e.g., dietary control, time of sample collection). The effects of pooling samples in the animal scenario are shown in Figure 4.

In general, the trends of the animal study simulations (Figure 4) are similar to the human scenario (Figure 1), where a larger pool size causes higher error rates for classifiers. The differences between classifier performances are also larger for bigger numbers of mocked markers in datasets. However, the classifiers produce increased misclassification rates compared to the human scenario despite the lower variance in the animal datasets. The lower variability is compromised by the effect of the sample size. We have investigated the performance of classifiers in the animal study scenario

with the same sample size as in the human setting. As expected, the classifiers in the animal scenario outperform the ones in the human setting (Figure 5).

5. Conclusions

In this work, we provide a systematic evaluation of pooling designs on the discriminating ability of classifiers. The performance of SVMs, RF, k-NN, PLR, and PAM was studied on mock datasets. The results highlight that pooling strategies generally lead to higher error rates of classifiers. Misclassification rates are likely to increase with pool sizes in a linear pattern, not exponentially. Moreover, with datasets having small number of makers, there is no statistically significant difference of the performance of classifiers between some pairs of pool sizes. Although being inferior to non-pooling design, these results suggest the consideration of pooling strategies for "omics" biomedical studies; especially, if there

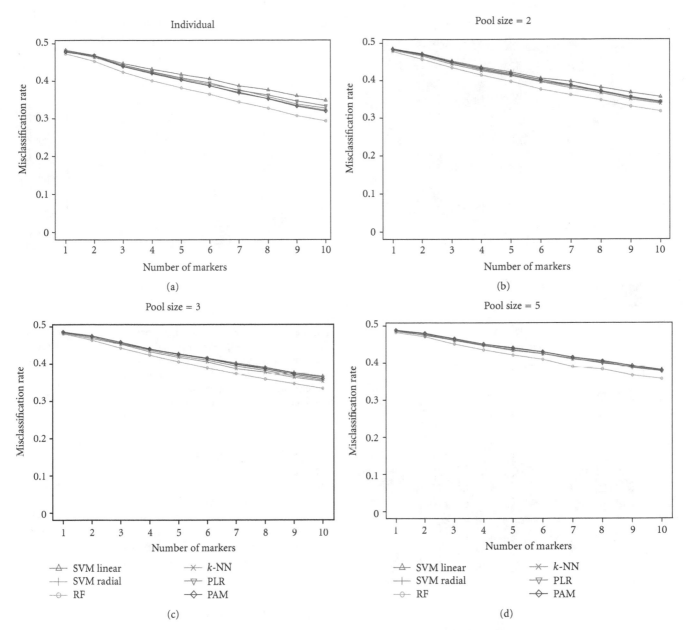

FIGURE 3: The performance of classifiers for various numbers of markers based on non-pooled and pooled data. Misclassification rates of classifiers are shown when the number of markers is increasing from 1 to 10. (a) shows the performance of classifiers on dataset of individual samples (90 controls and 90 cases). (b)–(d) show the performance of classifiers on pooled datasets when pool sizes are 2, 3, and 5, respectively.

are budgetary or time constraints that do not permit the analytical execution of individual sample runs (e.g., LC/MS-MS). Furthermore, a staged approach might also be considered where first a pooling design is used for global profiling of biomarkers in high-dimensional datasets and subsequent model building, followed by qualification steps where individual samples are analyzed and only a subset of biomolecules is targeted for analysis. This comparative study motivates scientists to consider and balance pros and cons of various designs prior to the execution of biomarker discovery studies. Thus, scientists are encouraged to make an informed decision to leverage pooling designs as a valid strategy to compensate for limited amounts of samples or high biologi-

cal variation, or as a remedy to improve analytical cost and time efficiency.

In this study, we applied various classifiers with and without feature selection, and systematically explored the effect of relevant parameters on their performance. In general, all considered designs aim at discovering a subset of features via an algorithm that is subsequently used to predict future outcome, such as the disease status. Our results show that RF mainly outperforms SVMs, k-NN, PLR, and PAM in our settings, while the latter provide comparable accuracy among themselves. SVMs perform better with a radial kernel compared to a linear one. We strongly recommend conducting feature selection prior to classification. It aids in

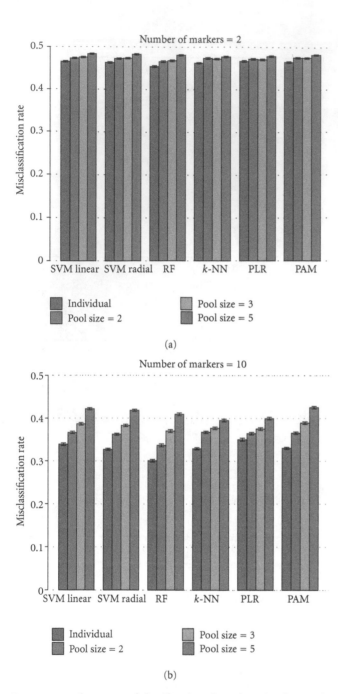

(a)

(b)

FIGURE 4: Performance of classifiers based on the animal scenario. Performance of classifiers for datasets of individual samples and pool sizes of 2, 3, and 5 are compared. Misclassification rates rise with larger pool sizes as the human scenario. (a) and (b) show the comparison when numbers of markers are 2 and 10, respectively. The height of bars indicates 95% confidence interval from 300 replications.

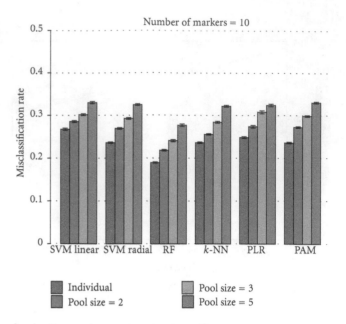

FIGURE 5: Performance of classifiers based on the animal scenario (sample size = 180). Performance of classifiers for datasets of individual samples and pool sizes of 2, 3, and 5 are compared when numbers of markers = 10 and sample size = 90 samples per class as performed in human scenario. The height of bars indicates 95% confidence interval from 300 replications.

of classifiers more than variance of the data in our setting. Therefore, even though data of the animal scenario has lower variance in this study, the classifiers do not perform better than in human datasets.

In future studies, we want to include skewed class distributions and correlations between features in our mock datasets and explore the effect of these properties as well as unbalanced study group sample sizes on the performance of classifiers.

Authors' Contributions

K. Kusonmano carried out the data simulation, established framework for feature selection and classification, analyzed the results, and drafted the paper. M. Netzer participated in implementation of the framework for feature selection and classification. A. Graber guided the design of the study. K. Kusonmano, A. Graber, M. Netzer, M. Dehmer, C. Baumgartner, and K. Liedl participated in discussion of the results and coordination to draft the paper. All authors read and approved the final paper.

Acknowledgments

K. Kusonmano thanks the Austrian Federal Ministry for Science and Research in the frame of ASEA UNINET for providing the scholarship during her study. The authors also acknowledge the support of the Austrian Genome Research Program GEN-AU (Bioinformatics Integration Network, BIN III) and COMET Center ONCOTYROL, and were

picking important features and reducing noise, which in turn yields better performance of classification algorithms. The results highlight the importance of applying feature selection and pooling design according to the individual properties of the classification algorithms. As a consequence of the selected data properties in the human and animal study scenarios, sample size influences and compromises the performance funded by the Federal Ministry for Transport Innovation and Technology (BMVIT) and the Federal Ministry of Economics and Labour (BMWA), the Tiroler Zukunftsstiftung (TZS) and the Styrian Business Promotion Agency (SFG) (and supported by the University for Health Sciences, Medical Informatics and Technology, the Graz University of Technology and Biomax Informatics).

References

[1] R. Clarke, H. W. Ressom, A. Wang et al., "The properties of high-dimensional data spaces: implications for exploring gene and protein expression data," *Nature Reviews Cancer*, vol. 8, no. 1, pp. 37–49, 2008.

[2] F. Molina, M. Dehmer, P. Perco et al., "Systems biology: opening new avenues in clinical research," *Nephrology Dialysis Transplantation*, vol. 25, no. 4, pp. 1015–1018, 2010.

[3] D. Agrawal, T. Chen, R. Irby et al., "Osteopontin identified as lead marker of colon cancer progression, using pooled sample expression profiling," *Journal of the National Cancer Institute*, vol. 94, no. 7, pp. 513–521, 2002.

[4] R. A. Jolly, K. M. Goldstein, T. Wei et al., "Pooling samples within microarray studies: a comparative analysis of rat liver transcription response to prototypical toxicants," *Physiological Genomics*, vol. 22, pp. 346–355, 2005.

[5] C. M. Kendziorski, Y. Zhang, H. Lan, and A. D. Attie, "The efficiency of pooling mRNA in microarray experiments," *Biostatistics*, vol. 4, no. 3, pp. 465–477, 2003.

[6] X. Peng, C. L. Wood, E. M. Blalock, K. C. Chen, P. W. Landfield, and A. J. Stromberg, "Statistical implications of pooling RNA samples for microarray experiments," *BMC Bioinformatics*, vol. 4, article no. 26, 2003.

[7] J. H. Shih, A. M. Michalowska, K. Dobbin, Y. Ye, T. H. Qiu, and J. E. Green, "Effects of pooling mRNA in microarray class comparisons," *Bioinformatics*, vol. 20, no. 18, pp. 3318–3325, 2004.

[8] S. D. Zhang and T. W. Gant, "Effect of pooling samples on the efficiency of comparative studies using microarrays," *Bioinformatics*, vol. 21, no. 24, pp. 4378–4383, 2005.

[9] W. Zhang, A. Carriquiry, D. Nettleton, and J. C. M. Dekkers, "Pooling mRNA in microarray experiments and its effect on power," *Bioinformatics*, vol. 23, no. 10, pp. 1217–1224, 2007.

[10] J. A. Cruz and D. S. Wishart, "Applications of machine learning in cancer prediction and prognosis," *Cancer Informatics*, vol. 2, pp. 59–77, 2006.

[11] J. Hayward, S. A. Alvarez, C. Ruiz, M. Sullivan, J. Tseng, and G. Whalen, "Machine learning of clinical performance in a pancreatic cancer database," *Artificial Intelligence in Medicine*, vol. 49, no. 3, pp. 187–195, 2010.

[12] M. Netzer, G. Millonig, M. Osl et al., "A new ensemble-based algorithm for identifying breath gas marker candidates in liver disease using ion molecule reaction mass spectrometry," *Bioinformatics*, vol. 25, no. 7, pp. 941–947, 2009.

[13] E. K. Lee, "Machine learning framework for classification in medicine and biology," in *Integration of AI and OR Techniques in Constraint Programming for Combinatorial Optimization Problems*, Springer, Berlin, Germany, 2009.

[14] A. Telaar, G. Nürnberg, and D. Repsilber, "Finding biomarker signatures in pooled sample designs: a simulation framework for methodological comparisons," *Advances in Bioinformatics*, vol. 2010, Article ID 318573, 8 pages, 2010.

[15] C. Kendziorski, R. A. Irizarry, K. S. Chen, J. D. Haag, and M. N. Gould, "On the utility of pooling biological samples in microarray experiments," *Proceedings of the National Academy of Sciences of the United States of America*, vol. 102, no. 12, pp. 4252–4257, 2005.

[16] T. Hastie, R. Tibshirani, and J. Friedman, *The Elements of Statistical Learning: Data Mining, Inference, and Prediction*, Springer, 2009.

[17] T. M. Mitchell, *Machine Learning*, McGraw-Hill, 1997.

[18] V. N. Vapnik, *Statistical Learning Theory*, John Wiley & Sons, New York, NY, USA, 1998.

[19] W. S. Noble, "What is a support vector machine?" *Nature Biotechnology*, vol. 24, no. 12, pp. 1565–1567, 2006.

[20] K. Kusonmano, M. Netzer, B. Pfeifer, C. Baumgartner, K. R. Liedl, and A. Graber, "Evaluation of the impact of dataset charactertics for classification problems in biological applications," in *Proceedings of the International Conference on Bioinformatics and Biomedicine*, pp. 741–745, Venice, Italy, 2009.

[21] L. Breiman, "Random forests," *Machine Learning*, vol. 45, no. 1, pp. 5–32, 2001.

[22] M. Y. Park and T. Hastie, "Penalized logistic regression for detecting gene interactions," *Biostatistics*, vol. 9, no. 1, pp. 30–50, 2008.

[23] J. Zhu and T. Hastie, "Classification of gene microarrays by penalized logistic regression," *Biostatistics*, vol. 5, no. 3, pp. 427–443, 2004.

[24] R. Tibshirani, T. Hastie, B. Narasimhan, and G. Chu, "Diagnosis of multiple cancer types by shrunken centroids of gene expression," *Proceedings of the National Academy of Sciences of the United States of America*, vol. 99, no. 10, pp. 6567–6572, 2002.

[25] C. Baumgartner and A. Graber, "Data mining and knowledge discovery in metabolomics," in *Successes and New Directions in Data Mining*, P. Poncelet, F. Masseglia, and M. Teisseire, Eds., pp. 141–166, IGI Global, 2008.

[26] Y. Saeys, I. Inza, and P. Larrañaga, "A review of feature selection techniques in bioinformatics," *Bioinformatics*, vol. 23, no. 19, pp. 2507–2517, 2007.

[27] B. Wu, T. Abbott, D. Fishman et al., "Comparison of statistical methods for classification of ovarian cancer using mass spectrometry data," *Bioinformatics*, vol. 19, no. 13, pp. 1636–1643, 2003.

[28] Y. Guo, A. Graber, R. N. McBurney, and R. Balasubramanian, "Sample size and statistical power considerations in high-dimensionality data settings: a comparative study of classification algorithms," *BMC Bioinformatics*, vol. 11, article no. 447, 2010.

[29] J. Quackenbush, "Microarray data normalization and transformation," *Nature Genetics*, vol. 32, no. 5, pp. 496–501, 2002.

[30] M. Slawski, M. Daumer, and A. L. Boulesteix, "CMA—a comprehensive Bioconductor package for supervised classification with high dimensional data," *BMC Bioinformatics*, vol. 9, article no. 439, 2008.

[31] W. Pan, "A comparative review of statistical methods for discovering differentially expressed genes in replicated microarray experiments," *Bioinformatics*, vol. 18, no. 4, pp. 546–554, 2002.

[32] A. Statnikov, L. Wang, and C. F. Aliferis, "A comprehensive comparison of random forests and support vector machines for microarray-based cancer classification," *BMC Bioinformatics*, vol. 9, article no. 319, 2008.

[33] R. Díaz-Uriarte and S. Alvarez de Andrés, "Gene selection and classification of microarray data using random forest," *BMC Bioinformatics*, vol. 7, article no. 3, 2006.

[34] R. Polikar, "Ensemble based systems in decision making," *IEEE Circuits and Systems Magazine*, vol. 6, no. 3, Article ID 1688199, pp. 21–44, 2006.

[35] R. N. McBurney, W. M. Hines, L. S. Von Tungeln et al., "The liver toxicity biomarker study: phase i design and preliminary results," *Toxicologic Pathology*, vol. 37, no. 1, pp. 52–64, 2009.

6

Extracting Physicochemical Features to Predict Protein Secondary Structure

Yin-Fu Huang and Shu-Ying Chen

Department of Computer Science and Information Engineering, National Yunlin University of Science and Technology, 123 University Road, Section 3, Touliu, Yunlin 640, Taiwan

Correspondence should be addressed to Yin-Fu Huang; huangyf@yuntech.edu.tw

Academic Editors: S. Jahandideh and J. Ni

We propose a protein secondary structure prediction method based on position-specific scoring matrix (PSSM) profiles and four physicochemical features including conformation parameters, net charges, hydrophobic, and side chain mass. First, the SVM with the optimal window size and the optimal parameters of the kernel function is found. Then, we train the SVM using the PSSM profiles generated from PSI-BLAST and the physicochemical features extracted from the CB513 data set. Finally, we use the filter to refine the predicted results from the trained SVM. For all the performance measures of our method, Q_3 reaches 79.52, SOV94 reaches 86.10, and SOV99 reaches 74.60; all the measures are higher than those of the SVMpsi method and the SVMfreq method. This validates that considering these physicochemical features in predicting protein secondary structure would exhibit better performances.

1. Introduction

Many issues on molecular biology have been addressed in the past decades, including genetics, structural biology, and drug design. A protein primary sequence is composed of amino acids; as we know, totally 20 different kinds of amino acids can be found in protein sequences. In this paper, we would investigate protein secondary structures based on protein sequences.

The secondary structure of a protein sequence comes from different folding of amino acids, due to the differences of their side chain sizes, shapes, reactivity, and the ability to form hydrogen bonds. Furthermore, owing to the differences of the side chain sizes, the number of electric charges, coupled with the affinity for water, the tertiary structures of protein sequences are not all the same. Thus, the exploration of molecular structures on protein sequences is divided into secondary, tertiary, and even quaternary structures. Given a protein primary sequence, its corresponding secondary structure can be revealed as follows:

Primary sequence:

MFKVYGYDSNIHKCVYCDNAKRLLTVKKQP-
FEFINIMPEKGV

Secondary structure:

CEEEEECCCCCCCCCHHHHHHHHHHHHCCCC-
EEEEECCCCTTC.

A protein sequence affects the structure and function; in other words, a protein sequence determines its structure, and the structure determines functions. If amino acids in a protein sequence are arranged in a different order in the skeleton branch of the side chain R group, the nature of the protein would reveal specific functions. Even for different species of proteins, if they have a similar structure, their functions would be also similar. Therefore, predicting the protein structure is crucial to the function analysis. Besides, the secondary structure refers to the relative position of the space between the atoms of a certain backbone. Traditional protein structure determination was done by protein X-ray crystallography or nuclear magnetic resonance (NMR). However, all experimental analysis costs much time. In order to shorten the time to help biologists, protein structure prediction by computers facilitates reaching this goal.

The prediction of protein secondary structure has been studied for decades. Early, the statistical analysis of secondary structure was done for a single amino acid. The most representative is the Chou and Fasman method [1], and the accuracy is only 50%. Next, the statistical analysis for amino acid segments was done further. A segment length is usually with 9~21 amino acids. Based on an amino acid segment, predicting the structure of central residues enables promoting the accuracy. The most representative is the GOR method [2], and the accuracy increases more than 10% (about 63%). At present, the prediction methods on protein secondary structure have evolved into using the PSI-BLAST program [3] to find the protein homology information, based on PSSM (position-specific scoring matrices) profiles. The accuracy of using PSSM to predict secondary structure has reached between 70 and 80% [4–7]. However, we believe that there still exists a great improvement in predicting protein secondary structure.

The rest of this paper is organized as follows. In Section 2, basic concepts used in the proposed methods are introduced first. In Section 3, we propose the methods and relevant features to predict the secondary structure of a protein sequence. Then, we make use of window sizes and tune parameters in the experiments in Section 4, in order to obtain better experimental results. Finally, we make a conclusion in Section 5.

2. Basic Concepts

2.1. Protein Secondary Structure. Protein secondary structure derived from the experimentally determined 3D structure has been defined using DSSP (Dictionary of Secondary Structures of Proteins) [8], STRIDE (STRuctural IDEntification) [9], and DEFINE (DEFINE_structure) [10]. DSSP is selected here so that our method can be compared with most existing methods, based on the same protein secondary structure definition. Eight secondary structure classes were defined there, that is, H(α-helix), G(310-helix), I(π-helix), E(β-strand), B(isolated β-bridge), T(turn), S(bend), and -(rest). The eight structure classes are usually reduced to three classes of helix (H), sheet (E), and coil (C). Five reductions could be performed as follows:

(1) H, G and I to H; E to E; the rest to C

(2) H, G to H; E, B to E; the rest to C

(3) H, G to H; E to E; the rest to C

(4) H to H; E, B to E; the rest to C

(5) H to H; E to E; the rest to C.

The first reduction was used in the PHD (Profile network from HeiDelberg) method [7] which is the early secondary structure prediction method using multiple sequence alignments of proteins homologous with a query protein sequence. We also use the first reduction in order to provide a fair comparison with other prediction methods.

2.2. SVM (Support Vector Machine). SVM was first investigated by Boser et al. in 1992 [11]. It solves linearly inseparable problems by nonlinearly mapping the vector in a low dimensional space to a higher dimensional feature space and constructs an optimal hyper-plane in the higher dimensional

space. Therefore, SVM has high performances in data classification. A classification task usually involves with training and testing data which consist of some data instances. Each instance in the training set contains one "target value" (i.e., class label) and several "attributes" (i.e., features). The goal of SVM is to produce a model which can predict the target value of data instances in the testing set by using the attributes.

3. Methods and Features

3.1. System Architecture. The system architecture of predicting protein secondary structure is divided into three steps, as illustrated in Figure 1. The first step is to determine/extract the relevant features in/from protein sequences. Then, in the second step, we feed the features into SVM, respectively, in the training and test phases. Finally, we use a filter method to refine the predicted results from the trained SVM. During the SVM training phase, we not only train the SVM using the training data, but also, in advance, find the optimal sliding window size and the cost and gamma parameters of SVM kernel function, using the entire data set. The details about each module in the system architecture are depicted in the following subsections.

3.2. Feature Extraction. Five relevant kinds of features are extracted from protein sequences to predict protein secondary structure, that is, (1) conformation parameters, (2) position specific scoring matrix (PSSM) profiles, (3) net charge, (4) hydrophobic, and (5) side chain mass. The process of feature extraction is shown in Figure 2.

3.2.1. Extracting Sequences. First, we extract amino acid and secondary structure sequences from the PDB website (http://www.rcsb.org/pdb/home/home.do), using the PDB codes of CB513 [12]. Then, we can further extract five different features from amino acid sequences as follows.

3.2.2. Conformation Parameters. Conformation parameters are the proportions that residues (or amino acids) tend to secondary structure. In general, protein secondary structure is divided into three types: α-helix (H), β-sheet (E), and coil (C), so that there are three values for each amino acid. In the feature extraction, all the conformation parameters are calculated from a data set. The conformation parameters for each amino acid S_{ij} are defined as follows:

$$S_{ij} = \frac{a_{ij}}{a_i}, \quad \text{where } i = 1, \ldots, 20, \ j = 1, 2, 3. \quad (1)$$

In this formula, i indicates the 20 amino acids, and j indicates the 3 types of secondary structure: H, E, and C. Here, a_i is the amount of the ith amino acid in a data set whereas a_{ij} is the amount of the ith amino acids with the jth secondary structure. The conformation parameters for each amino acid in a data set are shown in Table 1. The reason of using conformation parameters as features is that the folding of each residue has some correlation with forming a specific structure.

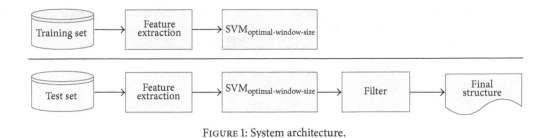

FIGURE 1: System architecture.

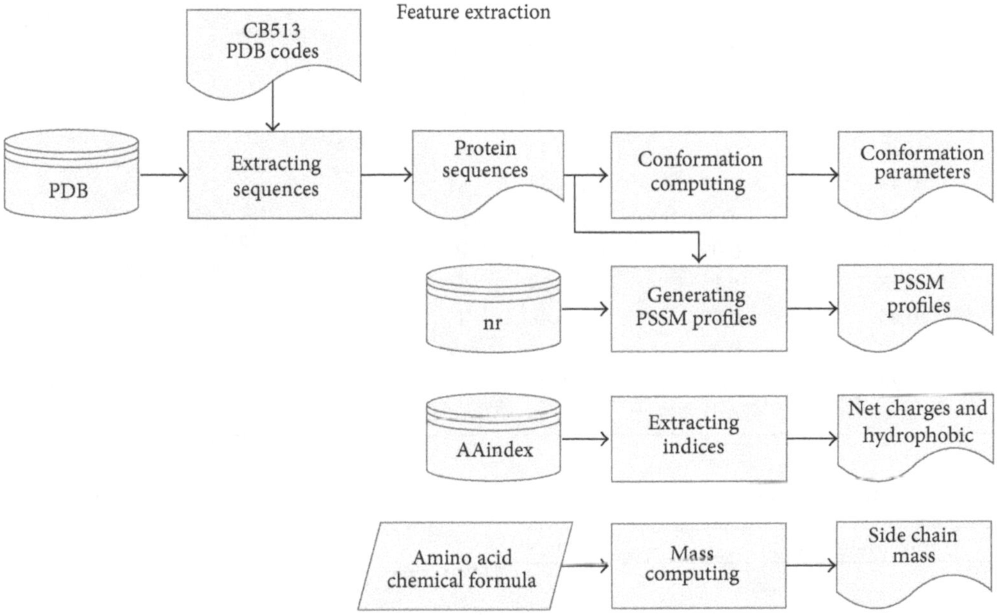

Feature extraction

FIGURE 2: Process of feature extraction.

3.2.3. PSSM Profiles. PSSM profiles are generated by PSI-BLAST (Position Specific Iterative-Basic Local Alignment Search Tool) program. Since PSSM profiles are involved with biological evolution, we consider them as features in our work. A PSSM profile has $L \times 20$ elements, where L is the length of a query sequence. These profiles are then used as the input features to feed an SVM, employing a sliding window method.

PSI-BLAST is based on BLAST which has been published by Altschul et al. in 1997 [3]. Since PSI-BLAST program is more sensitive than other methods, we can find a lot of low similarity sequences and similarity structure function of protein sequences. First, a database containing all known sequences (or nonredundant database) is selected. Then, low complexity regions are removed from the nr database. Finally, PSI-BLAST program is used to query each sequence in CB513 and generates PSSM profiles after three iterations. Here, multiple sequence alignment (MSA) and BLOSUM62 matrix [13] are used in this process.

The reason of using the sliding window method is to get more surrounding information of residues. We consider a sliding window of size 7~19 at which a predicted residue is centered to extract input features. The optimal window size yielding favorable predictive performances would be obtained experimentally. For the ith residue centered at

the sliding window of size 7, we can get 7×20 features $F_{i+n,j}$ where n is in the range $[-3, 3]$ and j is the PSSM column from 1 to 20.

3.2.4. Net Charges. There are five amino acids with charges, that is, R, D, E, H, and K. Since residues with similar electric charges repel each other and interrupt the hydrogen bond of main chain, they are adverse to α-helix formation. Besides, the continuous residues of β-sheet cannot be with similar charges. This information facilitates predicting the secondary structure. The net charge of amino acids can be taken from Amino Acid index database (or AAindex) [14–18], as shown in Table 2. A plus sign represents a positive charge and a minus sign represents a negative charge.

3.2.5. Hydrophobic. For protein folding, polar residues prefer to stay outside of protein to prevent non-polar (hydrophobic) residues from exposing to polar solvent, like water. Therefore, hydrophobic residues appearing periodically can be used for predicting protein secondary structure. In general, the residues in α-helix structure are made up of one segment of hydrophobic and one segment of hydrophilic. However, β-sheet structure is usually influenced by the environment, so

TABLE 1: Conformation parameters for each amino acid in a data set.

Amino acids	H	E	C
A	0.49	0.16	0.35
R	0.42	0.19	0.39
N	0.27	0.13	0.6
D	0.31	0.11	0.58
C	0.26	0.29	0.45
E	0.49	0.15	0.36
Q	0.46	0.16	0.38
G	0.16	0.14	0.7
H	0.3	0.22	0.48
I	0.35	0.37	0.28
L	0.45	0.24	0.31
K	0.4	0.17	0.43
M	0.44	0.23	0.33
F	0.35	0.3	0.35
P	0.18	0.09	0.74
S	0.28	0.19	0.54
T	0.25	0.27	0.48
W	0.37	0.29	0.35
Y	0.34	0.3	0.36
V	0.3	0.41	0.29

TABLE 2: Net charge of amino acids.

Amino acids	Mass
A	0
R	+1
N	0
D	−1
C	0
E	−1
Q	0
G	0
H	+1
I	0
L	0
K	+1
M	0
F	0
P	0
S	0
T	0
W	0
Y	0
V	0

TABLE 3: Hydrophobic values of amino acids.

Amino acids	Mass
A	1.8
R	−4.5
N	−3.5
D	−3.5
C	2.5
E	−3.5
Q	−3.5
G	−0.4
H	−3.2
I	4.5
L	3.8
K	−3.9
M	1.9
F	2.8
P	−1.6
S	−0.8
T	−0.7
W	−0.9
Y	−1.3
V	4.2

FIGURE 3: Basic structure of amino acids.

3.2.6. Side Chain Mass. Although the basic structure as shown in Figure 3 is the same for 20 amino acids, the size of the side chain R group still influences structure folding. Here, we explain the influences as follows. First, the side chain R group is distributed in the outside of the main chain of α-helix structure, but the continuous large R groups can make α-helix structure unstable, thereby disabling amino acids from forming α-helix structure. Next, the R group with ring structure like proline (P) is not easy to form α-helix structure. Proline is composed of 5 atoms in a ring, which is not easy to reverse and is also not easy to generate a hydrogen bond. Finally, we observe that the R group of β-sheet structure is smaller than those of other structures, in general. Therefore, we include the side chain mass as a feature, as shown in Table 4.

3.3. SVM (Finding the Optimal Window Size and Parameters). The SVM used in the experiments is a classifier for predicting the secondary structure H, E, and C. Threefold cross-validation is employed on the CB513 data set to find (1) the optimal window size in the range [7, 19] and (2) the optimal parameters of the kernel function, such as cost C and gamma γ. Here, the kernel function used in the SVM

this phenomenon is not obvious. In other words, hydrophobic affects the stability of secondary structure. The hydrophobic values of amino acids can also be obtained from Amino Acid index database (or AAindex) [14–18], as shown in Table 3. The more positive values are, the more hydrophobic is.

TABLE 4: Side chain mass of amino acids.

Amino acids	Mass
A	15.0347
R	100.1431
N	58.0597
D	59.0445
C	47.0947
E	73.0713
Q	72.0865
G	1.0079
H	81.0969
I	57.1151
L	57.1151
K	72.1297
M	75.1483
F	91.1323
P	41.0725
S	31.0341
T	45.0609
W	130.1689
Y	107.1317
V	43.0883

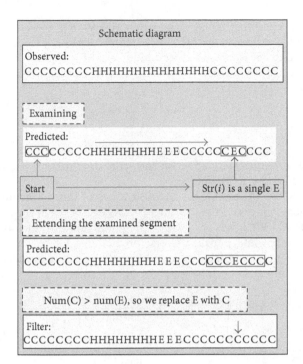

FIGURE 4: Schematic diagram for filtering 9INSb.

TABLE 5: Structures of the CB513 data set.

Structures	H	E	C	Total
Residues	29090	17950	37053	84093

is RBF (i.e., Radial Basis Function). To solve the multiclass problem confronted in the work, we employ the "one-against-one" approach. For 3 classes, we need 3 binary classifiers and set the labels of the secondary structure (H, E, C) to (−1, +1, +2). Then, we use the max-wins voting strategy to determine the class; in other words, each binary classifier casts a vote, and the winning class is with the highest number of votes. In the experiments, the LIBSVM tool kit proposed by Chang and Lin [19] would be used to implement the program. After the optimal window size and parameters are found, we would use the SVM for training and test.

3.4. Filter. A single residue in its natural state cannot be alone folded into α-helix or β-sheet. Thus, setting thresholds on the length of consensus secondary structure can be used to filter out incorrect predicted results. For example, at least three contiguous residues are for α-helix and at least two contiguous residues are for β-sheet. For the current scanning window ($i − 1, i, i + 1$) in the predicted secondary structure, two possible structures could happen at position i:

Case H: if str($i − 1$) and str($i + 1$) are H, then str(i) is not changed; otherwise, extend the examined segment to ($i − 3, i − 2, i − 1, i, i + 1, i + 2, i + 3$) and replace str($i$) with the majority structure in the examined segment.

Case E: if str($i − 1$) or str($i + 1$) is E, then str(i) is not changed; otherwise, extend the examined segment to ($i − 3, i − 2, i − 1, i, i + 1, i + 2, i + 3$) and replace str($i$) with the majority structure in the examined segment.

For the example as shown in Figure 4, after the filtering, Q_3 for 9INSb is improved from 76.7 to 80 and SOV99 is improved from 77.8 to 93.3 where Q_3 and SOV99 will be described in Section 4.2.

4. Experiments

4.1. Data Set. In the previous work, some typical data sets were frequently used in protein secondary structure prediction, such as RS126 [7], CB513 [12], CASP [20], and EVA [21]. Here, we consider the selected data set should be with low similarity; that is, the protein sequences within the data set are not similar to each other. Thus, the protein secondary structure prediction we develop would enable predicting an unknown protein sequence more accurately.

In our work, the data set we choose is nonhomologous CB513 data set constructed by Cuff and Barton and contains 513 protein chains. Almost all the sequences in the RS126 data set are also included in the CB513 data set. The CB513 data set contains 16 chains of ≤30 residues. Although very short chains would slightly decrease the accuracy for the hard definition of secondary structures, we still include them in the set for comprehensive study. We retrieve the CB513 data set from the website: http://paraschopra.com/projects/evoca_prot/index.php, which contains 84,093 residues where 34.59% of the residues is for helix, 21.35% for sheet, and 44.06% for coil, as shown in Table 5.

4.2. Performance Measures. Two kinds of performance measures are frequently used in protein secondary structure prediction; that is, Q_3 or accuracy (three-state overall per-residue accuracy) and SOV99 [22] (or SOV94 [23]) (Segment Overlap measure). Q_3 is a residue-based measure of three-structure overall percentage of correctly classified residues, which can be represented as

$$Q_3 = \frac{H_{pre} + E_{pre} + C_{pre}}{N_{total}}, \quad (2)$$

where N_{total} is the total number of predicted residues, H_{pre} is the correctly classified secondary structure for helix, E_{pre} for sheet, and C_{pre} for coil.

SOV99 is a segment-based measure of three structures, whose value is within the range $[0, 100]$, as shown in Formula (3). SOV99 differs from Q_3 in the prediction unit such that SOV99 would penalize wrong predictions; for example, a single helix predicted as a multiply-split helix is unrealistic prediction

$$SOV = 100 \times \left[\frac{1}{N} \sum_{i \in \{H,E,C\}} \sum_{S(i)} \frac{\min ov(s_1, s_2) + \delta(s_1, s_2)}{\max ov(s_1, s_2)} \right.$$

$$\left. \times len(s_1) \right], \quad (3)$$

where s_1 and s_2 denote segments of secondary structure i (H, E, or C), $S(i) = \{(s_1, s_2) : s_1 \cap s_2 \neq \varnothing, s_1 \text{ and } s_2 \text{ are both in structure } i\}$, N is a normalization value, $\min ov(s_1, s_2)$ is the length of actual overlap of s_1 and s_2, $\max ov(s_1, s_2)$ is the length of total extent for s_1 and s_2, and $\delta(s_1, s_2)$ can be represented as

$$\delta(s_1, s_2) = \min \begin{cases} \max ov(s_1, s_2) - \min ov(s_1, s_2) \\ \min ov(s_1, s_2) \\ int\left(\frac{len(s_1)}{2}\right) \\ int\left(\frac{len(s_2)}{2}\right). \end{cases} \quad (4)$$

The definition of δ and the normalization value N are different for SOV99 and SOV94.

4.3. Optimal Parameters and Window Sizes. As introduced in Section 2.2, we adopt the well-known LIBSVM developed by Chang and Lin [19] as an SVM classifier. The kernel function used here is RBF (Radial Basis Function) since it is more accurate and effective than the other kernel ones. The parameters C and γ are determined by the optimum performance of 6×6 combinations between $[2^0, \ldots, 2^5]$ and $[2^{-6}, \ldots, 2^{-1}]$ for each window size. Moreover, the feature vector is normalized in the range $[0, 1]$ and the number of features in a larger window size would become more. The optimal parameters and classification accuracy are evaluated in threefold cross-validation, as shown in Table 6.

According to the experimental results, we found the optimal parameters and window size are $C = 2^1, \gamma = 2^{-4}$, and $WS = 13$. Then, we use these parameters and window size to conduct the further experiments.

TABLE 6: Optimal parameters for different window sizes.

Window sizes	Features	Best C	Best γ	Accuracy (%)
7	146	2^0	2^{-3}	76.3203
9	186	2^1	2^{-4}	76.7935
11	226	2^0	2^{-4}	77.4464
13	266	2^1	2^{-4}	78.0029
15	306	2^1	2^{-4}	77.7806
17	346	2^1	2^{-5}	77.6549
19	386	2^1	2^{-4}	77.5796

TABLE 7: Confusion matrix without filtering.

Actual	Predicted			
	H	E	C	Recall (%)
H	22976	931	5183	78.98
E	1044	11569	5337	64.45
C	3451	3059	30543	82.43
Precision (%)	83.64	74.36	74.38	77.40

TABLE 8: Confusion matrix with filtering.

Actual	Predicted			
	H	E	C	Recall (%)
H	22372	818	5900	76.91
E	432	11776	5742	65.60
C	1514	2819	32720	88.31
Precision (%)	92.00	76.40	73.76	79.52

4.4. Experimental Results. In this section, we compare the experimental results without filtering and with filtering. For the classification results, a confusion matrix is employed to present the correct and false predictions based on the precision and recall, as shown in Tables 7 and 8. The precision and recall are expressed as follows:

Precision (i)

$$= \frac{\text{The number of correctly classified structure } i}{\text{The number of total predicted structure } i},$$

$$\text{for } i = H, E, C,$$

Recall (i)

$$= \frac{\text{The number of correctly classified structure } i}{\text{The number of total actual structure } i},$$

$$\text{for } i = H, E, C. \quad (5)$$

Obviously, the classification accuracy with filtering (i.e., 79.52%) is higher than that without filtering (i.e., 77.40%). The precision for H and the recall for C especially are improved from 83.64 to 92.00 (with filtering) and from 82.43 to 88.31 (with filtering), respectively. Therefore, the filter rules are required to improve the accuracy in predicting protein secondary structure.

TABLE 9: Comparisons between ours and other methods.

Methods	Q_3	SOV94	SOV99	R(H)	R(E)	R(C)
PHD (RS126) [7]	70.8	73.5	—	72.0	66.0	72.0
SVMfreq (RS126) [5]	71.2	74.6	—	73.0	58.0	73.0
SVMfreq (CB513) [5]	73.5	76.2	—	75.0	60.0	79.0
PMSVM (CB513) [4]	75.2	80.0	—	80.4	71.5	72.8
SVMpsi (RS126) [6]	76.1	79.6	72.0	77.2	63.9	81.5
SVMpsi (CB513) [6]	76.6	80.1	73.5	78.1	65.6	81.1
Ours without filtering (CB513)	77.40	90.20	71.10	78.98	64.45	82.43
Ours with filtering (CB513)	79.52	86.10	74.60	76.91	65.60	88.31

4.5. Comparing with Other Methods. Here, we compare our methods with other four methods; that is, PHD, SVMfreq, PMSVM, and SVMpsi as shown in Table 9. Both the PHD and SVMfreq methods are based on the frequency profiles with multiple sequence alignment; however, the classifier used in the PHD method is a neural network (or NN) whereas the classifier used in the SVMfreq method is a support vector machine (or SVM). Similarly, both the PMSVM and SVMpsi methods are based on the PSSM profiles generated from PSI-BLAST. Although they use the same-type classifier (or SVM), the former adopts one-versus-one classifier (i.e., H/E, E/C, C/H) and the latter adopts the one-versus-rest classifier (i.e., H/~H, E/~E, C/~C).

As shown in Table 9, we found that all the performance measures of our method (i.e., the version with filtering), including Q_3, SOV94, and SOV99, are higher than those of the other four methods, regardless using the CB513 or RS126 data sets. Q_3 for the version with filtering (or without filtering) is improved by 2.92 (or 0.8), SOV94 for the version with filtering (or without filtering) is improved by 6 (or 10.1), and SOV99 for the version with filtering is improved by 1.1, compared with the results of the SVMpsi method for CB513 (i.e., the next best one).

However, our method (i.e., the version with filtering) has lower R(H) than the SVMpsi method (i.e., 76.91 versus 78.1). One of the possible reasons is that the threshold on the length of consensus secondary structure (i.e., at least three contiguous residues for H) is set in the filter. Although the recall for H is decreased, the predicted structures are more structurally meaningful. Besides, we found that two SOV measures in the SVMpsi and our methods vary greatly. Although SOV94 is decreased (i.e., from 90.20 to 86.10) after applying the filter in our method, the latest definition (i.e., SOV99) is still the highest.

5. Conclusions

In this paper, we propose a protein secondary structure prediction method using PSSM profiles and four physicochemical features, including conformation parameters, net charges, hydrophobic, and side chain mass. In the experiments, the SVM with the optimal window size and the optimal parameters of the kernel function is found first. Then, we train the SVM using the PSSM profiles and physicochemical features extracted from the CB513 data set.

Finally, we use the filter to refine the predicted results from the trained SVM. For the experimental results, Q_3, SOV94, SOV99, and recall of our method are higher than those of the SVMpsi method based on the PSI-BLAST profiles as well as the SVMfreq method based on the frequency profiles with multiple sequence alignment for the CB513 data set. In summary, considering these physicochemical features in predicting protein secondary structure would exhibit better performances.

Acknowledgment

This work was supported by National Science Council of Taiwan under Grant NSC100-2218-E-224-011-MY3.

References

[1] P. Y. Chou and G. D. Fasman, "Empirical predictions of protein conformation," *Annual Review of Biochemistry*, vol. 47, pp. 251–276, 1978.

[2] J. Garnier, D. J. Osguthorpe, and B. Robson, "Analysis of the accuracy and implications of simple methods for predicting the secondary structure of globular proteins," *Journal of Molecular Biology*, vol. 120, no. 1, pp. 97–120, 1978.

[3] S. F. Altschul, T. L. Madden, A. A. Schäffer et al., "Gapped BLAST and PSI-BLAST: a new generation of protein database search programs," *Nucleic Acids Research*, vol. 25, no. 17, pp. 3389–3402, 1997.

[4] J. Guo, H. Chen, Z. Sun, and Y. Lin, "A novel method for protein secondary structure prediction using dual-layer SVM and profiles," *Proteins*, vol. 54, no. 4, pp. 738–743, 2004.

[5] S. Hua and Z. Sun, "A novel method of protein secondary structure prediction with high segment overlap measure: support vector machine approach," *Journal of Molecular Biology*, vol. 308, no. 2, pp. 397–407, 2001.

[6] H. Kim and H. Park, "Protein secondary structure prediction based on an improved support vector machines approach," *Protein Engineering*, vol. 16, no. 8, pp. 553–560, 2003.

[7] B. Rost and C. Sander, "Prediction of protein secondary structure at better than 70% accuracy," *Journal of Molecular Biology*, vol. 232, no. 2, pp. 584–599, 1993.

[8] W. Kabsch and C. Sander, "Dictionary of protein secondary structure: pattern recognition of hydrogen-bonded and geometrical features," *Biopolymers*, vol. 22, no. 12, pp. 2577–2637, 1983.

[9] D. Frishman and P. Argos, "Knowledge-based protein secondary structure assignment," *Proteins*, vol. 23, no. 4, pp. 566–579, 1995.

[10] F. M. Richards and C. E. Kundrot, "Identification of structural motifs from protein coordinate data: secondary structure and first-level supersecondary structure," *Proteins*, vol. 3, no. 2, pp. 71–84, 1988.

[11] B. E. Boser, I. M. Guyon, and V. N. Vapnik, "Training algorithm for optimal margin classifiers," in *Proceedings of the 5th Annual ACM Workshop on Computational Learning Theory*, pp. 144–152, July 1992.

[12] J. A. Cuff and G. J. Barton, "Evaluation and improvement of multiple sequence methods for protein secondary structure prediction," *Proteins*, vol. 34, no. 4, pp. 508–519, 1999.

[13] S. Henikoff and J. G. Henikoff, "Amino acid substitution matrices from protein blocks," *Proceedings of the National Academy of Sciences of the United States of America*, vol. 89, no. 22, pp. 10915–10919, 1992.

[14] S. Kawashima, H. Ogata, and M. Kanehisa, "AAindex: amino acid index database," *Nucleic Acids Research*, vol. 27, no. 1, pp. 368–369, 1999.

[15] S. Kawashima and M. Kanehisa, "AAindex: amino acid index database," *Nucleic Acids Research*, vol. 28, no. 1, p. 374, 2000.

[16] S. Kawashima, P. Pokarowski, M. Pokarowska, A. Kolinski, T. Katayama, and M. Kanehisa, "AAindex: Amino acid index database, progress report 2008," *Nucleic Acids Research*, vol. 36, no. 1, pp. D202–D205, 2008.

[17] K. Nakai, A. Kidera, and M. Kanehisa, "Cluster analysis of amino acid indices for prediction of protein structure and function," *Protein Engineering, Design and Selection*, vol. 2, no. 2, pp. 93–100, 1988.

[18] K. Tomii and M. Kanehisa, "Analysis of amino acid indices and mutation matrices for sequence comparison and structure prediction of proteins," *Protein Engineering*, vol. 9, no. 1, pp. 27–36, 1996.

[19] C.-C. Chang and C.-J. Lin, "LIBSVM: a library for support vector machines," http://www.csie.ntu.edu.tw/~cjlin/libsvm, 2001.

[20] J. Moult, J. T. Pedersen, R. Judson, and K. Fidelis, "A large-scale experiment to assess protein structure prediction methods," *Proteins*, vol. 23, no. 3, pp. ii–iv, 1995.

[21] V. A. Eyrich, M. A. Martí-Renom, D. Przybylski et al., "EVA: continuous automatic evaluation of protein structure prediction servers," *Bioinformatics*, vol. 17, no. 12, pp. 1242–1243, 2002.

[22] A. Zemla, C. Venclovas, K. Fidelis, and B. Rost, "A modified definition of SOV, a segment based measure for protein secondary structure prediction assessment," *Proteins*, vol. 34, no. 2, pp. 220–223, 1999.

[23] B. Rost, C. Sander, and R. Schneider, "Redefining the goals of protein secondary structure prediction," *Journal of Molecular Biology*, vol. 235, no. 1, pp. 13–26, 1994.

7

Gene Expression Profiles for Predicting Metastasis in Breast Cancer: A Cross-Study Comparison of Classification Methods

Mark Burton,[1,2] **Mads Thomassen,**[1,2] **Qihua Tan,**[1,2,3] **and Torben A. Kruse**[1,2]

[1] Research Unit of Human Genetics, Institute of Clinical Research, University of Southern Denmark, Sdr. Boulevard 29, 5000 Odense C, Denmark
[2] Department of Clinical Genetics, Odense University Hospital, Sdr. Boulevard 29, 5000 Odense C, Denmark
[3] Institute of Public Health, University of Southern Denmark, J. B. Winsløws Vej 9B, 5000 Odense C, Denmark

Correspondence should be addressed to Mark Burton, mark.burton@ouh.regionsyddanmark.dk

Academic Editors: M. A. Kon and K. Najarian

Machine learning has increasingly been used with microarray gene expression data and for the development of classifiers using a variety of methods. However, method comparisons in cross-study datasets are very scarce. This study compares the performance of seven classification methods and the effect of voting for predicting metastasis outcome in breast cancer patients, in three situations: within the same dataset or across datasets on similar or dissimilar microarray platforms. Combining classification results from seven classifiers into one voting decision performed significantly better during internal validation as well as external validation in similar microarray platforms than the underlying classification methods. When validating between different microarray platforms, random forest, another voting-based method, proved to be the best performing method. We conclude that voting based classifiers provided an advantage with respect to classifying metastasis outcome in breast cancer patients.

1. Introduction

The analysis of high-dimensional gene expression datasets has posed new computational challenges. These datasets have, for example, in breast cancer research, been applied to develop classifiers predicting metastasis outcome, disease recurrence, or breast cancer survival. Some of the classification methods most frequently applied to microarray data are logistic regression [1, 2], support vector machines (SVM) [3–12], neural networks (NNET) [1, 13], random forest (RF) [1, 12], and classifiers based on voting [1]. However, few studies have systematically compared the predictive performance of such methods using microarray gene expression datasets on breast cancer. In their studies, method comparisons have been done within the same datasets by, for example, 10-fold cross-validation, leave-one-out cross-validation, or hold-out procedures [14–18], addressing prediction of relapse within a 5-year period [14, 16, 19], or molecular subtype classification [15]. Furthermore, even fewer studies have compared cross-study validation between classification methods within the field of breast cancer research. Two studies addressed ER-positivity and molecular subtype classification [20, 21], while

another tested prediction of relapse within a 5-year period in a small group of 19 independent patients [22].

This study compares the performance of seven classification methods belonging to four different categories for predicting metastatic outcome in lymph negative breast cancer patients, which have not been treated with adjuvant systemic therapy. The classification methods used included an ensemble decision tree model (random forest), regression (logistic regression), four support vector machines and a neural network. To address various degrees of variation for such tasks, the comparisons were done either within the same dataset (internal) or between different datasets (external). Within the same dataset model building and classification were performed using 10-fold cross-validation. Across datasets the comparisons were done in two ways. The first is in which the validations are conducted between studies using the same microarray platform (classifiers developed from an Affymetrix dataset and validated on an independent Affymetrix dataset), while the second encompasses validations across studies with different platforms (classifiers developed from an Agilent dataset and validated on an independent Affymetrix dataset). Furthermore, we

TABLE 1: Overview of datasets used.

Dataset	Chip	Probes (K)	Patients	Outcome	Treatment	Define genes	Internal CV	External validation train	External validation test	Reference
Amsterdam	Agilent/Rosetta	25	295, N⁺, N⁻	DM	None, et, ct	√				[31]
Amsterdam (AM) (subset of the above)	Agilent/Rosetta	25	151, N⁻	DM	None	√	√	√		[31]
Rotterdam (RO)	Affymetrix HG-133A	22	286, N⁻	DM	None	√	√	√		[28]
HUMAC	Spotted oligonucleotides	29	60, N⁻	ME	None	√				[4]
Huang	Affymetrix 95av2	12	52, N⁺	RE	ct	√				[27]
Sotiriou 2003	Spotted cDNA	7.6	99, N⁺/N⁻	RE	et, ct	√				[24]
Sotiriou 2006	Affymetrix HG-133A	22	179, N⁺/N⁻	DM	et	√				[25]
Uppsala	Affymetrix HG-133A+B	44	236, N⁺/N⁻	DF	None, ct, et	√				[6]
Stockholm	Affymetrix HG-133A+B	44	159, N⁺/N⁻	RE	None, ct, et	√				[23]
TRANSBIG (TR)	Affymetrix HG-133A	22	147, N⁻	DM	None				√	[32]
Mainz (MA)	Affymetrix HG-133A	22	200, N⁻	DM	None				√	[33]

The columns show the following: "dataset": the individual names for the eight datasets; "chip": microarray chip used; "probes": number of probes on the chip measured in thousands ($K = 1000$); patients': number of patients in the study and their nodal status (N⁺ and N⁻ indicates number of node-positive and -negative patients; "outcome" covers the clinical outcome being DM: distant metastasis, ME: metastasis, RE: relapse, and DF: death from breast cancer; "treatment" shows patient treatments abbreviated by et: endocrine therapy, ct: chemo therapy, and none: no adjuvant therapy.

examined the effect of combining the classification results on each sample by the seven methods into one final classification determined by majority voting, and performances compared by internal and external validation as well.

2. Materials and Methods

2.1. Datasets Used in This Study. The following eight datasets were used for either defining the gene features and or training purposes in the further study: samples from the studies [23–27] and samples from the Gene Expression Omnibus- (GEO-) series GSE2034 [28], GSE4796 [4], and GSE3494 [6] (Table 1). A subset of 151 node-negative samples from the dataset by van de Vijver (AM) and the entire GSE2034 dataset [28] (abbreviated RO) were used for classifier development in the further study (Table 1). The following datasets were used as independent testing sets: the node-negative samples from GSE7390 [29] (abbreviated TR) and the GSE11121 dataset [30] (abbreviated MA) (Table 1).

2.2. Dataset Processing. The eight datasets above were downloaded and directly used for identification of rank-significant genes. Following this identification, the four datasets: AM, RO, TR, and MA were all standardized to have mean zero and standard deviation one. Calculations and classification were all conducted using the R free package. For random forest, logistic regression, support vector machines, and neural network we used the *randomForest*, *glm*, *e1071*, and *nnet* packages, respectively.

2.3. Identification of Cross-Study Rank-Significant Features. To determine which genes should be used to build gene expression classifiers, we used the eight publicly available datasets mentioned above, which were used in our two previous studies [34, 35]. This was done by applying the microarray meta-analysis described in [34], upon the individual gene expression values of each individual probe/gene in the eight datasets. This method ranks each individual gene in each dataset according to its signal-to-noise ratio, calculates the gene's mean rank across datasets, and determines if this mean rank is significantly high or low, according to a significance cutoff at FDR ≤ 0.05.

2.4. Classifier Building. The features within each training dataset were ranked according to their random forest variable importance measure. For each feature, this value reports the standardized drop in prediction accuracy when the classlabels are permuted [36]. For each feature, this rank was used for model building by subsequently adding one feature at a time in a "top-down" manner. To avoid creating bias, during gene selection and training of the final classifier, and on classification performance, we used ten-times repeated 10-fold cross-validation accuracies as a performance measure, as this metric has previously been shown to give an excellent bias-variance balance [37]. In this study, the models were developed to achieve the best mean sensitivity and specificity thus forcing the overall accuracy to give a balanced sensitivity and specificity. Seven different classification methods were used for model building which included: random forest (RF) [36], logistic regression, SVM with a radial- (R-SVM), a linear (L-SVM), polynomial (P-SVM), or a sigmoid-based kernel (S-SVM) [38], and a neural network with a single hidden layer (NNET). The voting approach is described in detail below. As all classification methods have hyperparameters, we optimized these parameters during model building using a grid-like search of parameter combinations. In random forest, we optimized the number of trees in the forest (*n*tree) from settings of 2000, 3000, 4000, and 5000 trees, and the number of subselected predictors for node splitting (mtry) with settings of: $1, 0.5 \cdot \sqrt{\text{(number of features)}}, 1 \cdot \sqrt{\text{(number of features)}}, 2 \cdot \sqrt{\text{(number of features)}}$, and total number of features. In all support vector machines, the slack variable penalizing cost parameter (C) was optimized using settings of 0.01, 0.1, 1, and 10, and the γ-parameter, controlling the spreading of samples in feature space, with the settings of 0.001, 0.01, 0.1, and 1, and for P-SVM also the polynomial degree using degrees of 2, 3, and 4.

2.5. Voting. The voting procedure can be regarded as a metamodel, where a sample is first fed to be predicted by each of the respective classification methods. These predictions are next fed to the final metamodel, combining each of these predictions into a final classification determined by majority voting.

The voting procedure, at the level of internal dataset prediction, consisted of two steps. In the first step, each sample is classified ten times during 10×10 CV, meaning that each sample is given 10 votes for classification within each classification method. To prevent ties, the nine first votes were used for class decision. In the second step the final votes from each of the seven classification methods are combined into one vote, thus creating the cross-classification voting result.

During external validation, every sample is classified once by each of the seven classification methods. The voting classification for each sample is determined by the winning class assigned by the seven classification methods (voters).

2.6. Classification Performance Assessment. We compared the bAcc, defined as the mean of sensitivity and specificity, of classifiers at two levels either internal or external. Internal performance was determined by the 10-times repeated 10-fold cross-validation classification accuracies. External performances obtained through transferring the trained classifier from the training sets to classify each of the independent samples are reported. In external validation, two different situations were examined: (1) between similar (RO on TR or MA) and (2) different microarray platforms (AM on TR or MA), covering Affymetrix-based classifiers validated on an Affymetrix dataset and Agilent-based classifiers validated on another Affymetrix dataset, respectively.

2.7. Endpoint/Outcome Definition. The outcome is defined as metastasis after time of diagnosis. As this study addresses outcome classification, we did not consider the time-to-event component or censoring, due to the fact that survival analysis sometimes can be misleading when considering classification, and because transformation of time-to-event into a binary outcome can blur prediction of the classes [39].

2.8. Comparison of External Validation Performance. There is to our knowledge no standard statistics for comparing classifier performance on unbalanced datasets using the balanced accuracy as a performance measure. Therefore, in order to test the significance of the performance difference between the classification methods (defined as a significant difference between correct predictions using method A versus using method B), we used a repeated downsampled binomial test approach consisting of five steps. (1) The classifiers classification results upon the entire test data were initially converted into a balanced test result by downsampling. Downsampling obtains a class-balanced dataset from an imbalanced dataset by removing a subset of randomly selected samples from the majority class, where the number of samples removed equals the difference in sample size between the major and the minor class. In this study the majority class is the nonmetastasis class; (2) the number of samples correctly classified by one classification method but incorrectly by the other classification method and vice versa is counted; (3) the significance of the difference in these counts is determined using a binomial χ^2-test; (4) the P-value of this test is stored. The steps 2 to 4 are repeated 1000 times; (5) from the 1000 tests, the median P value is reported as the statistical significance impact between the two compared methods.

3. Results

3.1. Features and Classifiers/Models. In this study the classifiers were developed to predict metastasis outcome using full follow-up time. To make the classifiers globally applicable and robust, we identified genes being significantly associated with outcomes across eight different studies using different microarray platforms and originating from different populations. These eight datasets are referred to as the "feature definers" (FD) (Table 1). In the further analysis, two of the

FD datasets were used as training sets. The first, Rotterdam (RO), is an Affymetrix-based dataset containing 286 samples, and the second, Amsterdam (AM), is a node-negative subset of 151 samples from the entire FD-Amsterdam dataset (Table 1). Two independent datasets, not used for feature selection or classifier development, were used as test sets. These comprise the TRANSBIG (TR) and Mainz (MA) datasets, which are based on the Affymetrix platform and consist of 147 and 200 samples, respectively.

As a preliminary feature selection step, we identified genes being significantly associated with outcomes across eight different studies using a rank-based method (as described in Section 2). This method led to identification of 519 rank-significant genes. By matching the 519 rank-significant genes and those present in AM, RO, TR, and MA, these genes were reduced to 283 (Figure 1) and were thus used for classifier building. The list of 283 genes is shown in Supplementary Table 1 in Supplementary Material available online at doi:10.1100/2012/380495.

In order to build the models, the 283 features within each training dataset were ranked according to their random forest variable importance measure (Figure 2). For a given feature, this measure reports the standardized drop in prediction accuracy when the class labels are permuted [36]. This rank was then used for model building by subsequently adding one feature at a time in a "top-down" forward manner (Figure 2).

3.2. Comparison of Classification Methods: Internal Validation Performance.

To reduce variability, and complexity and to keep validation parameters as constant as possible, the performance of the classifiers was tested within the same dataset by a ten-times repeated 10-fold cross-validation (Figure 2). This validation scheme partitions the training data into 10 nearly equal-sized folds. Subsequently, 10 iterations of training and validation are performed. During each of these iterations a different fold of the training data is left out for validation and the remaining are used for learning. The mean accuracy of all 10-folds validated is thus the 10-fold cross-validated (10×10 CV) accuracy of the model. By repeating this process 10 times a more robust and unbiased estimation of the performance is obtained. In our study, the balanced accuracy (bAcc), defined as the mean of sensitivity and specificity, was used as a performance measure. It should be noted that the individual classification performances are artificially elevated due to information leakages, caused by AM and RO being used for primary feature selection, and that the entire AM and RO datasets are used for importance ranking prior to cross-validation. However, the differences between the individual classification method performances are assumed, unaffected by these leakages.

The performances within the AM and RO by each classification method were combined, and the mean performance calculated. The classifiers based on NNET had the best performance achieving a mean 10×10 CV bAcc of 78%, followed by S-SVM, L-SVM, R-SVM, P-SVM, RF, and LR achieving mean 10×10 CV bAcc of 74.1%, 72.1%, 71.6%, 70.9%, 69.4%, and 68.0%, respectively (Figure 3 and Supplementary Table 2). The significance of these

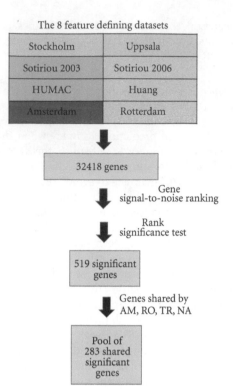

The 8 feature defining datasets

Stockholm	Uppsala
Sotiriou 2003	Sotiriou 2006
HUMAC	Huang
Amsterdam	Rotterdam

32418 genes

Gene signal-to-noise ranking

Rank significance test

519 significant genes

Genes shared by AM, RO, TR, NA

Pool of 283 shared significant genes

FIGURE 1: Feature selection. Eight breast cancer gene expression datasets (feature defining datasets), covering 32418 genes, were used to define a list of rank significant genes. Datasets using the Affymetrix platform, spotted oligonucleotides, and the Agilent platform are colored orange, blue, and red, respectively. These genes were first ranked within each of the eight datasets according to their signal-to-noise ratio, and their across dataset mean rank calculated. This mean rank was significance tested as described in Section 2, resulting in a list of 519 rank significant genes. These 519 genes were reduced to a pool of 283 genes shared by the two training sets (AM and RO) and the testing sets (TR and MA), used in the further study.

differences was tested using the down-sampling statistical test described in Section 2, showing that NNET significantly outperformed RF ($P = 0.011$), LR ($P = 1.2e^{-5}$), L-SVM ($P = 0.027$), and P-SVM ($P = 6.3e^{-4}$). NNET only borderline significantly outperformed R-SVM ($P = 0.07$) and S-SVM ($P = 0.10$). Furthermore, S-SVM also performed significantly better than RF ($P = 0.049$), LR ($P = 9.0e^{-5}$), and P-SVM ($P = 0.049$), and R-SVM outperformed RF ($P = 0.018$). No significant performance difference was found when comparing the other classification methods.

We next combined the cross-validated results by the seven methods into a voting procedure. This led to a mean 10×10 CV bAcc of 86.9%, which significantly outperformed all the seven underlying classification methods: RF ($P = 1.1e^{-19}$), LR ($P = 1.7e^{-18}$), R-SVM ($P = 4.2e^{-12}$), L-SVM ($P = 1.4e^{-14}$), P-SVM ($P = 8.9e^{-16}$), S-SVM ($P = 5.8e^{-11}$), and NNET ($P = 2.6e^{-4}$) (Figure 3 and Supplementary Table 2).

3.3. External Validation Performance between Similar Microarray Platforms.
The performance of the classifiers was validated in independent datasets based on the same

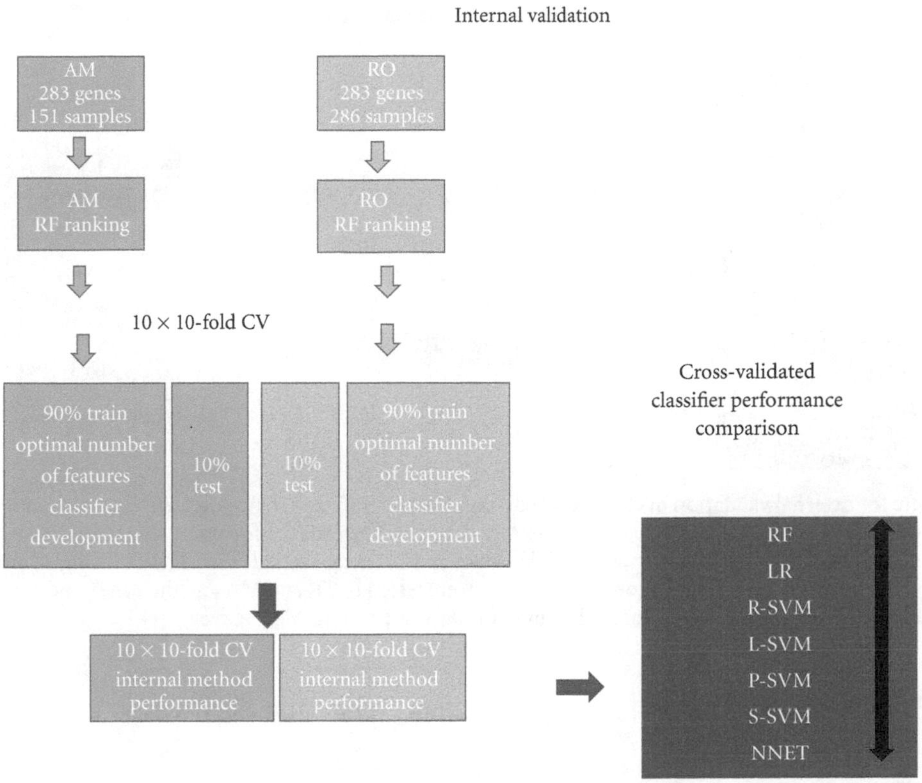

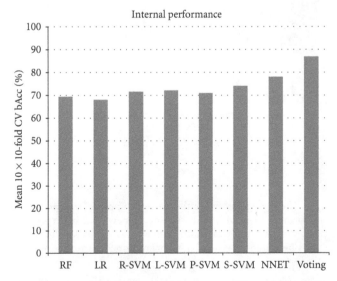

Internal validation

Cross-validated
classifier performance
comparison

FIGURE 2: Internal validation procedure. The two datasets, AM (blue) and RO (orange) composed of the 283 rank-significant genes and 151 or 286 samples, respectively, were used for internal performance evaluation. These datasets were first individually used to rank each feature by their random forest variable importance value (RF ranking). These ranks were separately used for selecting the optimal number of features by adding one feature using the same classification method, using a 10-times repeated 10-fold cross-validation procedure. The AM and RO 10-times cross-validation results using the same classification method were combined, and the mean classification performance of each method was compared.

FIGURE 3: Internal validation performance. Shown in blue histograms are the mean 10-times repeated 10-fold cross-validation balanced accuracy performance (bAcc) within the two training datasets: AM and RO. Methods used are random forest (RF), logistic regression (LR), support vector machines with a radial (R-SVM), linear (L-SVM), polynomial (P-SVM), sigmoid kernel (S-SVM), a neural network with a single hidden layer (NNET), or cross-method voting (Voting).

TABLE 2: Number of features in the models.

Dataset	AM	RO
Method	($n = 151$)	($n = 286$)
RF	21	21
LR	5	11
R-SVM	20	25
L-SVM	8	11
P-SVM	4	7
S-SVM	17	35
NNET	21	16

AM and RO are the Amsterdam and Rotterdam training sets and n shows the number of samples in the respective datasets. Methods used are as follows: RF: random forest, LR: logistic regression, R-, L-, P-, and S-SVM: support vector machine with a radial basis function, linear, polynomial, or sigmoid kernel, and NNET: neural network with a single hidden layer.

microarray platform (Affymetrix), which covers the validation of RO-based classifiers on the TR and MA test data (Figure 4), which contained between 7 to 35 features (Table 2). In this setting, the entire classifiers developed in the training set, using the features and rules associated with the classifiers, were used to classify the independent samples in the entire test sets, and the performance is defined as the mean test accuracy in TR and MA.

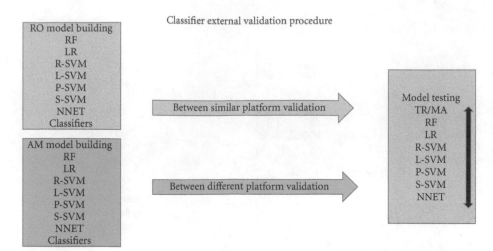

FIGURE 4: The procedure for external validation of classifiers. External classifier validation. Two datasets were used for training (AM and RO), and two others for testing (TR and MA). Datasets based on the Affymetrix and Agilent platforms are shown in orange and blue, respectively. RO and AM classifiers were used for evaluating external validation of classifiers developed from datasets using similar platform and using different microarray platforms, respectively. The models built in RO were tested in TR and MA and their mean performance calculated. This was done for all classification methods and compared. The same was done for testing AM models.

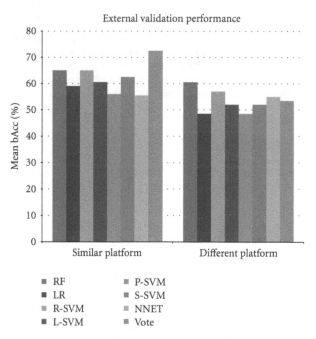

FIGURE 5: External validation performance. External classifier performance. The histogram shows the mean testing performance when classifiers are validated in test sets based on similar platforms or different platforms as from which they were developed. Each bar represents the mean balanced accuracy by random forest (RF), logistic regression (LR), support vector machines with a radial (R-SVM), linear (L-SVM), polynomial (P-SVM), sigmoid kernel (S-SVM), a neural network with a single hidden layer (NNET), or cross-method voting (VOTE), respectively.

RF and R-SVM had the best external classification performance achieving a mean bAcc of 65%, while NNET had the poorest performance (55.5% mean bAcc) (Figure 5). RF performed significantly better than LR ($P = 0.0085$), L-SVM ($P = 0.026$), P-SVM ($P = 0.0057$), and NNET ($P = 0.0012$), and R-SVM also performed significantly better than

LR ($P = 0.0064$), L-SVM ($P = 0.025$), P-SVM ($P = 0.013$) and NNET ($P = 0.0025$) (Figure 5).

The voting procedure increased the performance to a 72.5% mean bAcc and significantly outperformed the seven underlying methods: RF ($P = 6.1e^{-5}$), LR ($P = 1.5e^{-8}$), R-SVM ($P = 0.00026$), L-SVM ($P = 6.0e^{-8}$), P-SVM

($P = 2.1e^{-7}$), S-SVM ($P = 1.9e^{-6}$), and NNET ($P = 4.7e^{-7}$) (Figure 5). Detailed overview of the individual validation results is shown in Supplementary Table 3.

3.4. External Validation Performance between Different Microarray Platforms. The performance of the classifiers was finally validated in independent datasets (Affymetrix) based on a different microarray platform from the one used by training data (Agilent) and covers the validation of AM-based classifiers on the TR and MA test data. These classifiers contained 4 to 21 features (Table 2). As in the case of the between-similar-platform validation, the entire classifier developed in the training set, using the features and rules associated with the classifiers, was used to classify the independent samples in the entire test sets (Figure 4), and the performance is defined as the mean test accuracy in TR and MA.

Comparison of classifiers developed on an Agilent dataset and validated on an Affymetrix dataset revealed that the mean classification performances based on RF had the best performance amongst the seven methods, achieving a mean bAcc of 60.5%, while the poorest performances were achieved by the LR- and P-SVM classifiers, which obtained only 48.5% bAcc (Figure 5). RF performed significantly better than the other six methods: LR ($P = 3e^{-4}$), R-SVM ($P = 0.038$), L-SVM ($P = 0.0012$), P-SVM ($P = 9.8e^{-5}$), S-SVM ($P = 0.0015$), and NNET ($P = 0.032$) (Figure 5). In contrast to the between-similar-platforms validations, the voting procedure only obtained a mean bAcc performance of 53.5%, which was a borderline significantly inferior to RF ($P = 0.059$) (Figure 5). Detailed description of the individual between different platforms validation results is shown in Supplementary Table 4.

4. Conclusion and Discussion

This study compared seven classification methods and a voting procedure ability to predict metastasis outcome in lymph node-negative breast cancer patients. The results showed that during internal assessment and external validation— methods based on voting had the best performance.

Our study first compared the internal performance within a single dataset and showed that NNET had the best performance followed by the support vector machines, while RF and LR had the worst performances. This implies that at least for prediction of metastasis outcome within the same dataset—NNET and support vector machines displays superiority. This finding agrees well with other studies using cross- or hold-out procedures for performance comparisons. For example, one study comparing the performance of eight different classification methods showed that NNET and SVMs in general perform better than the other six methods for predicting outcome in eight different cancer microarray datasets [15]. Several studies confirm our finding of RF inferiority when using cross-validation [17, 18, 40]. Interestingly, a study conducting algorithm comparison on microarray gene expression based drug signatures showed that NNET and R-SVM had the best performance when

tested in the most heterogeneous datasets [41]. As the datasets used in our study are likely to be very heterogeneous, due to the nature and etiology of breast cancer, the superior performances of NNET and support vector machines could reflect the ability of these particular methods to distinguish outcome in such complex datasets.

Combining the classification results by each method into classification based on voting significantly increased the internal performance. The finding of voting superiority in the internal validations suggests that voting would be valuable when applied to datasets having a combination of limited technical variation (due to using same protocols and platforms) and biological heterogeneity. Although the patients in our study are limited to being node negative, they may still be very heterogeneous due to the existence of various breast cancer molecular subgroups and the disease etiology. Voting may therefore reduce the variation associated with this biological heterogeneity. This is in line with the above-mentioned study, showing that some classification methods are more suitable for prediction tasks in complex datasets [41].

Our finding of voting superiority agrees with four other studies: one using multiple different feature extraction methods in combination with SVM for gene microarray classification showed that using a voting-based method across all the examined combinations achieved a better 10-fold cross-validated classification performance compared to any single combination [33]; a second study showed that an SVM-based ensemble outperformed single SVM for microarray data classification [42]; a third study comparing the performance of principal component discriminant classifiers either with or without voting using cross-validation applied on a simulated dataset a leukemia microarray gene expression dataset, a Gaucher serum proteomics dataset and a grape extract metabolomics dataset, also showed that voting had a better performance than the nonvoting method [43]; a fourth study comparing the performance of single models to combined models in thirteen diverse microarray datasets, which included predictions of estrogen receptor positivity and complete pathological response to chemotherapy in breast cancer, found that the majority of combined multiple models had a better classification performance than the single models [21]. Furthermore, our findings also agree with a study by Taylor and Kim who, by splitting their original datasets into training and test parts, showed that voting based on nearest mean voters was a top performing method with respect to classification on lung or prostate cancer data. In contrast to our results, RF was found to perform equally well as the mean voter [44]. However, this discrepancy is likely caused by the difference in classification tasks. In contrast to our results, Statnikov and coworkers found that SVM-based ensemble/voting methods perform similar or worse compared to SVM nonensemble/voting methods, when tested on ten different human gene expression datasets by 10-fold cross-validation. However, these comparisons were primarily based on multicategory classification [45].

In the second experiment, we investigated the classifiers performance when tested in an external dataset based on a similar microarray platform. In this setup, RF and

R-SVM achieved the best performances, both significantly outperforming four of the five remaining classification methods. Furthermore, the voting procedure significantly outperformed the seven underlying classification methods. This suggests that every classifier in the voting committee agrees on most of the samples that are predicted correctly and that the majority of voters do not make the same misclassifications. The finding that voting and RF have the best performances could be explained by these methods' ability to reduce the cross-study prediction variance, without simultaneously increasing prediction bias [37]. Only a limited number of studies have compared the cross-study performance of multiple classification methods. A study by Tan and Gilbert compared the performance of single C4.5 classifiers with the voting-like C4.5 bagging and boosting classifiers on gene expression data cancer classification. In four of the experiments, an independent dataset measured on similar platforms was used for testing. Interestingly, one of the results found that bagging and boosting performed better than single C4.5 classifiers when predicting relapse within a 5-year period in a small group of 19 independent breast cancer patients, achieving 88.7%, 88.7%, and 75% bAcc, respectively [46]. These voting results are higher than the mean voting performance achieved in our two test sets (72.5% bAcc). This could be due to three factors: (1) the training and testing sets used by Tan and Gilbert originate from the same population (The Netherlands), and the sample preparations and gene expression measurements were performed using the same protocols; (2) the classification task also differs. It might be easier to predict relapse within a 5-year period than predicting if a patient would ever metastasize; (3) the voting methods used also differ. Another study deployed a committee of neural networks for gene expression based leukemia subclassification using three gene expression datasets measured on the same microarray platform. The study used a first dataset for feature selection, a second for network training and committee development, and a third independent test set for validating the committee. When compared to the performance by each of the underlying classifiers in the committee, the committee neural networks proved to perform better or equally well in the final testing set [47].

In the third experiment, the trained classifiers were externally validated on datasets based on a different microarray platform. With this setup, the performances dropped dramatically. This suggests that the data distributions in the Agilent and Affymetrix datasets are dissimilar. This is likely caused by biological and technical variation. The fact that the training and test samples originate from two different patient populations could make the data distributions dissimilar. The technical variation may originate from several sources, for example, the size of the oligonucleotides used, probe coverage, labeling, cross-hybridization, and detection limits by the scanner. Furthermore, the two platforms use different strategies for measuring the same RNA quantity. On the Agilent platform, this quantity is measured as the ratio of fluorescence intensities between a sample and a reference at each spot on the array, while the Affymetrix platform uses single channel measurements for a collection of probe

sets covering one gene, which are therefore not comparable. To circumvent this obstacle, we standardized the datasets. However, this standardization seemed not to be sufficient for avoiding a drop in performance by all the classification methods used. Therefore, it is likely that the data distributions of the training and test sets are very heterogeneous thus hampering the external application of the classifiers.

Although all classification methods experience a drop in performance when validating between datasets measured on different platforms, the results showed that RF remained the strongest method and significantly outperformed the six other methods. Surprisingly, the voting procedure performed poorly when validated on data measured on a different microarray platform and was a borderline significantly outperformed by RF. This is probably due to randomness by each method/voter. The finding of RF performing better than the cross-method voting procedure suggests that when tested on datasets using a different microarray technology for gene expression measurement, voting procedures based on the same classification algorithm, in the case of random forest being a collection of decision trees, are more advantageous than voting procedures based on diverse classification methods. This implies that RF compared to voting is more capable of reducing the prediction variance associated with validation across studies and platforms. Therefore, in a situation when validating between different microarray platforms and where voting is outperformed, an approach called bagging might prove advantageous. Bagging uses voters consisting of multiple classifiers developed by bootstrap resamplings from the same dataset and based on the same classification method (decisions trees in the case of random forest) [48]. Thus, bagged SVM, LR, and NNET might be considered ideal for cross-study-cross-platform validations. RF may also be powerful, as the method is based on multiple decision rules, which might be better at segregating a complex data structure. This situation is in line with a study showing that molecular classification of cancer achieves better or similar performance as other classification algorithms, when using decision rules based on a single gene or a gene pair [49].

In the literature, there has been a limited number of studies comparing the performance of multiple classification methods, applied to across the dataset and microarray platform validations. One study by Yoshida compared a nearest template prediction method (NTP) with CART (single decision tree method), weighted voting, SVM, and k-nearest neighbor classification (k-NN) across datasets using Agilent datasets for training and Affymetrix datasets for testing [20]. For prediction of estrogen receptor positivity in breast cancer, NTP had the best performance, while SVM had the worst performance. For predictions of breast cancer molecular subtypes, SVM had the best performance in two of three testing sets used for this purpose, while NTP had the best performance in the third dataset. The worst performing methods were achieved by CART and k-NN [20]. In our study, SVM was not a top performing method for cross-platform testing. These differences are likely due to two factors: first, the study by Hoshida did not apply the entire classifier to the test sets, but only the list of genes defined by the training datasets. This list was used to train and test a classifier in the validation dataset; second, the study addresses completely different classification tasks compared to our study.

Our results showed that when validation is applied between two datasets of similar or different microarray platforms, LR and NNET were among the poorest performing methods.

The general poor performance of LR could be due to several factors. First, a strong LR model is frequently composed of predictors being highly univariate significant and remains significant in the multivariate model. The fact that the list of 519 rank-significant genes defined by the eight feature definer datasets was reduced to a pool of 283 genes could have led to the exclusion of some highly significant genes, due to the only reason that they were not shared by the AM, RO, TR, and MA datasets, thus impairing the possibility for development of a stronger model. This could explain the poor performance by LR classifiers developed by the individual AM and RO datasets; second, an LR model requires a large sample size for providing robust maximum likelihood parameter estimation. Although the training datasets contain 151 and 286 samples, these sample sizes may not be sufficient for developing a strong model if some of the highly discriminative genes are absent; third, LR models rely on the assumption that there is no colinearity between the variables, meaning that the variables/features should be independent from each other. This assumption may be violated if predictors in a logistic model consist of, for example, gene expression features, some of which could be coregulated, thus leading to colinearity and weakening the model; finally, LR is sensitive to outliers. As we have not removed any samples from our datasets, and the possibility of outlier presence thus could be evident, this could also hamper the predictive power of the LR models.

The finding of NNET had a high internal 10-fold cross validation performance but a weak external validation performance could suggest that the NNET classifiers are not very generable. Another explanation could be that the transfer function used by the neural network was a sigmoid function, which is identical to that used in logistic regression, thus leading to some of the weaknesses observed in logistic regression, although the parameter estimation in neural networks is not conducted by maximum-likelihood but by a gradient descent algorithm. Interestingly, a study has compared the classification performance of four different single hidden layer feedforward neural networks on three microarray gene expression cancer dataset, showing that an SVD-neural classifier based on a *tansig* activation function and using single value decomposition for parameter estimation had a better performance compared to the three other methods and that this classifier outperformed support vector machines, principle component analysis classifiers, and Fisher discriminant analysis classifiers [50]. This implies that using another neural network type could achieve a better performance when applied for external validation in datasets based on similar or different microarray platforms.

In conclusion, voting-based classifiers provided an advantage with respect to classifying metastasis outcome in breast cancer patients. When testing was performed within the same dataset or between datasets using similar microarray platforms, combining class decisions by multiple classification methods significantly increased the classification performance. Random forest, a voting-like method, proved to be the strongest method when testing was performed in datasets based on a different microarray platform.

Conflict of Interests

The authors declare that they have no competing interests.

Acknowledgments

This work was funded by the Danish Ministry of Interior, the Danish Strategically Research Council and DBCG-TIBCAT, the Clinical Institute at the University of Southern Denmark and the Human Microarray Center associated with the Department of Clinical Genetics at the Odense University Hospital. Furthermore, the authors acknowledge authors and people making the microarray datasets used in this study publically available.

References

[1] E. Karlsson, U. Delle, A. Danielsson et al., "Gene expression variation to predict 10-year survival in lymph-node-negative breast cancer," *BMC Cancer*, vol. 8, article 254, 2008.

[2] H. Y. Chuang, E. Lee, Y. T. Liu, D. Lee, and T. Ideker, "Network-based classification of breast cancer metastasis," *Molecular Systems Biology*, vol. 3, article 140, 2007.

[3] Q. Tan, M. Thomassen, and T. A. Kruse, "Feature selection for predicting tumor metastases in microarray experiments using paired design," *Cancer Informatics*, vol. 3, pp. 133–138, 2007.

[4] M. Thomassen, Q. Tan, F. Eiriksdottir, M. Bak, S. Cold, and T. A. Kruse, "Prediction of metastasis from low-malignant breast cancer by gene expression profiling," *International Journal of Cancer*, vol. 120, no. 5, pp. 1070–1075, 2007.

[5] R. Sabatier, P. Finetti, N. Cervera et al., "A gene expression signature identifies two prognostic subgroups of basal breast cancer," *Breast Cancer Research and Treatment*, vol. 126, no. 2, pp. 407–420, 2011.

[6] L. D. Miller, J. Smeds, J. George et al., "An expression signature for p53 status in human breast cancer predicts mutation status, transcriptional effects, and patient survival," *Proceedings of the National Academy of Sciences of the United States of America*, vol. 102, no. 38, pp. 13550–13555, 2005.

[7] M. H. van Vliet, R. Fabien, H. M. Horlings, M. J. van de Vijver, M. J. T. Reinders, and L. F. A. Wessels, "Pooling breast cancer datasets has a synergetic effect on classification performance and improves signature stability," *BMC Genomics*, vol. 9, article 375, 2008.

[8] M. Thomassen, Q. Tan, F. Eiriksdottir, M. Bak, S. Cold, and T. A. Kruse, "Comparison of gene sets for expression profiling: prediction of metastasis from low-malignant breast cancer," *Clinical Cancer Research*, vol. 13, no. 18, part 1, pp. 5355–5360, 2007.

[9] N. Servant, M. A. Bollet, H. Halfwerk et al., "Search for a gene expression signature of breast cancer local recurrence in young women," *Clinical Cancer Research*, vol. 18, no. 6, pp. 1704–1715, 2012.

[10] T. Zeng and J. Liu, "Mixture classification model based on clinical markers for breast cancer prognosis," *Artificial Intelligence in Medicine*, vol. 48, no. 2-3, pp. 129–137, 2010.

[11] M. Garcia, R. Millat-carus, F. Bertucci, P. Finetti, D. Birnbaum, and G. Bidaut, "Interactome-transcriptome integration for predicting distant metastasis in breast cancer," *Bioinformatics*, vol. 28, no. 5, pp. 672–678, 2012.

[12] R. Díaz-Uriarte and A. S. de Andrés, "Gene selection and classification of microarray data using random forest," *BMC Bioinformatics*, vol. 7, article 3, 2006.

[13] L. J. Lancashire, D. G. Powe, J. S. Reis-Filho et al., "A validated gene expression profile for detecting clinical outcome in breast cancer using artificial neural networks," *Breast Cancer Research and Treatment*, vol. 120, no. 1, pp. 83–93, 2010.

[14] A. Statnikov and C. F. Aliferis, "Are random forests better than support vector machines for microarray-based cancer classification?" *AMIA Annual Symposium Proceedings*, pp. 686–690, 2007.

[15] M. Pirooznia, J. Y. Yang, M. Q. Qu, and Y. Deng, "A comparative study of different machine learning methods on microarray gene expression data," *BMC Genomics*, vol. 9, supplement 1, article S13, 2008.

[16] M. Zucknick, S. Richardson, and E. A. Stronach, "Comparing the characteristics of gene expression profiles derived by univariate and multivariate classification methods," *Statistical Applications in Genetics and Molecular Biology*, vol. 7, no. 1, article 7, 2008.

[17] A. Statnikov, L. Wang, and C. F. Aliferis, "A comprehensive comparison of random forests and support vector machines for microarray-based cancer classification," *BMC Bioinformatics*, vol. 9, article 319, 2008.

[18] J. Önskog, E. Freyhult, M. Landfors, P. Rydén, and T. R. Hvidsten, "Classification of microarrays; synergistic effects between normalization, gene selection and machine learning," *BMC Bioinformatics*, vol. 12, article 390, 2011.

[19] S. Y. Kim, "Effects of sample size on robustness and prediction accuracy of a prognostic gene signature," *BMC Bioinformatics*, vol. 10, article 147, 2009.

[20] Y. Hoshida, "Nearest template prediction: a single-sample-based flexible class prediction with confidence assessment," *PLoS One*, vol. 5, no. 11, Article ID e15543, 2010.

[21] M. Chen, L. Shi, R. Kelly, R. Perkins, H. Fang, and W. Tong, "Selecting a single model or combining multiple models for microarray-based classifier development?—a comparative analysis based on large and diverse datasets generated from the MAQC-II project," *BMC Bioinformatics*, vol. 12, supplement 10, Article ID S3, 2011.

[22] M. Zervakis, M. E. Blazadonakis, G. Tsiliki, V. Danilatou, M. Tsiknakis, and D. Kafetzopoulos, "Outcome prediction based on microarray analysis: a critical perspective on methods," *BMC Bioinformatics*, vol. 10, article 53, 2009.

[23] S. Calza, P. Hall, G. Auer et al., "Intrinsic molecular signature of breast cancer in a population-based cohort of 412 patients," *Breast Cancer Research*, vol. 8, no. 4, article R34, 2006.

[24] C. Sotiriou, S. Y. Neo, L. M. McShane et al., "Breast cancer classification and prognosis based on gene expression profiles from a population-based study," *Proceedings of the National Academy of Sciences of the United States of America*, vol. 100, no. 18, pp. 10393–10398, 2003.

[25] C. Sotiriou, P. Wirapati, S. Loi et al., "Gene expression profiling in breast cancer: understanding the molecular basis of histologic grade to improve prognosis," *Journal of the National Cancer Institute*, vol. 98, no. 4, pp. 262–272, 2006.

[26] M. J. van de Vijver, Y. D. He, L. J. van't Veer et al., "A gene-expression signature as a predictor of survival in breast cancer," *New England Journal of Medicine*, vol. 347, no. 25, pp. 1999–2009, 2002.

[27] E. Huang, S. H. Cheng, H. Dressman et al., "Gene expression predictors of breast cancer outcomes," *The Lancet*, vol. 361, no. 9369, pp. 1590–1596, 2003.

[28] Y. Wang, J. G. M. Klijn, Y. Zhang et al., "Gene-expression profiles to predict distant metastasis of lymph-node-negative primary breast cancer," *The Lancet*, vol. 365, no. 9460, pp. 671–679, 2005.

[29] M. Buyse, S. Loi, L. van't Veer et al., "Validation and clinical utility of a 70-gene prognostic signature for women with node-negative breast cancer," *Journal of the National Cancer Institute*, vol. 98, no. 17, pp. 1183–1192, 2006.

[30] M. Schmidt, D. Böhm, C. von Törne et al., "The humoral immune system has a key prognostic impact in node-negative breast cancer," *Cancer Research*, vol. 68, no. 13, pp. 5405–5413, 2008.

[31] L. J. van't Veer, H. Dai, M. J. van de Vijver et al., "Gene expression profiling predicts clinical outcome of breast cancer," *Nature*, vol. 415, no. 6871, pp. 530–536, 2002.

[32] C. Desmedt, F. Piette, S. Loi et al., "Strong time dependence of the 76-gene prognostic signature for node-negative breast cancer patients in the TRANSBIG multicenter independent validation series," *Clinical Cancer Research*, vol. 13, no. 11, pp. 3207–3214, 2007.

[33] L. Nanni, S. Brahnam, and A. Lumini, "Combining multiple approaches for gene microarray classification," *Bioinformatics*, vol. 28, no. 8, pp. 1151–1157, 2012.

[34] M. Thomassen, Q. Tan, and T. A. Kruse, "Gene expression meta-analysis identifies metastatic pathways and transcription factors in breast cancer," *BMC Cancer*, vol. 8, article 394, 2008.

[35] M. Thomassen, Q. Tan, and T. A. Kruse, "Gene expression meta-analysis identifies chromosomal regions and candidate genes involved in breast cancer metastasis," *Breast Cancer Research and Treatment*, vol. 113, no. 2, pp. 239–249, 2009.

[36] L. Breiman, "Random forests," *Machine Learning*, vol. 45, no. 1, pp. 5–32, 2001.

[37] T. Hastie, R. Tibshirani, and J. Friedman, *The Elements of Statistical Learning: Data Mining Inference and Prediction*, Springer, New York, NY, USA, 2nd edition, 2009.

[38] V. Vapnik, *The Nature of Statistical Learning Theory*, Springer, New York, Ny, USA, 1995.

[39] A. Dupuy and R. M. Simon, "Critical review of published microarray studies for cancer outcome and guidelines on statistical analysis and reporting," *Journal of the National Cancer Institute*, vol. 99, no. 2, pp. 147–157, 2007.

[40] R. Hewett and P. Kijsanayothin, "Tumor classification ranking from microarray data," *BMC Genomics*, vol. 9, supplement 2, article S21, 2008.

[41] G. Natsoulis, L. El Ghaoui, G. R. G. Lanckriet et al., "Classification of a large microarray data set: algorithm comparison and analysis of drug signatures," *Genome Research*, vol. 15, no. 5, pp. 724–736, 2005.

[42] Y. Peng, "A novel ensemble machine learning for robust microarray data classification," *Computers in Biology and Medicine*, vol. 36, no. 6, pp. 553–573, 2006.

[43] C. J. Xu, H. C. J. Hoefsloot, and A. K. Smilde, "To aggregate or not to aggregate high-dimensional classifiers," *BMC Bioinformatics*, vol. 12, article 153, 2011.

[44] S. L. Taylor and K. Kim, "A jackknife and voting classifier approach to feature selection and classification," *Cancer Informatics*, vol. 10, pp. 133–147, 2011.

[45] A. Statnikov, C. F. Aliferis, I. Tsamardinos, D. Hardin, and S. Levy, "A comprehensive evaluation of multicategory classification methods for microarray gene expression cancer diagnosis," *Bioinformatics*, vol. 21, no. 5, pp. 631–643, 2005.

[46] A. C. Tan and D. Gilbert, "Ensemble machine learning on gene expression data for cancer classification," *Appl Bioinformatics*, vol. 2, supplement 3, pp. S75–S83, 2003.

[47] M. S. Sewak, N. P. Reddy, and Z. H. Duan, "Gene expression based leukemia sub-classification using committee neural networks," *Bioinformatics and Biology Insights*, vol. 3, pp. 89–98, 2009.

[48] L. Breiman, "Bagging predictors," *Machine Learning*, vol. 24, no. 2, pp. 123–140, 1996.

[49] X. Wang and O. Gotoh, "Accurate molecular classification of cancer using simple rules," *BMC Medical Genomics*, vol. 2, article 64, 2009.

[50] H. T. Huynh, J. J. Kim, and Y. Won, "Performance comparison of SLFN training algorithms for DNA microarray classification," *Advances in Experimental Medicine and Biology*, vol. 696, pp. 135–143, 2011.

8

Ligand-Based Virtual Screening Using Bayesian Inference Network and Reweighted Fragments

Ali Ahmed,[1,2] **Ammar Abdo,**[1,3] **and Naomie Salim**[1]

[1] *Faculty of Computer Science and Information Systems, Universiti Teknologi Malaysia, 81310 Skudai, Malaysia*
[2] *Faculty of Engineering, Karary University, Khartoum 12304, Sudan*
[3] *Department of Computer Science, Hodeidah University, Hodeidah, Yemen*

Correspondence should be addressed to Ali Ahmed, alikarary@gmail.com

Academic Editors: M. A. Fischl and G. D. Morse

Many of the similarity-based virtual screening approaches assume that molecular fragments that are not related to the biological activity carry the same weight as the important ones. This was the reason that led to the use of Bayesian networks as an alternative to existing tools for similarity-based virtual screening. In our recent work, the retrieval performance of the Bayesian inference network (BIN) was observed to improve significantly when molecular fragments were reweighted using the relevance feedback information. In this paper, a set of active reference structures were used to reweight the fragments in the reference structure. In this approach, higher weights were assigned to those fragments that occur more frequently in the set of active reference structures while others were penalized. Simulated virtual screening experiments with MDL Drug Data Report datasets showed that the proposed approach significantly improved the retrieval effectiveness of ligand-based virtual screening, especially when the active molecules being sought had a high degree of structural heterogeneity.

1. Introduction

Virtual screening refers to the use of a computer-based method to process compounds from a library or database of compounds in order to identify and select ones that are likely to possess a desired biological activity, such as the ability to inhibit the action of a particular therapeutic target. The selection of molecules with a virtual screening algorithm should yield a higher proportion of active compounds, as assessed by experiment, relative to a random selection of the same number of molecules [1].

Over recent decades, drug discovery companies have used combinatorial chemistry approaches to create large and diverse libraries of structures; therefore large arrays of compounds are formed by combining sets of different types of reagents, called building blocks, in a systematic and repetitive way. These libraries can be used as a source of new potential drugs, since the compounds in the libraries can be randomly tested or screened to find good drug compounds. Increasing the capabilities of testing compounds using chemoinformatic technologies such as high-throughput screening (HTS) enables hundreds of thousands of these compounds to be tested in a short time. Computers can be used to aid this process in a number of ways; for example, in the creation of virtual combinatorial libraries which can be much larger than their real counterparts. There are two methods for screening those libraries, looking into active sites of interest and looking for similarities to a known active compound. Recently, searching chemical databases has been done using computers instead of experiment, and this is known as the virtual screening technique [2–9].

Chemical information systems offer three principal types of searching facility. Early systems provided two types of retrieval mechanisms: structure searching and substructure searching. These mechanisms were later complemented by another access mechanism: similarity searching. There are many studies in the literature associated with the measurement of molecular similarity [10–13]. However, the most common approaches are based on 2D fingerprints, with the similarity between a reference structure and a database structure computed using association coefficients such as the Tanimoto coefficient [1, 14].

Several methods have been used to further optimise the measures of similarity between molecules, including weighting, standardization, and data fusion [15–18].

The Bayesian inference network (BIN) was originally developed for text document retrieval systems [19]. Many studies in information retrieval (IR) have shown that the retrieval effectiveness of BIN can be improved by fragment reweighting. Fragments reweighting is one of the most useful query modification techniques in IR systems [20–22]. In our previous works, the retrieval performance of Bayesian inference network was observed to improve significantly when relevance feedback and turbo search screening were used [23].

In this paper, we enhanced the screening effectiveness of BIN using a weighting factor. In this approach, weighting factors are calculated for each fragment of the multireference input query based on the frequency of their occurrence in the set of references' input. This weighting factor is later used to calculate a new weight for each fragment of the reference structure.

2. Material and Methods

This study has compared the retrieval results obtained using three different similarity-based screening models. The first screening system was based on the tanimoto (TAN) coefficient, which has been used in ligand-based virtual screening for many years and is now considered a reference standard. The second model was based on a basic BIN [24] using the Okapi (OKA) weight, which was found to perform the best in their experiments and which we shall refer to as the conventional BIN model. The third model, our proposed model, is a BIN based on reweighted fragments, which we shall refer to as the BINRF model. In what follows, we give a brief description of each of these three models.

2.1. Tanimoto-Based Similarity Model. This model used the continuous form of the tanimoto coefficient, which is applicable to nonbinary data of fingerprint. $S_{K,L}$ is the similarity between objects or molecules K and L, which, using tanimoto, is given by (1):

$$S_{kL} = \frac{\sum_{j=1}^{M} w_{jk} w_{jl}}{\sum_{j=1}^{M} \left(w_{jk}\right)^2 + \sum_{j=1}^{M} \left(w_{jl}\right)^2 - \sum_{j=1}^{M} \left(w_k w_{jl}\right)}. \quad (1)$$

For molecules described by continuous variables, the molecular space is defined by an $M \times N$ matrix, where entry w_{ji} is the value of the jth fragments ($1 \leq j \leq M$) in the ith molecule ($1 \leq i \leq N$). The origins of this coefficient can be found in a review paper by Ellis et al. [25].

2.2. Conventional BIN Model. The conventional BIN model, as shown in Figure 1, is used in molecular similarity searching. It consists of three types of nodes: compound nodes as roots, fragment nodes, and a reference structure node as leaf. The roots of the network are the nodes without parent nodes and the leaves are the nodes without child nodes. Each compound node represents an actual compound

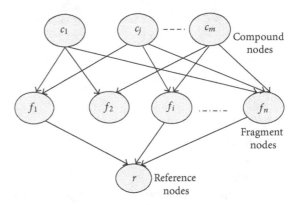

FIGURE 1: Bayesian inference network model.

in the collection and has one or more fragment nodes as children. Each fragment node has one or more compound nodes as parents and one reference structure node as a child (or more where multiple references are used). Each network node is a binary value, taking one of the two values from the set {true, false}. The probability that the reference structure is satisfied given a particular compound is obtained by computing the probabilities associated with each fragment node connected to the reference structure node. This process is repeated for all the compounds in the database.

The resulting probability scores are used to rank the database in response to a bioactive reference structure in the order of decreasing probability of similar bioactivity to the reference structure.

To estimate the probability associating each compound to the reference structure, the probability for the fragment and reference nodes must be computed. One particular belief function, called OKA, has been found to have the most effective recall [24]. This function was used to compute the probabilities for the fragment nodes and is given by (2):

$$\text{bel}_{\text{OKA}}(f_i) = \alpha + (1 - \alpha) \times \frac{ff_{ij}}{ff_{ij} + 0.5 + 1.5 \times |c_j| / |c_{\text{avg}}|}$$

$$\times \frac{\log[(m + 0.5)/cf_i]}{\log(m + 1.0)}, \quad (2)$$

where α = Constant; and experiments using the BIN show that the best value is 0.4 [26, 27], ff_{ij} = frequency of the ith fragment within the jth compound reference structure, cf_i = number of compounds containing the ith fragment, $|c_j|$ = the size (in terms of number of fragments) of the jth compound, $|C_{\text{avg}}|$ = the average size of all the compounds in the database, and m = the total number of compounds.

To produce a ranking of the compounds in the collection with respect to a given reference structure, a belief function from In Query, the SUM operator, was used. If $p1, p2, \ldots, pn$ represent the belief in the fragment nodes (parent nodes of r), then the belief at r is given by (3):

$$\text{bel}_{\text{sum}}(r) = \frac{\sum_{i=1}^{n} p_i}{n}, \quad (3)$$

TABLE 1: MDDR activity classes for DS1 dataset.

Activity index	Activity class	Active molecules	Pairwise similarity (mean)
31420	Renin inhibitors	1130	0.290
71523	HIV protease inhibitors	750	0.198
37110	Thrombin inhibitors	803	0.180
31432	Angiotensin II AT1 antagonists	943	0.229
42731	Substance P antagonists	1246	0.149
06233	Substance P antagonists	752	0.140
06245	5HT reuptake inhibitors	359	0.122
07701	D2 antagonists	395	0.138
06235	5HT1A agonists	827	0.133
78374	Protein kinase C inhibitors	453	0.120
78331	Cyclooxygenase inhibitors	636	0.108

TABLE 2: MDDR activity classes for DS2 dataset.

Activity index	Activity class	Active molecules	Pairwise similarity (mean)
07707	Adenosine (A1) agonists	207	0.229
07708	Adenosine (A2) agonists	156	0.305
31420	Renin inhibitors 1	1300	0.290
42710	CCK agonists	111	0.361
64100	Monocyclic-lactams	1346	0.336
64200	Cephalosporins	113	0.322
64220	Carbacephems	1051	0.269
64500	Carbapenems	126	0.260
64350	Tribactams	388	0.305
75755	Vitamin D analogous	455	0.386

where n = the number of the unique fragments assigned to reference structure r.

2.3. BINRF Model. The difference between the two models (BIN and BINRF) arises from the differences in the type of belief function used to produce the ranking of the compounds in the collection. In the conventional BIN model, the probability of the reference node is computed by summing the probabilities in the fragment nodes connected to the reference node. The fragment nodes participating in the final probability are scored equally (meaning that no extra weight given to any fragment node). This calculation is conducted using the SUM operator, as described above.

In the BINRF model, the reweighting factor is used to assign a new weight to the fragment. In order to produce this factor, it is necessary to start by analysing the occurrence of each fragment in the set of input references. The reweighing factor rwf_i is calculated using (4):

$$rwf_i = \frac{F_{f_i}}{\max F}, \tag{4}$$

TABLE 3: MDDR activity classes for DS3 dataset.

Activity index	Activity class	Active molecules	Pairwise similarity (mean)
09249	Muscarinic (M1) agonists	900	0.111
12455	NMDA receptor antagonists	1400	0.098
12464	Nitric oxide synthase inhibitors	505	0.102
31281	Dopamine-hydroxylase inhibitors	106	0.125
43210	Aldose reductase inhibitors	957	0.119
71522	Reverse transcriptase inhibitors	700	0.103
75721	Aromatase inhibitors	636	0.110
78331	Cyclooxygenase inhibitors	636	0.108
78348	Phospholipase A2 inhibitors	617	0.123
78351	Lipoxygenase inhibitors	2111	0.113

where F_{f_i} is the frequency of ith fragment in the set of references' input and $\max F$ is the maximum fragment frequency in the set of references' input.

New weights are then assigned to the fragments based on this factor, the new weight, nw_i, of the ith fragment, is given by (5):

$$nw_i = w_i + rwf_i, \tag{5}$$

where w_i is the original frequency of the ith fragment in the reference input.

Consequently, the use of (4) and (5) to assign the new weights shows that higher weights will be assigned to those that occur more frequently in the set of references' input structures.

2.4. Experimental Design. The searches were carried out on the MDL Drug Data Report (MDDR) database. The 102,516 molecules in the MDDR database were converted to Pipeline Pilot ECFC_4 fingerprints and folded to give 1024-element fingerprints [28].

For the screening experiments, three data sets (DS1–DS3) [29] were chosen from the MDDR database. Dataset DS1 contains 11 MDDR activity classes, with some of the classes involving actives that are structurally homogeneous and others involving actives that are structurally heterogeneous (structurally diverse). The DS2 dataset contains 10 homogeneous MDDR activity classes and the DS3 dataset contains 10 heterogeneous MDDR activity classes. Full details of these datasets are given in Tables 1–3. Each row in the tables contains an activity class, the number of molecules belonging to the class, and the class's diversity, which was computed as the mean pair-wise Tanimoto similarity calculated across all pairs of molecules in the class using ECFP6. The pair-wise similarity calculations for all datasets were performed using Pipeline Pilot software [28].

For each dataset (DS1–DS3), the screening experiments were conducted with 10 reference structures selected randomly from each activity class and the similarity measure used to obtain an activity score for all of its compounds.

TABLE 4: The recall is calculated using the top 1% and top 5% of the DS1 data sets when ranked using the TAN, BIN, and BINRF.

Activity index	1%			5%		
	TAN	BIN	BINRF	TAN	BIN	BINRF
31420	55.84*	74.08*	81.8**	85.49*	87.61**	84.12*
71523	22.26*	28.26*	43.86**	42.7*	52.72*	68.72**
37110	12.54*	26.05*	41.25**	24.11*	48.2*	71.05**
31432	33.36*	39.23*	46.5**	68.2*	77.57*	91.59**
42731	16.24*	21.68*	28.13**	32.81*	26.63*	42.39**
06233	14.23*	14.06*	16.75**	27.01*	23.49*	32.93**
06245	10.06**	6.31*	10.04*	22.9*	14.86*	28.8**
07701	8.91*	11.45*	19.75**	23.1*	27.79*	41.24**
06235	11.87*	10.84*	12.45**	24.54*	23.78*	31.89**
78374	16.75*	14.25*	25.49**	24.26*	20.2*	39.18**
78331	8.05*	6.03*	8.14**	16.83**	11.8*	11.20*
Mean	**19.10**	**22.93**	**30.38**	**35.63**	**37.69**	**49.73**
Share cells	1	0	10	1	1	9

TABLE 5: The recall is calculated using the top 1% and top 5% of the DS2 data sets when ranked using the TAN, BIN, and BINRF.

Activity index	1%			5%		
	TAN	BIN	BINRF	TAN	BIN	BINRF
07707	78.3**	72.18*	72.33*	91.08**	74.81*	74.17*
07708	74.01*	96*	100**	88.52*	99.61*	100**
31420	46.44*	79.82*	82.71**	77.6*	95.46*	97.15**
42710	57.22*	76.27*	95.36**	67.59*	92.55*	99.36**
64100	93.22*	88.43**	87.75*	97.89*	99.22**	98.93*
64200	63.39*	70.18*	71.79**	89.82*	99.2**	99.12*
64220	73.56*	68.32*	82.47**	92.05*	91.32*	98.89**
64500	60.75*	81.2*	96.56**	74.98*	94.96*	99.28**
64350	76.69*	81.89*	93.67**	90.34*	91.47*	98.24**
75755	95.99*	98.06*	98.26**	98.78**	98.33*	98.33*
Mean	**71.957**	**81.235**	**88.09**	**86.86**	**93.69**	**96.34**
Share cells	1	1	8	2	2	6

These activity scores were then sorted in descending order with the recall of the active compounds, meaning the percentage of the desired activity class compounds that are retrieved in the top 1% and 5% of the resultant sorted activity scores, providing a measure of the performance of our similarity method.

3. Results and Discussion

Our goal was to identify different retrieval effectiveness of using different search approaches. In this study, we tested the TAN, BIN, and BINRF models against the MDDR database using three different datasets (DS1–DS3). The results of the searches of DS1–DS3 are presented in Tables 4-6, respectively, using cutoffs at both 1% and 5%.

In these tables, the first column from the left contains the results for the TAN, the second column contains the corresponding results when BIN is used, and the last column of each table contains the corresponding results when BINRF is used.

Each row in the tables lists the recall for the top 1% and 5% of a sorted ranking when averaged over the ten searches for each activity class; and the penultimate row in each table corresponds to the mean value for that similarity method when averaged over all of the activity classes for a dataset. The similarity method with the best recall rate in each row is strongly ($**$), and the recall value is boldfaced; any similarity method with an average recall within 1% and 5% of the value for the best similarity method is shown lightly ($*$). The bottom row in a table corresponds to the total number of ($*$ and $**$) cells for each similarity method across the full set of activity classes.

Visual inspection of the recall values in Tables 4–6 enables comparisons to be made between the effectiveness of the various search models. However, a more quantitative approach is possible using the Kendall W test of concordance [30].

This test shows whether a set of judges make comparable judgments about the ranking of a set of objects; here, the activity classes were considered the judges and the recall rates

TABLE 6: The recall is calculated using the top 1% and top 5% of the DS3 data sets when ranked using the TAN, BIN, and BINRF.

Activity index	1%			5%		
	TAN	BIN	BINRF	TAN	BIN	BINRF
09249	25.09**	15.33*	15.51*	40.21**	25.72*	29.08*
12455	7.7*	9.37*	11.59**	19.08**	14.65*	16.77*
12464	9.02*	8.45*	11.67**	14.56*	16.55*	27.1**
31281	27.53*	18.29*	44.48**	44*	28.29*	59.9**
43210	11.1**	7.34*	9.41*	26.37**	14.41*	21.27*
71522	2.35*	4.08*	11.39**	6.28*	8.44*	23.62**
75721	24.02*	20.41*	28.24**	28.97*	30.02*	56.39**
78331	6.27*	7.51*	10.11**	15.79*	12.03*	18.82**
78348	4.69*	9.79**	8.99*	13.16*	20.76*	24.15**
78351	4.31*	13.68*	16.64**	10.55*	12.94*	20.16**
Mean	**12.21**	**11.42**	**16.80**	**21.90**	**18.38**	**29.72**
Share cells	2	1	7	3	0	7

TABLE 7: Rankings of weighting functions based on Kendall W test results: DS1–DS3 Top 1% and 5%.

Dataset	Recall type	W	P	Ranking
DS1	1%	0.75	<0.01	BINRF > BIN > TAN
	5%	0.71	<0.01	BINRF > TAN > BIN
DS2	1%	0.39	>0.01	BINRF > BIN > TAN
	5%	0.28	<0.01	BINRF > BIN > TAN
DS3	1%	0.37	<0.01	BINRF>TAN>BIN
	5%	0.39	<0.01	BINRF>TAN>BIN

TABLE 8: Number of ($*$ and $**$) cells for mean recall of actives using different search models for DS1–DS3 Top 1% and 5%.

Dataset	TAN	BIN	BINRF
Top 1%			
DS1	1	0	10
DS2	1	1	8
DS3	2	1	7
Top 5%			
DS1	1	1	9
DS2	2	2	6
DS3	3	0	7

of the various search models the objects. The outputs of this test are the value of the Kendall coefficient and the associated significance level, which indicates whether this value of the coefficient could have occurred by chance. If the value is significant (for which we used cutoff values of both 0.01 and 0.05), then it is possible to give an overall ranking of the objects that have been ranked. The results of the Kendall analyses (for DS1–DS3) are reported in Table 7 and describe the top 1% and top 5% rankings for the various weighting functions. In Table 7, the columns show the dataset type, the recall percentage, the value of the coefficient, the associated probability, and the ranking of the methods.

Some of the activity classes, such as low-diversity activity classes, may contribute disproportionally to the overall value of mean recall. Therefore, using the mean recall value as the evaluation criterion could be impartial in some methods but not in others. To avoid this bias, the effective performances of the different methods have been further investigated based on the total number of ($*$ and $**$) cells for each method across the full set of activity classes, as shown in the bottom rows of Tables 4–6. These ($*$ and $**$) cell results are also listed in Table 8 (the results shown in the bottom rows of Tables 4–6 form the lower part of the results in Table 8).

Inspection of the DS1 search in Table 4 shows that BINRF produced the highest mean values when compared to the BIN and TAN. In addition, according to the total number of ($*$ and $**$) cells in Table 4, BINRF is the best performing

search across the 11 activity classes in terms of mean recall. Table 7 shows that the value of the Kendall coefficient for DS1 top 1% and 5%, 0.752, is significant at the 0.01 and 0.05 levels of statistical significance. Given that the result is significant, we can conclude that the overall ranking of the different procedures are BINRF > BIN > TAN and BINRF > TAN > BIN for the DS1 top 1% and 5%, respectively.

The good performance of the BINRF method is not restricted to DS1 since it also gives the best results for the top 1% and 5% for DS2 and DS3.

The DS3 searches are of particular interest since they involve the most heterogeneous activity classes in the three datasets used, and thus provide a tough test of the effectiveness of a screening method. Hert et al. [29] found that TSS (group fusion) was not preferred to the conventional similarity search for DS3 activity classes. However, when BINRF is used on this dataset, Tables 6 and 7 show that it gives the best performance of all the methods for this dataset at both cutoffs.

Visual inspection of the results in Tables 4–8 shows very clearly that reweighting reference fragments can significantly increase the effectiveness of the BIN method and the results are presented for the original search using TAN, BIN, and BINRF. A very surprising pattern of behaviour is observed in the DS3 results presented in Table 6 as the degree of enhancement in this more challenging screening task is remarkable.

In conclusion, we have introduced a new technique for utilising the effectiveness of retrieval when applying a BIN for ligand-based virtual screening. Simulated virtual screening experiments with MDDR datasets showed that the proposed techniques described here provide simple ways of enhancing the cost effectiveness of ligand-based virtual screening in chemical databases.

4. Conclusion

In this paper, we further investigated the impact of reweighting fragments on the Bayesian inference network performance for ligand-based virtual screening. Simulated virtual screening experiments with MDL Drug Data Report datasets showed that the proposed approach significantly improved the retrieval effectiveness of ligand-based virtual screening, especially when the active molecules being sought had a high degree of structural heterogeneity. This finding is in line with our previous study, in which the relevance feedback information was used to reweight the fragments. However, it should be pointed out that while using relevance feedback information is limited only by computational cost, using a set of reference structures implies the availability of bioactivities.

Acknowledgment

This work is supported by Ministry of Higher Education (MOHE) and Research Management Centre (RMC) at the Universiti Teknologi Malaysia (UTM) under Research University Grant Category (VOT Q.J130000.7128.00H72).

References

[1] M. A. Johnson and G. M. Maggiora, *Concepts and Application of Molecular Similarity*, John Wiley & Sons, New York, NY, USA, 1990.

[2] P. Willett, J. M. Barnard, and G. M. Downs, "Chemical similarity searching," *Journal of Chemical Information and Computer Sciences*, vol. 38, no. 6, pp. 983–996, 1998.

[3] W. P. Walters, M. T. Stahl, and M. A. Murcko, "Virtual screening—an overview," *Drug Discovery Today*, vol. 3, no. 4, pp. 160–178, 1998.

[4] B. Waszkowycz, T. D. J. Perkins, R. A. Sykes, and J. Li, "Large-scale virtual screening for discovering leads in the postgenomic era," *IBM Systems Journal*, vol. 40, no. 2, pp. 360–378, 2001.

[5] M. A. Miller, "Chemical database techniques in drug discovery," *Nature Reviews Drug Discovery*, vol. 1, no. 3, pp. 220–227, 2002.

[6] H. Eckert and J. Bajorath, "Molecular similarity analysis in virtual screening: foundations, limitations and novel approaches," *Drug Discovery Today*, vol. 12, no. 5-6, pp. 225–233, 2007.

[7] R. P. Sheridan, "Chemical similarity searches: when is complexity justified?" *Expert Opinion on Drug Discovery*, vol. 2, no. 4, pp. 423–430, 2007.

[8] H. Geppert, M. Vogt, and J. Bajorath, "Current trends in ligand-based virtual screening: molecular representations, data mining methods, new application areas, and performance evaluation," *Journal of Chemical Information and Modeling*, vol. 50, no. 2, pp. 205–216, 2010.

[9] R. P. Sheridan and S. K. Kearsley, "Why do we need so many chemical similarity search methods?" *Drug Discovery Today*, vol. 7, no. 17, pp. 903–911, 2002.

[10] N. Nikolova and J. Jaworska, "Approaches to measure chemical similarity—a Review," *QSAR & Combinatorial Science*, vol. 22, no. 9-10, pp. 1006–1026, 2003.

[11] A. Bender and R. C. Glen, "Molecular similarity: a key technique in molecular informatics," *Organic and Biomolecular Chemistry*, vol. 2, no. 22, pp. 3204–3218, 2004.

[12] A. G. Maldonado, J. P. Doucet, M. Petitjean, and B. T. Fan, "Molecular similarity and diversity in chemoinformatics: from theory to applications," *Molecular Diversity*, vol. 10, no. 1, pp. 39–79, 2006.

[13] A. R. Leach and V. J. Gillet, *An Introduction to Chemoinformatics*, Springer, 2007.

[14] P. Willett, "Enhancing the effectiveness of ligand-based virtual screening using data fusion," *QSAR & Combinatorial Science*, vol. 25, no. 12, pp. 1143–1152, 2006.

[15] L. Hodes, "Clustering a large number of compounds. 1. Establishing the method on an initial sample," *Journal of Chemical Information and Computer Sciences*, vol. 29, pp. 66–71, 1989.

[16] P. Willett and V. Winterman, "A comparison of some measures for the determination of inter-molecular structural similarity measures of inter-molecular structural similarity," *Quantitative Structure-Activity Relationships*, vol. 5, no. 1, pp. 18–25, 1986.

[17] P. A. Bath, C. A. Morris, and P. Willett, "Effect of standardization on fragment–based measures of structural similarity," *Journal of chemometrics*, vol. 7, pp. 543–550, 1993.

[18] J. D. Holliday, C. Y. Hu, and P. Willett, "Grouping of coefficients for the calculation of inter-molecular similarity and dissimilarity using 2D fragment bit-strings," *Combinatorial Chemistry & High Throughput Screening*, vol. 5, no. 2, pp. 155–166, 2002.

[19] H. Turtle and W. B. Croft, "Evaluation of an inference network-based retrieval model," *ACM Transactions on Information Systems*, vol. 9, pp. 187–222, 1991.

[20] D. Haines and W. B. Croft, "Relevance feedback and inference networks," in *Proceedings of the 16th Annual International ACM SIGIR Conference on Research and Development in Information Retrieval (SIGIR '93)*, pp. 2–11, July 1993.

[21] L. M. De Campos, J. M. Fernández-Luna, and J. F. Huete, "Implementing relevance feedback in the Bayesian network retrieval model," *Journal of the American Society for Information Science & Technology*, vol. 54, no. 4, pp. 302–313, 2003.

[22] J. Xin and J. S. Jin, "Relevance feedback for content-based image retrieval using Bayesian network," in *Proceedings of the Pan-Sydney Area Workshop on Visual Information Processing (VIP '05)*, pp. 91–94, 2004.

[23] A. Abdo, N. Salim, and A. Ahmed, "Implementing relevance feedback in ligand-based virtual screening using bayesian inference network," *Journal of Biomolecular Screening*, vol. 16, no. 9, pp. 1081–1088, 2011.

[24] A. Abdo and N. Salim, "New fragment weighting scheme for the Bayesian inference network in ligand-based virtual screening," *Journal of Chemical Information and Modeling*, vol. 51, no. 1, pp. 25–32, 2011.

[25] D. Ellis, J. F. Hines, and P. Willett, "Measuring the degree of similarity between objects in text retrieval systems," *Perspectives in Information Management*, vol. 3, pp. 128–149, 1993.

[26] A. Abdo and N. Salim, "Similarity-based virtual screening with a bayesian inference network," *ChemMedChem*, vol. 4, no. 2, pp. 210–218, 2009.

[27] B. Chen, C. Mueller, and P. Willett, "Evaluation of a Bayesian inference network for ligand-based virtual screening," *Journal of Cheminformatics*, vol. 1, article 5, 2009.

[28] *Pipeline Pilot*, Accelrys Software, San Diego, Calif, USA, 2008.

[29] J. Hert, P. Willett, D. J. Wilton et al., "New methods for ligand-based virtual screening: use of data fusion and machine learning to enhance the effectiveness of similarity searching," *Journal of Chemical Information and Modeling*, vol. 46, no. 2, pp. 462–470, 2006.

[30] S. Siegel and N. J. Castellan, *Nonparametric Statistics for the Behavioral Sciences*, McGraw-Hill, 1988.

9

Survival Analysis by Penalized Regression and Matrix Factorization

Yeuntyng Lai, Morihiro Hayashida, and Tatsuya Akutsu

Bioinformatics Center, Institute for Chemical Research, Kyoto University, Gokasho, Uji, Kyoto 611-0011, Japan

Correspondence should be addressed to Morihiro Hayashida; morihiro@kuicr.kyoto-u.ac.jp
and Tatsuya Akutsu; takutsu@kuicr.kyoto-u.ac.jp

Academic Editors: H.-W. Chang, Y.-H. Cheng, L.-Y. Chuang, Y. Liu, and C.-H. Yang

Because every disease has its unique survival pattern, it is necessary to find a suitable model to simulate followups. DNA microarray is a useful technique to detect thousands of gene expressions at one time and is usually employed to classify different types of cancer. We propose combination methods of penalized regression models and nonnegative matrix factorization (NMF) for predicting survival. We tried L_1- (lasso), L_2- (ridge), and L_1-L_2 combined (elastic net) penalized regression for diffuse large B-cell lymphoma (DLBCL) patients' microarray data and found that L_1-L_2 combined method predicts survival best with the smallest logrank P value. Furthermore, 80% of selected genes have been reported to correlate with carcinogenesis or lymphoma. Through NMF we found that DLBCL patients can be divided into 4 groups clearly, and it implies that DLBCL may have 4 subtypes which have a little different survival patterns. Next we excluded some patients who were indicated hard to classify in NMF and executed three penalized regression models again. We found that the performance of survival prediction has been improved with lower logrank P values. Therefore, we conclude that after preselection of patients by NMF, penalized regression models can predict DLBCL patients' survival successfully.

1. Introduction

Survival analysis is a branch of statistics that is of interest to researchers in when patients' death will occur after some therapies [1]. So far there are many methods to analyze survival data, for example, Kaplan-Meier curve, logrank test, Cox proportional hazards model, and so on. We often have information about patients' survival status and survival time. However, censored data cannot offer complete information; that is to say, the survival time of live patient is only partially known. Because of such censored data, survival analysis becomes more complicated than other studies.

The Kaplan-Meier curve is the most popular illustration of survival pattern, and it only considers the survival time data of dead patients (excluding the censored data). By Kaplan-Meier curve, we can estimate the survival rate at different survival time. The logrank test is a useful method to compare the survival distributions, where we can consider the logrank test as a modified chi-squared test. The Cox proportional hazards model is the most famous regression

model in survival analysis. Its main concept is to analyze the relationships between multiple covariates and survival time. The covariates may be internal factors such as patients' age, sex, or gene expression, whereas external factors may include environmental influences like smoke, food, or life style. Since survival time is most likely not normally distributed, we cannot directly use original multiple regression to simulate regression models. The survival patterns usually display as exponential or Weibull distributions. In addition, the survival data have the "censored" problem; therefore, we need a special regression method, like Cox regression model, to perform survival analysis. We will discuss it in detail in Section 2.

So far there is some research in linking gene expression profiles to survival data, such as predictions of therapy outcome in kidney [2], lung [3], and breast cancer [4]. The traditional procedures are utilizing Cox regression model to select significant genes [5] or separating patients into different risk levels by hierarchical clustering [2]. Because of high dimension of microarray data, some researchers introduce partial least squares [6] or least angle regression

[7] to reduce the dimension. An optimized set of guidelines has been published to utilize penalized regression dealing with gene expression data [8]. Sparse kernel methods also have been employed as survival SVM and IVM and could get better results than Cox regression [9]. Some researchers apply Bayesian approach to add flexibility accounting for nonlinear relationships between survival time and gene expression level [10]. Unlike focusing on the problem of high dimension within microarray data, selecting patients whose survival patterns are extremely different also can improve survival prediction performance [11]. Here we are trying to use microarray data to predict survival by combining two kinds of methods: (1) penalized regression models and (2) nonnegative matrix factorization.

Furthermore, we choose the disease, diffuse large B-cell lymphoma (DLBCL) to analyze, because this disease has diagnostic discrepancies if only based on clinical morphology [12]. DLBCL is the most common subtype of non-Hodgkin's lymphoma and accounts for approximately 40% in adults. The DLBCL patients can be cured by chemotherapy with only 35 to 40 percent. The dataset [13] can be downloaded from http://llmpp.nih.gov/DLBCL. It contains a total of 240 patients with untreated DLBCL, and all of the patients have no previous history of lymphoma. The median followup is 2.8 years for total patients and 7.3 years for survived patients. During this study 138 patients (57%) unfortunately died. The tumor samples of DLBCL patients are collected and tested by DNA microarray experiment. The cDNA clones on the Lymphochip microarray are composed of genes that are considered to express in lymphoid cells and some genes that are thought or confirmed to play a role in cancer or immune function. Each microarray datum of each patient comprises 7395 different genes, but some genes of some patients have too weak fluorescent signals (compared with dot's surrounding) and are denoted as missing values. There are only 434 genes without missing values among total 240 patients. The Cy5/Cy3 ratios are log transformed by base 2 and stored in a table to construct gene expression profiles.

2. Methods

2.1. Cox Proportional Hazards Model.
The Cox proportional hazards model is constructed by Cox [14] and widely used in the analysis of survival data. The Cox regression model demonstrates that the hazard function $h(t)$, which means the risk of death at time t for an individual with gene expression profiles, is given by

$$h(t \mid \mathbf{X}) = h_0(t) \exp \left(\sum_{i=1}^{p} \beta_i x_i \right) = h_0(t) \exp \left({}^\top\boldsymbol{\beta}\mathbf{X} \right), \quad (1)$$

where $h_0(t)$ is the baseline hazard, $\boldsymbol{\beta} = {}^\top(\beta_1, \ldots, \beta_p)$ is the column vector of regression parameters, and ${}^\top\boldsymbol{\beta}$ means its transpose. $\mathbf{X} = {}^\top(x_1, \ldots, x_p)$ denotes the gene expression levels of p genes. The term $h_0(t)$ is the hazard when all gene expression levels are equal to zero. Or we can think the Cox proportional hazards model as another form:

$$\log \frac{h(t \mid \mathbf{X})}{h_0(t)} = {}^\top\boldsymbol{\beta}\mathbf{X}. \quad (2)$$

In Cox regression model, there is no assumption about the probability distribution of the hazard. It just assumes that the ratio of hazard functions of different observations does not depend on time [1]. The other assumption is that there is a log-linear relationship between covariates (gene expression levels) and hazard function. Finally we can presume the Cox proportional hazards model as a modified "simple" linear regression model. Like other statistical methods using likelihood function to estimate parameters from a dataset, in Cox proportional hazards model, the Cox partial likelihood is also derived by Cox [14] as follows:

$$L(\boldsymbol{\beta}) = \prod_{r \in D} \frac{\exp \left({}^\top\boldsymbol{\beta}\mathbf{X}^{(r)} \right)}{\sum_{j \in R_r} \exp \left({}^\top\boldsymbol{\beta}\mathbf{X}^{(j)} \right)}, \quad (3)$$

where D is the set of indices of patient death and R_r denotes the set of indices of the individuals at risk for death at time t_r [7]. For many applications of likelihood function, the term that takes logarithm of likelihood is more convenient than the original likelihood function. Thus, taking the logarithm of the Cox partial likelihood, we have the following log partial likelihood:

$$l(\boldsymbol{\beta}) = \sum_{r \in D} \left({}^\top\boldsymbol{\beta}\mathbf{X}^{(r)} - \log \left(\sum_{j \in R_r} \exp \left({}^\top\boldsymbol{\beta}\mathbf{X}^{(j)} \right) \right) \right). \quad (4)$$

Next we follow the normal maximum likelihood estimation method to calculate unknown parameters. Our goal is to estimate the regression coefficients $\boldsymbol{\beta}$, so we can maximize the log partial likelihood function over $\boldsymbol{\beta}$.

2.2. Lasso, Ridge, and Other Penalized Regression.
In usual cases that the patient size n is bigger than covariate number p, we can compute $\boldsymbol{\beta}$ by maximizing the log partial likelihood. However, some research has indicated that the Cox proportional hazards model cannot be applied directly to predict survival time when $p \gg n$ (e.g., in microarray case) [7, 15]. It is because of the high-dimensional space of the predictors and high collinearity of some genes. When we use microarray data to do survival analysis, the dataset always composes thousands of gene expression data. The huge gene numbers make the prediction model a very high dimensional and cause the difficulty of computing. The second problem usually happens in biological research, because the expression levels of some genes are highly correlated. These genes may belong to the same biological pathway or play similar roles in different reactions. To solve these problems, we apply several kinds of penalized regression methods.

All of the penalized regression models are based on the Cox proportional hazards model. The idea is to add a regularization term in the Cox partial likelihood function and control the over-fitting. There are two popular kinds of penalized regression methods. The first one is L_1-penalized regression; it is also called the least absolute shrinkage and selection operator (lasso) estimation, which was first proposed by Tibshirani [16]. Because of some constraints in lasso's principles, it tends to convert some coefficients to zero finally. According to this special characteristic, the lasso estimation is often applied in parameter shrinkage to build simpler models. The second penalized regression method is L_2-penalized regression, which is usually called ridge regression [17]. Unlike lasso estimation, ridge regression conserves all parameters to construct prediction models.

To add regularization term into the Cox regression model, the log partial likelihood function will be rewritten as the following. L_1-penalized (lasso) log partial likelihood is given by

$$l(\boldsymbol{\beta}) - \sum_{j=1}^{p} \lambda |\beta_j|, \tag{5}$$

and L_2-penalized (ridge) log partial likelihood is written as

$$l(\boldsymbol{\beta}) - \sum_{j=1}^{p} \lambda \beta_j^2, \tag{6}$$

where λ is a tuning parameter and p is the number of genes. There is another simple penalized likelihood method combined with L_1- and L_2-penalized regression. It is named the elastic net, and its log partial likelihood is

$$l(\boldsymbol{\beta}) - \sum_{j=1}^{p} \left(\lambda_1 |\beta_j| + \lambda_2 \beta_j^2 \right), \tag{7}$$

where λ_1 and λ_2 are corresponding tuning parameters of L_1 and L_2 penalties, respectively. We can find that the elastic net method just adds L_1 and L_2 penalties together to create a new regularization term. The elastic net performs feature selection and parameter estimation as the lasso regression. However, by adding the L_2 penalty it distributes weight to more variables; hence, the elastic net may select more parameters than the lasso regression [18].

In order to select variables, we first randomly divided 240 patients into training group (160 patients) and testing group (80 patients). Although the whole microarray datum contains 7395 genes for each patient, we primarily used the 434 complete genes (without missing values among all patients) to build penalized regression models. All experiments were executed on R platform by using libraries of "survival" and "penalized". We initially established L_1-, L_2-, and L_1-L_2 combined penalized regression models by training data. No doubt it is necessary to set the tuning parameter λ first, and we can use the cross-validation method encompassed in the "penalized" package to find optimal values. If we set tuning parameters too small, the algorithm may run very slowly and fail to converge especially for high-dimensional data. In this study, we set $\lambda = 10$ in lasso regression model and $\lambda = 20$ in ridge regression model. In L_1-L_2 combined penalized regression model, we set $\lambda_1 = 10$ and $\lambda_2 = 20$. After computing on R platform, we got out 21 nonzero coefficients in lasso regression model and 27 ones in elastic net model. In other words, we selected out 21 and 27 important genes.

2.3. Nonnegative Matrix Factorization. The nonnegative matrix factorization (NMF) method has been introduced first to decompose images, and its goal is to factorize a matrix into two nonnegative matrices [19]. In NMF, it makes the constraint about nonnegativity of matrices. It is because not only most data in the real world are nonnegative but also we can only explain their meanings in nonnegative way [20]. The other characteristic of NMF is the additive property; that is to say, the NMF model does not allow subtraction. This special signature makes NMF illustrate quantitatively each component. Or we can say NMF is a part-based representation method. While zero value represents the absence of some components or events, the positive value may denote the presence of the same ones.

Lee and Seung first used NMF to do image decomposition [21]. They analyzed a face figure with NMF and compared the result with principal component analysis (PCA) and vector quantization (VQ). They showed that NMF can do part-based representation, whereas PCA and VQ represented the face image holistically. In other words, NMF decomposed the face image successfully into several facial parts, like nose, lips, and eyes. Suppose we have the image data matrix V of size $n \times m$ that contains m facial images, where each image has n nonnegative pixels. Our goal is to factorize the matrix V into two nonnegative matrices, W and H:

$$V \approx WH. \tag{8}$$

The sizes of the matrices W and H are $n \times k$ and $k \times m$, respectively. The rank k is usually chosen to be smaller than n and m, so that W and H are smaller than the original matrix V. The rank k is similar to the basis image that identifies parts of the face image.

The NMF method starts by randomly initializing nonnegative matrices W and H. Similar the values of V and WH are, the distance between V and WH approaches approximately to zero. A useful distance measurement is to calculate the square of the Euclidean distance between them. The equation can be written as

$$\|V - WH\|^2 = \sum_{ij} \left(V_{ij} - (WH)_{ij} \right)^2. \tag{9}$$

Another similarity measurement is to test the "divergence" of V from WH, which is denoted as a divergence function:

$$D(V \| WH) = \sum_{ij} \left(V_{ij} \log \frac{V_{ij}}{(WH)_{ij}} - V_{ij} + (WH)_{ij} \right). \tag{10}$$

Unlike the Euclidean distance, it assumes that V and WH are not symmetric. To minimize the Euclidean distance or the divergence function, Lee and Seung created the following "multiplicative update rules" to ease implementation and accelerate computing speed [21]. The Euclidean distance $\|V - WH\|$ is nonincreasing under the update rules:

$$H_{au} \longleftarrow H_{au} \frac{(^\top WV)_{au}}{(^\top WWH)_{au}},$$

$$W_{ia} \longleftarrow W_{ia} \frac{(V^\top H)_{ia}}{(WH^\top H)_{ia}}. \tag{11}$$

Furthermore, the divergence $D(V\|WH)$ is nonincreasing under the update rules:

$$H_{au} \longleftarrow H_{au} \frac{\sum_i W_{ia} V_{iu}/(WH)_{iu}}{\sum_k W_{ka}},$$

$$W_{ia} \longleftarrow W_{ia} \frac{\sum_u H_{au} V_{iu}/(WH)_{iu}}{\sum_v H_{av}}. \qquad (12)$$

Therefore, we can iteratively update W and H to minimize the Euclidean distance or the divergence function by upper coupled update rules.

It has been indicated that NMF is very useful when analyzing data that have multiple attributes, and these attributes are often ambiguous and hard to predict. Because of this property, NMF has been applied much in text data mining. The same word may have other different meanings just depending on the different locations in the sentence or document. It resembles the biological data so that the same gene may play different roles in different biological pathways. To deal with the gene complexity of multiple functions, NMF method has been exploited to process the biomedical data such as microarray data [22].

In microarray case, we first consider the gene expression matrix A, which is composed by N genes in M patients. In other words, the size of matrix A is $N \times M$. Then, we want to factorize matrix A into two matrices with nonnegative entries, $A \approx WH$. It means to find a small number of genes (which are called metagenes) to represent the whole gene expression pattern of patients [23]. That is to say, we can approximate the gene expression pattern as positive linear combinations of these metagenes. Like to find the essential face components (eyes, nose, and lips) from the entire face image, we try to figure out the representative metagenes that may provide biological insight into sparse microarray data. Each column of W of size $N \times k$ defines a metagene and each column of H of size $k \times M$ defines the metagene expression pattern of the corresponding patient, where the ijth elements w_{ij} and h_{ij} represent the coefficient of gene i in metagene j and the expression level of metagene i in patient j, respectively.

Figure S1 (see Supplementary Material available online at http://dx.doi.org/10.1155/2013/632030) shows a simple example when rank $k = 2$. We can see the original gene expression matrix A is decomposed into two smaller matrices W and H. There are two ways to analyze the gene expression pattern— the matrix W-based aspect and the matrix H-based aspect. In W-based view, the total N genes can be grouped into some clusters according to the value of entries w_{ij}. If we reorder the N genes by the coefficients of every gene in corresponding metagene, the inherent special expression pattern of some genes may be uncovered. In H-based view, the M patients can be clustered into k groups by the expression levels of metagene for all patients. As Figure S1 shows, metagene expression profiles are illustrated in two significant distributions (red line and blue line). By this unique distribution, we can cluster patients into cluster 1 and cluster 2 separately. Because of this distinctive character, nonnegative matrix factorization can be employed as a clustering method in microarray data. Moreover by reason of the dual-way aspect of W and H

matrices, some research has proved it is practicable to analyze the microarray data in the biclustering way [24].

Since we can set any rank k to group patients into k clusters, the key point is to find k that can partition patients into meaningful clusters. To solve this problem, we apply the method of consensus clustering [23]. The different initial matrices of W and H on each run may cause different clustering forms of patients. However, if rank k is strong enough, we may expect that patient assignment to clusters would vary a little from run to run. For each run, the patient assignment can be defined by a connectivity matrix C. The size of matrix C is $M \times M$, and entry $c_{ij} = 1$ if patient i and patient j belong to the same cluster. Whereas entry $c_{ij} = 0$ if patient i and patient j belong to different clusters. Then, we compute the average connectivity matrix C over 100 runs and denote it as the consensus matrix $\overline{C}$. Since c_{12} takes 1 or 0 over 100 runs as shown in Figure S2, the average of c_{12} will be within the region between 1 and 0. Therefore, all the entries of $\overline{C}$ may range from 0 to 1 and reflect the probability that patient i and patient j are assigned to the same cluster. Next, we can reorder all patients by their assignment probability and then construct a new consensus clustering matrix by heat map presentation coloring from 0 (deep blue, patients in different groups) to 1 (dark red, patients in the same group). Through heat map result, we can evaluate the validity of any setting rank k. All experiments were executed on R platform by using the library of "NMF".

The gene expression levels in microarray are displayed as Cy5/Cy3 log-2 ratios, and these values are distributed dispersedly as positives or negatives. Additionally, there are only 434 genes without missing values among total 240 patients. Since the missing values are caused by the too weak fluorescent signals to detect, we may think these values are approximately equal to zero. So, we refilled all the missing values in the gene expression profiles as zero [25]. Next procedure is to transform all of the ratios into nonnegative values; therefore, we used each ratio as an exponent by base 2 [22].

2.4. Lasso Regression after NMF Selection. According to the consensus clustering results by NMF, we found some patients cannot be clustered into the same group over all 100 runs. We may suggest that these patients will become noise in the following computing. Therefore, we excluded the patients whose value in $\overline{C}$ is smaller than 0.9. We finally excluded 15 patients from the training group and 7 patients from the testing group. Next, we built L_1-, L_2-, and L_1-L_2 combined penalized regression models again.

To compare the prediction performance of the three penalized regression models, we should define the criteria of prediction assessment initially. However, there are no determinate criteria that have been stipulated for survival analysis [26]. Furthermore, many comparative studies of survival prediction have indicated that different criteria may influence the conclusion about evaluations of different prediction models [15, 27]. We chose one simple evaluation criteria that has been reported in many survival studies. A common way to assess the effect of one prediction model is

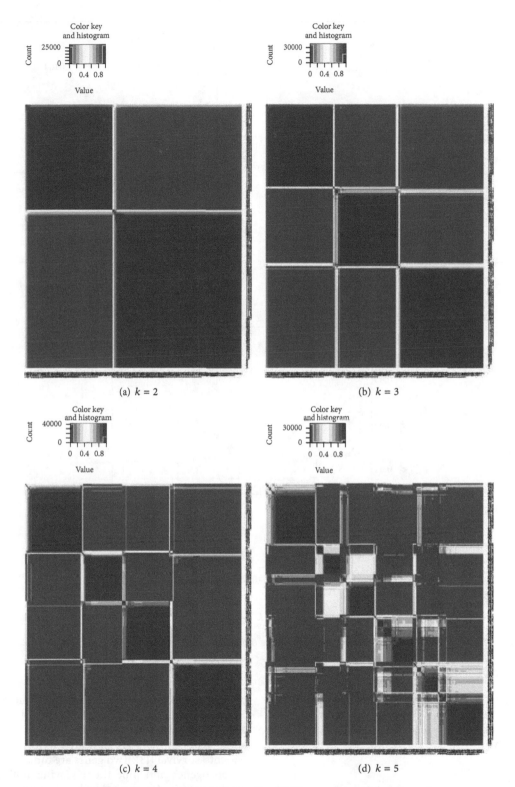

FIGURE 1: Consensus clustering results of 7395 genes for rank $k = 2, \ldots, 5$.

to check whether or not the assignments of patients, such as "high-risk" group or "low-risk" group, are correct. In clinic, patients are always concerned about whether or not they are at risk for death after some therapies.

Let $\widehat{\beta}_{\text{train}}$ denote the vector of estimated regression coefficients obtained from training data. For each patient i in the testing group, this estimate is then used together with its vector of gene expression values $\mathbf{X}^{(i)}$ to derive a prognostic index η_i for the patient, given by $\eta_i = {}^\top\widehat{\beta}_{\text{train}}\mathbf{X}^{(i)}$ [27]. Then, we found the median of the prognostic indices of 80 patients. If the prognostic index is bigger than the median, the patient is assigned to the high-risk group, whereas smaller than the

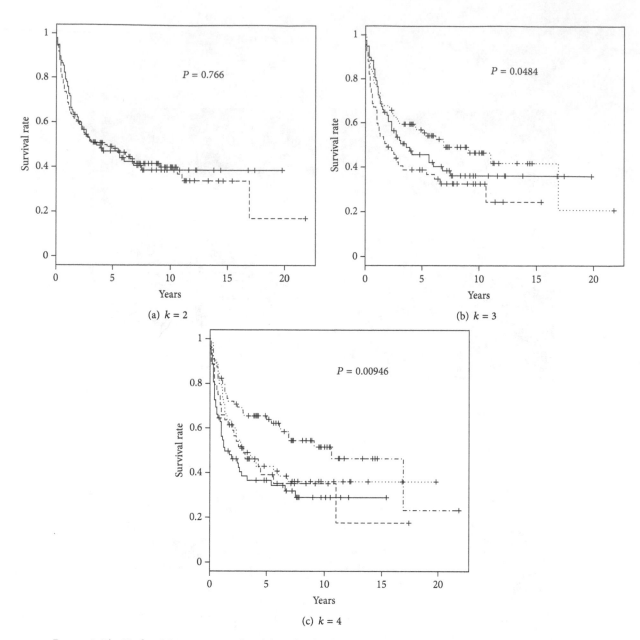

FIGURE 2: The Kaplan-Meier curve results of three kinds of patients' divisions corresponding to rank $k = 2, \ldots, 4$.

median the patient is assigned to the low-risk group. We can compare the results of L_1- (lasso), L_2- (ridge), and L_1-L_2 combined (elastic net) penalized regression model by the Kaplan-Meier curve.

3. Results

3.1. Important Genes Selected out by Lasso Regression. We have described in Section 2 that there are 21 genes selected out by lasso regression model and 27 genes selected out by elastic net model. Moreover, the 21 genes are overall included in the 27 genes. It implies that these 21 genes (see Table 1) may play important roles in patients' survival. To understand these genes more comprehensively, we investigated their

biological functions and discriminated whether or not they are involved in carcinogenesis. We found that there are 10 genes that have been reported to relate to some cancers, and 5 genes of them are indicated to influence the DLBCL patients' survival [13]. Two genes are tumor suppressor genes or oncogenes and hint them playing noticeable roles in carcinogenesis. On the other hand, there are 9 genes that have biological functions concerned to fundamental immune functions, such as MHC class II or antigen processing. We may infer that genes with these special biological functions will cause DLBCL pathogenesis and even affect patients' survival eventually. Unfortunately, the biological functions of two genes within the 21 genes have not been known clearly so far. However, total 17 genes among the 21 genes (about 80 percent) are correlated to carcinogenesis or important

TABLE 1: 21 important genes selected by lasso regression model.

UNIQID in microarray	Name	Biological function	Correlated cancer or carcinogenesis	coef. in lasso	coef. in elastic net
24432		Unknown		0.1987	0.0864
17316	RPS21	Ribosomal protein	HCC	0.1367	0.0705
15841	MYC	Transcription factor	Many cancers (e.g. DLBCL)	0.0818	0.0713
29250	AARS	tRNA synthase		0.1979	0.0874
30040	PHB2	Mitochondrial morphology	Breast cancer	0.0074	0.0356
30347	SIT1	Lymphoid cell marker		−0.0440	−0.0248
19373	HLA-DQA1	MHC class II alpha chain	DLBCL	−0.1279	−0.1115
28197	HLA-DPA1	MHC class II alpha chain	DLBCL	−0.0920	−0.0799
24396	HLA-DRB1	MHC class II beta chain	DLBCL	−0.1345	−0.0877
31957	CD22	B-cell receptor signalling	DLBCL, cancer drug	−0.0895	−0.0597
27091	ST6GAL1	Glycosyltransferase	Colorectal cancer	0.1062	0.0741
31316	FCRL3	New CD molecule		0.0324	0.0207
27379	LRMP	Germinal center marker		−0.0562	−0.0499
26361		Unknown		−0.0070	−0.0037
17723	IGKC	Immunoglobulin light chain		0.0341	0.0360
34407	PTPN6	Protein tyrosine phosphatase	Anaplastic large-cell lymphoma	0.0611	0.0434
24400	MGLL	Monoglyceride lipase		0.0131	0.0216
24395	IFI30	MHC class II Ag processing		−0.0889	−0.0635
16972	TXNIP	Interact with thioredoxin	Tumor suppressor gene	0.0659	0.0372
34814	IL23A	Cytokine	Oncogene or tumor suppressor gene	−0.0114	−0.0128
17475	HSPA1A	Heat shock protein	Many cancers	−0.0211	−0.0166

immune functions. It makes us believe that the L_1- and L_1-L_2 combined penalized regression models may select out significant genes associated to the DLBCL patients' survival.

3.2. Divide DLBCL into 4 Subgroups by NMF.

We initially used 434 gene expression profiles (without missing values) to run matrix factorization 100 times for rank $k = 2, \ldots, 5$ and got the consensus matrix. The reordered consensus clustering results are illustrated by heat maps in Figure S3. We found that the clustering pattern is better when rank $k = 3$ or 4 and is the worst when rank $k = 5$. It suggests that 3 or 4 groupings of DLBCL patients may have some biological meaning, so we next plotted the Kaplan-Meier curve of two-divided, three-divided, and four-divided results as Figure S4 shows to compare their survival distributions. Using logrank test, we also calculated the P value of each result and got 0.927, 0.13, and 0.00365 from rank $k = 2$ to 4. We found that only when rank $k = 4$ the survival curves separate significantly among four patient groups (the P value is smaller than 0.05), meaning that the fourth division of DLBCL patients has some biological implications that may generate different survival patterns of patients.

Since the survival curves did not separate significantly in two-division and three-division results, we changed to use all of the 7395 genes (missing values approximated to zero) to analyze again. Similarly after running 100 nonnegative matrix factorizations, the heat maps of the consensus matrix for rank $k = 2, \ldots, 5$ are shown in Figure 1. We found that the clustering pattern is good when rank $k = 2, 3$, or 4 and is the worst when rank $k = 5$. However, comparing with the results of 434 genes generally, all clustering results of 7395

genes are much better. Next, we plotted likewise the Kaplan-Meier curve of two-divided, three-divided, and four-divided results in Figure 2 and compared their survival distributions. By using logrank test again, we measured each P value of survival curves, which yielded 0.766, 0.0484, and 0.00946 from rank $k = 2$ to 4. We discovered that the P values of not only rank $k = 4$ but also $k = 3$ are smaller than 0.05. It implies that the survival patterns can be distinguished significantly when DLBCL patients are divided into 3 or 4 groups.

3.3. Survival Prediction of Lasso Model is Improved by Preselection of NMF.

We compared the survival predictions of L_1- (lasso), L_2- (ridge), and L_1-L_2 combined (elastic net) penalized regression models by the Kaplan-Meier curve as showing in Figure 3. Using logrank test, we also calculated the P value of each model and got 0.139, 0.352, and 0.0364 from top to bottom. In all three models, the patients' survival rates of low-risk group are always higher than the survival rates of high-risk group. We found that only in L_1-L_2 combined penalized regression model, the survival curves separate significantly between high-risk group and low-risk group (the P value is smaller than 0.05), meaning that the elastic net model successfully predicts followups with high risk or low risk of death.

After exclusion of noise patients by NMF, we tested L_1-, L_2-, and L_1-L_2 combined penalized regression models again. Similarly plotting the Kaplan-Meier curve in Figure 4, we yielded the P values as 0.0208, 0.209, and 0.043 by logrank test. The P values of L_1- and L_2- penalized regression models became smaller, whereas bigger in L_1-L_2 combined model. However, the survival distributions in L_1-L_2 combined

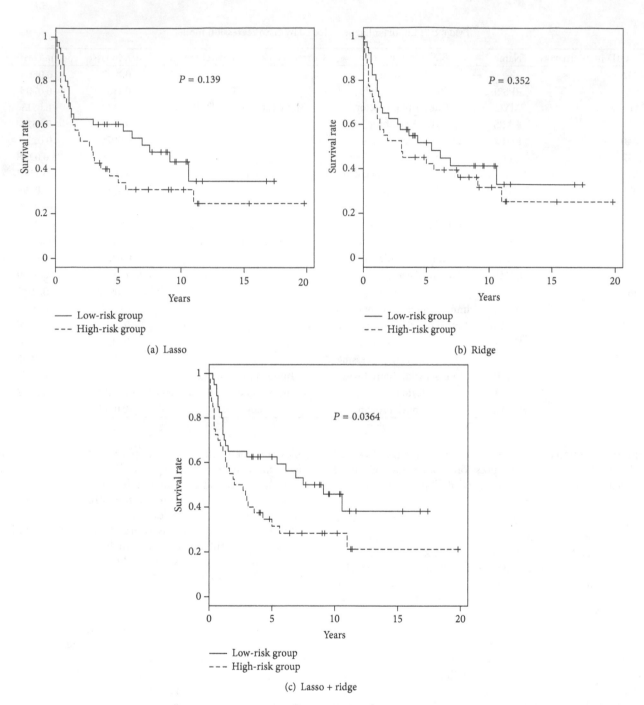

FIGURE 3: The Kaplan-Meier curve results of three penalized regression models, lasso, ridge, and elastic net, for low- and high- risk groups, respectively.

penalized regression model are still significant between high-risk and low-risk groups. Consequently, we may conclude that the prediction performance can be improved (especially in lasso regression model) by previously excluding some patients who are considered hard to classify in NMF.

4. Discussion

Through three penalized regression methods based on Cox proportional hazards model, we analyzed the microarray data of DLBCL patients and tried to predict the patients' survival. We found that without preselection of NMF, L_1-L_2 combined (elastic net) penalized regression model yields better prediction performance than L_1- (lasso) and L_2- (ridge) penalized regression models because of the smallest P value. It seems that the elastic net method combines the advantages of both lasso and ridge regression methods. Furthermore, the elastic net method reserves the merit of lasso regression that can sort out the important genes that may influence the patients' survival. To improve the prediction performance of

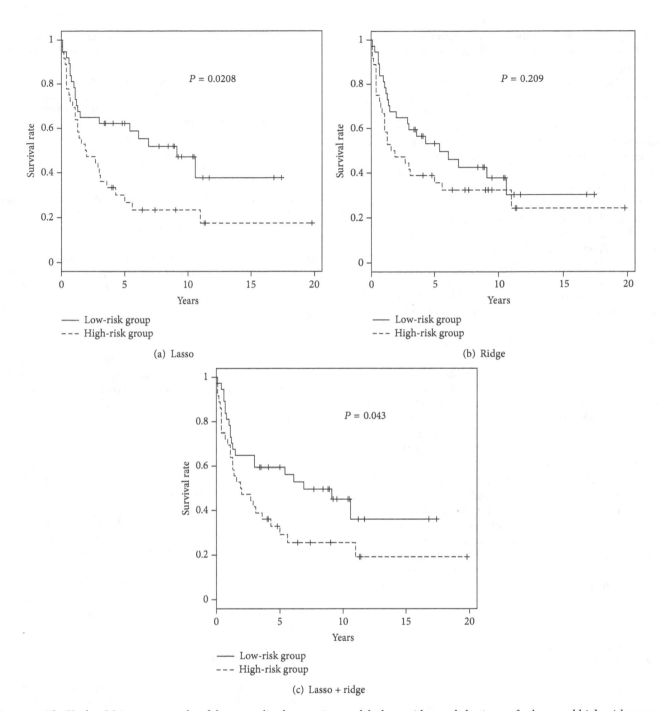

FIGURE 4: The Kaplan-Meier curve results of three penalized regression models, lasso, ridge, and elastic net, for low- and high- risk groups, respectively, after preselection of NMF.

L_1-L_2 combined penalized regression model, different kinds of combination or modification should be developed.

21 genes were selected out by L_1- and L_1-L_2 combined penalized regression models. Among them, MYC, HLA-DQA1, HLA-DPA1, HLA-DRB1, and CD22 have been reported to be used in prediction of DLBCL patients' survival [13]. Moreover, MYC has been indicated as an oncogenic transcription factor that regulates expressions of a great number of genes. CD22 is a B-cell marker and regulates the signaling pathways within B cell. Recent research shows that CD22 is a potential drug target in many cancers.

In this study, we only utilized gene expression data as predictors. However, prediction performance may be improved by adding other covariates such as age, sex, and stage [5]. Unfortunately, the DLBCL dataset does not contain detailed information about clinical data. Nevertheless not only clinical factors but also published gene signatures that are employed in some cancer prediction chips are proved to increase the predictive strength [28].

We employed the nonnegative matrix factorization to naturally cluster DLBCL patients into some groups and then compared the survival distributions within different groupings. Not only complete gene expression profiles but also total gene expression profiles indicate that the patient grouping of 4 has some biological meaning. It implies that the disease DLBCL may have 4 subtypes that have a little different survival patterns. Moreover, if we observe the heat maps of consensus clustering matrix more carefully, we will find some patients with values near to 1 but not equal to 1 (the orange or yellow color). It means these patients do not always belong to the same group and may suggest that they have unusual gene expression profiles because of special constitutions or other unknown diseases.

The R package of "NMF" provides other distance calculation methods to execute, such as nsNMF, offset, pe-NMF and snmf. Examining these different algorithms may get different consensus clustering results. Another useful NMF algorithm which is called Semi-NMF can handle clustering while input data contain negative values. Its plug-in for a microarray data analysis tool has even been introduced [25]. Of course, NMF can deal with other kinds of data different from microarray data. Array comparative genomic hybridization data are also utilized to analyze patients' survival [29].

The DLBCL dataset that we used in this study has been analyzed by hierarchical clustering before [12, 13]. Although they claim to cluster DLBCL patients into 2 or 3 groups, our NMF results prefer 4 groups. It may be because of distinct algorithms within two methods. Nevertheless, the consistent results are also reported in lung cancer case [22].

An obvious problem in microarray data is the existence of missing values. To make full use of gene expression profiles, we should employ some methods to estimate missing values. For example, a nearest neighbor technique has been employed to approximate missing values in DLBCL microarray dataset and then predict patients' survival well [7, 30].

There is a growing tendency in research about survival analysis for the last several decades. Many new ideas from different fields have been introduced to predict survival according to gene expression profiles. For instance, topology has been employed to handle the high-dimensional data and uncover the shape characteristic of data [31]. Through survival analysis using advanced information technologies for kinds of diseases, potential therapies will be developed and patients may expect better outcome in future.

Acknowledgment

This work was partially supported by Grants-in-Aid no. 22240009 and no. 24500361 from MEXT, Japan.

References

[1] D. G. Kleinbaum and M. Klein, *Survival Analysis: A Self-Learning Text*, Springer, New York, NY, USA, 2nd edition, 2005.

[2] J. R. Vasselli, J. H. Shih, S. R. Iyengar et al., "Predicting survival in patients with metastatic kidney cancer by gene-expression profiling in the primary tumor," *Proceedings of the National Academy of Sciences of the United States of America*, vol. 100, no. 12, pp. 6958–6963, 2003.

[3] R. S. Herbst, J. V. Heymach, and S. M. Lippman, "Molecular origins of cancer: lung cancer," *The New England Journal of Medicine*, vol. 359, no. 13, pp. 1367–1380, 2008.

[4] C. Sotiriou and L. Pusztai, "Gene-expression signatures in breast cancer," *The New England Journal of Medicine*, vol. 360, no. 8, pp. 752–800, 2009.

[5] K. Shedden, J. M. G. Taylor, S. A. Enkemann et al., "Gene expression-based survival prediction in lung adenocarcinoma: a multi-site, blinded validation study," *Nature Medicine*, vol. 14, no. 8, pp. 822–827, 2008.

[6] D. V. Nguyen and D. M. Rocke, "Partial least squares proportional hazard regression for application to DNA microarray survival data," *Bioinformatics*, vol. 18, no. 12, pp. 1625–1632, 2002.

[7] J. Gui and H. Li, "Penalized Cox regression analysis in the high-dimensional and low-sample size settings, with applications to microarray gene expression data," *Bioinformatics*, vol. 21, no. 13, pp. 3001–3008, 2005.

[8] L. Waldron, M. Pintilie, M.-S. Tsao, F. A. Shepherd, C. Huttenhower, and I. Jurisica, "Optimized application of penalized regression methods to diverse genomic data," *Bioinformatics*, vol. 27, no. 24, pp. 3399–3406, 2011.

[9] L. Evers and C.-M. Messow, "Sparse kernel methods for high-dimensional survival data," *Bioinformatics*, vol. 24, no. 14, pp. 1632–1638, 2008.

[10] V. Bonato, V. Baladandayuthapani, B. M. Broom, E. P. Sulman, K. D. Aldape, and K.-A. Do, "Bayesian ensemble methods for survival prediction in gene expression data," *Bioinformatics*, vol. 27, no. 3, Article ID btq660, pp. 359–367, 2011.

[11] H. Liu, J. Li, and L. Wong, "Use of extreme patient samples for outcome prediction from gene expression data," *Bioinformatics*, vol. 21, no. 16, pp. 3377–3384, 2005.

[12] A. A. Alizadeh, M. B. Elsen, R. E. Davis et al., "Distinct types of diffuse large B-cell lymphoma identified by gene expression profiling," *Nature*, vol. 403, no. 6769, pp. 503–511, 2000.

[13] A. Rosenwald, G. Wright, W. C. Chan et al., "The use of molecular profiling to predict survival after chemotherapy for diffuse large-B-cell lymphoma," *The New England Journal of Medicine*, vol. 346, no. 25, pp. 1937–1947, 2002.

[14] D. R. Cox, "Regression models and life-tables," *Journal of the Royal Statistical Society B*, vol. 34, no. 2, pp. 187–220, 1972.

[15] M. Schumacher, H. Binder, and T. Gerds, "Assessment of survival prediction models based on microarray data," *Bioinformatics*, vol. 23, no. 14, pp. 1768–1774, 2007.

[16] R. Tibshirani, "Regression shrinkage and selection via the lasso," *Journal of the Royal Statistical Society B*, vol. 58, no. 1, pp. 267–288, 1996.

[17] A. E. Hoerl and R. W. Kennard, "Ridge regression: biased estimation for nonorthogonal problems," *Technometrics*, vol. 12, no. 1, pp. 55–67, 1970.

[18] A. Benner, M. Zucknick, T. Hielscher, C. Ittrich, and U. Mansmann, "High-dimensional cox models: the choice of penalty as part of the model building process," *Biometrical Journal*, vol. 52, no. 1, pp. 50–69, 2010.

[19] D. D. Lee and H. S. Seung, "Algorithms for non-negative matrix factorization," *Advances in Neural Information Processing Systems*, vol. 13, pp. 556–562, 2001.

[20] A. Cichocki, R. Zdunek, A. H. Phan, and S. Amari, *Nonnegative Matrix and Tensor Factorizations: Applications to Exploratory Multi-Way Data Analysis and Blind Source Separation*, John Wiley & Sons, New York, NY, USA, 2009.

[21] D. D. Lee and H. S. Seung, "Learning the parts of objects by non-negative matrix factorization," *Nature*, vol. 401, no. 6755, pp. 788–791, 1999.

[22] K. Inamura, T. Fujiwara, Y. Hoshida et al., "Two subclasses of lung squamous cell carcinoma with different gene expression profiles and prognosis identified by hierarchical clustering and non-negative matrix factorization," *Oncogene*, vol. 24, no. 47, pp. 7105–7113, 2005.

[23] J.-P. Brunet, P. Tamayo, T. R. Golub, and J. P. Mesirov, "Metagenes and molecular pattern discovery using matrix factorization," *Proceedings of the National Academy of Sciences of the United States of America*, vol. 101, no. 12, pp. 4164–4169, 2004.

[24] P. Carmona-Saez, R. D. Pascual-Marqui, F. Tirado, J. M. Carazo, and A. Pascual-Montano, "Biclustering of gene expression data by non-smooth non-negative matrix factorization," *BMC Bioinformatics*, vol. 7, article 78, 2006.

[25] Q. Qi, Y. Zhao, M. Li, and R. Simon, "Non-negative matrix factorization of gene expression profiles: a plug-in for BRB-ArrayTools," *Bioinformatics*, vol. 25, no. 4, pp. 545–547, 2009.

[26] H. M. Bøvelstad and Ø. Borgan, "Assessment of evaluation criteria for survival prediction from genomic data," *Biometrical Journal*, vol. 53, no. 2, pp. 202–216, 2011.

[27] H. M. Bøvelstad, S. Nygård, H. Størvold et al., "Predicting survival from microarray data—a comparative study," *Bioinformatics*, vol. 23, no. 16, pp. 2080–2087, 2007.

[28] X. Zhao, E. A. Rødland, T. Sørlie et al., "Combining gene signatures improves prediction of breast cancer survival," *PLoS One*, vol. 6, no. 3, article e17845, 2011.

[29] D. R. Carrasco, G. Tonon, Y. Huang et al., "High-resolution genomic profiling of chromosomal aberrations using Infinium whole-genome genotyping," *Cancer Cell*, vol. 16, no. 9, pp. 313–325, 2006.

[30] O. Troyanskaya, M. Cantor, G. Sherlock et al., "Missing value estimation methods for DNA microarrays," *Bioinformatics*, vol. 17, no. 6, pp. 520–525, 2001.

[31] M. Nicolau, A. J. Levine, and G. Carlsson, "Topology based data analysis identifies a subgroup of breast cancers with a unique mutational profile and excellent survival," *Proceedings of the National Academy of Sciences*, vol. 108, no. 17, pp. 7265–7270, 2011.

10

A Comparative Genomic Study in Schizophrenic and in Bipolar Disorder Patients, Based on Microarray Expression Profiling Meta-Analysis

Marianthi Logotheti,[1,2,3] **Olga Papadodima,**[2] **Nikolaos Venizelos,**[1] **Aristotelis Chatziioannou,**[2] **and Fragiskos Kolisis**[3]

[1] *Neuropsychiatric Research Laboratory, Department of Clinical Medicine, Örebro University, 701 82 Örebro, Sweden*
[2] *Metabolic Engineering and Bioinformatics Program, Institute of Biology, Medicinal Chemistry and Biotechnology, National Hellenic Research Foundation, 48 Vassileos Constantinou Avenue, 11635 Athens, Greece*
[3] *Laboratory of Biotechnology, School of Chemical Engineering, National Technical University of Athens, 15780 Athens, Greece*

Correspondence should be addressed to
Aristotelis Chatziioannou; achatzi@eie.gr and Fragiskos Kolisis; kolisis@chemeng.ntua.gr

Academic Editors: N. S. T. Hirata, M. A. Kon, and K. Najarian

Schizophrenia affecting almost 1% and bipolar disorder affecting almost 3%–5% of the global population constitute two severe mental disorders. The catecholaminergic and the serotonergic pathways have been proved to play an important role in the development of schizophrenia, bipolar disorder, and other related psychiatric disorders. The aim of the study was to perform and interpret the results of a comparative genomic profiling study in schizophrenic patients as well as in healthy controls and in patients with bipolar disorder and try to relate and integrate our results with an aberrant amino acid transport through cell membranes. In particular we have focused on genes and mechanisms involved in amino acid transport through cell membranes from whole genome expression profiling data. We performed bioinformatic analysis on raw data derived from four different published studies. In two studies postmortem samples from prefrontal cortices, derived from patients with bipolar disorder, schizophrenia, and control subjects, have been used. In another study we used samples from postmortem orbitofrontal cortex of bipolar subjects while the final study was performed based on raw data from a gene expression profiling dataset in the postmortem superior temporal cortex of schizophrenics. The data were downloaded from NCBI's GEO datasets.

1. Introduction

Schizophrenia (SZ) and bipolar disorder (BD) are approached and studied as diseases with aberrant functions of the neurotransmitter systems, as neurodevelopmental diseases or generally complex diseases caused by multiple genetic and environmental factors. Recently they have started to be studied as systemic diseases; thus a combination of disturbed biological systems and genes of small contribution is believed to cause their expression [1, 2].

Altered membrane composition of the cells, aberrant membrane phospholipid metabolism [3, 4], dysfunctional tyrosine, and other amino acid (AA) transport systems [5–11]

evidence the systemic nature of SZ disease. Moreover, failure of niacin skin test implying reduced arachidonic acid (ARA) in cell membranes of schizophrenics [12] and abnormalities in muscle fibers [13] constitute such indications. The same holds for BD, which can also be considered a systemic disease. Aberrant tyrosine, and other AA transport systems, in cells from BD disorder patients [14, 15], aberrant signal transduction [16], and abnormal membrane composition and metabolism support the notion of BD being a systemic disease as well [17, 18].

Studying these disorders through this holistic approach, we presume the membrane phospholipid hypothesis, namely, that aberrant AA transport mechanisms and the disturbed cell membrane composition are highly correlated. AAs are transported though cell membranes with specific transporter/protein transport systems, which perform active transport of AAs from one side of the cell membrane to the other [19]. These AA transporters are embedded in the cell membranes; thus their structure and functionality interact with the membrane composition and functionality, as well as with membrane fluidity and enzymatic activity [9, 20]. Particularly, a membrane defect would impact, for example, the functionality of the tyrosine transporters as well as the permeability of the membranes [2, 5].

The Membrane Theory. The membrane theory of mental diseases is related with two primary abnormalities: an increased rate of removal of essential fatty acids (EFA) from the membrane phospholipids, combined with a reduced rate of incorporation of fatty acids (FA) into membrane phospholipids [21]. Some SZ study findings that relate the expression of the disease with the membrane hypothesis are studies based on postmortem and blood samples showing reduction of docosahexaenoic acid (DHA) and ARA in cell membranes independently of the disease state and magnetic resonance spectroscopy (MRS) studies revealing decreased levels of phosphomonoesters (phospholipid membrane synthesis precursors) and higher levels of phosphodiesters (phospholipid metabolism products) in SZ patients compared to control patients [22]. Also, the niacin skin flush test is indicative of a membrane dysfunction resulting in an inflammatory dysfunction [12]. In addition, phospholipase A2 (PLA) calcium (Ca) dependent type has been shown to have an increased activity and PLA Ca independent type a decreased activity. The latter is considered quite important finding, as the A2 enzyme catalyzes the breakdown of FA [23].

Similar findings suggest cell membrane dysfunction in BD. 31P-MRS magnetic resonance spectroscopy (MRS) measures phosphorus metabolites in the organs [24]. Phosphomonoester levels are measured in BD depressed patients with MRS. Phosphomonoesters are measured as being higher in these patients compared to control subjects and lower in asymptomatic patients. Abnormal functionalities in signal transduction pathways are also repeated in several studies including overactivated phosphatidylinositol and G-protein pathways, as well as altered membrane protein kinase C and adenyl cyclase enzyme pathways. PLA enzyme activity and Ca release are involved in the membrane hypothesis of BD [17].

Amino Acid Transporters. The transport of AAs into the cell membranes of the blood brain barrier (BBB) is mediated by many transport systems. Three basic active transporters result in the AA flux from and into all types of cells (including brain cells). The primary active transport mechanism is an adenosine triphosphatase (ATPase) that exchanges sodium (Na) and potassium (K) ions, contributing in the maintenance of the ion gradients of the cells, known as sodium-potassium adenosine triphosphatase (Na,K-ATPase). These ion gradients in combination with other ions and gradients are utilized by the secondary active transport mechanisms for the influx of specific AAs into the cells. The secondary

active transport through these AA influxes sets also an AA concentration gradient in the cells, which, in combination with Na+ exchange, is further utilized by the tertiary active transport mechanisms for transport of another group of AAs in and out of the cells. AAs may be transported via different AA transport mechanisms. An alteration in any of the active transport mechanisms could result in an aberrant AA transport into the cells [10, 25].

Aim of the Study. The aim of our meta-analysis was to interpret the results of comparative genomic profiling studies in schizophrenic patients as compared to healthy controls and in patients with BD and try to relate and integrate our results with an aberrant AA transport through cell membranes.

2. Materials and Methods

2.1. Microarray Datasets. Four human datasets were used, by downloading submitted raw data (Cel files) from corresponding studies, available at the Gene Expression Omnibus (GEO) database of National Center for Biotechnology Information (NCBI) [26].

(1) The first study has the GEO Accession number GSE12654 and the microarrays preparation followed the guidelines of MIAME in the way it is described in [27]. RNA from postmortem brain tissues (Brodmann's Area 10) of 15 schizophrenic and 15 BD affected patients and 15 control healthy subjects was hybridized on Affymetrix HG-U95 Arrays. After quality control stage in this study, 11 schizophrenic, 11 BD and 15 control subjects were used for further bioinformatic analysis.

(2) The second study has the GEO Accession number GSE5389, and the microarrays preparation followed the guidelines of MIAME in the way it is described in [28]. RNA extracted from human postmortem brain tissue (Brodmann's Area 11) from 15 adult subjects with BD and 15 healthy control subjects was hybridized to Affymetrix HG-U133A GeneChip to identify differentially expressed (DE) genes in the disease state. After quality control in this study, 10 BD and 11 control subjects were used for further bioinformatic analysis.

(3) The third study has the GEO Accession number GSE21935, and the microarrays preparation followed the guidelines of MIAME in the way it is described in [29]. 60 postmortem RNA samples derived from brain tissue (Brodmann's Area 22) of schizophrenic and control patients were hybridized to the Affymetrix HG-U133 Plus 2.0 Array. After quality control stage samples from 19 control and 23 SZ subjects were subjected to bioinformatic analysis.

(4) The fourth study has the GEO Accession number GSE12649, and the microarrays preparation followed the guidelines of MIAME in the way it is described in [30]. RNA samples were extracted from postmortem brain tissue (Brodmann's Area 46) of 35 BD subjects, 35 SZ subjects, and 35 healthy control subjects.

The RNA was applied to the Affymetrix HG-U133A GeneChip. After quality control stage in this study, 35 SZ, 33 BD samples, and 34 control samples were finally subjected to bioinformatic analysis.

2.2. Analysis of Microarray Data. The raw signal intensity data of each study were imported into the Gene Automated and Robust MicroArray Data Analysis (Gene ARMADA) software tool [31] for versatile, microarray data analysis. In order to extract the signal intensities from the raw data, specific steps were followed: background correction was performed with the gcRMA method and was followed by Quantile normalization. The negative intensity values were treated with the minimum positive and noise method and then summarization followed with the Median Polish method. The data were transformed in $\log_2$ values. In each analysis two experimental conditions were always selected: the disease condition and its corresponding control condition. Genes that were characterized as absent in more than 40% of the samples in each experimental condition were excluded from further analysis. The missing values were imputed using the k-nearest neighbor (k-NN) algorithm. All the steps of the microarray analysis were common for all the extracted datasets.

2.3. Statistical Analysis. The probe sets that were differentially expressed in the disease samples compared to the control healthy samples were selected by two-tailed Student's t-test. The lists of the DE probe sets were defined by applying the following criteria in each dataset: (i) 1.3 or greater-fold change (FC) of the mean expression in all studies, except for the fourth study of BD samples compared to controls with FC > 1.2 (small number of DE genes with stricter cutoff) and (ii) P value threshold below 0.05. The P value distribution for each gene list was used to estimate the False Discovery Rate (FDR) levels. The final gene list corresponds to an FDR < 0.05. The statistical analysis was also performed in the Gene ARMADA software.

2.4. Prioritized Pathway/Functional Analysis of Differentially Expressed Genes. In order to derive better insight into the biological processes related to the DE genes, the lists of significant genes from each microarray analysis were subjected to statistical enrichment analysis using the Statistical Ranking Annotated Genomic Experimental Results (StRAnGER) web application [22]. This bioinformatic tool is using gene ontology term (GOT) annotations and KEGG pathways as well as statistical overrepresentation tests further corrected by resampling methods, aiming to select in a prioritized fashion those GOTs and pathways related to the DE genes, that do not just have a high statistical enrichment score, but also bear a high biological information, in terms of differential expression. Specifically gene ontology (GO) based analysis and KEGG-based analysis result in a list of GO terms and KEGG pathways, respectively, based on hypergeometric tests with values <0.05, which have been reordered according to bootstrapping to correct for statistical distribution-related bias.

2.5. Prioritizations of Putative Disease Genes. In order to prioritize the gene list of interest according to the functional involvement of genes in various cellular processes, thus indicating candidate hubgenes, after inferring the theoretical topology of the GOT-gene interaction network delineated, we used the online tool GOrevenge [32] with the following settings: Aspect: BP (Biological Process), Distance: Resnik, Algorithm: BubbleGene, and Relaxation: 0.15. By adopting these settings we are able to exclude from the interaction network the bias relating to the presence of functionally redundant terms, describing the same cellular phenotypic trait, and thus assessing the centrality, namely, the correlation of the specific genes to certain biological phenotypes in an objective way.

Finally, BioGraph [33] is a data integration and data mining platform for the exploration and discovery of biomedical information. The platform offers prioritizations of putative disease genes, supported by functional hypotheses. BioGraph can retrospectively confirm recently discovered disease genes and identify potential susceptibility genes, without requiring prior domain knowledge, outperforming other text-mining applications in the field of biomedicine.

3. Results and Discussion

3.1. Differentially Expressed Probesets. After the microarray analysis and the statistical selection, lists of DE probesets for each dataset occurred. From the first and fourth studies' analysis, four lists of significantly differentiated probesets were generated: two after comparison of SZ and control subjects and two after comparison of BD and control subjects. The second study (comparison of BD patients to control subjects) resulted also in a list of DE probesets and the third study in another list of DE probesets (SZ subjects compared to control subjects). The differentiated probesets from each case are depicted in representative volcano plots (Figure 1).

3.1.1. Differentially Expressed Genes in Each Study. In postmortem studies the alterations in the gene expression are usually lower than twofold [29]. For each study, transcripts of interest and of particular expression alterations are described in the following paragraphs. The lists of DE genes for each study are presented in Supplementary Tables 1–6 (available online at doi:10.1155/2013/685917). Information about the protein products arising from the DE genes has been provided mainly from the Reference Sequence (RefSeq) database of NCBI [34].

First Study. Statistical analysis of the gene expression profile of SZ and BD patients as compared to controls is summarized in Table 1. The number of DE genes is 196 and 134 respectively.

In SZ patients, transcripts related to the membrane hypothesis show altered expression. Lipases LPL and LIPA, downregulated phosphodiesterases ENPP2 and PDE8A, downregulated phosphoinositide PIK3R4, PNPLA4 phospholipase are related to membrane metabolic processes ENPP2 and PDE8A dysregulation could also be related to

A Comparative Genomic Study in Schizophrenic and in Bipolar Disorder Patients, Based on Microarray Expression
Profiling Meta-Analysis

81

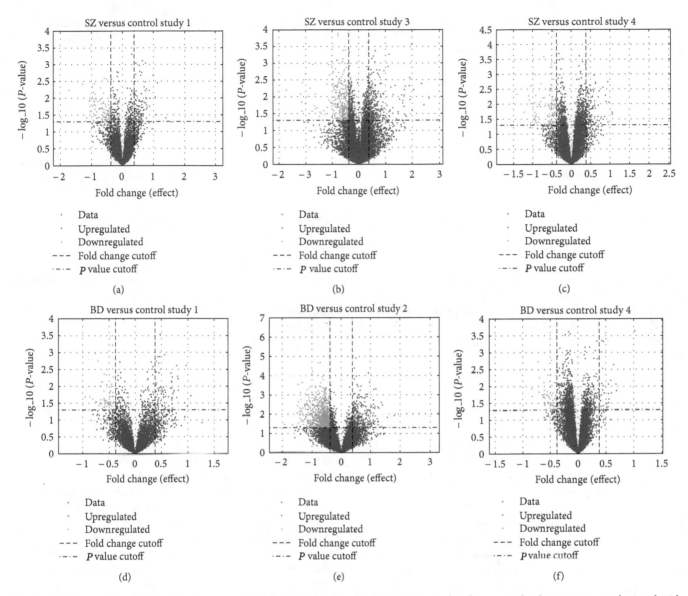

FIGURE 1: Volcano plots of DE probesets, generated from two-tailed Student's t-test. Upregulated genes in the disease state are depicted with red-colored spots and downregulated genes with green-colored spots. The first three plots (a, b, c) represent DE genes in SZ patients from first, third, and fourth studies, respectively, and the following three plots (d, e, f) represent DE genes in BD patients from first, second, and fourth studies, respectively. FC ratio between gene expression in disease state and healthy state is depicted in the horizontal axes for each dataset in $\log_2$ scale, and P values in $-\log_{10}$ scale are depicted in vertical axes. All plots are similar in most studies, except for plot (e), which shows more green and red spots. This fact means that the number of DE genes is similar in most studies but in study 2 there is a greater number of statistically significant genes in comparison to other plots.

previous MRS studies revealing different levels of phospho-diesters in SZ patients [23]. Some genes encoding proteins of signal transduction pathways, for example, downregulated G protein-coupled receptors GPR37 and GPRC5B, downregulated kinase activity encoding genes PIK3R4 and AATK, or SST somatostatin and CX3CR1 chemokine receptor can also be related to membrane dysfunctions [17]. Genes encoding ion homeostasis seem to be dysregulated as well. NPY, GRIN2A, and CACNA1C all annotated to Ca ion transport (provided by Gene Ontology Annotation UniProt Database) are DE. Also expression of manganese ion binding genes and copper ion binding genes (provided by Gene Ontology

Annotation UniProt Database), such as MT1X, is affected. KCNQ2 encoding K voltage-gated channel is overexpressed.

In BD patients of the same study transcript ATP1A3, expressing Na,K-ATPase is downregulated. This ATPase is very important for the normal regulation of the primary active transport mechanism of the cells [29]; thus it affects indirectly the normal function of the AA active transport into the cells. Other dysregulated genes contribute to abnormal K binding and transport (provided by Gene Ontology Annotation UniProt Database): SLC12A5, KCNK3, and KCNK1 are downregulated. POLR2 K encoding phosphodiesterase 6D is upregulated. This fact complies with dysregulated

TABLE 1: Number of DE genes and probesets, in SZ and BD patients as compared to healthy controls. Genes are characterized as overexpressed when they present positive FC > |0.37| in $\log_2$ scale and as downregulated when they present negative FC respectively. Out of 63000 probesets and 10000 genes of the Affymetrix HG-U95 platform, we derived a much smaller number of probesets and genes.

Disease versus control	Overexpressed genes	Downregulated genes	Total DE genes	Total probesets
SZ versus control	103	93	196	203
BD versus control	74	60	134	134

TABLE 2: Number of DE genes and probesets, occurring from comparison of BD gene expression profile and control expression profile. Genes are characterized as overexpressed when they present positive FC > |0.37| in $\log_2$ scale and as downregulated when they present negative FC, respectively. Out of 45000 probesets and 33000 genes of the Affymetrix HG-U133A GeneChip, we derived a much smaller number of probesets and genes.

Disease versus control	Overexpressed genes	Downregulated genes	Total DE genes	Total probesets
BD versus control	303	732	1035	1162

membrane phospholipid metabolism, as phosphodiesters are products of this metabolic pathway [17]. SLC7A8 gene is overexpressed. The importance of this gene relies on the fact that it is encoding transmembrane Na-independent AA transport proteins of the L system. LAT1 protein complex, which is specifically expressed from SL7A8 gene, is a tertiary active transporter and mediates tyrosine, tryptophan, and other neutral AA transport systems through cell membranes [19].

Second Study. Statistical analysis of the gene expression profile of BD patients as compared to controls is summarized in Table 2. The number of DE genes is 1035.

Many transcripts regulating ion transport are shown to be downregulated in this study: SCN1A, KCNK1, TRPC1, ATP6V1A, and ATP5G3. Many metallothionein encoding genes (provided by Gene Ontology Annotation UniProt Database) (MT1X, MT2A, MT1E, MT1M, MT1H, MT3, MT1A, and MT1G) are overexpressed. The latter genes combined with downregulated genes COX11, PAM, and RNF7 seem to result in abnormal copper ion binding, because their protein products are involved in this pathway (provided by Gene Ontology Annotation UniProt Database). Genes, encoding ATPases related to Ca++ (ATP2B1, ATP2B2) and H+ (ATP5G3, ATP6AP2, ATP6V1A, ATP6V1D, ATP6V1G2) transporting (provided by Gene Ontology Annotation UniProt Database), are downregulated. The protein encoded by the overexpressed ATP1B1 gene is a member of the family of Na+/K+ and H+/K+ ATPases, as well as a member of the subfamily of responsible proteins for establishing and maintaining the electrochemical gradients of Na and K ions across the plasma membranes [29]. PLA2G5 gene encodes an enzyme that belongs to PLA family. It catalyzes the membrane phospholipid hydrolysis to free FA, and in this study it is overexpressed. Overexpressed PLA2G4A also encodes an enzyme of A2 family. It hydrolyzes phospholipids to ARA (provided by RefSeq). ARA is subsequently metabolized into eicosanoids. Prostaglandins and leukotrienes belong to the eicosanoids, and they are lipid-based cell hormones that regulate inflammation pathways and cellular thermodynamics. The catalyzed hydrolysis also

results in lysophospholipids that are further utilized as platelet-activating factors. High Ca++ levels and phosphorylation activate the enzyme (provided by RefSeq). 37 genes encoding proteins involved in magnesium ion binding (provided by Gene Ontology Annotation UniProt Database) show altered expression. Phosphoinositide-3-kinases encoded by downregulated genes PIK3C3, PIK3CB, and PIK3R1 encode phosphoinositide 3-kinases (PI3 K). These kinases are involved in signaling pathways, and their receptors are located on the outer cell membranes [17].

Third Study. Statistical analysis of the gene expression profile of SZ patients as compared to controls is summarized in Table 3. The number of DE genes is 122.

The membrane-related protein encoded by the overexpressed ABCA1 gene is a member of ATP-binding cassette (ABC) transporter proteins superfamily. ABC proteins mediate transport of many molecules across extra- and intracellular membranes. ABC1 transporter subfamily's substrate is cholesterol; thus its function is affecting the cellular lipid removal pathway. This gene is related to Tangier's disease and familial high-density lipoprotein deficiency (provided by RefSeq). Apart from ABCA1 gene, also SLC27A3, HSD11B1, CHPT1, and GM2A genes encoding proteins associated with lipid metabolic processes (provided by Gene Ontology Annotation UniProt Database) present a different expression in SZ patients compared to controls. In the DE list CACNB2 is present as an overexpressed gene. This gene encodes a subunit of a voltage-dependent Ca channel protein which is a member of the voltage-gated Ca channel superfamily (provided by RefSeq). CACNA1B, encoding another Ca channel that regulates neuronal release of neurotransmitter, has been proved to be involved in BD and SZ (provided by RefSeq).

Fourth Study. Statistical analysis of the gene expression profiles of SZ and BD patients as compared to controls is summarized in Table 4. The number of DE genes is 216 and 205, respectively.

In SZ patients of these study genes ATP2B2 and ATP2B4 are downregulated and upregulated, respectively. These genes encode proteins that belong to the family of P-type ATPases.

A Comparative Genomic Study in Schizophrenic and in Bipolar Disorder Patients, Based on Microarray Expression Profiling Meta-Analysis

83

TABLE 3: Number of DE genes and probesets, occurring from comparison of SZ gene expression profile and control expression profile. Genes are characterized as overexpressed when they present positive FC > |0.37| in $\log_2$ scale and as downregulated when they present negative FC, respectively. Out of 54921 probesets and 38500 genes of Affymetrix HG-U133 Plus 2.0 Array, we derived a much smaller number of probesets and genes.

Disease versus control	Overexpressed genes	Downregulated genes	Total DE genes	Total probesets
SZ versus control	88	34	122	128

TABLE 4: Number of DE genes and probesets, occurring from comparison of SZ or BD gene expression profile and control expression profile. In case of SZ vs control samples genes are characterized as overexpressed when they present positive FC > |0.37| in $\log_2$ scale and in case of BD vs control when they present FC > |0.26| in $\log_2$ scale. Genes are characterized as downregulated when they present the negative FCs respectively. Out of 45000 probesets and 33000 genes of the Affymetrix HG-U133A GeneChips, we derived a much smaller number of probesets and genes.

Disease versus control	Overexpressed genes	Downregulated genes	Total DE genes	Total probesets
SZ versus control	113	103	216	227
BD versus control	69	136	205	210

These enzymes regulate primary ion transport. These two specific ATPases are very important for the homeostasis of Ca in the cell, as they catalyze cellular efflux of bivalent Ca ions from cells against great concentration gradients (provided by RefSeq). Ca ion homeostasis and Ca ion transport (provided by Gene Ontology Annotation UniProt Database) are also dependent on some other genes dysregulated in this study, such as upregulated NPY, RYR3, and ITPR2 and downregulated CXCL12. Two metallothionein encoding genes MT1X and MT1H are overexpressed. After pathway analysis, these genes, in concert with the differentiated expression of several other genes, seem to affect zinc ion binding and copper ion binding (provided by Gene Ontology Annotation UniProt Database).

In BD patients of the fourth study ATP1A2 is overexpressed. The protein expressed by this gene is a member of P-type cation transport ATPases and belongs to the subfamily of Na,K-ATPases. It belongs to integral membrane proteins, responsible for establishing and maintaining the electrochemical gradients of Na and K ions across the plasma membrane. These gradients are very important for osmoregulation, for Na-coupled transport of many organic and inorganic molecules, and for nerve and muscle electrical excitability. The catalytic subunit of Na,K-ATPase is encoded by multiple genes (provided by RefSeq). PLA2G16 is downregulated. The protein encoded by this gene belongs to a superfamily of PLA enzymes. PLA regulates adipocyte lipolysis and release of FA through a G-protein coupled pathway involving prostaglandin and prostaglandin receptors. It belongs to the phospholipase C enzymes that are activated by G-coupled regulatory pathways, such as serotoninergic 5-HT2 pathways (provided by RefSeq). Finally overexpressed metallothioneins MT1X, MT1M, MT1H, and MT1M may result in copper ion binding dysfunctions, as they are involved in this biological function (provided by Gene Ontology Annotation UniProt Database).

3.1.2. Common Differentially Expressed Genes in the Examined Studies. In the first and fourth study SZ gene expressions and BD gene expressions are compared to the same control

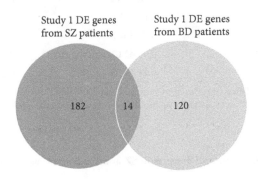

FIGURE 2: Venn diagram drawn based on DE genes in SZ and BD patients compared with controls of the first study from Brodmann's Area 10 (cognitive functions, goal formation functions). The common DE genes are represented by the intersection of the two circles.

gene expressions. Common DE genes in SZ and BD patients compared to the same control subjects, for example, in the first (Figure 2) and fourth (Figure 3) examined studies are depicted in Tables 5 and 6, respectively. The genes present in lists of statistical significant genes derived from SZ patients' expression profiles are given in Table 8. The common genes in all DE genes of BD patients compared to control groups from all related studies are presented in Table 7. MT1X gene is overexpressed in all studies, in all gene expression comparisons, except for the second study, where it is not among the statistical significant genes as shown in Figure 4.

Among the common DE genes in BD and SZ patients of the first study HTR2C is an interesting gene. Serotonergic pathway is highly related to psychiatric disease expressions. The neurotransmitter serotonin (5-hydroxytryptamine, 5-HT) causes many physiological functions after binding to receptor subtypes, such as 5-HT2 family of seven-transmembrane-spanning, G-protein-coupled receptors. These receptors activate phospholipase C and D signaling pathways. This gene encodes the 2C subtype of serotonin receptor, and its RNA editing is predicted to alter AAs within the second intracellular loop of the 5-HT2C receptor and generate receptor isoforms that differ in their ability to

TABLE 5: The fourteen common DE genes in schizophrenic and BD samples compared to control samples derived from the first study.

Gene symbol	FC (log$_2$) SZ versus control	FC (log$_2$) BP versus control	Gene title
SLC25A1	−0.624219	−0.627028	"Solute carrier family 25 (mitochondrial carrier; citrate transporter), member 1"
HTR2C	−0.511652	−0.515884	5-hydroxytryptamine (serotonin) receptor 2C
SYP	−0.506666	−0.644315	Synaptophysin
SERINC5	−0.476598	−0.564567	Serine incorporator 5
CGRRF1	**0.388505**	**0.443519**	Cell growth regulator with ring finger domain 1
SF3B1	**0.434178**	**0.435295**	Splicing factor 3b, subunit 1, 155 kDa
ADD2	**0.476098**	**0.529755**	Adducin 2 (beta)
GRK5	**0.554659**	−0.593328	G protein-coupled receptor kinase 5
UCHL3	**0.587522**	**0.701958**	ubiquitin carboxyl-terminal esterase L3 (ubiquitin thiolesterase)
DARC	**0.642385**	**0.498777**	Duffy blood group, chemokine receptor
SEPT11	**0.651131**	−0.551204	septin 11
MT1X	**0.754667**	**0.966154**	Metallothionein 1X
CEBPD	**0.774212**	**0.726239**	CCAAT/enhancer binding protein (C/EBP), delta
LGALS3	**0.892986**	**0.636527**	Lectin, galactoside-binding, soluble, 3

Downregulation of genes in each disease state compared with controls is represented with negative FC values (fold decrease) and upregulation with positive FC values. Most statistically significant genes, common in SZ and BD, are differentiated in similar way.

TABLE 6: Common DE genes in SZ and BD patients as compared to control samples derived from the fourth study. Top twenty genes (BD) are shown.

Gene symbol	FC (log$_2$) SZ versus control	FC (log$_2$) BD versus control	Gene title
DERL1	−0.9218	−0.59278	Der1-like domain family, member 1
DDX27	−0.58735	−0.55081	DEAD (Asp-Glu-Ala-Asp) box polypeptide 27
NELL1	−0.48395	−0.49181	NEL-like 1 (chicken)
WDR41	−0.561422	−0.47103	WD repeat domain 41
SST	−0.56168	−0.47692	Somatostatin
ZYX	−0.55832	−0.4319	Zyxin
SSR1	−0.79829	−0.41544	Signal sequence receptor, alpha fibronectin
FSD1	−0.4133	−0.39578	Type III and SPRY domain containing 1
TRIM27	−0.51857	−0.39195	Tripartite motif-containing
TESC	−0.546183	−0.364501	27 Tescalcin
HES1	**0.383441**	**0.32929**	Hairy and enhancer of split 1
MT1H	**0.477326**	**0.329479**	(Drosophila) metallothionein 1H
GJA1	**0.694821**	**0.332313**	Gap junction protein, alpha 1, 43 kDa
TRIL	**0.405464**	**0.343382**	TLR4 interactor with leucine-rich repeats
MT1X	**0.60052**	**0.35402**	Metallothionein 1X
AGXT2L1	**0.816962**	**0.375859**	Alanine-glyoxylate aminotransferase 2-like 1
GREB1	**0.623598**	**0.418634**	Growth regulation by estrogen in breast cancer 1
EMX2	**0.975302**	**0.545582**	Empty spiracles homeobox
GPC5	**0.772653**	**0.591493**	2 glypican 5
ALDH1L1	**1.0583**	**0.599394**	Aldehyde dehydrogenase 1 family, member L1

Downregulation of genes in each disease state is represented with negative FC values (fold decrease) and upregulation with positive FC values. Most statistically significant genes, common in SZ and BD, are differentiated in similar way.

TABLE 7: Genes present in all gene lists from all studies including comparison of gene expression between BD samples and control samples.

Gene symbol	FC BD versus control (Study 1)	FC BD versus control (Study 2)	FC BD versus control (Study 4)	Gene title
SDC4	**0.403522**	**0.79702**	**0.323976**	Syndecan 4
MT1X	**0.440635**	**1.1129**	**0.35402**	Metallothionein 1X channel
KCNK1	*−0.416116*	*−0.5935*	*−0.280259*	Potassium, SubfamilyK, Member 1
MT1H	**0.684202**	**1.09618**	**0.329479**	Metallothionein 1H
POLR3C	**0.563585**	**1.28172**	*−0.335122*	Polymerase (RNA) III (DNA directed) PolypeptideC (62 kDa)

Downregulation of genes in each disease state is represented with negative FC values (fold decrease) and upregulation with positive FC values. Most statistical significant genes, common in all BD studies are differentiated in similar way.

TABLE 8: Genes present in DE gene lists from all studies including comparison of gene expression between SZ samples with control samples.

Gene symbol	FC SZ versus control (Study 1)	FC SZ versus control (Study 3)	FC SZ versus control (Study 4)	Gene title
SRGN	**0.777085**	**0.42152**	—	Serglycin
PRPF4B	**0.563723**	—	**0.415853**	PRP4 pre-mRNA processing factor 4 homolog B (yeast)
MT1X	**0.754667**	—	**0.60052**	Metallothionein 1X
GYG2	**0.754525**	—	*0.686934*	Glycogenin 2
NR4A2	*−0.90769*	—	*−0.550066*	Nuclear receptor subfamily 4, group A, member 2
NPY	*−0.568144*	—	*−0.406243*	Neuropeptide Y
SST	*−0.83089*	—	*−0.561683*	Somatostatin
PALLD	—	**0.509794**	**0.401231**	Paladin, cytoskeletal Associated protein
AQP4	—	**0.449303**	**0.714565**	Aquaporin 4
ARPC1B	—	**0.392173**	*−0.597327*	Actin-related protein 2/3 complex, subunit 1B, 41 kDa
PVALB	—	*−0.403296*	*−0.432033*	Parvalbumin
HSD11B1	—	*−0.413042*	*−0.538573*	Hydroxysteroid(11-beta)dehydrogenase1
PHLDA2	—	*−0.452704*	*−0.455578*	Pleckstrin homology-like domain, family A

Downregulation of genes in each disease state is represented with negative FC values (fold decrease) and upregulation with positive FC values. Most statistical significant genes, common in SZ studies are differentiated in similar way.

interact with G proteins and the activation of phospholipase C and D signaling cascades, thus modulating serotonergic neurotransmission in the central nervous system. Studies in humans have reported abnormalities in patterns of 5-HT2C editing in depressed suicide victims. Three transcript variants encoding two different isoforms have been found for this gene. This gene is downregulated in both diseases [17]. Serotonin neurotransmitter has been proved to play an important role in emotional, sexual, and eating behavior and in other symptoms of mental diseases, such as hallucinations. Many drugs used for the treatment of these diseases are serotonin agonists. Upregulated ADD2, GGRRF1, and MT1X encode proteins related to metal ion binding. HTR2C, DARC, and GRK5 products participate in signal transduction pathway.

The protein encoded by SDC4 gene is a transmembrane heparan sulfate proteoglycan that functions as a receptor in intracellular signaling. Downregulated KCNK1 gene encodes one of the members of the superfamily of K channel proteins, and it has been previously reported as dysregulated in BD patients [35]. The downregulation of this gene may affect the passive transport of K into the cells.

NPY (neuropeptide) and GABA-system-related SST (somatostatin) are downregulated in two of our SZ studies. These genes have been reported in many studies as candidate psychosis genes [36]. They have also been related to SZ. Earlier studies reveal also downregulation of these specific genes. Neuropeptide genes are involved in working memory functions [37]. In psychiatric diseases working memory and neurodegeneration have been suggested as possible abnormal functions of the prefrontal cortex. These genes seem to be implicated in these functions [36]. PALLD gene, myocardial infarction-related gene, has also been reported as dysregulated in SZ [38]. The protein encoded by AQP4 gene is involved in the regulation of the water homeostasis. Upregulation of this gene has been already reported and has

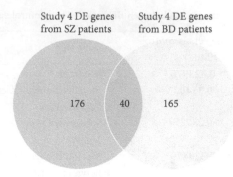

FIGURE 3: Venn diagram drawn based on DE genes in SZ and BD patients compared with controls of the fourth study from Brodmann's Area 46 (attention and working memory functions). The common DE genes are represented by the intersection of the two circles.

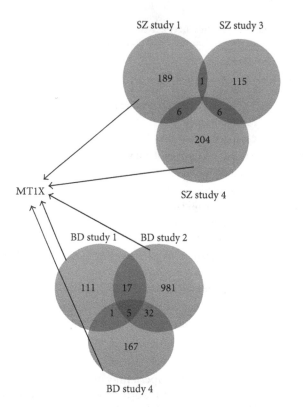

FIGURE 4: Venn diagram drawn based on DE genes in SZ and BD patients compared with controls. Red circles represent number of DE genes of SZ samples and blue circles represent number of DE genes of BD samples. MT1X is DE in all studies apart from study 3. All studies include samples from frontal cortices, apart from study 3.

been related to white matter hyperintensity, observed in MRS studies of BD patients [27]. Generally there are no common genes in all three SZ datasets. This could be explained by the fact that there are region-specific alterations in SZ, and our SZ raw data were extracted from different brain regions.

3.2. Pathway Analysis. The lists of statistical significant genes of each study were submitted to StrAnGER web application

elucidating overrepresented GO terms. The results of GO-analysis for each dataset are presented in Supplementary Tables 7–12.

In the first study, StRAnGER analysis in the SZ-related DE gene list indicated that K ion binding and transport are two of the statistical significant altered GO terms. These processes are very important for the maintenance of K ion gradients in the cells. K ion transport regulates the fluxes of K ions from and into the cells via some transport proteins or pores [19, 25].

StRAnGER analysis in the BD-related DE gene list indicated altered synaptic pathways. Synaptic pathways and genes have been reported earlier as possible dysfunction factors in BD [39]. G-protein pathways are also related to neurotransmitter receptors and particularly to serotonergic receptors, most studied in BD as part of serotonergic pathway [17]. Ca transport, protein tyrosine kinase, and phosphoinositide binding are involved in signal transduction pathways. Several studies of BD patients have shown abnormalities in the phosphoinositol/protein kinase C (PKC) signaling system. One such study has demonstrated significantly higher concentrations of 4,5-bisphosphate (PIP2) in the platelet membranes of patients in the manic phase of BD; they also found that the levels of PIP2 increased when cycling from the euthymic state into the manic state. Additionally, the activity of platelet PKC was found elevated in patients, during a manic episode of BD. Additionally several independent studies have shown increased concentrations of the stimulatory alpha subunit (G_{as}) of G-protein in the brains of BD patients, specifically in the frontal, temporal, and occipital cortices. Other studies have suggested there is also increased presence/activity of G-proteins in the leukocytes of untreated manic patients and the mononuclear leukocytes of bipolar, but not unipolar, patients. Currently, there is no evidence to indicate that the increased concentration of G_{as} is caused by gene mutations; it has been suggested that they could be caused by a change in any of the biochemical pathways leading to the transcription and translation of the G_{as} gene [40]. Copper ion binding belongs to the significant GOTs as well.

In the second study copper ion binding, magnesium ion binding, chloride channel activity, chloride transport, postsynaptic membrane, and inositol or phosphatidylinositol phosphatase activity represent significantly differentiated GOTs.

In study 3 and 4 defense response, immune response, and inflammatory response GOTs are present in the over-represented GOTs. The inflammatory system is strongly related to these mental disorders, and the immune underlying mechanisms remain mainly obscure [41]. Lipid metabolic process is also a statistically significant GOT altered in study 3.

Dysregulated neurotransmitter systems in the central nervous system of BD and SZ patients have been systematically reported [2, 4]; thus central nervous system development is among the GO terms resulting from pathway analysis of study 3 BD DE list. Copper ion binding, chloride ion binding, and signal transduction pathways seem to be affected.

TABLE 9: Overrepresented GO terms extracted from the union of 68 common genes either of BD patients or of SZ patients.

GO annotation	GOT P-value	Enrichment
Protein amino acid phosphorylation	0.000254537	6/424
ATP binding	0.000266417	10/1063
Protein binding	0.000833654	19/3248
Transferase activity	0.001557772	8/925
Nucleotide binding	0.001893973	10/1348
Cytoplasm	0.002264782	10/1379
Extracellular region	0.005570074	5/547
Metabolic process	0.0076371	4/414
Multicellular organismal development	0.011932632	5/644
Endoplasmic reticulum	0.018083004	4/514
Zinc ion binding	0.024540778	8/1430
Plasma membrane	0.034457754	4/610

Copper ion binding is present in almost all lists of significantly altered GO terms. Signaling pathways are among the KEGG pathways that appear more often as overrepresentative pathways (Supplementary Table 13).

We also performed GO analysis in the 68 genes, shown schematically in Figure 4, that were present in at least two of the BD or SZ DE lists. Table 9 summarizes the GO terms of this pathway analysis. ATP binding is essential for the maintenance of the ion gradients in the cell. ATP is universally an important coenzyme and enzyme regulator [19].

3.3. Identification of Candidate Hub Genes.

In order to expand our knowledge regarding which genes have critical role among the common DE genes in BD datasets, we used the online tool GOrevenge [32], which performs prioritization of the gene list taking into consideration the centrality of each gene, as described in the GO tree. The 68 genes found differentiated in at least two BD- or SZ-related studies were submitted to GOrevenge, and the analysis was performed based on GO annotations for Homo sapiens as described in materials and methods section. A prioritized list of genes, containing candidate linker genes, that is, genes participating in many different cellular processes, was derived (Table 10). Among them, three genes, namely, APOE, RELA, and NPY, have also been found as statistically significantly differentiated in at least two of either SZ or BD DE gene lists.

3.4. Prioritizations of Putative Disease Genes.

By setting SZ and BD as concept, the relation of each gene with the BD and SZ was assessed, and the 68 genes found differentiated in at least two BD- or SZ-related studies were prioritized by BioGraph algorithm as shown in Tables 11 and 12, respectively. The genes are prioritized according to their score which is a statistical enrichment measure of the relevance of each gene with the inquired context (here specified as either BD or SZ) to the total relations (references) of the gene in the universe of terms. In this way, the user can derive which of its genes are already associated and in what extent with a given disease or generally biological term and which of

TABLE 10: GOrevenge prioritization. The second column refers to the number of GO terms remaining after GOrevenge pruning, reflecting the centrality of each gene, while the third column refers to the original number of biological process category GO terms of each gene. Top 20 genes are shown. Genes presented in italics are among the statistically significant differentiated genes in at least two of either SZ or BD DE gene lists.

Gene symbol	Remaining GO terms	Original GO terms
TGFB1	56	126
CTNNB1	53	117
BCL2	50	121
SHH	45	142
AKT1	44	73
PSEN1	39	70
WNT5A	38	98
APOE	38	54
BMP4	37	128
TNF	37	88
FGF10	36	102
IL1B	35	75
AGT	34	63
P2RX7	33	68
SFRP1	32	81
RELA	32	50
TGFB2	32	66
BMP2	32	59
PPARG	31	51
EP300	31	46

them represent novel findings with respect to the investigated pathological phenotype. APOE, RELA, and NPY have also high scores and are among the ten top genes related either to the BD or SZ after the prioritization of genes in BioGraph. These three genes have been shown to play a major role in the examined studies, after different bioinformatic analyses. NPY has been reported as a candidate psychosis gene, as aforementioned.

APOE regulates cholesterol of the central nervous system; thus any alteration in APOE levels may result in abnormal brain function. APOE has been mostly related to Alzheimer's disease [42].

Genotyping studies and Western plot analysis have shown differences of APOE in SZ patients. Abnormal cholesterol metabolism has been associated with SZ as well. High levels of three different apolipoproteins in brains of patients with psychiatric disorders may indicate aberrant central nervous system lipid metabolism. Additionally, APOE has been implicated in inflammation pathways, after studies on mice revealing possible action of APOE as inflammatory response inhibitor. Inflammation pathways are considered candidate mechanisms responsible for the pathogenesis of several mental disorders and mainly of SZ [42].

RELA, v-rel reticuloendotheliosis viral oncogene homolog A (avian), is also involved in immune and inflammatory responses, as it encodes the main component of the

TABLE 11: Prioritization of the genes presented in table 11, by Bio-Graph exploiting unsupervised methodologies for the identification of causative SZ-associated genes. Genes with the higher nineteen scores are shown.

Gene symbol	Score
PVALB	0.172895
SYN2	0.084975
APOE	0.013519
RELA	0.00034
CRK	0.000246
NTRK2	0.000219
MAPT	0.000136
TRIP13	0.000127
NPY	$7.39E-05$
MT1X	$6.19E-05$
NR4A2	$4.25E-05$
SDC4	$3.57E-05$
PGK1	$3.29E-05$
PRPF4B	$3.21E-05$
SST	$2.35E-05$
TRPC1	$2.28E-05$
LGALS3	$2.19E-05$
DUSP6	$1.96E-05$
BGN	$1.66E-05$

TABLE 12: Prioritization of the genes presented in table 12, by Bio-Graph exploiting unsupervised methodologies for the identification of causative BD-associated genes. Genes with the higher nineteen scores are shown.

Gene symbol	Score
PVALB	1.930909595
NTRK2	0.520432786
MAPT	0.000852042
RELA	0.000381239
CRK	0.0002833
NPY	0.000109408
APOE	$8.79036E-05$
SYN2	$6.07336E-05$
NR4A2	$5.57465E-05$
TRPC1	$4.28846E-05$
SDC4	$3.78467E-05$
HSD11B1	$3.34794E-05$
TRIP13	$2.26339E-05$
SLC12A5	0.000021501
LGALS3	0.000020488
MT1X	$1.88525E-05$
SST	$1.75935E-05$
DUSP6	0.000015482
AQP4	$1.50416E-05$

NF-κB complex. NF-κB has been related indirectly to SZ, as it is highly correlated to SZ involved cytokines: interleukin-1β (IL-1β), IL-1 receptor antagonist (IL-1RA), IL-6, and tumor necrosis factor-α (TNF-α). NF-κB is a regulator of cytokines' expression, and proinflammatory cytokines activate NF-κB. NF-κB is present in synaptic terminals and participates in regulation of neuronal plasticity. NF-κB regulates genes that encode subunits of N-methyl-D-aspartate receptors, voltage-dependent Ca channels and the Ca-binding protein calbindin, cell survival factors, including Bcl-2, Mn-SOD, and inhibitor of apoptosis proteins (IAPs) and cell death factors, including Bcl-x(S) and Bax. All these genes are related to neurotransmission, and altered expression of several of them has been reported in previous SZ postmortem brain studies [43].

4. Conclusions

The aim of the study was to interpret the results of comparative genomic profiling studies in schizophrenic patients as compared to healthy controls and in patients with BD and try to relate and integrate our results with an aberrant AA transport through cell membranes. Starting from genomewide expression data, the analysis focused on genes and mechanisms involved in AA transport through cell membranes. We performed transcriptomic computational analysis on raw data derived from four different studies. Moreover, a multistage, translational bioinformatic computational framework is employed, previously utilized for the molecular analysis of transcriptomic data of atherosclerotic mice models [44], exploiting different methods in order to identify critical altered molecular mechanisms and important central players. In this way, the results derived here do not rely solely on a single stage of significance. They are complying to a systematic screening of the results, exploiting various statistical measures, in a unified analysis pipeline. These measures either exploit the stringent FDR estimations at the single gene level, further filtered to keep those common in between diseases or studies comparisons. Moreover, the consensus gene lists thus derived are corrected through a rigorous, bootstrapping framework, applied in the statistical enrichment analysis of the significant biological processes. Moreover, critical regulatory genes, prioritized by their total number of GO annotations, to the resulting significant GOTs list, are highlighted. It is also examined, whether these genes have been associated with the disease phenotypes of SZ or BD in the broader biomedical literature. The results were eventually analyzed, complying with a meta-analysis context, giving emphasis on common functional patterns mined amid the various studies.

Our bioinformatic analyses of the downloaded datasets demonstrate genes and GOTs associated with ion transport dysregulation (K, Na, Ca, and other ion transports and bindings) resulting in a disturbed primary active transport, suggesting a deficit in transmembrane Na+ and K+ gradients maintenance. Characteristic downregulation of Na+ and K+ transporting ATPases, enzymes responsible for establishing and maintaining the electrochemical gradients of Na and K ions across the plasma membrane, is indicated in the DE gene lists of two of our datasets. They are also upregulated in one dataset (BD patients' expression profiles). Also downregulation of P-type ATPases is reported in the datasets.

A Comparative Genomic Study in Schizophrenic and in Bipolar Disorder Patients, Based on Microarray Expression Profiling Meta-Analysis

89

Altered distribution of specific ions in the cells may affect distributions of other ion groups. A statistical integration of many studies has previously related published data of Na,K-ATPase activity in erythrocytes of BD patients with the expression of the disease [45]. Decreased activity of Na,K-ATPase has been also related to SZ in previous studies [38]. The disturbed primary active transport observed in our study indicates difficulty in maintaining transmembrane ion gradients. This fact should result in disrupted, secondary, active AA transporter Systems A, X-AG, N, and y+, as they couple AA transport to the electrical and chemical gradients initiated by primary active transport. AA exchangers, systems ASC, y+L and L, that transport AAs by antiport mechanisms, may suffer from a deficit of secondary, actively transported AAs they need for the exchange, resulting in a disrupted transport of AAs mainly transported through this third mechanism.

Genes and pathways related to Ca transport agree with abnormalities in Ca signaling, that have been implicated in BD; findings show elevated intracellular Ca concentrations in the platelets, lymphocytes, and neutrophils of BD patients. Ca is very important in most intracellular signaling pathways and in the regulation of neurotransmitter synthesis and release [40].

Phospholipase activity may be dysregulated in BD and SZ diseases, as indicated by altered expression of the genes encoding this enzyme in this study. This alteration has obvious impacts on the phospholipid metabolism of the membrane, as it is a crucial enzyme in this metabolic pathway [23].

A consistent upregulation of MT1X and generally of metallothionein genes is consistent in different datasets. The functional role of metallothioneins in the brain has not been very well characterized [36]. The main function of metallothioneins is to protect neurons from pathological stressing factors. Abnormal expression of genes encoding these proteins may indicate an endogenous reaction to constant oxidative stress [46]. Several studies have suggested involvement of metallothioneins in functions of the central nervous system, such as neuroprotection, regeneration, and cognitive function. Other studies reported that metallothioneins are involved in cellular response, immunoregulation, cell survival, and brain functional restoration. Metallothioneins are mainly produced in astrocytes. Metallothionein overexpression has been also reported as a contributing factor in brain pathologies, such as excitotoxic injury, amyotrophic lateral sclerosis, Alzheimer's disease, and Parkinson's disease. Animal studies have associated substance dependences and learning procedures with metallothioneins. Other prefrontal cortex (PFC) studies have revealed overexpression of metallothioneins in SZ patients. All these studies indicate involvement of metallothioneins in neuroprotection and cognitive functions. A possible neurodegenerative function in the PFC may affect cognitive function in BD and SZ patients. Overexpression of these genes could then be a defense mechanism against these adverse processes. Metallothioneins have also been proposed as possible medical treatment as they have been tested in animal models and have been proved nontoxic [36].

The observed small number of common DE genes among the different studies reflects heterogeneity among the datasets analyzed, which could be explained by both biological and technical reasons. The brain area under study, the microarray platform used, and the selection of patients and controls could contribute to the heterogeneity and should be taken into consideration and duly addressed, ideally at the stage of the experimental design, whenever analogous meta-analysis tasks are envisioned. Highlighting genes that present different expression in different cases, but in the context of a multitiered systematic framework, like the one presented here, could result in molecular interactions, linked with causative, universal, and molecular pathways in mental disorders.

Abbreviations

ATPase:	Adenosine triphosphatase
AA:	Amino acid
ARA:	Arachidonic acid
ARMADA:	Automate Robust Microarray Data Analysis
BD:	Bipolar disorder
DHA:	Docosahexaenoic acid
EFA:	Essential fatty acids
FA:	Fatty acids
FC:	Fold change
FDR:	False discovery rate
GEO:	Gene expression omnibus
GO:	Gene ontology
GOT:	Gene ontology term
k-NN:	k-nearest neighbor
MRS:	Magnetic resonance spectroscopy
NCBI:	National Center for Biotechnology Information
PLA:	Phospholipase A2
Na,K-ATPase:	Sodium-potassium adenosine triphosphatase
StRAnGER:	Statistical Ranking Annotated Genomic Experimental Results
SZ:	Schizophrenia
Ca:	Calcium
Na:	Sodium
K:	Potassium
G_{as}:	alpha subunit of G protein
DE:	Differentially expressed
PFC:	Prefrontal cortex.

References

[1] A. Sawa and S. H. Snyder, "Schizophrenia: diverse approaches to a complex disease," *Science*, vol. 296, no. 5568, pp. 692–695, 2002.

[2] M. L. Persson, J. Johansson, R. Vumma et al., "Aberrant amino acid transport in fibroblasts from patients with bipolar disorder," *Neuroscience Letters*, vol. 457, no. 1, pp. 49–52, 2009.

[3] D. F. Horrobin, "Schizophrenia as a membrane lipid disorder which is expressed throughout the body," *Prostaglandins Leukotrienes and Essential Fatty Acids*, vol. 55, no. 1-2, pp. 3–7, 1996.

[4] T. M. Du Bois, C. Deng, and X. F. Huang, "Membrane phospholipid composition, alterations in neurotransmitter systems and schizophrenia," *Progress in Neuro-Psychopharmacology and Biological Psychiatry*, vol. 29, no. 6, pp. 878–888, 2005.

[5] F. A. Wiesel, J. L. R. Andersson, G. Westerberg et al., "Tyrosine transport is regulated differently in patients with schizophrenia," *Schizophrenia Research*, vol. 40, no. 1, pp. 37–42, 1999.

[6] F. A. Wiesel, G. Edman, L. Flyckt et al., "Kinetics of tyrosine transport and cognitive functioning in schizophrenia," *Schizophrenia Research*, vol. 74, no. 1, pp. 81–89, 2005.

[7] R. Vumma, F. A. Wiesel, L. Flyckt, L. Bjerkenstedt, and N. Venizelos, "Functional characterization of tyrosine transport in fibroblast cells from healthy controls," *Neuroscience Letters*, vol. 434, no. 1, pp. 56–60, 2008.

[8] E. Olsson, F. A. Wiesel, L. Bjerkenstedt, and N. Venizelos, "Tyrosine transport in fibroblasts from healthy volunteers and patients with schizophrenia," *Neuroscience Letters*, vol. 393, no. 2-3, pp. 211–215, 2006.

[9] L. Flyckt, N. Venizelos, G. Edman, L. Bjerkenstedt, L. Hagenfeldt, and F. A. Wiesel, "Aberrant tyrosine transport across the cell membrane in patients with schizophrenia," *Archives of General Psychiatry*, vol. 58, no. 10, pp. 953–958, 2001.

[10] L. Flyckt, G. Edman, N. Venizelos, and K. Borg, "Aberrant tyrosine transport across the fibroblast membrane in patients with schizophrenia -indications of maternal inheritance," *Journal of Psychiatric Research*, vol. 45, no. 4, pp. 519–525, 2011.

[11] C. N. Ramchand, M. Peet, A. E. Clark, A. E. Gliddon, and G. P. Hemmings, "Decreased tyrosine transport in fibroblasts from schizophrenics: implications for membrane pathology," *Prostaglandins Leukotrienes and Essential Fatty Acids*, vol. 55, no. 1-2, pp. 59–64, 1996.

[12] P. E. Ward, J. Sutherland, E. M. T. Glen, and A. I. M. Glen, "Niacin skin flush in schizophrenia: a preliminary report," *Schizophrenia Research*, vol. 29, no. 3, pp. 269–274, 1998.

[13] L. Flyckt, J. Borg, K. Borg et al., "Muscle biopsy, macro EMG, and clinical characteristics in patients with schizophrenia," *Biological Psychiatry*, vol. 47, no. 11, pp. 991–999, 2000.

[14] R. Vumma, J. Johansson, T. Lewander, and N. Venizelos, "Tryptophan Transport in human fibroblast cells: a functional characterization," *International Journal of Tryptophan Research*, vol. 4, pp. 19–27, 2011.

[15] D. Raucoules, J. M. Azorin, A. Barre, and R. Tissot, "Plasma levels and red blood cell membrane transports of L-tyrosine and L-tryptophan in depressions. Assessment at baseline and recovery," *Encephale*, vol. 17, no. 3, pp. 197–201, 1991.

[16] Y. Bezchlibnyk and L. T. Young, "The neurobiology of bipolar disorder: focus on signal transduction pathways and the regulation of gene expression," *Canadian Journal of Psychiatry*, vol. 47, no. 2, pp. 135–148, 2002.

[17] P. M. Kidd, "Bipolar disorder as cell membrane dysfunction. Progress toward integrative management," *Alternative Medicine Review*, vol. 9, no. 2, pp. 107–135, 2004.

[18] D. F. Horrobin and C. N. Bennett, "Depression and bipolar disorder: relationships to impaired fatty acid and phospholipid metabolism and to diabetes, cardiovascular disease, immunological abnormalities, cancer, ageing and osteoporosis. Possible candidate genes," *Prostaglandins Leukotrienes and Essential Fatty Acids*, vol. 60, no. 4, pp. 217–234, 1999.

[19] R. Hyde, P. M. Taylor, and H. S. Hundal, "Amino acid transporters: roles in amino acid sensing and signalling in animal cells," *Biochemical Journal*, vol. 373, no. 1, pp. 1–18, 2003.

[20] L. Bjerkenstedt, L. Farde, L. Terenius, G. Edman, N. Venizelos, and F. A. Wiesel, "Support for limited brain availability of tyrosine in patients with schizophrenia," *International Journal of Neuropsychopharmacology*, vol. 9, no. 2, pp. 247–255, 2006.

[21] D. F. Horrobin, "The membrane phospholipid hypothesis as a biochemical basis for the neurodevelopmental concept of schizophrenia," *Schizophrenia Research*, vol. 30, no. 3, pp. 193–208, 1998.

[22] A. Chatziioannou and P. Moulos, "Exploiting statistical methodologies and controlled vocabularies for prioritized functional analysis of genomic experiments: the StRAnGER web application," *Frontiers in Neuroscience*, vol. 5, pp. 1–14, 2011.

[23] D. L. Scott, S. P. White, Z. Otwinowski, W. Yuan, M. H. Gelb, and P. B. Sigler, "Interfacial catalysis: The mechanism of phospholipase A2," *Science*, vol. 250, pp. 1541–1546, 1990.

[24] A. Klemm, R. Rzanny, R. Fünfstück et al., "31P-Magnetic resonance spectroscopy (31P-MRS) of human allografts after renal transplantation," *Nephrology Dialysis Transplantation*, vol. 13, no. 12, pp. 3147–3152, 1998.

[25] S. Bröer, "Adaptation of plasma membrane amino acid transport mechanisms to physiological demands," *Pflügers Archiv. European Journal of Physiology*, vol. 444, no. 4, pp. 457–466, 2002.

[26] T. Barrett, D. B. Troup, S. E. Wilhite et al., "NCBI GEO: archive for high-throughput functional genomic data," *Nucleic Acids Research*, vol. 37, no. 1, pp. D885–D890, 2009.

[27] K. Iwamoto, C. Kakiuchi, M. Bundo, K. Ikeda, and T. Kato, "Molecular characterization of bipolar disorder by comparing gene expression profiles of postmortem brains of major mental disorders," *Molecular Psychiatry*, vol. 9, no. 4, pp. 406–416, 2004.

[28] M. M. Ryan, H. E. Lockstone, S. J. Huffaker, M. T. Wayland, M. J. Webster, and S. Bahn, "Gene expression analysis of bipolar disorder reveals downregulation of the ubiquitin cycle and alterations in synaptic genes," *Molecular Psychiatry*, vol. 11, no. 10, pp. 965–978, 2006.

[29] M. R. Barnes, J. Huxley-Jones, P. R. Maycox et al., "Transcription and pathway analysis of the superior temporal cortex and anterior prefrontal cortex in schizophrenia," *Journal of Neuroscience Research*, vol. 89, no. 8, pp. 1218–1227, 2011.

[30] K. Iwamoto, M. Bundo, and T. Kato, "Altered expression of mitochondria-related genes in postmortem brains of patients with bipolar disorder or schizophrenia, as revealed by large-scale DNA microarray analysis," *Human Molecular Genetics*, vol. 14, no. 2, pp. 241–253, 2005.

[31] A. Chatziioannou, P. Moulos, and F. N. Kolisis, "Gene ARMADA: an integrated multi-analysis platform for microarray data implemented in MATLAB," *BMC Bioinformatics*, vol. 10, article 1471, p. 354, 2009.

[32] K. Moutselos, I. Maglogiannis, and A. Chatziioannou, "GOrevenge: a novel generic reverse engineering method for the identification of critical molecular players, through the use of ontologies," *IEEE Transactions on Bio-Medical Engineering*, vol. 58, no. 12, pp. 3522–3527, 2011.

[33] A. M. L. Liekens, J. De Knijf, W. Daelemans, B. Goethals, P. De Rijk, and J. Del-Favero, "Biograph: unsupervised biomedical knowledge discovery via automated hypothesis generation," *Genome Biology*, p. R57, 2011.

[34] K. D. Pruitt, T. Tatusova, W. Klimke, and D. R. Maglott, "NCBI reference sequences: current status, policy and new initiatives," *Nucleic Acids Research*, vol. 37, no. 1, pp. D32–D36, 2009.

[35] N. Matigian, L. Windus, H. Smith et al., "Expression profiling in monozygotic twins discordant for bipolar disorder reveals

A Comparative Genomic Study in Schizophrenic and in Bipolar Disorder Patients, Based on Microarray Expression Profiling Meta-Analysis

91

dysregulation of the WNT signalling pathway," *Molecular Psychiatry*, vol. 12, no. 9, pp. 815–825, 2007.

[36] K. H. Choi, M. Elashoff, B. W. Higgs et al., "Putative psychosis genes in the prefrontal cortex: combined analysis of gene expression microarrays," *BMC Psychiatry*, vol. 8, article 87, 2008.

[37] T. Hashimoto, D. Arion, T. Unger et al., "Alterations in GABA-related transcriptome in the dorsolateral prefrontal cortex of subjects with schizophrenia," *Molecular Psychiatry*, vol. 13, no. 2, pp. 147–161, 2008.

[38] N. Petronijević, D. Mićić, B. Duricić, D. Marinković, and V. R. Paunović, "Substrate kinetics of erythrocyte membrane Na, K-ATPase and lipid perosides in schizophrenia," *Progress in Neuro-Psychopharmacology & Biological Psychiatry*, vol. 27, no. 3, pp. 431–440, 2003.

[39] C. A. Ogden, M. E. Rich, N. J. Schork et al., "Candidate genes, pathways and mechanisms for bipolar (manic-depressive) and related disorders: an expanded convergent functional genomics approach," *Molecular Psychiatry*, vol. 9, no. 11, pp. 1007–1029, 2004.

[40] H. K. Manji and R. H. Lenox, "The nature of bipolar disorder," *Journal of Clinical Psychiatry*, vol. 61, no. 13, pp. 42–57, 2000.

[41] S. Hope, I. Melle, P. Aukrust et al., "Similar immune profile in bipolar disorder and schizophrenia: selective increase in soluble tumor necrosis factor receptor I and von Willebrand factor," *Bipolar Disorders*, vol. 11, no. 7, pp. 726–734, 2009.

[42] E. A. Thomas and J. G. Sutcliffe, "The neurobiology of apolipoproteins in psychiatric disorders," *Molecular Neurobiology*, vol. 26, no. 2-3, pp. 369–388, 2002.

[43] R. Hashimoto, K. Ohi, Y. Yasuda et al., "Variants of the RELA gene are associated with schizophrenia and their startle responses," *Neuropsychopharmacology*, vol. 36, no. 9, pp. 1921–1931, 2011.

[44] O. Papadodima, A. Sirsjö, F. N. Kolisis, and A. Chatziioannou, "Application of an integrative computational framework in trancriptomic data of atherosclerotic mice suggests numerous molecular players," *Advances in Bioinformatics*, vol. 2012, Article ID 453513, 9 pages, 2012.

[45] S. W. Looney and R. S. Ei-Mallakh, "Meta-analysis of erythrocyte Na, K-ATPase activity in bipolar illness," *Depression and Anxiety*, vol. 5, no. 2, pp. 53–65, 1997.

[46] E. Mocchegiania, C. Bertoni-Freddarib, F. Marcellinic, and M. Malavolta, "Brain, aging and neurodegeneration: role of zinc ion availability," *Progress in Neurobiology*, vol. 75, pp. 367–390, 2005.

11

Novel Computational Methodologies for Structural Modeling of Spacious Ligand Binding Sites of G-Protein-Coupled Receptors: Development and Application to Human Leukotriene B4 Receptor

Yoko Ishino[1] and Takanori Harada[2]

[1] Graduate School of Innovation & Technology Management, Yamaguchi University, 2-16-1 Tokiwadai, Ube, Yamaguchi 755-8611, Japan
[2] Graduate School of Biomedical Sciences, Hiroshima University, 1-2-3 Kasumi, Minami-Ku, Hiroshima 734-8551, Japan

Correspondence should be addressed to Yoko Ishino, ishino.y@yamaguchi-u.ac.jp

Academic Editors: S. Jahandideh, P. Jain, and M. Liu

This paper describes a novel method to predict the activated structures of G-protein-coupled receptors (GPCRs) with high accuracy, while aiming for the use of the predicted 3D structures in *in silico* virtual screening in the future. We propose a new method for modeling GPCR thermal fluctuations, where conformation changes of the proteins are modeled by combining fluctuations on multiple time scales. The core idea of the method is that a molecular dynamics simulation is used to calculate average 3D coordinates of all atoms of a GPCR protein against heat fluctuation on the picosecond or nanosecond time scale, and then evolutionary computation including receptor-ligand docking simulations functions to determine the rotation angle of each helix of a GPCR protein as a movement on a longer time scale. The method was validated using human leukotriene B4 receptor BLT1 as a sample GPCR. Our study demonstrated that the proposed method was able to derive the appropriate 3D structure of the active-state GPCR which docks with its agonists.

1. Introduction

G-protein-coupled receptors (GPCRs), the largest family of membrane proteins (around 800 in humans), are involved in a variety of biological and pathological processes such as development and proliferation [1], neurological disorders [2], angiogenesis [3], and metabolic disorders [4]. GPCRs transmit molecular information from the extracellular side to the intracellular side of the cell, thus mediating many intracellular responses. Although nearly one half of currently marketed drugs target GPCRs [5], only 10% of these receptors have endogenous ligands [6]. Structurally, all GPCRs share an architecture formed by seven transmembrane (TM) helices connected by extracellular and intracellular loops. GPCRs can recognize structurally diverse ligands ranging from photons to ions, amino acids, small organic molecules, lipids, peptides, or proteins [7].

Due to limitations in the purification and crystallization of GPCRs, until recently only a limited number of three-dimensional (3D) structures of GPCRs have been resolved at high resolution by X-ray crystallography: rhodopsin [8], the β-adrenergic receptors (β_2AR [9, 10], β_1AR [11]), the adenosine A_{2A} receptor [12], and the opioid receptors (κ [13], μ [14]). The highly conserved general architecture including the TM helical bundle and some universally conserved residues allows predicting the 3D structure of unknown GPCRs by homology modeling, while using a few known GPCR structures as a template [15]. However, great cautions are needed when utilizing the homology-based models for detailed GPCR structural and functional annotations since helix kinks are often different in different receptors. Modeling these subtle distinctions, which is essential for ligand docking and screening, remains a major challenge [16]. In addition, since almost all known GPCR structures have been found in their inactive forms, the homology modeling has shown little power to practically predict the 3D structure of GPCRs in the active forms. It is known that the agonist-bound GPCRs take the active forms, whereas the antagonist-bound or inverse agonist-bound GPCRs take the inactive forms.

Ligand-induced activation of GPCRs results in multiple allosteric conformational changes that propagate throughout the receptor structure, ultimately triggering different signaling cascades [17]. In contrast to inactive states of GPCRs, no crystal structures of active states were available until 2011. Given the absence of experimental structural information, several investigators have applied computational strategies to predict activated models of GPCRs [18–22]. Therein, it is reported that applying an appropriate long-term molecular dynamics (MD) simulation after homology modeling could predict plausible 3D structures of activated GPCRs in view of the induced fit mechanism [21, 22]. However, this approach needs to impose appropriate structural constraints prior to the MD simulation, which requires both the skills and experience of an MD specialist. Moreover, MD simulations on ordinary personal computers are generally limited to timescales up to the microsecond order in long-term studies, yet structural changes from fitting-induced fluctuations require calculations on the millisecond order. Due to its time-consuming nature, it is virtually impossible to simulate all processes involved in structural changes using only MD on common computers. For this reason, currently no high-accuracy methods are available for predicting the activated structure of GPCRs.

This paper describes a novel method to predict activated GPCR structures with high accuracy on standard workstations, while aiming for the use of the predicted 3D structures in *in silico* virtual screening in the future. First, we have developed a new method for modeling thermal fluctuations in GPCRs by using combinations of fluctuations with different time scales. Based on this model, we propose a novel computational method to search for one of the best 3D structures of an activated GPCR.

2. Model and Framework

Proteins undergo thermal fluctuations of considerable magnitude. The time scale of thermal fluctuations in proteins ranges from femtoseconds to minutes, or even longer timescales [23]. In terms of spatial considerations, various levels of fluctuations exist, which include rapid motions within microspace (such as thermal oscillations between atoms and rotations of amino acid side chains), and relatively slow but large structural changes (such as local unfolding). Not all of these motions can be simulated because of the physical limits of currently available MD calculations. We therefore propose a new method for modeling GPCR thermal fluctuations, in which fluctuations are combined on different time scales. In this approach, we first simulate the oscillations and fluctuations of various atoms at the picosecond and nanosecond levels to obtain native structure within a short time span. We then simulate the thermal fluctuations

of GPCRs in terms of their characteristic rotational motions around helical axes, which represent fluctuations of greater time scales. In our approach, some information on GPCRs that is known *a priori* is utilized. For instance, we know that TM helices are immobilized in a cell membrane, so their mobility is certainly low. Furthermore, this approach is based on the previous findings that when a GPCR is activated in a cell membrane, its structural changes occur by rotations around the axes of TM helices [24], and that especially TM3, TM5, and TM6 play an important role in the activation process in some GPCRs [18, 21]. Although this method does not guarantee the optimum from an exhaustive chemical calculation approach, it does have the clear advantage of reducing calculation load without sacrificing the quality of the solution obtained. We specifically focus on predicting the central part of the 7-TM helical bundle, a spacious ligand binding site, with good quality, while aiming for the use of the predicted 3D structures in *in silico* virtual screening in the future.

Based on this model, we propose a framework for structural search which comprises three stages, namely: (i) obtaining initial structures of a target GPCR by homology modeling using known GPCRs in their inactive forms as a template, (ii) obtaining average structures of a GPCR in a stable state after simulating fluctuations from several hundred picoseconds to a nanosecond using MD simulations, and (iii) obtaining a best 3D structure of a target GPCR in the active form through a machine-learning technique including evolutionary computation and modularized ligand-binding simulations. Our proposed method employs a real-coded genetic algorithm (GA) as an evolutionary computation to search appropriate rotation angles of helices of a target GPCR, in which discrete steps employ receptor-ligand docking simulations to evaluate the goodness of the rotation angles of the GPCR.

The core idea of the framework is that an MD simulation is used to calculate the 3D coordinates of all atoms of a target GPCR in a relaxed state in terms of heat fluctuation on the picosecond or nanosecond time scale, after which the evolutionary computation is used to determine the best ligand-bound rotation angles of helices of a GPCR as a movement on a longer time scale.

3. Methodology to Predict 3D Structure of Activated GPCR

The detailed procedure of the proposed structural search method is described as follows.

(1) *Determination of an initial structure:* a known GPCR such as rhodopsin or beta-adrenergic receptor is used as a template. After alignment of the primary amino acid sequences of the template and target GPCR, the inactivated structure of the target GPCR is generated by regular homology modeling, which results in an initial structure.

(2) *Average molecular structures with respect to fluctuations on a short-time scale:* an appropriate amount of water molecules are added to the surroundings of the

target GPCR. The fluctuations of GPCR molecules are then calculated by MD simulations at the level of several hundred picoseconds. The average structures are defined as those for which the energy values stabilize.

(3) *Structural changes with respect to rotational motions of helices:* hypothetical rotational motions around the axes of helices constituting the target GPCR (as fluctuations of greater-time scale) are generated. These are fed into a real-coded GA [25], as explained above, including simulations of binding with known ligands to determine optimal values. Details of the steps are described as follows. In addition, the schemes for generation alternation and offspring creation are shown in Figure 1.

(3.1) *Generation of initial populations.* Individuals are assigned real-number vectors representing rotational angle changes relative to the average structures of various helices. These real-number vectors are treated as values within the space adjoining the two ends of the search space (i.e., toroidal space.) An initial population of m individuals is randomly generated.

(3.2) *Creation of offspring for each generation.* Parents (two individuals) for random crossover of population pools are selected to match with a third parent, so as to generate offspring by the unimodal normal distribution crossover (UNDX) method [26]. The third parent is used to determine the standard deviation of normal distribution in UNDX. This procedure is repeated n times to provide n offspring individuals. In total, the number of individuals in a generation is $n + 2$ (offspring and two parents).

(3.3) *Selection in each generation.* To evaluate each individual, receptor-ligand docking simulations are conducted using a known agonist and a known antagonist. An individual's real-valued vector translates into a corresponding 3D structure, with its side chains optimized before the binding simulations. An evaluation function has been established to represent how good the binding is. For a single individual, ligand-GPCR docking simulations are conducted up to k times, and each evaluation score is recorded. Upon obtaining the top score for each individual, the scores are then used to rank all individuals in a generation. The two individuals highest in ranking are selected (elite strategy) to replace the two parents in the population.

(3.4) *Reiteration.* Steps (3.2) and (3.3) are repeated until some stop criteria are met.

The values for m and n can be determined based on previous researches and/or preliminary experiments. In our proposed search method, generation transition is achieved

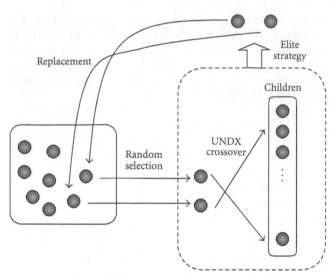

FIGURE 1: Schemes for generation alternation.

via the minimal generation gap (MGG) method [27]. MGG has good compatibility with UNDX and contributes to maintaining diversity in the population.

4. Test Case of Human Leukotriene B4 Receptor BLT1

This study reports on a novel approach to molecular modeling of 7-TM proteins that has been developed to build plausible active states of any given GPCR by using evolutionary computation. This heuristic approach starts from the amino-acid sequence of a target GPCR. We performed a validation test, where human leukotriene B4 receptor BLT1 was used as a sample target GPCR.

4.1. Leukotriene Receptor. Leukotriene (LT) is a bioactive lipid that serves as an important mediator of host defense, though it is also known to be implicated in bronchial asthma as a pathogenetic or precipitating factor. To date, four types of LT receptors have been cloned. One of these receptors, the high-affinity human LTB4 receptor BLT1 (GPCRDB entry ID: LT4R1_HUMAN; UniProt entry ID: Q15722), was selected as a target GPCR in our experiments. The length of the amino-acid sequence of BLT1 is 352aa.

4.2. Experimental Procedure. The sequence of BLT1 was retrieved from the UniProt database. ClustalX software [28] was used to align the sequence with the crystal structure of the bovine rhodopsin (UniProt entry ID: P02699) with which it shares a sequence similarity of more than 54%. One 3D structure of BLT1 obtained after running homology modeling using the bovine rhodopsin (PDB ID: 1L9H) as a template was selected from ModBase [29] as an initial rough 3D structure. ModBase is an open database of comparative protein structure models, theoretically calculated by the modeling pipeline ModPipe, which is maintained by Sali [30].

After annealing for atomic relaxation, MD simulations having distance restraints similar to a way proposed by Gouldson et al. [22] were run by using the TINKER software (ver. 4.2) [31]. The simulation conditions used were: force field = AMBER99; temperature = 310 K; pressure = 1 atm; time step = 1.0 fs. An average structure was determined after reaching a stable state, at which no steep drop in the molecular energy was observed. MD simulations for several hundred picoseconds were needed to achieve such a stable state.

The following are the processes of an evolutionary computation method in terms of optimizing the rotation angles of TM helices. The previous work performing amino-acid residue substitution analysis and spectroscopic experiments found that "TM3, TM5, and TM6 play an important role in activation of the leukotriene receptor [32]." This let us bound the free rotation space searched to these three helices; hence, the solutions we seek are the rotation angles of the three helices. Our proposed method employs a real-coded GA as a search algorithm and the ligand-binding simulation as an evaluation tool. An individual, which is defined as a real number vector representing the rotational angles of TM3, TM5, and TM6, has a unique value. In the evolutionary search process, the genetic operations mentioned in the previous section are repeated until the point when the stop criteria are met (the maximum generation number is 200, determined based on a preliminary experiment). The computational parameters in the evolutionary search are as follows: the initial population size is 50, and the number of offspring in a generation is 8. For evaluation of individuals, two sets of ligand-binding simulations are independently performed using a BLT1 agonist 12-keto-LTB4 (PubChem CID: 5280876) and a BLT1 antagonist pranlukast (PubChem CID: 115100). Docking of these ligands into the 3D structure of each individual, which is restored from the individual's vector representing the rotational angles of three helices to the 3D structure through structural relaxation by an *ab initio* (first-principle approach) computational method, is carried out with the GOLD software (ver. 3.1) [33]. The evaluation function in the evolutionary process is determined using the GOLD scores obtained from the docking simulations. The maximum GOLD scores derived from the docking with the BLT1 agonist and the BLT1 antagonist are assigned as x_1 and x_2, respectively. The evaluation function value is shown below.

When $x_2 > 0$, evaluation function value = $x_1 - x_2$; for all cases other than this condition, evaluation function value = x_1.

Finally, a best BLT1 structure obtained through the proposed method is evaluated by executing the docking simulations with many ligands other than ligands used in the evolutionary search process.

4.3. Results and Discussion. A computer with an Intel Xeon 3.6 GHz CPU (dual processor) was used for computation. For MD processing of 219.3-ps simulations, 524 hours were required. We investigated the changes in GPCR molecular energy values (kcal/mol) for every 0.1 ps time elapsed in

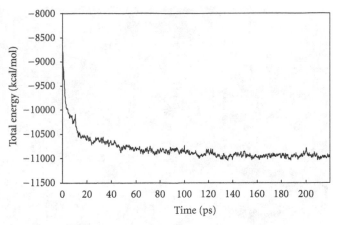

FIGURE 2: Molecular energy change of BLT1 through MD simulations.

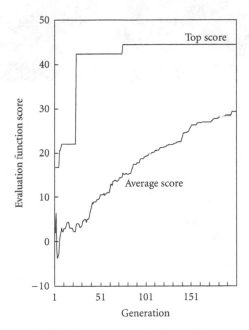

FIGURE 3: Evaluation function score in the evolutionary computation.

MD, as shown in Figure 2. Lower-energy values suggest corresponding increases in structural stability. At the point of approximately 200 ps, energy values ceased to further fall, which suggests that a region of stability had been reached. As our study focused on MD simulations for structural changes on a short-time scale (meaning that the objectives were to simulate structural relaxation), we considered 200 ps to be a sufficient level and therefore stopped at 219.3 ps.

For subsequent evolutionary computation, 899 hours were required for calculations for 200 generations. Figure 3 shows the trends of scores in evolutionary computation (the higher the scores, the better). The optimal solutions for rotational angles after 200 generations were: TM3 = 11°, TM5 = 14°, and TM6 = 255°.

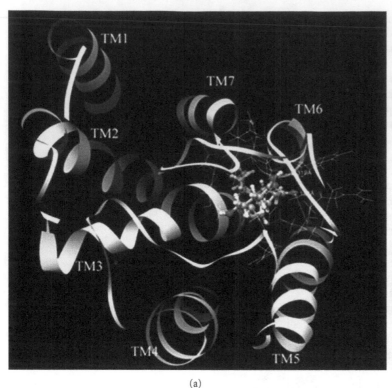

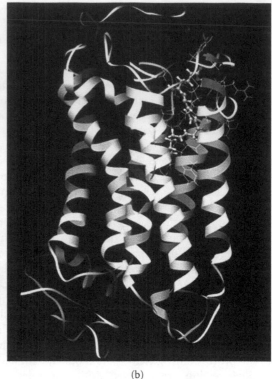

(a)   (b)

FIGURE 4: A best 3D structure of active-state BLT1.

Figure 4 shows the state of binding between the LT receptor and its agonist in one of the best 3D structures computed. The 3D structures of binding are shown in Figure 4(a) with a view from above the cell plasma membrane and in Figure 4(b) with a cross-section of the membrane (the upper part being the extracellular space). In order to highlight receptor-ligand interactions, the main chains (backbones) of the helices are shown as ribbons, while the BLT1 agonist 12-keto-LTB4 is drawn as a ball-and-stick structure. From Figure 4, it is clear that the BLT1 agonist binds to a recessed region (pocket) formed by TM3, TM5, and TM6. Upon further analysis regarding the binding state of the LT receptor and its ligand, these helices responsible for interacting with the LT ligand are composed mostly of hydrophobic amino acid residues, suggesting that the BLT1 ligand is drawn into a strongly hydrophobic environment. Since the BLT1 agonist has many hydrophobic groups, it is likely that ligand-receptor binding is contributed to mainly by hydrophobic interactions, though several hydrogen bonding sites contribute to the binding. The following interactions are worth detailing.

(i) Hydrophobic interactions between TM3 and the alkyl side chain near the central carbonyl (–C=O) group of the BLT1 agonist.

(ii) Hydrophobic interactions between TM5 and the alkyl side chain near the central carbonyl group of the BLT1 agonist.

(iii) Hydrogen bonding between the –OH group in the carboxyl (–COOH) group of the BLT1 ligand and the

carbonyl group of Asn241 on TM6 (C=O$\cdots$H–O intermolecular distance 2.32 Å.).

(iv) Hydrogen bonding between the central carbonyl group of the BLT1 agonist and the main chain (–N–H peptide bond) of Gly246 on the loop joining TM6 and TM7 (C=O$\cdots$H–O intermolecular distance 2.13 Å.).

(v) Hydrophobic interactions between TM6 and all alkyl side chains of the BLT1 agonist.

In addition to TM3, TM5, and TM6, we speculate that TM7 also contributes to hydrophobic interactions with the alkyl side chains of the BLT1 agonist.

At the beginning of evaluation, we calculated the root mean square deviation (RMSD) of BLT1 structures to investigate the structure change. Firstly, we obtained initial structures from homology modeling as structure I, MD relaxed structures as structure II, and structures generated from post-MD evolutionary computation as structure III to calculate the RMSD of 1,316 atoms forming the backbones. The resultant RMSDs were 4.49 Å for structures I and II, 1.55 Å for structures II and III, and 4.63 Å for structures I and III. Based on these values, the transition from structure I to structure II involved a large change. The reason why the transition from structure II to structure III was a smaller change is that the evolutionary search process only altered the rotation angle of TM3, TM5, and TM6. Nevertheless, what is interesting is that in the transition from structure II to structure III, the amount of rotational angle change in TM6 was clearly large compared with the other two TM

Novel Computational Methodologies for Structural Modeling of Spacious Ligand Binding Sites of G-Protein-Coupled Receptors: Development and Application to Human Leukotriene B4 Receptor

97

helices: TM3 = 11°, TM5 = 14°, and TM6 = 255°. This is consistent with other previous research showing that the TM6 region plays a very important role in the transition from inactive-state to active-state rhodopsin [34]. Since GPCRs including the leukotriene receptor are allosteric proteins, the conformational change from inactive to active state likely affects the state of engagement with the associated G-protein. However, details of this mechanism require additional research.

In order to check the validity of LT receptor structures obtained by our method, we further used 6 known BLT1 agonists (including 12-keto-LTB4) and 14 known BLT1 antagonists (including pranlukast) to independently perform binding simulations with BLT1 of the optimal 3D structure, from which the corresponding maximum GOLD scores were determined. The results are as shown in Figure 5 such that the agonists and antagonists are plotted in order of decreasing scores. The agonist group produced scores that were visibly higher than those of the antagonist group. By using the Wilcoxon signed rank test (which makes no assumptions on normality of distribution), the GOLD scores of the agonist group and the antagonist group were found to be significantly different ($P = 0.00046$). This strongly suggests that the binding pocket obtained by our search method selectively binds with the BLT1 agonists.

Next, in order to assess the quality of the agonist binding states, we have challenged the best 3D structure model with a set of 144 GPCR ligands to determine whether the structure indeed shows a good preference for BLT1 agonists. The ligand set included 6 BLT1 agonists (including 12-keto-LTB4), 14 BLT1 antagonists (including pranlukast), and 124 other GPCR ligands (32 against serotonin receptors, 17 against histamine receptors, 17 against adenosine receptors, 14 against prostanoid receptors, 10 against dopamine receptor, 8 against adrenoceptors, 8 against angiotensin receptors, 7 against cannabinoid receptors, and 11 against other GPCRs), as shown in Table 1. Being GPCR ligands, these ligands automatically have "drug-like" properties, so the only filtering on the ligand selection was to ensure that BLT1- and non-BLT1 ligands had a similar molecular mass distribution. The ligand-binding simulations were individually performed using the GOLD software. The overall docking results for the most highly ranked conformations are shown in Figure 6. Based on the GOLD binding score (higher indicates better binding), all 6 BLT1 agonists were ranked in the top 11. The enrichment curve in Figure 6 shows that there is immediate enrichment, and the results are good compared to related studies [22, 35]. This also suggests that the binding pocket obtained by our search method selectively binds with the BLT1 agonists.

Consequently, we have developed a search method capable of predicting the 3D structures of active forms of GPCRs, which is broadly consistent with known facts of the target proteins and is reasonably persuasive as a model.

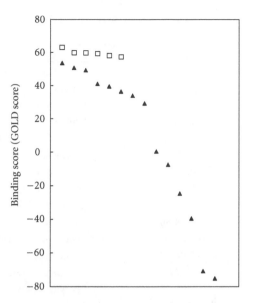

FIGURE 5: Ligand-receptor docking score (GOLD score) when docking with known agonists and antagonists of BLT1. Open squares show docking scores of known BLT1 agonists. Filled triangles show docking scores of known BLT1 antagonists. PubChem ID of BLT1 agonists (descending order): 5280492, 5280745, 5283156, 5280876, 5283129, 5280877. PubChem ID of BLT1 antagonists (descending order): 159476, 3081307, 6444688, 6439064, 6449854, 6540750, 132425, 6439436, 115100, 6442838, 204055, 177941, 196905, 192617.

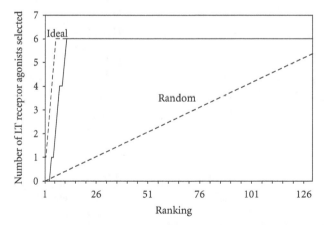

FIGURE 6: Enrichment curve for various GPCR ligands docked into the predicted active-state BLT1 structure.

5. Discussion and Conclusions

With no crystal structures of active-state GPCRs other than mutant rhodopsin [34], it is indispensable to develop a practical method to predict 3D structures of activated GPCRs from their sequence information. In this study, we proposed a method for finding one of the best structures of an activated GPCR at a level of accuracy acceptable to virtual screening. The method was validated using human leukotriene B4 receptor BLT1 as a sample GPCR. Our study demonstrated that the proposed method including homology modeling,

TABLE 1: Ligands used for evaluation.

No.	PubChem ID	Receptor name	Ligand	GLIDA ID	Molecular weight
1	5280492	Leukotriene receptor	Agonist	L000354	336
2	5280745	Leukotriene receptor	Agonist	L000056	352
3	5283156	Leukotriene receptor	Agonist	L000050	320
4	5280876	Leukotriene receptor	Agonist	L000049	334
5	5283129	Leukotriene receptor	Agonist		336
6	5280877	Leukotriene receptor	Agonist	L000055	366
7	159476	Leukotriene receptor	Antagonist	L001349	304
8	3081307	Leukotriene receptor	Antagonist	L011298	414
9	6444688	Leukotriene receptor	Antagonist	L002037	502
10	6439064	Leukotriene receptor	Antagonist	L002263	360
11	6449854	Leukotriene receptor	Antagonist	L000610	361
12	6540750	Leukotriene receptor	Antagonist	L015882	346
13	132425	Leukotriene receptor	Antagonist	L006854	358
14	6439436	Leukotriene receptor	Antagonist	L009515	536
15	115100	Leukotriene receptor	Antagonist	L000493	481
16	6442838	Leukotriene receptor	Antagonist	L001488	455
17	204055	Leukotriene receptor	Antagonist	L006005	537
18	177941	Leukotriene receptor	Antagonist	L001468	544
19	196905	Leukotriene receptor	Antagonist	L006944	539
20	192617	Leukotriene receptor	Antagonist	L011726	600
21	68555	Dopamine receptor	Agonist	L013392	307
22	55483	Dopamine receptor	Agonist	L013398	356
23	5760	Dopamine receptor	Agonist	L000836	303
24	3341	Dopamine receptor	Agonist	L000254	306
25	5281878	Dopamine receptor	Antagonist	L000188	434
26	4748	Dopamine receptor	Antagonist	L000919	403
27	28864	Dopamine receptor	Antagonist	L000349	338
28	5265	Dopamine receptor	Antagonist	L000569	395
29	2818	Dopamine receptor	Antagonist	L000195	327
30	5074	Dopamine receptor	Antagonist	L001003	477
31	4038180	Adrenoceptors	Agonist	L000090	309
32	3251	Adrenoceptors	Agonist	L000768	581
33	13109	Adrenoceptors	Agonist	L000895	312
34	2419	Adrenoceptors	Antagonist	G000137	385
35	3372	Adrenoceptors	Antagonist	L000257	437
36	5640	Adrenoceptors	Antagonist	L000080	401
37	47811	Adrenoceptors	Antagonist	L000474	314
38	2369	Adrenoceptors	Antagonist	L000125	307
39	2790	Histamine receptor	Antagonist	L000192	308
40	55482	Histamine receptor	Antagonist	L000593	441
41	41376	Histamine receptor	Antagonist	L000313	321
42	3219	Histamine receptor	Antagonist	L001093	302
43	5533	Histamine receptor	Antagonist	L000771	371
44	65895	Histamine receptor	Antagonist	L000115	380
45	3947	Histamine receptor	Antagonist	L000944	418
46	2678	Histamine receptor	Antagonist	L000655	388
47	3957	Histamine receptor	Antagonist	L000667	382
48	2342	Histamine receptor	Antagonist	L000844	404
49	4830	Histamine receptor	Antagonist	L000727	375
50	475096	Histamine receptor	Antagonist	L000558	440

Novel Computational Methodologies for Structural Modeling of Spacious Ligand Binding Sites of G-Protein-Coupled Receptors: Development and Application to Human Leukotriene B4 Receptor

99

TABLE 1: Continued.

No.	PubChem ID	Receptor name	Ligand	GLIDA ID	Molecular weight
51	4940	Histamine receptor	Antagonist	L000807	340
52	4066	Histamine receptor	Antagonist	L000704	322
53	3348	Histamine receptor	Antagonist	L000869	501
54	124488	Histamine receptor	Antagonist	L001444	608
55	5282450	Histamine receptor	Antagonist	L001378	392
56	132059	Serotonin receptor	Agonist	L000336	411
57	127728	Serotonin receptor	Agonist	L000873	465
58	197706	Serotonin receptor	Agonist	L000746	403
59	57347	Serotonin receptor	Agonist	L000797	415
60	219050	Serotonin receptor	Agonist	L001062	346
61	3408722	Serotonin receptor	Agonist	L000428	365
62	4440	Serotonin receptor	Agonist	L000432	335
63	56971	Serotonin receptor	Agonist	L000682	401
64	91273	Serotonin receptor	Agonist	L000863	383
65	71351	Serotonin receptor	Agonist	L001106	420
66	5311258	Serotonin receptor	Agonist	L000364	351
67	5761	Serotonin receptor	Agonist	L000352	323
68	5311097	Serotonin receptor	Agonist	L000365	351
69	37816	Serotonin receptor	Agonist	L000794	340
70	3292447	Serotonin receptor	Agonist	L001346	486
71	16362	Serotonin receptor	Antagonist	L000494	461
72	3559	Serotonin receptor	Antagonist	L000288	375
73	55216	Serotonin receptor	Antagonist	L000503	346
74	4431	Serotonin receptor	Antagonist	L000685	393
75	5073	Serotonin receptor	Antagonist	L000510	410
76	2726	Serotonin receptor	Antagonist	L000182	318
77	55752	Serotonin receptor	Antagonist	L000720	440
78	5684	Serotonin receptor	Antagonist	L000012	422
79	28693	Serotonin receptor	Antagonist	L000396	403
80	4106	Serotonin receptor	Antagonist	L000397	356
81	68848	Serotonin receptor	Antagonist	L000394	362
82	37459	Serotonin receptor	Antagonist	L000016	361
83	107780	Serotonin receptor	Antagonist	L000275	497
84	3378093	Serotonin receptor	Antagonist	L000538	520
85	1229	Serotonin receptor	Agonist	L000011	321
86	3654103	Serotonin receptor	Agonist	L000142	406
87	4585	Serotonin receptor	Antagonist	L000455	312
88	133083	Angiotensin receptor	Antagonist	L008043	490
89	114899	Angiotensin receptor	Antagonist	L000467	480
90	3749	Angiotensin receptor	Antagonist	L000319	428
91	60921	Angiotensin receptor	Antagonist	L000533	610
92	2541	Angiotensin receptor	Antagonist	L000156	440
93	5281037	Angiotensin receptor	Antagonist	L000248	424
94	60846	Angiotensin receptor	Antagonist	L000621	435
95	5833	Angiotensin receptor	Antagonist	L001221	416
96	472880	Follicle stimulating hormone	Agonist	L000979	352
97	125672	Melanocortin hormone	Agonist	L000639	342
98	6434259	Prostanoid receptor	Agonist	L000194	424
99	6436393	Prostanoid receptor	Agonist	L000160	350
100	5311027	Prostanoid receptor	Agonist	L001211	415

TABLE 1: Continued.

No.	PubChem ID	Receptor name	Ligand	GLIDA ID	Molecular weight
101	5311503	Prostanoid receptor	Agonist	L000634	384
102	119304	Prostanoid receptor	Agonist	L000151	368
103	5311493	Prostanoid receptor	Agonist	L024041	350
104	6433212	Prostanoid receptor	Agonist	L000478	354
105	6439022	Prostanoid receptor	Agonist	L000570	362
106	122021	Prostanoid receptor	Antagonist	L000153	459
107	160	Prostanoid receptor	Antagonist	L000705	354
108	5311213	Prostanoid receptor	Antagonist	L024043	442
109	50294	Prostanoid receptor	Antagonist	L001326	371
110	132836	Prostanoid receptor	Agonist	L000098	388
111	5311035	Prostanoid receptor	Agonist	L000150	408
112	164437	Adenosine receptor	Agonist	L000290	388
113	104795	Adenosine receptor	Agonist	L000437	308
114	164305	Adenosine receptor	Agonist	L001390	363
115	93205	Adenosine receptor	Agonist	L000708	385
116	123807	Adenosine receptor	Agonist	L000165	369
117	3086599	Adenosine receptor	Agonist	L001283	499
118	5311506	Adenosine receptor	Antagonist	L000893	337
119	1329	Adenosine receptor	Antagonist	L000233	304
120	393595	Adenosine receptor	Antagonist	L000629	403
121	176408	Adenosine receptor	Antagonist	L000548	345
122	5697	Adenosine receptor	Antagonist	L000963	428
123	64627	Adenosine receptor	Antagonist	L001406	356
124	1970	Adenosine receptor	Agonist	L001216	399
125	9576912	Adenosine receptor	Agonist	L001516	393
126	122246	Adenosine receptor	Agonist	L000951	521
127	5287468	Adenosine receptor	Agonist	L000058	526
128	123739	Adenosine receptor	Antagonist	L001123	386
129	16078	Cannabinoid receptor	Agonist	L000023	314
130	5281969	Cannabinoid receptor	Agonist	L000111	347
131	5689	Cannabinoid receptor	Agonist	L000626	426
132	5488671	Cannabinoid receptor	Agonist	L000222	395
133	104895	Cannabinoid receptor	Agonist	L000004	376
134	39860	Cannabinoid receptor	Agonist	L000994	372
135	5311257	Cannabinoid receptor	Antagonist	L000363	383
136	4172142	Melatonin receptor	Agonist	L000306	348
137	4004	Melatonin receptor	Antagonist	L001138	330
138	5311198	Melatonin receptor	Antagonist	L000326	376
139	6024	Calcitonin receptor	Agonist	L000905	396
140	91498	Calcitonin receptor	Agonist	L024117	421
141	446284	Metabotropic glutamate group I	Agonist	L001256	302
142	6324636	Metabotropic glutamate group I	Antagonist	L000366	323
143	5311262	Metabotropic glutamate group I	Antagonist	L000372	383
144	123885	GABA-B subtype 1	Antagonist	L000172	401

MD simulations, and evolutionary computing was able to provide the appropriate 3D structure of the activated leukotriene receptor to specifically dock with its agonists.

The first remarkable feature of this study is that the proposed method models GPCR thermal fluctuations on multiple time scales: the short-term heat fluctuation on the picosecond or nanosecond time scale and the rotational motions of TM helices on a longer time scale. This is a kind of coarse approximation compared with other methods like rigorous long-term MD simulations. However, the proposed method provides a significant reduction in computational cost when predicting the 3D structure of GPCRs and finally leads us to obtain the structure on common personal computers.

The second feature is that a machine learning technique including evolutionary computation and modularized ligand-binding simulations is employed for the structural prediction. Though to date, there have been methods using GAs to generate various conformations of ligands to explore a most suitable conformation in ligand-receptor docking [36], our method is the first approach using a GA employing a modularized ligand-binding simulation to find a best conformation on the receptor side.

However, some improvements might remain in the evaluation function of our evolutionary computing. Essentially, a scoring system capable of closely reflecting the binding-free energy would be desirable for the conformation evaluation. In our method, the GOLD scores produced by the GOLD software are directly used for the evaluation function. Although the GOLD scores are related with the values of the binding-free energy, they are not identical. We should accordingly investigate this issue in the future.

In addition, it should be noted that our method has a tendency to predict the central part of the 7-TM helical bundle, a spacious ligand binding site, with good quality. That is, small deviations would be observed in a spacious binding pocket area, whereas larger deviations would be observed in the distal section of the helices and even larger in the loop regions. This is because the evaluation function in evolutionary computing is naturally based on the ligand-binding score, closely related with the binding free energy. Hence, our method may predict another structure having energetically highly evaluated conformations of seven helices and the loops as a best structure if another search is performed. However, the structure of the spacious ligand-binding site would emerge again. We originally have the purpose of using the predicted 3D structure for virtual screening of candidate chemicals. Our method is able to provide 3D structure accurately enough for this purpose as shown in the case of the leukotriene receptor, since the structural information of the spacious binding pocket area is the most important for virtual screening.

We anticipate that parallelization of the proposed algorithm would contribute to an improvement in computation time. Future study designs will incorporate such. Furthermore, we plan to use GPCRs other than the leukotriene receptor to test the applicability and robustness of our search method. For such investigations, it would be important to carefully select an appropriate target GPCR. Based on sequence similarity within the seven TMs, GPCRs can be grouped into six families: the rhodopsin family A, the secretin family B, the glutamate receptor family C, the fungal pheromone family D, the cAMP receptor family E, and the frizzled/smoothened receptor family F [37]. In general, GPCRs belonging to class A fit the prediction, because all known GPCRs used as templates in homology modeling are classified into the class A. In contrast, other GPCRs having low amino-acid homology would need extra processing at the preliminary stage of homology modeling.

Acknowledgment

This work was in part supported by the Grant-in-Aid for Scientific Research from the Ministry of Education, Culture, Sports, Science, and Technology of Japan.

References

[1] V. L. Lowes, N. Y. Ip, and Y. H. Wong, "Integration of signals from receptor tyrosine kinases and G protein-coupled receptors," *NeuroSignals*, vol. 11, no. 1, pp. 5–19, 2002.

[2] K. J. Miller, B. J. Murphy, and M. A. Pelleymounter, "Central G-protein coupled receptors (GPCR)s as molecular targets for the treatment of obesity: assets, liabilities and development status," *Current Drug Targets*, vol. 3, no. 5, pp. 357–377, 2004.

[3] S. L. Parker, M. S. Parker, R. Sah, and F. Sallee, "Angiogenesis and rhodopsin-like receptors: a role for N-terminal acidic residues?" *Biochemical and Biophysical Research Communications*, vol. 335, no. 4, pp. 983–992, 2005.

[4] G. V. Rayasam, V. K. Tulasi, J. A. Davis, and V. S. Bansal, "Fatty acid receptors as new therapeutic targets for diabetes," *Expert Opinion on Therapeutic Targets*, vol. 11, no. 5, pp. 661–671, 2007.

[5] J. Drews, "Drug discovery: a historical perspective," *Science*, vol. 287, no. 5460, pp. 1960–1964, 2000.

[6] D. K. Vassilatis, J. G. Hohmann, H. Zeng et al., "The G protein-coupled receptor repertoires of human and mouse," *Proceedings of the National Academy of Sciences of the United States of America*, vol. 100, no. 8, pp. 4903–4908, 2003.

[7] K. Lundstrom, "Structural genomics and drug discovery: molecular pharmacology," *Journal of Cellular and Molecular Medicine*, vol. 11, no. 2, pp. 224–238, 2007.

[8] K. Palczewski, T. Kumasaka, T. Hori et al., "Crystal structure of rhodopsin: a G protein-coupled receptor," *Science*, vol. 289, no. 5480, pp. 739–745, 2000.

[9] V. Cherezov, D. M. Rosenbaum, M. A. Hanson et al., "High-resolution crystal structure of an engineered human β2-adrenergic G protein-coupled receptor," *Science*, vol. 318, no. 5854, pp. 1258–1265, 2007.

[10] D. M. Rosenbaum, V. Cherezov, M. A. Hanson et al., "GPCR engineering yields high-resolution structural insights into β2-adrenergic receptor function," *Science*, vol. 318, no. 5854, pp. 1266–1273, 2007.

[11] T. Warne, M. J. Serrano-Vega, J. G. Baker et al., "Structure of a β1-adrenergic G-protein-coupled receptor," *Nature*, vol. 454, no. 7203, pp. 486–491, 2008.

[12] V. P. Jaakola, M. T. Griffith, M. A. Hanson et al., "The 2.6 angstrom crystal structure of a human A2A adenosine receptor bound to an antagonist," *Science*, vol. 322, no. 5905, pp. 1211–1217, 2008.

[13] H. Wu, D. Wacker, M. Mileni et al., "Structure of the human κ-opioid receptor in complex with JDTic," *Nature*, vol. 485, pp. 327–332, 2012.

[14] A. Manglik, A. C. Kruse, T. S. Kobilka et al., "Crystal structure of the μ-opioid receptor bound to a morphinan antagonist," *Nature*, vol. 485, pp. 321–326, 2012.

[15] J. Moult, K. Fidelis, A. Kryshtafovych, B. Rost, and A. Tramontano, "Critical assessment of methods of protein structure prediction-Round VIII," *Proteins*, vol. 77, no. 9, pp. 1–4, 2009.

[16] M. Michino, E. Abola, C. L. Brooks III, J. S. Dixon, J. Moult,

and R. C. Stevens, "Community-wide assessment of GPCR structure modelling and ligand docking: GPCR Dock 2008," *Nature Reviews Drug Discovery*, vol. 8, no. 6, pp. 455–463, 2009.

[17] M. R. Whorton, M. P. Bokoch, S. G. F. Rasmussen et al., "A monomeric G protein-coupled receptor isolated in a high-density lipoprotein particle efficiently activates its G protein," *Proceedings of the National Academy of Sciences of the United States of America*, vol. 104, no. 18, pp. 7682–7687, 2007.

[18] C. Altenbach, A. K. Kusnetzow, O. P. Ernst, K. P. Hofmann, and W. L. Hubbell, "High-resolution distance mapping in rhodopsin reveals the pattern of helix movement due to activation," *Proceedings of the National Academy of Sciences of the United States of America*, vol. 105, no. 21, pp. 7439–7444, 2008.

[19] F. Fanelli and D. Dell'Orco, "Rhodopsin activation follows precoupling with transducin: inferences from computational analysis," *Biochemistry*, vol. 44, no. 45, pp. 14695–14700, 2005.

[20] B. Isin, A. J. Rader, H. K. Dhiman, J. Klein-Seetharaman, and I. Bahar, "Predisposition of the dark state of rhodopsin to functional changes in structure," *Proteins: Structure, Function and Genetics*, vol. 65, no. 4, pp. 970–983, 2006.

[21] M. Y. Niv, L. Skrabanek, M. Filizola, and H. Weinstein, "Modeling activated states of GPCRs: the rhodopsin template," *Journal of Computer-Aided Molecular Design*, vol. 20, no. 7-8, pp. 437–448, 2006.

[22] P. R. Gouldson, N. J. Kidley, R. P. Bywater et al., "Toward the active conformations of rhodopsin and the β-adrenergic receptor," *Proteins: Structure, Function and Genetics*, vol. 56, no. 1, pp. 67–84, 2004.

[23] H. Saitô, Y. Kawase, A. Kira et al., "Surface and dynamic structures of bacteriorhodopsin in a 2D crystal a distorted or disrupted lattice, as revealed by site-directed solid-state 13C NMR," *Photochemistry and Photobiology*, vol. 83, no. 2, pp. 253–262, 2007.

[24] Z. L. Lu and E. C. Hulme, "A network of conserved intramolecular contacts defines the off-state of the transmembrane switch mechanism in a seven-transmembrane receptor," *Journal of Biological Chemistry*, vol. 275, no. 8, pp. 5682–5686, 2000.

[25] L. J. Eshelman and J. D. Schaffer, "Real-coded genetic algorithms and interval-schemata," *Foundations of Genetic Algorithms*, vol. 2, pp. 187–202, 1993.

[26] I. Ono, H. Sato, and S. Kobayashi, "A real-coded genetic algorithm for function optimization using the unimodal normal distribution crossover," *The Japanese Society for Artificial Intelligence*, vol. 14, pp. 1146–1155, 1999.

[27] H. Sato, I. Ono, and S. Kobayashi, "A new generation alternation model of genetic algorithms and its assessment," *The Japanese Society for Artificial Intelligence*, vol. 12, pp. 734–744, 1997.

[28] J. D. Thompson, T. J. Gibson, F. Plewniak, F. Jeanmougin, and D. G. Higgins, "The CLUSTAL X windows interface: flexible strategies for multiple sequence alignment aided by quality analysis tools," *Nucleic Acids Research*, vol. 25, no. 24, pp. 4876–4882, 1997.

[29] U. Pieper, N. Eswar, B. M. Webb et al., "MODBASE, a database of annotated comparative protein structure models and associated resources," *Nucleic Acids Research*, vol. 37, no. 1, pp. D347–D354, 2009.

[30] A. Sali, "ModPipe: a software to calculate protein structure models," 2012, http://salilab.org/modpipe/.

[31] J. W. Ponder, "Tinker: a software for molecular design," 2012, http://dasher.wustl.edu/tinker/.

[32] A. Sabirsh, R. P. Bywater, J. Bristulf, C. Owman, and J. Z. Haeggström, "Residues from transmembrane helices 3 and 5 participate in leukotriene B4 binding to BLT1," *Biochemistry*, vol. 45, no. 18, pp. 5733–5744, 2006.

[33] M. L. Verdonk, J. C. Cole, M. J. Hartshorn, C. W. Murray, and R. D. Taylor, "Improved protein-ligand docking using GOLD," *Proteins: Structure, Function and Genetics*, vol. 52, no. 4, pp. 609–623, 2003.

[34] J. Standfuss, P. C. Edwards, A. D'Antona et al., "The structural basis of agonist-induced activation in constitutively active rhodopsin," *Nature*, vol. 471, no. 7340, pp. 656–660, 2011.

[35] C. Bissantz, P. Bernard, M. Hibert, and D. Rognan, "Protein-based virtual screening of chemical databases. II. Are homology models of G-protein coupled receptors suitable targets?" *Proteins: Structure, Function and Genetics*, vol. 50, no. 1, pp. 5–25, 2003.

[36] C. M. Oshiro, I. D. Kuntz, and J. S. Dixon, "Flexible ligand docking using a genetic algorithm," *Journal of Computer-Aided Molecular Design*, vol. 9, no. 2, pp. 113–130, 1995.

[37] J. C. Mobarec and M. Filizola, "Advances in the development and application of computational methodologies for structural modeling of G-protein-coupled receptors," *Expert Opinion on Drug Discovery*, vol. 3, no. 3, pp. 343–355, 2008.

12

A Novel Partial Sequence Alignment Tool for Finding Large Deletions

Taner Aruk,[1] Duran Ustek,[2] and Olcay Kursun[3]

[1] Scientific and Technological Research Council of Turkey (TUBITAK), 41470 Kocaeli, Turkey
[2] Genetics Department, Institute for Experimental Medicine, Istanbul University, 34093 Istanbul, Turkey
[3] Computer Engineering Department, Istanbul University, 34320 Istanbul, Turkey

Correspondence should be addressed to Olcay Kursun, okursun@istanbul.edu.tr

Academic Editors: M. L. Bauman, S. Mastana, and D. E. Wells

Finding large deletions in genome sequences has become increasingly more useful in bioinformatics, such as in clinical research and diagnosis. Although there are a number of publically available next generation sequencing mapping and sequence alignment programs, these software packages do not correctly align fragments containing deletions larger than one kb. We present a fast alignment software package, BinaryPartialAlign, that can be used by wet lab scientists to find long structural variations in their experiments. For BinaryPartialAlign, we make use of the Smith-Waterman (SW) algorithm with a binary-search-based approach for alignment with large gaps that we called partial alignment. BinaryPartialAlign implementation is compared with other straightforward applications of SW. Simulation results on mtDNA fragments demonstrate the effectiveness (runtime and accuracy) of the proposed method.

1. Introduction

In bioinformatics, sequence alignment is a way of arranging the sequences of DNA, RNA, or protein to identify regions of similarity that may be a consequence of functional, structural, or evolutionary relationships between the sequences [1]. Next Generation sequencing (NGS) technology produces terabytes of sequencing data in an inexpensive way [2]. However, among these sequences, most NGS software such as Path, UGENE, JAligner, SSEARCH, Water, and others based on the well-known Smith-Waterman algorithm (SW) [3–5] is designed to align sequences with small gaps and may not be suitable when large deletions are present. Finding such large deletions (and the related counterpart, finding large insertions) has become increasingly more useful in bioinformatics [6, 7]. It has been long known that chromosomal deletions can lead to developmental and malformation disorders [6, 8, 9] and have a significant role both in the genetics of complex traits such as autism [10] and in genome evolution [11, 12].

In the Smith-Waterman algorithm, to find the optimal local alignment between a query and a reference sequence, a scoring system including a set of specified gap penalties is used. However, when a sequence subjected to a large deletion is used as a query sequence, its alignment with the reference is problematic because the query sequence must be first divided into two parts: the one before the deletion that we will refer to as the "former part" and the one after the deletion that we will call the "latter part" of the query (Figure 1). Otherwise, the classical SW algorithm encounters with the large deletion, and then it will start using gaps. As each gap used contributes penalty points to the alignment score, SW cannot bridge these two parts to be aligned with far apart loci in the reference sequence, and, for example, it can align not only the former part of the query but also an intermix of gaps and some nucleotides from the latter part that match the deleted fragment by chance. Therefore, the basic Smith-Waterman algorithm has a big error in the estimated deletion position; we will refer to this error as EDPE (Estimated Deletion Position Error), which is measured in number of bases (bp).

The paper is organized as follows. The classical SW method is explained in Section 2 along with an example demonstrating that it fails when query sequences have large deletions. In Section 3, with a small modification SW is used in an incremental way (called IncrementalPartialAlign). Then,

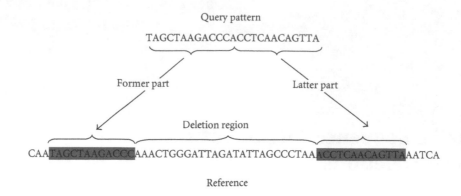

FIGURE 1: A demonstrative example of large deletion.

in Section 4, to reduce its long runtime for completing many repetitions of SW alignment runs, we propose a better partial sequence alignment method that we called BinaryPartialAlign. In Section 5, we present our experimental simulations on mtDNA fragments and we conclude in Section 6.

2. The Smith-Waterman Alignment Algorithm

The Smith-Waterman (SW) algorithm [3] is an algorithm for performing local sequence alignment, considering segments of all possible lengths to optimize the similarity measure (score). A typical use of SW needs a query sequence as input to be searched within a longer reference sequence, for example, the mithecondrial (mtDNA) reference [13]. To identify where the best match/alignment takes place, SW utilizes a scoring matrix to assign a score to the corresponding nucleotide pairs of the query and the relevant fragment of the reference (it also includes gap penalties). After finding the best alignment (possibly with gaps), it gives the similarity ratio as the fraction (percentage) of bases in the query sequence that were matched with the reference.

Let l_{former} and l_{latter} denote the lengths of the former and the latter parts of the query sequence. Also let $[a, b]$ denote the fragment from base position a to the base position b in the reference that best aligns with the former part of the query (of course, $a < b$). Similarly, let $[c, d]$ denote the fragment from base position c to the base position d in the reference that best aligns with the latter part of the query ($c < d$). For the sake of simplicity, let us assume $b < c$ (and in fact $b \ll c$ for the large deletions). Then, it follows that $[b + 1, \ c - 1]$ is the part of the sequence subjected to the deletion (and thus not visible in the query sequence). The length of the deletion can be defined as

$$l_{deletion} = |[b + 1, \ c - 1]| = c - b - 1. \tag{1}$$

In Figure 2, we give an example with 40 bp query pattern with a large deletion at base position 27 (i.e., some large fragment was actually removed from between what now appears to be the 27th and the 28th nucleotides). That is, the first 27 bp of the query pattern (the former part) relates to the fragment of the reference from 1401st to 1427th nucleotides, and its last 13 bp (the latter part of the query) is from 2071st

to 2083rd nucleotides of the reference sequence. This implies that there was a deletion of length $2071 - 1427 - 1 = 643$ (1).

We aligned the query pattern with basic SW to find these two fragments and the location of the large deletion. We used BLOSUM 62 [14] as the scoring matrix, the open gap penalty of 10, the extend gap penalty of 0.5. As shown in Figure 2, the classical SW could not find the large deletion. Instead of 27, it returns 37 bases mapped in the optimal local alignment. This shows that SW has a large estimated deletion position error (EDPE) of 10 bp.

3. The Incremental Partial Align Algorithm

To alleviate this problem in a most basic manner, we used SW in an incremental approach and we named this method "IncrementalPartialAlign". This method takes four input parameters, query sequence, reference sequence, similarity ratio threshold, and minimum sequence length. After aligning the query, if the similarity ratio is found to be below the given threshold, considering that this can be due to the presence of a large gap (small gaps would be tolerated by the classical SW anyway), we try splitting the query into a former and a latter part in all possible ways. We start with the shortest possible former part, the length of which is determined by the minimum sequence length. For example, if the minimum sequence length parameter is 20, we take the first 20 bases of the query pattern. Starting with such a short former part results in a high similarity ratio, but then, we repeatedly increase its length (one by one) until the similarity ratio becomes smaller than the threshold value, at which position we assume that the deletion starts. Then we align the remaining (latter) part of the query pattern with the reference (see Algorithm 1).

The query pattern used in Figure 2, for which the classical SW failed, was also aligned using this IncrementalPartialAlign method (see Figure 3). IncrementalPartialAlign found the deletion at the 27th base correctly (EDPE = 0). The former part is correctly mapped to the 1401st and 1427th, and the latter part is correctly mapped to the 2071st and 2083rd base positions of the reference sequence. However, even though the query pattern was very short (designated for a demonstration only), IncrementalPartialAlign takes 187 msecs for the extensively repetitive use of SW. For longer

Query pattern:

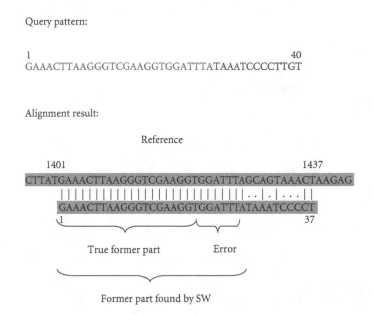

FIGURE 2: Failure of the classical Smith-Waterman alignment in detecting the large deletion at base position 27. In this simulated experiment, the former part is actually known to be the first 27 nucleotides printed in blue in the "Query pattern". In "Alignment result", bases shown in red do actually belong to the latter part but were aligned together with the nucleotides of the former part of the query. SW gives the deletion position estimate of 37, which results in an EDPE of 10 bp.

Query pattern:

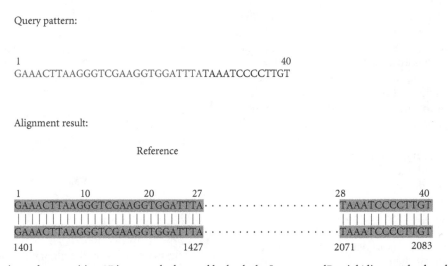

FIGURE 3: The large deletion at base position 27 is correctly detected by both the IncrementalPartialAlign method and the BinaryPartialAlign method.

query patterns (especially when the deletion is present towards the end of the query pattern), alignment would take much longer as many more iterations of SW are used. We propose to modify it using a binary search-based approach [15] that we named BinaryPartialAlign.

4. Proposed Partial Alignment Method Based on Binary Search

Having seen that the classical SW fails in finding large deletions and IncrementalPartialAlign takes more iterations and long time for completing many repetitions of SW runs, we

developed a partial sequence alignment method that we called BinaryPartialAlign. The BinaryPartialAlign method uses the same set of four input parameters (query sequence, reference sequence, similarity ratio threshold, and minimum sequence length) as the IncrementalPartialAlign method does. Again, similarly, BinaryPartialAlign is also based on repetitive use of SW. However, unlike IncrementalPartialAlign, it shifts the boundary between the former and latter parts by more than one base in every iteration based on an approach that resembles binary search.

The binary search is a fast way to search a key within a sorted array. Firstly we check the element in the middle. If the key is equal to that, the search is finished. If the key is less than

```
Input
reference sequence: r,
query pattern: q,
minimum sequence length: m,
threshold similarity ratio: t
Output
location(index) of deletion: f
sr = SWSR of r and q
//SWSR stands for Smith-Waterman similarity ratio of r and q;
if sr > t then
    exit;         // no deletion
else
    sr is SWSR of r and [q0, qm];
    iteration = 1;
    f = m + iteration;
    while sr > t
            sr is SWSR of r and [q0, qf];
            iteration ++;
    end while
        return f;
end if
```

ALGORITHM 1: IncrementalPartialAlign pseudocode.

the middle element, we perform a binary search for the key within the first half. Otherwise (if it is greater), we perform a binary search within the second half. This procedure is demonstrated for searching 96 in a sample integer sequence in Figure 4. Binary search is an efficient search algorithm with a time complexity of $O(\log_2 n)$. Given n elements to search within, the binary search method takes at most $\log_2 n$ iterations (i.e., makes $\log_2 n$ comparisons with the key in the worst case, with each comparison reducing the search space to its half).

After aligning the query, if the similarity ratio is above the given threshold, similar to IncrementalPartialAlign, we conclude that there is no deletion in this query and terminate the algorithm. Otherwise, in contrast to the IncrementalPartialAlign, we divide the query pattern into two equal length parts: first half is called the former part and the second half is called the latter part of the query as before. In other words, let l_{query} be the total length of the query; we start with a former part and a latter part of length $l_{\text{query}}/2$.

Then, we align both parts separately and get two similarity ratios to compare with the given similarity ratio threshold. If both of them are above the threshold, we assume that deletion position is found and terminate the algorithm with the current former and latter parts as the output.

If only one of the similarity ratios is greater than the threshold, we lengthen the part with the bigger similarity ratio (and thus shorten the other one) by

$$k = \frac{l_{\text{query}}}{2^{i+1}}, \qquad (2)$$

where i is the number of the current iteration (the algorithm starts i with an initial value of 1 and increments it until both ratios go above the threshold; see Algorithm 2).

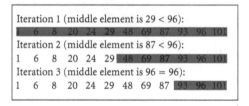

FIGURE 4: Binary search demonstration. The searched item is 96. The binary search finds the item in 3 comparisons; however, a sequential search would take 11 comparisons.

To demonstrate the alignment procedure of BinaryPartialAlign, we used the same query pattern as in demonstration of the classical SW and IncrementalPartialAlign methods. BinaryPartialAlign correctly found the deletion at position 27 with an EDPE of 0 (see Figure 3).

The steps taken by the algorithm can be outlined as follows. Firstly, the query is split into two subsequences with lengths 20 and 20 (former and latter parts, resp.). Then, we increase the length of the former part as its similarity ratio is above the threshold and it is below for the latter part. We obtain 30–10 splits this time. Then, the former part has a similarity ratio below the threshold, which means that the latter part is lengthened. Thus, we obtain 25–15 splits. Then procedure is iterated similarly and stops at 27–13 splits, a perfect partial alignment with EDPE = 0.

When we aligned the query pattern with IncrementalPartialAlign, the alignment time was 187 msecs, which improves to 109 msecs with BinaryPartialAlign. If the query pattern is long and a large deletion occurred towards the end of the query, the alignment would take much more time with IncrementalPartialAlign; however, the BinaryPartialAlign method is not badly affected by neither the position of deletion or the length of the query as it is an $O(\log_2 n)$ algorithm.

```
Input
reference sequence: r,
query pattern: q,
minimum sequence length: m,
threshold similarity ratio: t
Output
location(index) of deletion: f
sr = SWSR of r and q
//SWSR stands for Smith-Waterman similarity ratio of r and q
l is length of the query pattern;
if sr > t then
    exit;        // no deletion
else
    i = 1;       // iteration
    f = 1/2;
    repeat
        sr1 = SWSR of r and [q₀, q_f];
        sr2 = SWSR of r and [q_{f+1}, q_l];
        k = 1 × (1/2)^{(i + 1)} ;
        if sr1 > t and sr2 < t then
          f = f + k;
        else if sr1 < t and sr2 > t then
          f = f - k;
        else if sr1 < t and sr2 > t then
          exit;
        end if
        i++;
    until (sr1 ≤ t and sr2 ≤ t)
    return f;
end if
```

ALGORITHM 2: BinaryPartialAlign pseudocode.

TABLE 1: Alignment times of BinaryPartialAlign, IncrementalPartialAlign, and classical SW.

	Alignment time (mean ± standard deviation in msec)			Base error in estimated deletion position (mean ± standard deviation in bp)		
Sequence length	BinaryPartialAlign	IncrementalPartialAlign	Classical SW	BinaryPartialAlign	IncrementalPartialAlign	Classical SW
100–199	226.7 ± 95.2	3149.0 ± 2460.3	106.6 ± 22.4	9.8 ± 12.3	12.9 ± 11.1	38.6 ± 40.6
200–299	418.3 ± 148.0	6896.9 ± 5484.0	176.1 ± 21.6	13.1 ± 12.3	23.7 ± 20.3	67.1 ± 73.0
300–399	611.0 ± 203.1	16295.1 ± 13346.4	241.4 ± 21.1	21.8 ± 22.8	37.1 ± 30.2	76.0 ± 96.8
400–499	741.6 ± 237.1	28763.0 ± 20988.4	247.0 ± 63.4	29.3 ± 27.9	51.9 ± 33.4	85.9 ± 95.8
500–599	798.8 ± 259.6	38638.7 ± 29724.3	284.3 ± 85.2	37.4 ± 38.9	69.4 ± 50.3	92.2 ± 99.5
600–699	932.9 ± 327.4	60640.8 ± 44106.5	321.3 ± 106.3	41.5 ± 41.1	83.2 ± 53.2	107.6 ± 123.9
700–799	1177.9 ± 413.2	71953.8 ± 59874.8	359.1 ± 128.7	46.2 ± 35.7	94.0 ± 59.8	125.4 ± 167.5
800–899	1241.5 ± 432.4	81953.1 ± 64055.2	395.1 ± 148.0	51.6 ± 46.7	102.9 ± 59	143.7 ± 205.3
900–999	1366.1 ± 482.5	117779.0 ± 84950.1	679.1 ± 33.6	50.9 ± 52.1	127.2 ± 72.5	242.4 ± 285.8

5. Simulation Results

In order to test and compare these three alignment techniques, the classical SW, IncrementalPartialAlign, and BinaryPartialAlign were implemented in Java language using the JAligner package [16]. These executables are made publicly available on the site http://ce.istanbul.edu.tr/bioinformatics/PartialAlignment/.

We performed our simulations using 900 samples obtained from the mtDNA reference sequence [13]. Two subsequences selected from the mtDNA reference sequence were concatenated to form a single query pattern. The lengths and positions of these mtDNA subsequences were selected randomly. This way, we created query patterns with lengths varying in the range of 100 to 999 bases. Specifically, to evaluate the effect of the query pattern length, we created 10 length intervals: 100–199, 200–299, ..., and 900–999. We formed 100 query patterns from each length interval.

We aligned these 900 sequences with the classical SW, IncrementalPartialAlign, and BinaryPartialAlign. For each length interval, we calculated the average and standard deviation of alignment times and EDPE (estimated deletion position error), which are shown in Table 1. We obtained the runtimes of these three methods using single thread on an Intel Core 2 Duo CPU with 2.50 GHz clock and 3 GB RAM. As clearly seen in Table 1, the BinaryPartialAlign method gives the lowest EDPE within shorter runtime than IncrementalPartialAlign. The classical SW is the fastest one but with a very high EDPE.

6. Conclusions

Sequence database searching is among the most important and challenging tasks in bioinformatics. One special case of sequence searching is when large deletions are present in the query fragments, which is called partial or large-gap alignment. Partial alignment has become a need in bioinformatics as they are associated with developmental and malformation disorders, emergence of complex genetic traits, and genome evolution. Although the best choice of sequence search algorithm is Smith-Waterman's, if a sequence is subjected to a large deletion, to find the deletion location with the classical Smith-Waterman (SW) algorithm is inconclusive. In order to handle this problem, one basic approach is to use SW for various splits of the query pattern repeatedly in a systematic, incremental way. This approach that we called the IncrementalPartialAlign method works better, but, for longer query patterns (especially when the deletion is present towards the end of the query pattern), the procedure would take much longer time as it has many more iterations of SW that are used. Therefore, we proposed the BinaryPartialAlign method based on the binary search idea.

Considering the (partial) alignment time and error in estimated deletion position, the BinaryPartialAlign method gives better results than both IncrementalPartialAlign and the classical SW. Despite the runtime of the IncrementalPartialAlign method is badly affected by the query length and where the deletion occurs within the query, being an $O(\log_2 n)$ algorithm, the proposed BinaryPartialAlign is more robust to these factors.

The executable application, a short user-manual, and the query sequences used for simulations are made publicly available on the site http://ce.istanbul.edu.tr/bioinformatics/PartialAlignment/. These tools will be beneficial to researchers for finding large deletions in investigating their role in the genetics of complex traits and in genome evolution.

References

[1] D. M. Mount, *Bioinformatics: Sequence and Genome Analysis*, Cold Spring Harbor Laboratory Press, Cold Spring Harbor, NY, USA, 2nd edition, 2004.

[2] M. Margulies, M. Egholm, W. E. Altman et al., "Genome sequencing in microfabricated high-density picolitre reactors," *Nature*, vol. 437, no. 7057, pp. 376–380, 2005, Erratum in: *Nature*, vol. 441, no. 7089, pp. 120, 2006.

[3] T. F. Smith and M. S. Waterman, "Identification of common molecular subsequences," *Journal of Molecular Biology*, vol. 147, no. 1, pp. 195–197, 1981.

[4] T. Rognes, "Faster Smith-Waterman database searches with inter-sequence SIMD parallelisation," *BMC Bioinformatics*, vol. 12, article 221, 2011.

[5] M. A. Muratet, "Comparing the speed and accuracy of the Smith and Waterman algorithm as implemented by MPSRCH with the BLAST and FASTA heuristics for sequence similarity searching," *The Scientific World Journal*, vol. 2, no. S2, pp. 21–22, 2002.

[6] D. F. Conrad, T. D. Andrews, N. P. Carter, M. E. Hurles, and J. K. Pritchard, "A high-resolution survey of deletion polymorphism in the human genome," *Nature Genetics*, vol. 38, no. 1, pp. 75–81, 2006.

[7] K. Ye, M. H. Schulz, Q. Long, R. Apweiler, and Z. Ning, "Pindel: a pattern growth approach to detect break points of large deletions and medium sized insertions from paired-end short reads," *Bioinformatics*, vol. 25, no. 21, pp. 2865–2871, 2009.

[8] R. D. Schmickel, "Contiguous gene syndromes: a component of recognizable syndromes," *Journal of Pediatrics*, vol. 109, no. 2, pp. 231–241, 1986.

[9] R. J. Gardner and G. R. Sutherland, *Chromosomes Abnormalities and Genetic Counseling*, Oxford University Press, Oxford, UK, 2004.

[10] C. E. Yu, G. Dawson, J. Munson et al., "Presence of large deletions in kindreds with autism," *American Journal of Human Genetics*, vol. 71, no. 1, pp. 100–115, 2002.

[11] D. A. Petrov, "Mutational equilibrium model of genome size evolution," *Theoretical Population Biology*, vol. 61, no. 4, pp. 531–544, 2002.

[12] M. V. Olson, "When less is more: gene loss as an engine of evolutionary change," *American Journal of Human Genetics*, vol. 64, no. 1, pp. 18–23, 1999.

[13] http://www.ncbi.nlm.nih.gov/pubmed/7219534?dopt=Citation.

[14] http://www.ncbi.nlm.nih.gov/Class/FieldGuide/BLOSUM62.txt.

[15] T. H. Cormen, C. E. Leiserson, R. L. Rivest, and C. Stein, *Introduction to Algorithms*, MIT Press and McGraw-Hill, 2nd edition, 2001.

[16] http://jaligner.sourceforge.net/.

NCK2 Is Significantly Associated with Opiates Addiction in African-Origin Men

Zhifa Liu,[1] Xiaobo Guo,[1,2] Yuan Jiang,[3] and Heping Zhang[1]

[1] *Department of Biostatistics, Yale University School of Public Health, New Haven, CT 06520, USA*
[2] *Department of Statistical Science, School of Mathematics and Computational Science, Sun Yat-sen University, Guangzhou 510275, China*
[3] *Department of Statistics, Oregon State University, Corvallis, OR 97331, USA*

Correspondence should be addressed to Heping Zhang; heping.zhang@yale.edu

Academic Editors: J. Ma and B. Shen

Substance dependence is a complex environmental and genetic disorder with significant social and medical concerns. Understanding the etiology of substance dependence is imperative to the development of effective treatment and prevention strategies. To this end, substantial effort has been made to identify genes underlying substance dependence, and in recent years, genome-wide association studies (GWASs) have led to discoveries of numerous genetic variants for complex diseases including substance dependence. Most of the GWAS discoveries were only based on single nucleotide polymorphisms (SNPs) and a single dichotomized outcome. By employing both SNP- and gene-based methods of analysis, we identified a strong (odds ratio = 13.87) and significant (P value = $1.33E-11$) association of an SNP in the *NCK2* gene on chromosome 2 with opiates addiction in African-origin men. Codependence analysis also identified a genome-wide significant association between *NCK2* and comorbidity of substance dependence (P value = $3.65E-08$) in African-origin men. Furthermore, we observed that the association between the *NCK2* gene (P value = $3.12E-10$) and opiates addiction reached the gene-based genome-wide significant level. In summary, our findings provided the first evidence for the involvement of *NCK2* in the susceptibility to opiates addiction and further revealed the racial and gender specificities of its impact.

1. Introduction

Substance dependence is believed to result from a combination of genetic and environmental factors. Since substance dependence is a chronic brain disease, with high relapse rates, it causes serious social, economic, and medical consequences [1–3]. The World Health Organization (WHO) and the United Nations Office on Drugs and Crime (UNODC) reported that opiates dependence is associated with a high risk of HIV infection when opiates are injected using contaminated injection equipment [4]. Paulozzi et al. in 2006 reported that the number of deaths which involved prescription opioid analgesics increased from 2,900 in 1999 to at least 7,500 in 2004, an increase of 160% in just 5 years [5]. All available evidence indicated that the increasing numbers of deaths are significantly correlated to the increasing use of prescription drugs, especially opioid painkillers, among

people during the working years of life. While exposure to drugs is the prerequisite for addiction, the most important question is as follows: who will be addicted after the exposure? Genes are believed to be a major factor, although it is most likely that there are multiple genes as well as gene-environment interactions. For this reason, understanding the genetic mechanisms behind vulnerability to drug addiction is critical to improve the quality of overall health and life.

Linkage and genome-wide association studies (GWASs) have implicated many regions and genes for dependence on alcohol, tobacco, and opiates. GABRA2, CHRM2, ADH4, PKNOX2, GABRG3, TAS2R16, SNCA, OPRK1, and PDYN have all been associated with alcohol dependence with various degrees of replication [6–21]. Associations of other candidate alcohol dependence genes, such as KIAA0040, ALDH1A1, and MANBA [18, 20, 22–25], remain to be confirmed. Several groups reported CHRNA5, CHRNA3,

CHRNB4, and CSMD1 to be associated with nicotine dependence [26–34]. Meanwhile, recent studies also reported that a group of genes, such as OPRM1 [35–37], OPRD1, OPRK1 [21, 38, 39], HTR1B [40], SLC6A4 [41], GABRG2 [42], and BDNF [43], to be associated or in linkage with opiates addiction.

Complex diseases may involve heterogeneous genetic effects in different ethnic and gender groups [7, 44–47]. Luo et al. [44] reported that African-origin smokers become dependent at a lower threshold (number of cigarettes per day) than European-origin smokers. Hartel et al. [46] found that men are more vulnerable to addiction when compared to women. In addition, Chen et al. [7] revealed that *PKNOX2* is associated with drug addiction in European-origin women. These examples underscore the necessity to consider demographic or even other covariates in genetic association studies.

Many of the reported genetic variants have been identified through single SNP association tests. Despite many of the successes, a single SNP tends to have a small effect, and the single SNP-based association tests require a very stringent significance level, which is likely a key factor to the so-called "missing heritability" problem [48, 49]. To overcome some of these limitations, gene-based analysis [50–52] has emerged to jointly analyze the SNPs within genes. Gene-based methods are less affected by the heterogeneity of a single locus; hence the results may be more robust across populations [53], which increases the likelihood of replication. Hence, we performed both single SNP-based and gene-based association analyses for the data from the Study of Addiction: Genetics and Environment (SAGE) [6] which includes well-characterized phenotypic data on substance dependence including addiction to nicotine, alcohol, marijuana, cocaine, opiates, and other drugs. In our analysis, we find a genome-wide significant association of *NCK2* gene on chromosome 2 with opiates dependence in African-origin men at both the SNP and gene levels. *NCK2* is a member of NCK family of adaptor proteins, which is associated with tyrosine-phosphorylated growth factor receptors of their cellular substrates [54]. However, to the best of our knowledge, *NCK2* has not been reported to be associated with any drug addiction outcomes in humans.

2. Materials and Methods

Phenotypes for multisubstance dependency and genome-wide SNP data from SAGE [6] were downloaded from dbGaP (http://www.ncbi.nlm.nih.gov/gap). SAGE is a large case-control association study which investigates the genetic variants for drug addiction. The samples were collected from three large-scale genome-wide association studies: Collaborative Study on the Genetic of Alcoholism (COGA), the Family Study of Cocaine Dependence (FSCD), and the Collaborative Genetic Study of Nicotine Dependence (COGEND) [16, 44, 55, 56]. The original data set contains 4,121 subjects with six categories of substance dependence data: addiction to alcohol, cocaine, marijuana, nicotine, opiates, and other drugs. Lifetime dependence on these six substances is diagnosed by the Diagnostic and Statistical Manual of Mental Disorders, Fourth Edition (DSM-IV). The genotyping was

TABLE 1: Descriptive statistics of the key variables in the SAGE dataset stratified by sex and race.

	Black men	White men	Black women	White women	Overall
n	535	1131	568	1393	3627
Age (SD) yr.	40.9 (8.2)	38.7 (10.3)	39.7 (6.7)	38.2 (9.1)	39 (9.1)
Alcohol (%)	62.1	62.3	39.4	31.1	46.7
Cocaine (%)	46.4	27.3	36.3	12.5	25.8
Marijuana (%)	25.4	25.2	13.7	8.7	17.1
Nicotine (%)	47.5	46.7	47.7	41.1	44.8
Opiates (%)	8.2	9.9	6.2	4.8	7.1
Other drugs (%)	11.4	18	6.5	9.4	11.9
No drug (%)	27.1	31	38.9	50.1	39

performed by the illumina Human 1 M platform. In this study, we followed a quality control/quality assurance process similar to previous analyses [7, 57]. Individuals with call rates <90% and SNPs with minor allele frequency MAF <1% were excluded from the analysis. The P value for the Hardy-Weinberg equilibrium was set up by >0.0001. These steps reduced the level of noise in genotypes and increased the efficiency of analysis. There are 60 duplicate genotype samples and 9 individuals with ethnic backgrounds other than African origin or European origin. All of those individuals were removed from the subject list. Finally, there were a total of 3,627 unrelated samples with 859,185 autosomal SNPs for our final analysis. To alleviate the confounding by population substructure, we stratified the sample by race and sex. Finally, there are four sub-samples: 1,393 European-origin women, 1,131 European-origin men, 568 African-origin women and 535 African-origin men. The distribution of subjects diagnosed with lifetime dependence on substances in each of the six categories: nicotine, alcohol, marijuana, cocaine, opiates, or other drugs are presented in Table 1.

3. Methods

Figure 1 displays the flow chart of our analytic strategy, and the details of the association analysis methods are described later.

3.1. Statistical Analysis for Single Trait. The SNP-based association is performed by the standard allelic test and logistic regression to obtain the P values for individual SNPs, and PLINK software (version 1.07) was used for analysis [58]. Meanwhile, a list of SNP pairs in linkage disequilibrium (LD) ($r^2 > 0.2$) is calculated for the gene-based association test.

For the gene-based analysis, we used the open-source tool: Knowledge-Based Mining System for Genome-Wide Genetic Studies (KGG, version 2.0)—based on the SNP association test results and LD files produced by PLINK. The procedure was performed as the following. We first calculate the effective number m_e of independent P value among m SNPs within a gene. Then, we sort the SNPs and calculate the effective number $m_{e(j)}$ of independent P-values among the

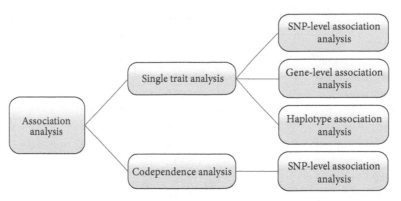

FIGURE 1: The pipeline of the association analysis.

top j significant SNPs. Finally, the modified Simes test [51] was employed to obtain a gene-based P value as follows,

$$P_G = \text{Min}\left(\frac{m_e P_{(j)}}{m_{e(j)}}\right), \qquad (1)$$

where $P_{(j)}$ is the jth most significant among the m SNPs within a gene. We refer the interested readers to [51] for details.

In the gene-based method, SNPs within 20 kilo bases (kb) $5'$ upstream and 10 kilo bases (kb) $3'$ downstream of a gene's coding regions [59] were assigned to the gene. In addition, we included other SNPs if they are in strong LD ($r^2 > 0.9$) with the initially mapped SNPs within the gene [60].

Since there are about 20,000 protein coding genes in human genome, we used $0.05/20,000 = 2.5 \times 10^{-6}$ as the genome-wide significance threshold for the gene-based association test. In contrast, we used 5.0×10^{-8} as the genome-wide significance threshold for the SNP-based association test [61].

3.2. Codependence Association Analysis. Although logistic regression is commonly used to study a binary outcome, it is not suitable to evaluate comorbidity involving multiple outcomes. We use a nonparametric association test based on Kendall's tau [62] to study the comorbidity. The Kendall's tau-based association test proceeds as follows.

Suppose that we observe a p-dimensional vector of traits $Y_i = (Y_i^{(1)}, \ldots, Y_i^{(p)})^T$, genotype G_i, and a q-dimensional vector of covariates $Z_i = (Z_i^{(1)}, \ldots, Z_i^{(q)})^T$ for the ith subject in a population-based study with n subjects, and $\{(Y_i, G_i, Z_i) : i = 1, \ldots, n\}$ are independent samples. For subjects i and j, let Y_i and Y_j be their vectors of traits, respectively, and analogously, G_i and G_j and Z_i and Z_j are their genotypes and covariates. Generalized from Kendall's tau, a U statistic is defined to measure the association between Y and G as follows:

$$U = \binom{n}{2}^{-1} \sum_{i<j} \left(Y_i - Y_j\right)\left(G_i - G_j\right). \qquad (2)$$

Without considering the covariates and conditioning on all phenotypes, U follows an asymptotically normal distribution

in the absence of association [63]. To accommodate covariates, a weighted U statistic has been developed [64, 65]. We refer to Jiang and Zhang [64] for a detailed description of the method. For the purpose of comparison, we present the results with and without considering age as the covariate. Recall that our analysis is stratified by ethnicity and gender.

4. Results

4.1. Association Analysis at SNP Level. Table 2 summarizes the top four significant SNPs (with $P < 1.0 \times 10^{-4}$) in gene *NCK2* on chromosome 2 (2q12) for opiates dependence in African-origin men. We identified a genome-wide significant SNP (rs2377339 with $P = 1.33 \times 10^{-11}$) for the opiates dependence in African-origin men by the allelic test. Logistic regression also yielded strong evidence for the association between the SNP rs2377339 ($P = 1.01 \times 10^{-7}$) and opiates dependence although the P-value did not reach the genome-wide significance threshold. In addition, Table 2 presents the association results for the other five addictions with the four candidate SNPs. None of the four SNPs appeared significantly associated with the other five substance addictions.

4.2. Association Analysis at Gene Level. The gene-based association results are displayed in the last two rows of Table 2. Specifically, we included 39 SNPs in NCK2. The P values from the gene-*NCK2*-based tests that were obtained through the standard allelic test and logistic regression are 3.12×10^{-10} and 2.70×10^{-6}, respectively. The gene-based P value from the standard allelic test reached the genome-wide significance at gene level. The gene-based P value through logistic regression is very close to the gene-based genome-wide significance level. Therefore, both methods provided significant evidence that supports the association between the *NCK2* gene and opiates dependence in African-origin men. For the addiction of the other five substances in African-origin men, nicotine dependence had the most significant association with the *NCK2* gene ($P = 9.56 \times 10^{-3}$).

4.3. Haplotypes Analysis. We also examined association of haplotypes with opiate addiction in *NCK2* region. Figure 2 displays the linkage disequilibrium (LD) heat map of 14 SNPs

TABLE 2: Association of the most significant SNPs in the NCK2 gene with the six substances dependence in African-origin sen.

Gene	SNP	Method	Alcohol	Cocaine	Marijuana	Nicotine	Opiates	Others
NCK2	rs2377339	Logistic regression	$2.46E-2$	$5.09E-2$	$4.48E-2$	$7.01E-2$	**$1.10E-7$**	$3.84E-3$
		Standard allelic test	$6.03E-3$	$4.34E-2$	$3.89E-2$	$6.25E-2$	**$1.33E-11$**	$1.78E-3$
	rs7589342	Logistic regression	$2.84E-1$	$8.79E-1$	$9.35E-1$	$8.60E-1$	$1.45E-4$	$4.26E-1$
		Standard allelic test	$2.81E-1$	$8.78E-1$	$9.34E-1$	$8.59E-1$	$5.39E-5$	$4.22E-1$
	rs12995333	Logistic regression	$1.71E-1$	$7.51E-1$	$7.16E-1$	$9.86E-1$	$1.89E-4$	$4.69E-1$
		Standard allelic test	$1.68E-1$	$7.51E-1$	$7.15E-1$	$9.86E-1$	$7.82E-5$	$4.67E-1$
	rs12053259	Logistic regression	$1.39E-1$	$9.43E-1$	$7.42E-1$	$9.01E-1$	$2.31E-4$	$4.86E-1$
		Standard allelic test	$1.33E-1$	$9.42E-1$	$7.39E-1$	$9E-1$	$8.67E-5$	$4.80E-1$
NCK2	—	KGG-logistic	$1.83E-1$	$8.15E-1$	$5.92E-1$	$9.56E-3$	**$2.70E-6$**	$9.45E-2$
NCK2	—	KGG- Standard allelic test	$1.41E-1$	$8.16E-1$	$4.83E-1$	$8.71E-3$	**$3.12E-10$**	$4.17E-2$

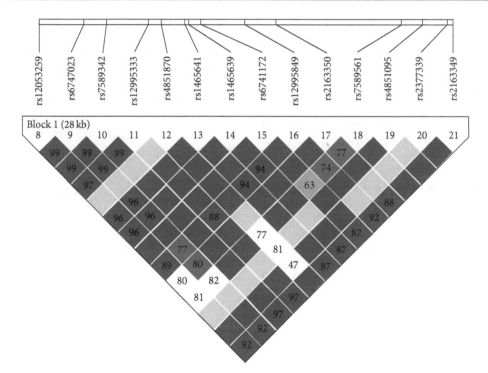

FIGURE 2: Linkage disequilibrium heat map near SNP rs2377339 on chromosome 2.

TABLE 3: Allele counts of rs2377339 in cases (opiates dependence) and controls (nonopiates dependence) in African-origin men.

	Genotype AA	Genotype AG	Genotype GG	Total
Case	35	9	0	44
Control	483	8	0	491

in 28 kb region [66]. Haplotype "AGTTCAGATCTCGT" with probability 0.016 yielded a P value of 1.66×10^{-11}. The genome-wide significant association between this haplotype and opiate addiction reduces the chance of a false discovery at the peak of a single SNP.

4.4. Contingency Table Analysis. We further examined the relationship between SNP rs2377339 and the opiates dependence in African-origin men. Table 3 depicts the allele frequencies of SNP rs2377339. The proportion of individuals

having minor allele G is 21.43% in the case group and 1.63% in the control group. The odds ratio of SNP rs2377339 is 13.87, indicating that those who have the risk allele (G) for rs2377339 are at a significantly increased risk of being diagnosed with opiates dependence.

4.5. Stratification Analysis. Furthermore, in Table 4, we investigated the racial specificity and sex difference in the association between SNP rs2377339 and opiates dependence. This scrutiny required us to include all racial and gender groups. We observed that the MAF and P values vary between different races and genders. The association between rs2377339 and opiates dependence becomes less significant in the overall cohort, after we adjusted race and gender in logistic regression.

4.6. Codependence Association Analysis. In Table 5, we also presented the association results for *NCK2* and comorbidity

TABLE 4: Association between SNP rs2377339 and opiates dependence by race and sex.

	MAF	P value	OR
African-origin men	1.59%	$1.33E-11$	13.87
African-origin women	1.14%	$1.64E-1$	2.82
European-origin men	6.77%	$8.13E-2$	0.55
European-origin women	6.64%	$6.95E-1$	1.14
Combined*	5.04%	$4.37E-1$	1.17

*Logistic regression is used to adjust for sex and race.

TABLE 5: Association of most significant SNPs in NCK2 with codependence of six individual substances dependence outcomes (P value).

Gene	SNP	position	P value for unadjusted	P value for adjusted
	rs2377339	105823723	**3.65E − 8**	**2.03E − 8**
NCK2	rs6747023	105798288	$5.43E-3$	$2.58E-2$
	rs7589342	105799910	$3.13E-3$	$1.68E-2$
	rs12995333	105802798	$3.81E-3$	$1.83E-2$

of substance dependence. The most significant signal in *NCK2* was observed for SNP rs2377339 in men of African-origin with $P = 3.65 \times 10^{-8}$ in adjusted association test and $P = 2.03 \times 10^{-8}$ in unadjusted association test. P values of SNPs in *NCK2* for other ethnicity by gender groups were far from the genome-wide significance level and, hence, are omitted here.

5. Discussion

We found a genome-wide significant association between SNP rs2377339 and opiates dependence in African-origin men. The *NCK2* gene that contains SNP rs2377339 also achieved the genome-wide significance for opiates dependence at the gene level. For the addiction of the other five substances, nicotine dependence had the most significant association but not significant at the genome-wide level.

NCK2, a member of NCK family of adaptor proteins, is reported to be associated with tyrosine-phosphorylated growth factor receptors of their cellular substrate [54]. The association between *NCK2* and nicotine dependence has been suggested in humans [67, 68]. Our finding coupled with those human studies enhances the plausibility of a causality relationship between *NCK2* and drug addiction.

Importantly, about one-fifth of opiates addiction subjects in the African-origin men carried minor allele G of SNP rs2377339, which is more than 10-fold of the frequency in the nonopiates dependence group. This suggested that the minor allele G in SNP rs2377339 potentially elevates the risk for opiates dependence in African-origin men. We acknowledge that our analysis included only 44 African-origin men with opiates dependence. Therefore, it is important and necessary to validate our finding through independent and larger cohort studies. Specifically, there are two possible strategies to validate our finding. The direct approach is to replicate the

association between SNP rs2377339 and opiates dependence in a larger cohort. An indirect approach is to evaluate whether SNP rs2377339 is associated with any substance dependence (opiates, alcohol, marijuana, etc.) as presented in Table 2.

A distinction of our analysis is to consider simultaneously multiple substance addictions rather than a single substance. This approach, which is a realistic depiction of substance dependence, confirmed that a novel susceptibility gene, *NCK2* is significantly associated with substance dependence in African-origin men.

This study has several limitations. First, we stratified by ethnicity and sex, which reduced sample sizes and affected the power of our analysis. Nonetheless, the significant associations revealed in African-origin men are consistent with the notion that men may be socially more prone to environmental influences that promote substance use and thus more vulnerable to addiction [46]. Second, for SNP rs2377339, we observed heterogeneous genetic effects, suggesting interactions between race, sex, and the gene, because the association is much weakened after adjusting for race and gender. Such interactions have been suggested in other addiction research [44, 45, 47]. Again, our result further supports the importance to examine interactions among genes, race, and sex in addiction.

Conflict of Interests

The authors declare that they have no conflict of interests.

Authors' Contribution

Zhifa Liu and Xiaobo Guo contributed equally.

Acknowledgments

This work was supported by Grant R01 DA016750-09 from the National Institute on Drug Abuse. Funding support for the Study of Addiction: Genetics and Environment (SAGE) was provided through the NIH Genes, Environment and Health Initiative (GEI) (U01 HG004422). SAGE is one of the genome-wide association studies funded as part of the Gene Environment Association Studies (GENEVA) under GEI. Assistance with phenotype harmonization and genotype cleaning, as well as with general study coordination, was provided by the GENEVA Coordinating Center (U01 HG004446). Assistance with data cleaning was provided by the National Center for Biotechnology Information. Support for collection of datasets and samples was provided by the Collaborative Study on the Genetics of Alcoholism (COGA; U10 AA008401), the Collaborative Genetic Study of Nicotine Dependence (COGEND; P01 CA089392), and the Family Study of Cocaine Dependence (FSCD; R01 DA013423). Funding support for genotyping, which was performed at the Johns Hopkins University Center for Inherited Disease Research, was provided by the NIH GEI (U01HG004438), the National Institute on Alcohol Abuse and Alcoholism, the National Institute on Drug Abuse, and the NIH Contract "High Throughput

Genotyping for Studying the Genetic Contributions to Human Disease" (HHSN268200782096C). The datasets used for the analyses described in this paper were obtained from dbGaP at http://www.ncbi.nlm.nih.gov/projects/gap/cgi-bin/study.cgi?study_id=phs000092.v1.p1 through dbGaP Accession no. phs000092.v1.p.

References

[1] K. R. Merikangas, M. Stolar, D. E. Stevens et al., "Familial transmission of substance use disorders," *Archives of General Psychiatry*, vol. 55, no. 11, pp. 973–979, 1998.

[2] W. R. True, A. C. Heath, J. F. Scherrer et al., "Interrelationship of genetic and environmental influences on conduct disorder and alcohol and marijuana dependence symptoms," *American Journal of Medical Genetics*, vol. 88, no. 4, pp. 391–397, 1999.

[3] G. E. Uhl and I. Gregory, "Genetic influences in drug abuse," in *Psychopharmacology: The Fourth Generation of Progress*, pp. 1793–1806, 1995.

[4] The World Health Organization, "Substitution maintenance therapy in the management of opioid dependence and HIV/AIDS prevention," Annual Report World Health Organization, 2004.

[5] L. J. Paulozzi, D. S. Budnitz, and Y. Xi, "Increasing deaths from opioid analgesics in the United States," *Pharmacoepidemiology and Drug Safety*, vol. 15, no. 9, pp. 618–627, 2006.

[6] L. J. Bierut, A. Agrawal, K. K. Bucholz et al., "A genome-wide association study of alcohol dependence," *Proceedings of the National Academy of Sciences of the United States of America*, vol. 107, no. 11, pp. 5082–5087, 2010.

[7] X. Chen, K. Cho, B. H. Singer, and H. Zhang, "The nuclear transcription factor PKNOX2 is a candidate gene for substance dependence in European-Origin Women," *PLoS ONE*, vol. 6, no. 1, Article ID e16002, 2011.

[8] J. Clarimon, R. R. Gray, L. N. Williams et al., "Linkage disequilibrium and association analysis of α-synuclein and alcohol and drug dependence in two American Indian populations," *Alcoholism: Clinical and Experimental Research*, vol. 31, no. 4, pp. 546–554, 2007.

[9] D. M. Dick, H. J. Edenberg, X. Xuei et al., "Association of GABRG3 with alcohol dependence," *Alcoholism: Clinical and Experimental Research*, vol. 28, no. 1, pp. 4–9, 2004.

[10] H. J. Edenberg, D. M. Dick, X. Xuei et al., "Variations in GABRA2, encoding the α2 subunit of the GABA a receptor, are associated with alcohol dependence and with brain oscillations," *American Journal of Human Genetics*, vol. 74, no. 4, pp. 705–714, 2004.

[11] H. J. Edenberg and T. Foroud, "The genetics of alcoholism: identifying specific genes through family studies," *Addiction Biology*, vol. 11, no. 3-4, pp. 386–396, 2006.

[12] H. J. Edenberg, J. Wang, H. Tian et al., "A regulatory variation in OPRK1, the gene encoding the κ-opioid receptor, is associated with alcohol dependence," *Human Molecular Genetics*, vol. 17, no. 12, pp. 1783–1789, 2008.

[13] T. Foroud, L. F. Wetherill, T. Liang et al., "Association of alcohol craving with α-synuclein (SNCA)," *Alcoholism: Clinical and Experimental Research*, vol. 31, no. 4, pp. 537–545, 2007.

[14] J. Gelernter, R. Gueorguieva, H. R. Kranzler et al., "Opioid receptor gene (OPRM1, OPRK1, and OPRD1) variants and response to naltrexone treatment for alcohol dependence:

results from the VA Cooperative Study," *Alcoholism: Clinical and Experimental Research*, vol. 31, no. 4, pp. 555–563, 2007.

[15] T. Reich, "A genomic survey of alcohol dependence and related phenotypes: results from the Collaborative Study on the Genetics of Alcoholism (COGA)," *Alcoholism: Clinical and Experimental Research*, vol. 20, supplement 8s, pp. 133–137, 1996.

[16] T. Reich, H. J. Edenberg, A. Goate et al. et al., "Genome-wide search for genes affecting the risk for alcohol dependence," *American Journal of Medical Genetics*, vol. 81, no. 3, pp. 207–215, 1998.

[17] J. Song, D. L. Koller, T. Foroud et al., "Association of GABAA receptors and alcohol dependence and the effects of genetic imprinting," *American Journal of Medical Genetics*, vol. 117, no. 1, pp. 39–45, 2003.

[18] B. Tabakoff, L. Saba, M. Printz et al. et al., "Genetical genomic determinants of alcohol consumption in rats and humans," *BMC Biology*, vol. 7, article 70, 2009.

[19] J. C. Wang, A. L. Hinrichs, S. Bertelsen et al., "Functional variants in TAS2R38 and TAS2R16 influence alcohol consumption in high-risk families of African-American origin," *Alcoholism: Clinical and Experimental Research*, vol. 31, no. 2, pp. 209–215, 2007.

[20] K. S. Wang, X. F. Liu, Q. Y. Zhang, Y. Pan, N. Aragam, and M. Zeng, "A meta-analysis of two genome-wide association studies identifies 3 new loci for alcohol dependence," *Journal of Psychiatric Research*, vol. 45, no. 11, pp. 1419–1425, 2011.

[21] H. Zhang, H. R. Kranzler, B. Z. Yang, X. Luo, and J. Gelernter, "The OPRD1 and OPRK1 loci in alcohol or drug dependence: OPRD1 variation modulates substance dependence risk," *Molecular Psychiatry*, vol. 13, no. 5, pp. 531–543, 2008.

[22] G. Kalsi, P. H. Kuo, F. Aliev et al., "A systematic gene-based screen of chr4q22–q32 identifies association of a novel susceptibility gene, DKK2, with the quantitative trait of alcohol dependence symptom counts," *Human Molecular Genetics*, vol. 19, no. 12, pp. 2497–2506, 2010.

[23] G. Kalsi, P. H. Kuo, F. Aliev et al., "A systematic gene-based screen of chr4q22–q32 identifies association of a novel susceptibility gene, DKK2, with the quantitative trait of alcohol dependence symptom counts," *Human Molecular Genetics*, vol. 19, no. 20, pp. 4121–2506, 2010.

[24] P. H. Kuo, G. Kalsi, C. A. Prescott et al., "Association of ADH and ALDH genes with alcohol dependence in the Irish affected sib pair study of alcohol dependence (IASPSAD) sample," *Alcoholism: Clinical and Experimental Research*, vol. 32, no. 5, pp. 785–795, 2008.

[25] L. J. Zuo, J. Gelernter, C. K. Zhang et al. et al., "Genome-wide association study of alcohol dependence implicates IAA0040 on chromosome 1q," *Neuropsychopharmacology*, vol. 37, no. 2, pp. 557–566, 2012.

[26] L. J. Bierut, "Genetic variation that contributes to nicotine dependence," *Pharmacogenomics*, vol. 8, no. 8, pp. 881–883, 2007.

[27] L. J. Bierut, P. A. F. Madden, N. Breslau et al., "Novel genes identified in a high-density genome wide association study for nicotine dependence," *Human Molecular Genetics*, vol. 16, no. 1, pp. 24–35, 2007.

[28] N. Caporaso, F. Gu, N. Chatterjee et al., "Genome-wide and candidate gene association study of cigarette smoking behaviors," *PLoS ONE*, vol. 4, no. 2, Article ID e4653, 2009.

[29] L. S. Chen, E. O. Johnson, N. Breslau et al., "Interplay of genetic risk factors and parent monitoring in risk for nicotine dependence," *Addiction*, vol. 104, no. 10, pp. 1731–1740, 2009.

[30] N. L. Saccone, S. F. Saccone, A. L. Hinrichs et al., "Multiple distinct risk loci for nicotine dependence identified by dense coverage of the complete family of nicotinic receptor subunit (CHRN) genes," *American Journal of Medical Genetics B*, vol. 150, no. 4, pp. 453–466, 2009.

[31] S. F. Saccone, A. L. Hinrichs, N. L. Saccone et al., "Cholinergic nicotinic receptor genes implicated in a nicotine dependence association study targeting 348 candidate genes with 3713 SNPs," *Human Molecular Genetics*, vol. 16, no. 1, pp. 36–49, 2007.

[32] G. R. Uhl, T. Drgon, C. Johnson et al., "Genome-wide association for smoking cessation success: participants in the patch in practice trial of nicotine replacement," *Pharmacogenomics*, vol. 11, no. 3, pp. 357–367, 2010.

[33] G. R. Uhl, Q. R. Liu, T. Drgon et al., "Molecular genetics of successful smoking cessation: convergent genome-wide association study results," *Archives of General Psychiatry*, vol. 65, no. 6, pp. 683–693, 2008.

[34] R. B. Weiss, T. B. Baker, D. S. Cannon et al., "A candidate gene approach identifies the CHRNA5-A3-B4 region as a risk factor for age-dependent nicotine addiction," *PLoS Genetics*, vol. 4, no. 7, Article ID e1000125, 2008.

[35] I. Deb, J. Chakraborty, P. K. Gangopadhyay, S. R. Choudhury, and S. Das, "Single-nucleotide polymorphism (A118G) in exon 1 of OPRM1 gene causes alteration in downstream signaling by mu-opioid receptor and may contribute to the genetic risk for addiction," *Journal of Neurochemistry*, vol. 112, no. 2, pp. 486–496, 2010.

[36] S. Kapur, S. Sharad, R. A. Singh, and A. K. Gupta, "A118G polymorphism in mu opioid receptor gene (OPRM1): association with opiate addiction in subjects of Indian origin," *Journal of Integrative Neuroscience*, vol. 6, no. 4, pp. 511–522, 2007.

[37] M. J. Kreek, G. Bart, C. Lilly, K. S. Laforge, and D. A. Nielsen, "Pharmacogenetics and human molecular genetics of opiate and cocaine addictions and their treatments," *Pharmacological Reviews*, vol. 57, no. 1, pp. 1–26, 2005.

[38] G. Gerra, C. Leonardi, E. Cortese et al., "Human kappa opioid receptor gene (OPRK1) polymorphism is associated with opiate addiction," *American Journal of Medical Genetics B*, vol. 144, no. 6, pp. 771–775, 2007.

[39] V. Yuferov, D. Fussell, K. S. LaForge et al., "Redefinition of the human kappa opioid receptor gene (OPRK1) structure and association of haplotypes with opiate addiction," *Pharmacogenetics*, vol. 14, no. 12, pp. 793–804, 2004.

[40] D. Proudnikov, K. S. LaForge, H. Hofflich et al., "Association analysis of polymorphisms in serotonin 1B receptor (HTR1B) gene with heroin addiction: a comparison of molecular and statistically estimated haplotypes," *Pharmacogenetics and Genomics*, vol. 16, no. 1, pp. 25–36, 2006.

[41] G. Gerra, L. Garofano, G. Santoro et al., "Association between low-activity serotonin transporter genotype and heroin dependence: behavioral and personality correlates," *American Journal of Medical Genetics*, vol. 126, no. 1, pp. 37–42, 2004.

[42] E. W. Loh, N. L. S. Tang, D. T. S. Lee, S. I. Liu, and A. Stadlin, "Association analysis of GABA receptor subunit genes on 5q33 with heroin dependence in a Chinese male population," *American Journal of Medical Genetics B*, vol. 144, no. 4, pp. 439–443, 2007.

[43] C. Y. Cheng, C. J. Hong, Y. W. Y. Yu, T. J. Chen, H. C. Wu, and S. J. Tsai, "Brain-derived neurotrophic factor (Val66Met) genetic polymorphism is associated with substance abuse in males," *Molecular Brain Research*, vol. 140, no. 1-2, pp. 86–90, 2005.

[44] Z. Luo, G. F. Alvarado, D. K. Hatsukami, E. O. Johnson, L. J. Bierut, and N. Breslau, "Race differences in nicotine dependence in the Collaborative Genetic study of Nicotine Dependence (COGEND)," *Nicotine and Tobacco Research*, vol. 10, no. 7, pp. 1223–1230, 2008.

[45] N. Breslau, E. O. Johnson, E. Hiripi, and R. Kessler, "Nicotine dependence in the United States: prevalence, trends, and smoking persistence," *Archives of General Psychiatry*, vol. 58, no. 9, pp. 810–816, 2001.

[46] D. M. Hartel, E. E. Schoenbaum, Y. Lo, and R. S. Klein, "Gender differences in illicit substance use among middle-aged drug users with or at risk for HIV infection," *Clinical Infectious Diseases*, vol. 43, no. 4, pp. 525–531, 2006.

[47] D. L. Karch, L. Barker, and T. W. Strine, "Race/ethnicity, substance abuse, and mental illness among suicide victims in 13 US states: 2004 data from the national violent death reporting system," *Injury Prevention*, vol. 12, no. 2, pp. 22–27, 2006.

[48] E. E. Eichler, J. Flint, G. Gibson et al., "Missing heritability and strategies for finding the underlying causes of complex disease," *Nature Reviews Genetics*, vol. 11, no. 6, pp. 446–450, 2010.

[49] T. A. Manolio, F. S. Collins, N. J. Cox et al., "Finding the missing heritability of complex diseases," *Nature*, vol. 461, no. 7265, pp. 747–753, 2009.

[50] X. Guo, Z. Liu, X. Wang, and H. Zhang, "Genetic association test for multiple traits at gene level," *Genetic Epidemiology*, vol. 37, no. 1, pp. 122–129, 2013.

[51] M. X. Li, H. S. Gui, J. S. H. Kwan, and P. C. Sham, "GATES: a rapid and powerful gene-based association test using extended Simes procedure," *American Journal of Human Genetics*, vol. 88, no. 3, pp. 283–293, 2011.

[52] J. Z. Liu, A. F. McRae, D. R. Nyholt et al., "A versatile gene-based test for genome-wide association studies," *American Journal of Human Genetics*, vol. 87, no. 1, pp. 139–145, 2010.

[53] B. M. Neale and P. C. Sham, "The future of association studies: gene-based analysis and replication," *American Journal of Human Genetics*, vol. 75, no. 3, pp. 353–362, 2004.

[54] G. M. Rivera, S. Antoku, S. Gelkop et al., "Requirement of Nck adaptors for actin dynamics and cell migration stimulated by platelet-derived growth factor B," *Proceedings of the National Academy of Sciences of the United States of America*, vol. 103, no. 25, pp. 9536–9541, 2006.

[55] H. Begleiter, T. Reich, V. Hesselbrock et al., "The collaborative study on the genetics of alcoholism," *Alcohol Health & Research World*, vol. 19, no. 3, pp. 228–236, 1995.

[56] L. J. Bierut, J. R. Strickland, J. R. Thompson, S. E. Afful, and L. B. Cottler, "Drug use and dependence in cocaine dependent subjects, community-based individuals, and their siblings," *Drug and Alcohol Dependence*, vol. 95, no. 1-2, pp. 14–22, 2008.

[57] X. Guo, Z. Liu, X. Wang, and H. Zhang, "Large scale association analysis for drug addiction: results from SNP to gene," *The Scientific World Journal*, vol. 2012, Article ID 939584, 6 pages, 2012.

[58] S. Purcell, B. Neale, K. Todd-Brown et al., "PLINK: a tool set for whole-genome association and population-based linkage analyses," *American Journal of Human Genetics*, vol. 81, no. 3, pp. 559–575, 2007.

[59] I. Menashe, J. D. Figueroa, M. Garcia-Closas et al. et al., "Large-scale pathway-based analysis of bladder cancer genome-wide association data from five studies of European background," *Plos One*, vol. 7, no. 1, Article ID e29396, 2012.

[60] A. Christoforou, M. Dondrup, M. Mattingsdal et al. et al., "Linkage-disequilibrium-based binning affects the interpretation of GWASs," *American Journal of Human Genetics*, vol. 90, no. 4, pp. 727–733, 2012.

[61] F. Dudbridge and A. Gusnanto, "Estimation of significance thresholds for genomewide association scans," *Genetic Epidemiology*, vol. 32, no. 3, pp. 227–234, 2008.

[62] H. Zhang, C. T. Liu, and X. Wang, "An association test for multiple traits based on the generalized Kendall's tau," *Journal of the American Statistical Association*, vol. 105, no. 490, pp. 473–481, 2010.

[63] D. Rabinowitz and N. Laird, "A unified approach to adjusting association tests for population admixture with arbitrary pedigree structure and arbitrary missing marker information," *Human Heredity*, vol. 50, no. 4, pp. 211–223, 2000.

[64] Y. Jiang and H. Zhang, "Propensity score-based nonparametric test revealing genetic variants underlying bipolar disorder," *Genetic Epidemiology*, vol. 35, no. 2, pp. 125–132, 2011.

[65] H. Zhao, T. R. Rebbeck, and N. Mitra, "A propensity score approach to correction for bias due to population stratification using genetic and non-genetic factors," *Genetic Epidemiology*, vol. 33, no. 8, pp. 679–690, 2009.

[66] J. C. Barrett, B. Fry, J. Maller, and M. J. Daly, "Haploview: analysis and visualization of LD and haplotype maps," *Bioinformatics*, vol. 21, no. 2, pp. 263–265, 2005.

[67] M. Akiyama, K. Yatsu, M. Ota et al., "Microsatellite analysis of the GLC1B locus on chromosome 2 points to NCK2 as a new candidate gene for normal tension glaucoma," *British Journal of Ophthalmology*, vol. 92, no. 9, pp. 1293–1296, 2008.

[68] S. Bonovas, K. Filioussi, A. Tsantes, and V. Peponis, "Epidemiological association between cigarette smoking and primary open-angle glaucoma: a meta-analysis," *Public Health*, vol. 118, no. 4, pp. 256–261, 2004.

14

Biomedical Informatics for Computer-Aided Decision Support Systems: A Survey

Ashwin Belle,[1] **Mark A. Kon,**[2] **and Kayvan Najarian**[1]

[1] *Department of Computer Science, Virginia Commonwealth University, Richmond, VA 23284, USA*
[2] *Department of Mathematics and Statistics, Boston University, Boston, MA 02215, USA*

Correspondence should be addressed to Kayvan Najarian; knajarian@vcu.edu

Academic Editors: J. Bajo, Y. Cai, and J. B. T. Rocha

The volumes of current patient data as well as their complexity make clinical decision making more challenging than ever for physicians and other care givers. This situation calls for the use of biomedical informatics methods to process data and form recommendations and/or predictions to assist such decision makers. The design, implementation, and use of biomedical informatics systems in the form of computer-aided decision support have become essential and widely used over the last two decades. This paper provides a brief review of such systems, their application protocols and methodologies, and the future challenges and directions they suggest.

1. Introduction

Over the past several decades the uses and applications of biomedical informatics for computer-aided medical diagnostics and decision support systems have become ubiquitous in clinical settings. Adaptations of decision support systems powered by biomedical informatics in either complex or simple forms were seen as early as the 1970s. A 1994 survey [1] indicates that the literature relevant to this field dates back to as early as the mid-1950s.

With advances in technologies related to medical signal and image acquisition, it can be seen that there has been an escalation of complexity in collected medical data. Apart from medical data being inherently more complex, the sheer volume of such data collected per patient is growing rapidly. Currently medical devices and high-throughput measurement systems produce thousands of images and large volumes of other data per patient in seconds, making it difficult for physicians to parse through the information while providing timely diagnoses and prognoses. There is a present significant need for development and improvement of computer-aided decision support systems in medicine, with an expected amplification in the future.

Clinical implementations of biomedical informatics methods in the form of computer-based decision support systems were seen as early as 1971, when Dombal's system AAPhelp, developed at Leeds University, attempted to automate the diagnosis of acute abdominal pain [2]. In 1974 a system called INTERNIST-I [3], a rule-based expert system designed to aid the diagnosis of complex medical problems in internal medicine, was developed. These represent prominent developments in early implementations of biomedical informatics systems, among many computer-based diagnostic decision support systems. Since their inception there has been a substantial evolution, with wide acknowledgment of their success in improving practitioners' performance and patient outcomes.

With broad research conducted in the area, there have been review studies on related topics. A book by Greenes [4] outlines general concepts and future directions for clinical decision support systems. Similarly, an article by Madabhushi et al. [5] describes development of computer-aided prognosis systems for predicting patient and disease outcomes using multiscale, multimodal medical data. Miller's article in 1994 provides a comprehensive list of important work conducted on diagnosis and decision support between 1954 and 1993

[1]. Similarly, a more recent article by Pearson et al. provides a systematic review of computerized clinical decision support systems between 1990 and 2007 [6]. In this work 56 different studies are considered, of which 38 are on systems used in therapy initiation, 23 involve computer-based monitoring of patients during therapy, and three study conditions for termination of therapy. From their outcomes, the authors infer that the most consistently effective computer-based systems are those that initiate advice to fine-tune existing therapies by improving patient safety, adjusting the doses, durations forms of prescribed drugs, or increasing the laboratory testing rates for patients on long-term therapies.

Some previous studies also provide insights into more specific subgenres of biomedical informatics methods and their implementations in the form of computer-aided diagnosis systems. Tourassi discusses systems that provide diagnostic interpretations based on image texture analysis [7] and Stivaros et al. [8] focus on the impacts of decision support systems in clinical radiological practice.

This paper provides a general survey of applications and methodologies in biomedical informatics that have been implemented as computer-aided decision support systems and discusses the resulting challenges, for example, in validation of such systems, and in adoption levels among end users. The paper is organized as follows. some major application areas for the above-mentioned systems are described, followed by a discussion of important methodologies employed. Then there is a brief look at the validation and success criteria for these systems, followed by the conclusion and discussion of future directions.

2. Applications

There are a number of application areas medicine for which computer-aided decision support systems have become designed and implemented. Some of the major application areas are discussed below.

2.1. Radiology. Here, computer-based image processing and analysis have been an active research area. Combining visualization, image processing, and machine learning for decision-making has provided an added advantage for clinical applications. With multiple technologies for medical imaging such as computed tomography (CT), X-rays, magnetic resonance imaging (MRI), and functional MRI (FMRI), numerous biomedical informatics methods have been designed for application-specific solutions. A study by Van Ginneken et al. surveys over 150 publications before 2001 on computer-aided diagnosis in chest radiography [9]. This survey emphasizes the continued interest in computer-aided diagnosis for chest radiography. There are also several studies on developing decision-making systems using automated analysis of CT scans. These include Chen et al.'s [10, 11] study, which focuses on developing a computer aided diagnostic system that automatically analyses brain CT scans of patients with traumatic brain injury (TBI). The system also automatically estimates the level of the intracranial pressure (ICP) within the brain. Another study by Davaluri et al. discusses the

development of computer-assisted decision-making systems for pelvic injuries [12]. Wu et al. focus on fracture detection in traumatic pelvic injury patients and discusses an automated method for quantifying the size of fractures from CT images of patients with pelvic injuries [13]. Stivaros et al. provide an overview of underlying design and functionality of radiological decision support systems, with supporting examples of the development and evolution of such systems in the past 40 years [8].

2.2. Emergency Medicine and Intensive Care Units. One of the most active areas of research in the realm of biomedical informatics and decision support systems is emergency medicine. For patients in intensive care units (ICU) and emergency rooms, it is critical that diagnosis and treatment are provided in a timely manner. Since critical care units typically experience a heavy strain on resources, it becomes important to manage and dispense resources to critically ill patients who need it the most. Computer-aided decision support systems play a vital role in reducing diagnosis time, improving resource allocation efficiency, and decreasing patient mortality. Ji et al. describe a study that provides a comparative analysis of computer-assisted decision-making systems for traumatic injuries [14]. Systems such as one developed by Frixea et al. show how case-based reasoning techniques for the estimation of patient outcomes and resource utilizations can improve patient care dramatically in ICUs [15]. Kumar et al.'s study [16] presents a clinical decision support system which combines both case-based reasoning and rule-based reasoning and that performs well with real and simulated ICU data. Raschke et al. describe a computer alert system which is designed to recognize averse drug events (AEDs) in hospital settings [17]. This system is reported to be capable of generating alerts for patients with increased risk of AEDs. The study states that during the 6-month trial of the system, a total of 265 (44%) of the 596 true positive alerts were unrecognized by the physicians prior to the alert notification, hence showing a great promise for applications in continuous patient monitoring.

2.3. Cardiovascular Medicine. Having continuous or interventional monitoring of cardiovascular signals for diagnosing ailments or predicting impending cardiac events can be an extremely useful tool. Currently there are several research biomedical informatics studies attempting to develop computer-aided solutions for various aspects of cardiovascular medicine. A study conducted by Polat et al. describes a computer-aided diagnosis system that automatically identifies and classifies arrhythmia from the analysis of patients' electrocardiograph (ECG) signals [18]. The authors claim 100% accuracy in classification within the dataset used. Watrous reviews various studies which use auscultation signal of the heart for analysis and provide diagnostics decision support to physicians [19, 20]. Shandilya et al. present their work on the design and development of a nonlinear method for analysis of ventricular fibrillation using ECG signals to predict high yields accuracy for defibrillation success [21]. The study also describes the incorporation of PetCO2 signal to noticeably increase the predictive models robustness.

2.4. Dental Applications. Computerized clinical diagnosis and decision support systems have also seen much success in the field of dentistry. Firestone et al. describe a clinical decision support system on observer performance which was a knowledge-based system performing image analysis on radiographic images [22]. This study involved 102 approximal surface radiographic images and sixteen general practitioners for identifying the presence of caries and whether restoration was required. The paper states that those dental practitioners who used the system to produce their diagnoses showed significant increases in their ability to diagnose caries correctly, with an increased overall diagnostic accuracy and recommendation for restoration of detected cavitated surfaces. Similarly, Olsen et al. propose a computer-aided caries detection system using image analysis of data from intraoral cameras [23]. This paper describes a feasibility study of using advanced image processing and machine learning techniques to identify caries from digital images.

2.5. Cancer. Biomedical informatics has begun to play an important role in cancer detection and treatment. In a study conducted by Lisboa and Taktak, a systematic review of several studies involving decision-making tools in the field of cancer is presented [24]. In particular, the review focuses on those studies that apply artificial neural network methods. Using 27 studies which were either clinical trials or randomized controlled trials, the paper reports that 21 of those studies show benefits in treatment while the remaining 6 did not. Another study by Jesneck discusses an approach to optimize computer-aided decision-making for cancer diagnosis by combining heterogeneous information from different modalities [25]. The authors claim that their proposed method at times outperforms two popular machine-learning techniques, that is, linear discriminant analysis and artificial neural networks. A study by Madabhushi et al. briefly discusses four different computer-aided support systems for cancer diagnosis and prognosis [26]. The first system is an image-based risk score algorithm for predicting the outcome of the estrogen receptor marker for breast cancer patients based on digitized biopsy. The second system is discussed in the paper segments and determines the extent of lymphocytic infiltration from digitized histopathology. The third method described distinguishes patients with varying Gleason grades of prostate cancer, from needle biopsy specimens. The final system integrates quantitative image features extracted from digitized histopathology with protein expression measurements obtained from mass spectrometry, in order to distinguish between low and high risk patients with prostate cancer recurrence following radical prostatectomy. Jiang et al. published a paper evaluating the reduction of interobserver variability in the interpretation of mammograms while using computer-aided diagnosis tools [27]. The authors state that using computer-aided diagnosis tools has the potential to reduce variability amongst expert opinions as well as improve diagnostic accuracy for the interpretation of mammograms. Similarly, another study by Cheng et al. summarizes and compares the methods used in various enhancement and segmentation algorithms, mammographic feature extraction, classifiers, and their performances for detection and classification of microcalcification clusters [28]. A paper by Mazurowski et al. describes an optimization framework for improving case-based computer-aided decision systems used for screening mammography [29]. The paper claims that the proposed method significantly improves the overall performance and breast mass detection rates of such systems. Cai et al.'s paper describes a study based on classification of cancer subtypes and survival prediction in diffuse large B-cell lymphoma (DLBCL) using levels of genes [30]. Research by Rangayyan et al. describes refined methodologies that have been developed in computer-aided breast cancer diagnostic systems [31]. The research presents new detection techniques for identifying subtle signs of breast cancer addressing difficult problems such as focal architecture distortion and global bilateral asymmetry.

2.6. Pediatric Medicine. Computer-aided diagnosis and decision support systems have become popular for a variety of applications in neonatal and pediatric care units. A study by Ramnarayan et al. discusses the potential of diagnostic and decision support systems in pediatric settings with a case study of a web-based pediatric differential diagnostic tool [32]. Ramnarayan also explains the various usages of such diagnostic aid systems and outlines its future direction for research in another article [33]. Frizea et al. discuss an artificial intelligence-based system which uses case-based reasoning for estimating medical outcomes and resource utilization. The paper explains how such a system was initially intended for adult ICU care units and then was modified to function in neonatal ICUs. The paper reports that the results from a short clinical pilot study performed in neonatal ICU were very encouraging and captured the interests of physicians for their potential clinical usefulness. Tan et al. published a review paper on clinical decision support systems for neonatal care [34]. The objective of this review was to find whether the use of clinical decision support systems had any effect on the mortality and morbidity rate of newborn infants, and to see if there was any change in the performance of the physicians treating these infants. Mack et al. also published a similar review study of decision support systems available in pediatric intensive care units [35]. The paper provides a look into the factors that are involved in the applications of such systems in pediatric practices, including liability, human factors, audit trails, engineering, and alert fatigue. The paper concludes that selecting and implementing such systems in clinical practice requires a great deal of caution, though when done correctly it has good potential for benefiting and improving clinical practice in pediatric intensive care units.

3. Methodology

There are several fundamental computational methodologies used toward developing these biomedical informatics and computer-aided diagnosis support systems. The types of techniques and methods are based on application areas and required performance metrics. Some of the major aspects of such systems are discussed below.

3.1. Expert Systems, Case-Based Reasoning, and Rule-Based Systems. Methods such as rule-based systems (fuzzy and crisp), expert systems, and case-based reasoning are formed from the knowledge accumulated from experts of a given field. Opinions, diagnoses, and prognoses, among other components, are compiled to form rule-based analysis structures, based on which specific concepts for diagnosis solutions are developed. Kumar et al. present a hybrid decision support system which was designed based on both case-based and rule-based reasoning [16], which is applied to ICU facilities for aiding physicians in decision making. Another study by Innocent describes an approach to computer-aided medical diagnosis systems for clinical contexts using fuzzy logic [36]. In this system, knowledge from experts is compiled into fuzzy cognitive maps and logical structures to estimate a stage of disease using temporal information in symptom durations.

3.2. Signal and Image Processing. Some computerized diagnostic aid systems use a variety of patient data for analysis in developing diagnostic suggestions. These systems analyze raw patient signals and images to extract useful features and trends based on which diagnostic and decision support information is computed and presented to physicians. For instance, Polat et al. describe a signal processing system that analyzes ECG to classify cases of arrhythmia in diseased persons [18]. The signal processing system, developed by Shandillya et al., detects the ideal time to defibrillate patients undergoing cardiac arrest or ventricular fibrillation [21, 37]. Davaluri et al. proposes an image processing system which uses CT images of patients with pelvic injuries to produce a quantitative and qualitative assessment of detected hemorrhaging [38]. Similarly, Wu's work on developing a computer-assisted fracture detection system automatically processes several CT slices of pelvic injury patients to identify and quantify potential fractures [39].

3.3. Machine Learning. Due to the continuous advancements in the field of machine learning, more complex and sophisticated biomedical informatics systems are being designed. Systems that have the ability to predict and classify diseases fundamentally rely on some type of machine learning methodology. There is no one superior machine learning technique that can be applied toward all learning problems; instead the best method depends on the type of application. For example, Lisboa's study provides a systematic review of neural networks in decision support systems for cancer diagnosis and treatment [24]. Jesneck et al. describe how a customized machine learning technique outperforms standard techniques such as artificial neural networks and linear discriminant analysis in their study using cancer datasets [25]. Ji et al. compare a variety of machine learning techniques used in decision-making systems for traumatic injury assessment [40].

4. Impact of Computer-Aided Decisions in Bioinformatics

In the last two decades, bioinformatics has emerged as a vibrant and rapidly growing field. However, as shown above, the majority of computer-aided decision support systems is implementations of biomedical informatics systems, so that very few of the currently used computer-aided support systems are based on bioinformatics approaches, which is understandable given the age of the field.

A study by Maojo et al. provides a comparison of histories, fundamental foundations, and scientific approaches of the two complementary yet separate fields, that is, of medical informatics and bioinformatics [41]. With most computerized clinical diagnostic aids being developed under the umbrella of biomedical informatics, Maojo et al. explain how inclusion of knowledge from bioinformatics can strengthen applications development for healthcare. The authors emphasize that future research designed as a hybrid of both informatics subdisciplines is the key to making significant advances in clinical practice and biomedical research.

The effort to combine multimodal data and to combine biomedical informatics and bioinformatics has already shown a great promise. As mentioned, Madabhushi et al. describe research on computer-aided prognosis and diagnosis systems using multi-modal data fusion, including computerized image analysis and digitized patient data such as tissue and genomic information for predicting outcomes and survival [5]. These projects use protein expression and other data, processed by typical biomedical informatics methods, to diagnose and develop prognoses for cancer cases. Huang et al. analyzed and published a time series microarray gene expression profiles dataset to predict how patients respond to pegylated interferon treatment [42, 43]. Computer-aided decision systems adapted with bioinformatics knowledge have begun to show positive impact on virological research. For instance a paper by Huang et al. describes a computational method in identifying the underlying mechanisms for HIV-1 resistance in some people based on gene expression profiles and the analysis of the network of virus-host interaction [44]. Similarly, another study describes a novel approach in diagnosing liver cirrhosis and hepatocellular diseases using a network based analysis [45].

5. Validation and Criteria for Success

With numerous clinical implementations of decision support systems for a variety of medical applications, it is essential to have a systematic method to verify, validate, and compare different systems and their performances. For instance, Berner et al. compare the performance of four computer-based diagnostic systems applied towards internal medicine applications, namely: Dxplain, Iliad, Meditel, and QMR [46]. These systems have all been noted in various publications in their phases of development, evaluation, and applications [47, 48]. The authors have tested these systems on identical diagnostically challenging cases and measured the performances of each of these systems on several developed measurement scales. Estimates of performance were provided with a prospectively determined set of test specifications, using cases with a range of content and difficulty. Another study by Manotti et al. assesses the performance of another decision support system pertinent to oral anticoagulant treatment [49]. In this paper the authors describe a clinical trial of

TABLE 1: Stregnths and weaknesses of existing computer-aided decision support systems and research in different application areas.

Application areas	Strengths	Weaknesses
Cancer	(i) An abundance of molecular assays and data are available for many cancer cases; these can be used towards developing strong decision support systems	(i) More should be done to integrate knowledge from molecular-based and image-based sources available for cancer detection (ii) There is a need to develop better schemes and methods for validating the effectiveness of the existing and upcoming systems in this area
Radiology	(i) A variety of effective computational techniques exists for many applications in radiology (ii) It is one of the fastest growing fields using applications of computer-aided decision systems	(i) Most of the research in this area suffers from lack of comprehensive datasets (ii) Most of these studies do not include knowledge of illness/injury/complication into the decision-making process
Emergency medicine	(i) Although there are only a few systems that have been adopted into clinical practices, the existing systems have shown a positive impact on the cost and quality of healthcare (ii) There is a significant potential for computer-aided systems in this area since emergency medicine and trauma are very time and resource critical aspects of healthcare	(i) Accuracies of existing systems may not be sufficient for clinical uses (ii) A variety of illnesses and injuries have not yet been addressed by computer-aided decision support systems (iii) There is a lack of comprehensive validation of the short-/long-term impacts on these systems using sufficiently large datasets
Cardiovascular medicine	(i) Since heart disease is among the leading causes of death, computer-aided decision systems here have potentially very high impact on world health (ii) While most cardiovascular-based intelligent decision support systems suffer from high false positives, they often help detect disease at early stages	(i) These systems usually incorporate only a portion of available patient information. More variety in information sources may be required in the decision-making process to reduce false positives (ii) There is a lack of a comprehensive validation process. Existing research claims need to be tested in more real-world settings
Dental	(i) Existing systems have shown capability for detecting dental complications at early stages (ii) Such early detection facilitates better practice of preventive care	(i) Some of the technologies used for capturing the information for computer-aided decision support systems are relatively expensive and hence preventing them from being widely adopted in practice

the system with several patients across multiple clinics, to test whether the computer-based decision support system is efficient in stabilizing patients undergoing oral anticoagulant treatment by initiating and maintaining therapy. With statistical analysis of performance measures the paper reports that the decision support system improves the quality of anticoagulant treatment, both during long-term treatments and in early, unstable phases of treatment.

Several publications also explain the various criteria that need to be considered for successful development and application of a computer-assisted decision support system. Along these lines, Kaplan reviews the literature related to clinical decision support systems with an emphasis on evaluation criteria [50]. In the paper the author explains that with the success seen so far there is a general enthusiasm amongst physicians and researchers with the potential of computerized clinical decision support systems to improve the quality of healthcare. Nonetheless, there is a lack of theoretical understanding especially from a nonphysician's perspective of such systems and also as to why certain diagnostic aid systems may not be effective. Similarly Dreiseitl and Binder consider the effects of decision support systems on physicians' opinions, in particular to see whether

they, doctors, value its opinion when it contradicts theirs [50]. They conclude that physicians are fairly susceptible to accepting recommendations of such decision support systems, making quality assurance and validation of more paramount importance. Ramnarayan et al. highlight the importance of developing a reliable and valid composite scoring system to measure the impact of diagnostic decision support on the quality of healthcare [32]. They claim that the scoring systems they describe can be further used in assessing outcome measures of other study types, involving computer-assisted diagnostic systems. Song et al. discuss the various approaches, goals, and characteristics of computer-aided healthcare workflows [51]. The authors analyze the workflow application issues and software challenges in the perspective of medical informatics and software engineering. Niès et al. published a paper listing four key characteristics pertaining to the content of diagnosis support that are associated with the success of computerized clinical decision support systems [52]. The paper provides a systematic review of published trials to identify the characteristics of the adopted methodologies and technicalities of those studies that assess the efficacy of clinical decision support systems.

6. Conclusion and Future Directions

Table 1 describes the overall strengths and weakness of existing computer-aided decision support systems, and research in some of the application areas discussed in this paper.

With the sheer number of biomedical informatics methods implemented as computer-assisted diagnosis and decision support systems, along with the vast amount of research in this field, such systems are inevitably becoming an inherent part of medicine. The systems are becoming capable of solving more complex and sophisticated clinical problems. By establishing systematic processes for validation and verification, these computer-aided systems can become much more reliable and thereby improve quality of diagnostic decisions, as well as reduce variance among physicians' opinions. The unique capabilities of these systems allow care givers and researchers to gain insight into current clinical issues in ways that would have been impossible in the past.

Furthermore, it is becoming advantageous to fuse information derived from medical data with multiple modalities to provide more robust diagnoses and treatment plan suggestions [5, 10, 40]. The current fusion of biomedical informatics and bioinformatics techniques will accelerate the formation of a new generation of system-biologic computer-aided decision support systems, that will process and combine information in molecular data, signals and images, and demographics, among others. These and many other sources of patient data will allow such systems to form much more specific and personalized recommendations.

Applying advances in computational methods and techniques towards such systems can help in problems such as overfitting of outputs towards specific types of data, susceptibility to incomplete/missing data, and presence of conflicting information from different sources. These advances in the computational methods can also improve the quality of information accessed from feature extraction and feature selection—this improvement is often a critical step prior to classification and/or clustering.

While computerized diagnostic and prognostic decision support systems have proved to be instrumental in medicine, it appears that an even more significant contribution of these systems can be expected when they further evolve to process and integrate newer and even broader types of patient data.

References

[1] R. A. Miller, "Medical diagnostic decision support systems—past, present, and future: a threaded bibliography and brief commentary," *Journal of the American Medical Informatics Association*, vol. 1, no. 1, pp. 8–27, 1994.

[2] F. T. de Dombal, D. J. Leaper, J. R. Staniland, A. P. McCann, and J. C. Horrocks, "Computer-aided diagnosis of acute abdominal pain," *British Medical Journal*, vol. 2, no. 5804, pp. 9–13, 1972.

[3] J. D. Myers, "The background of INTERNIST I and QMR," in *Proceedings of ACM Conference on History of Medical Informatics*, pp. 195–197, 1987.

[4] R. A. Greenes, *Clinical Decision Support: The Road Ahead*, Academic Press, 2007.

[5] A. Madabhushi, S. Agner, A. Basavanhally, S. Doyle, and G. Lee, "Computer-aided prognosis: predicting patient and disease outcome via quantitative fusion of multi-scale, multi-modal data," *Computerized Medical Imaging and Graphics*, vol. 35, pp. 506–514, 2011.

[6] S. A. Pearson, A. Moxey, J. Robertson et al., "Do computerised clinical decision support systems for prescribing change practice? A systematic review of the literature (1990–2007)," *BMC Health Services Research*, vol. 9, article 154, 2009.

[7] G. D. Tourassi, "Journey toward computer-aided diagnosis: role of image texture analysis," *Radiology*, vol. 213, no. 2, pp. 317–320, 1999.

[8] S. M. Stivaros, A. Gledson, G. Nenadic, X. J. Zeng, J. Keane, and A. Jackson, "Decision support systems for clinical radiological practice—towards the next generation," *British Journal of Radiology*, vol. 83, no. 995, pp. 904–914, 2010.

[9] B. Van Ginneken, B. M. Ter Haar Romeny, and M. A. Viergever, "Computer-aided diagnosis in chest radiography: a survey," *IEEE Transactions on Medical Imaging*, vol. 20, no. 12, pp. 1228–1241, 2001.

[10] W. Chen, C. Cockrell, K. R. Ward, and K. Najarian, "Intracranial pressure level prediction in traumatic brain injury by extracting features from multiple sources and using machine learning methods," in *Proceedings of the IEEE International Conference on Bioinformatics and Biomedicine (BIBM '10)*, pp. 510–515, December 2010.

[11] W. Chen, C. Cockrell, K. Ward, and K. Najarian, "Predictability of intracranial pressure level in traumatic brain injury: features extraction, statistical analysis and machine learning based evaluation," *Journal of Data Mining and Bioinformatics*. In press.

[12] P. Davuluri, J. Wu, K. R. Ward, C. H. Cockrell, K. Najarian, and R. S. Hobson, "An automated method for hemorrhage detection in traumatic pelvic injuries," in *Proceedings of the International Conference of the IEEE Engineering in Medicine and Biology Society (EMBC '11)*, pp. 5108–5111, 2011.

[13] J. Wu, Y. Tang, P. Davuluri et al., "Fracture detection and quantitative measure of displacement in pelvic CT images," in *Proceedings of the IEEE International Conference on Bioinformatics and Biomedicine Workshops (BIBMW '11)*, pp. 600–606, 2011.

[14] S. Y. Ji, R. Smith, T. Huynh, and K. Najarian, "A comparative analysis of multi-level computer-assisted decision making systems for traumatic injuries," *BMC Medical Informatics and Decision Making*, vol. 9, no. 1, article 2, 2009.

[15] M. Frize and R. Walker, "Clinical decision-support systems for intensive care units using case-based reasoning," *Medical Engineering and Physics*, vol. 22, no. 9, pp. 671–677, 2000.

[16] K. A. Kumar, Y. Singh, and S. Sanyal, "Hybrid approach using case-based reasoning and rule-based reasoning for domain independent clinical decision support in ICU," *Expert Systems with Applications*, vol. 36, no. 1, pp. 65–71, 2009.

[17] R. A. Raschke, B. Gollihare, T. A. Wunderlich et al., "A computer alert system to prevent injury from adverse drug events: development and evaluation in a community teaching hospital," *Journal of the American Medical Association*, vol. 280, no. 15, pp. 1317–1320, 1998.

[18] K. Polat, B. Akdemir, and S. Güneş, "Computer aided diagnosis of ECG data on the least square support vector machine," *Digital Signal Processing*, vol. 18, no. 1, pp. 25–32, 2008.

[19] R. L. Watrous, "Computer-aided auscultation of the heart: from anatomy and physiology to diagnostic decision support," in

Proceedings of the 28th Annual International Conference of the IEEE Engineering in Medicine and Biology Society (EMBS '06), pp. 140–143, September 2006.

[20] R. L. Watrous, W. R. Thompson, and S. J. Ackerman, "The impact of computer-assisted auscultation on physician referrals of asymptomatic patients with heart murmurs," *Clinical Cardiology*, vol. 31, no. 2, pp. 79–83, 2008.

[21] S. Shandilya, K. Ward, M. Kurz, and K. Najarian, "Non-linear dynamical signal characterization for prediction of defibrillation success through machine learning," *BMC Medical Informatics and Decision Making*, vol. 12, p. 116, 2012.

[22] A. R. Firestone, D. Sema, T. J. Heaven, and R. A. Weems, "The effect of a knowledge-based, image analysis and clinical decision support system on observer performance in the diagnosis of approximal caries from radiographic images," *Caries Research*, vol. 32, no. 2, pp. 127–134, 1998.

[23] G. F. Olsen, S. S. Brilliant, D. Primeaux, and K. Najarian, "An image-processing enabled dental caries detection system," in *Proceedings of the International Conference on Complex Medical Engineering (ICME '09)*, pp. 1–8, April 2009.

[24] P. J. Lisboa and A. F. G. Taktak, "The use of artificial neural networks in decision support in cancer: a systematic review," *Neural Networks*, vol. 19, no. 4, pp. 408–415, 2006.

[25] J. L. Jesneck, *Optimized Decision Fusion of Heterogeneous Data for Breast Cancer Diagnosis*, 2007.

[26] A. Madabhushi, S. Agner, A. Basavanhally, S. Doyle, and G. Lee, "Computer-aided prognosis: predicting patient and disease outcome via quantitative fusion of multi-scale, multi-modal data," *Computerized Medical Imaging and Graphics*, vol. 35, pp. 506–514, 2011.

[27] Y. Jiang, R. M. Nishikawa, R. A. Schmidt, A. Y. Toledano, and K. Doi, "Potential of computer-aided diagnosis to reduce variability in radiologists' interpretations of mammograms depicting microcalcifications," *Radiology*, vol. 220, no. 3, pp. 787–794, 2001.

[28] H. D. Cheng, X. Cai, X. Chen, L. Hu, and X. Lou, "Computer-aided detection and classification of microcalcifications in mammograms: a survey," *Pattern Recognition*, vol. 36, no. 12, pp. 2967–2991, 2003.

[29] M. A. Mazurowski, P. A. Habas, J. M. Zurada, and G. D. Tourassi, "Decision optimization of case-based computer-aided decision systems using genetic algorithms with application to mammography," *Physics in Medicine and Biology*, vol. 53, no. 4, pp. 895–908, 2008.

[30] Y. D. Cai, T. Huang, K. Y. Feng, L. Hu, and L. Xie, "A unified 35-gene signature for both subtype classification and survival prediction in diffuse large B-cell lymphomas," *PloS one*, vol. 5, no. 9, p. e12726, 2010.

[31] R. M. Rangayyan, F. J. Ayres, and J. E. Leo Desautels, "A review of computer-aided diagnosis of breast cancer: toward the detection of subtle signs," *Journal of the Franklin Institute*, vol. 344, no. 3-4, pp. 312–348, 2007.

[32] P. Ramnarayan, R. R. Kapoor, M. Coren et al., "Measuring the impact of diagnostic decision support on the quality of clinical decision making: development of a reliable and valid composite score," *Journal of the American Medical Informatics Association*, vol. 10, no. 6, pp. 563–572, 2003.

[33] P. Ramnarayan and J. Britto, "Paediatric clinical decision support systems," *Archives of Disease in Childhood*, vol. 87, no. 5, pp. 361–362, 2002.

[34] K. Tan, P. R. Dear, and S. J. Newell, "Clinical decision support systems for neonatal care," *Cochrane Database of Systematic Reviews*, no. 2, Article ID CD004211, 2005.

[35] E. H. Mack, D. S. Wheeler, and P. J. Embi, "Clinical decision support systems in the pediatric intensive care unit," *Pediatric Critical Care Medicine*, vol. 10, no. 1, pp. 23–28, 2009.

[36] P. R. Innocent and R. I. John, "Computer aided fuzzy medical diagnosis," *Information Sciences*, vol. 162, no. 2, pp. 81–104, 2004.

[37] S. Shandilya, K. R. Ward, and K. Najarian, "A time-series approach for shock outcome prediction using machine learning," in *Proceedings of the IEEE International Conference on Bioinformatics and Biomedicine Workshops (BIBMW '10)*, pp. 440–446, December 2010.

[38] P. Davuluri, Y. Tang, J. Wu et al., "A hybrid approach for hemorrhage segmentation in pelvic CT scans," in *Proceedings of the IEEE International Conference on Bioinformatics and Biomedicine Workshops (BIBMW '11)*, pp. 548–554, 2011.

[39] J. Wu, P. Davuluri, K. R. Ward, C. Cockrell, R. Hobson, and K. Najarian, "Fracture detection in traumatic pelvic CT images," *Journal of Biomedical Imaging*, vol. 2012, Article ID 327198, 10 pages, 2012.

[40] S. Y. Ji, R. Smith, T. Huynh, and K. Najarian, "A comparative analysis of multi-level computer-assisted decision making systems for traumatic injuries," *BMC Medical Informatics and Decision Making*, vol. 9, no. 1, article 2, 2009.

[41] V. Maojo and C. A. Kulikowski, "Bioinformatics and medical informatics: collaborations on the road to genomic medicine?" *Journal of the American Medical Informatics Association*, vol. 10, no. 6, pp. 515–522, 2003.

[42] T. Huang, K. Tu, Y. Shyr, C. C. Wei, L. Xie, and Y. X. Li, "The prediction of interferon treatment effects based on time series microarray gene expression profiles," *Journal of Translational Medicine*, vol. 6, article 44, 2008.

[43] X. Zhang, C. Chen, M. Wu et al., "Plasma microRNA profile as a predictor of early virological response to interferon treatment in chronic hepatitis B patients," *Antiviral Therapy*, vol. 17, pp. 1243–1253, 2012.

[44] T. Huang, Z. Xu, L. Chen, Y. D. Cai, and X. Kong, "Computational analysis of HIV-1 resistance based on gene expression profiles and the virus-host interaction network," *PLoS ONE*, vol. 6, no. 3, Article ID e17291, 2011.

[45] T. Huang, J. Wang, Y. D. Cai, H. Yu, and K. C. Chou, "Hepatitis C virus network based classification of hepatocellular cirrhosis and carcinoma," *PloS One*, vol. 7, Article ID e34460, 2012.

[46] E. S. Berner, G. D. Webster, A. A. Shugerman et al., "Performance of four computer-based diagnostic systems," *The New England Journal of Medicine*, vol. 330, no. 25, pp. 1792–1796, 1994.

[47] G. O. Barnett, J. J. Cimino, J. A. Hupp, and E. P. Hoffer, "DXplain. An evolving diagnostic decision-support system," *Journal of the American Medical Association*, vol. 258, no. 1, pp. 67–74, 1987.

[48] R. Miller and F. Masarie Jr Jr., "The quick medical reference (QMR) relationships function: description and evaluation of a simple, efficient "multiple diagnoses" algorithm," in *Proceedings of the World Conference on Medical Informatics (Medinfo '92)*, pp. 512–518, 1992.

[49] C. Manotti, M. Moia, G. Palareti, V. Pengo, L. Ria, and A. G. Dettori, "Effect of computer-aided management on the quality of treatment in anticoagulated patients: a prospective, randomized, multicenter trial of APROAT (Automated Program for

Oral Anticoagulant Treatment)," *Haematologica*, vol. 86, no. 10, pp. 1060–1070, 2001.

[50] B. Kaplan, "Evaluating informatics applications—clinical decision support systems literature review," *International Journal of Medical Informatics*, vol. 64, pp. 15–37, 2001.

[51] X. Song, B. Hwong, G. Matos et al., "Understanding requirements for computer-aided healthcare workflows: experiences and challenges," in *Proceedings of the 28th International Conference on Software Engineering (ICSE '06)*, pp. 930–934, May 2006.

[52] J. Niès, I. Colombet, P. Degoulet, and P. Durieux, "Determinants of success for computerized clinical decision support systems integrated into CPOE systems: a systematic review," in *Proceedings of the American Medical Informatics Association Annual Symposium (AMIA '06)*, p. 594, 2006.

15

A Hierarchical Method for Removal of Baseline Drift from Biomedical Signals: Application in ECG Analysis

Yurong Luo,[1] Rosalyn H. Hargraves,[2] Ashwin Belle,[1] Ou Bai,[3] Xuguang Qi,[1]
Kevin R. Ward,[4] Michael Paul Pfaffenberger,[1] and Kayvan Najarian[1]

[1] Department of Computer Science, School of Engineering, Virginia Commonwealth University, 401 West Main Street,
Richmond, VA 23284, USA

[2] Department of Electrical and Computer Engineering, School of Engineering, Virginia Commonwealth University,
401 West Main Street, Richmond, VA 23284, USA

[3] Department of Biomedical Engineering, School of Engineering, Virginia Commonwealth University, 401 West Main Street,
Richmond, VA 23284, USA

[4] Department of Emergency Medicine and Michigan Critical Injury and Illness Research Center, University of Michigan,
Ann Arbor, MI 48109, USA

Correspondence should be addressed to Ashwin Belle; bellea@vcu.edu

Academic Editors: G. Koch, J. Ma, and V. Positano

Noise can compromise the extraction of some fundamental and important features from biomedical signals and hence prohibit accurate analysis of these signals. Baseline wander in electrocardiogram (ECG) signals is one such example, which can be caused by factors such as respiration, variations in electrode impedance, and excessive body movements. Unless baseline wander is effectively removed, the accuracy of any feature extracted from the ECG, such as timing and duration of the ST-segment, is compromised. This paper approaches this filtering task from a novel standpoint by assuming that the ECG baseline wander comes from an independent and unknown source. The technique utilizes a hierarchical method including a blind source separation (BSS) step, in particular independent component analysis, to eliminate the effect of the baseline wander. We examine the specifics of the components causing the baseline wander and the factors that affect the separation process. Experimental results reveal the superiority of the proposed algorithm in removing the baseline wander.

1. Introduction

The electrocardiogram (ECG) is an important physiological signal that helps determine the state of the cardiovascular system; however, this signal is often corrupted by interfering noise. Baseline wander is a commonly seen noise in ECG recordings and can be caused by respiration, changes in electrode impedance, and motion. Baseline wander can mask important information from the ECG, and if it is not properly removed, crucial diagnostic information contained in the ECG will be lost or corrupted. Therefore, it is vital to effectively eliminate baseline wander before any further processing of ECG such as feature extraction.

The simplest method of baseline wander (drift) removal is the use of a high-pass filter that blocks the drift and passes all main components of ECG though the filter. The main components of ECG include the P-wave, QRS-complex, and T-wave. Specifically, the PR-Segment, ST-Segment, PR-Interval, and QT-Interval are considered as the main segments of the ECG. Each of these intervals/segments has its corresponding frequency components, and according to the American Health Association (AHA), the lowest frequency component in the ECG signal is at about 0.05 Hz [1]. However, a complete baseline removal requires that the cut-off frequency of the high-pass filter be set higher than the lowest frequency in the ECG; otherwise some of the baseline drift will pass through the filter. The frequency of the baseline wander high-pass filter is usually set slightly below 0.5 Hz. Therefore, knowing that the actual ECG signal has components between 0.05 Hz and 0.5 Hz, the forementioned simple approach for baseline removal distorts and deforms the ECG signal. In particular, it affects the ST-segment that has very low frequency components. Furthermore, ectopic beats occurring in the ECG during the course of different types of diseases and injuries change the frequency spectrum of both the baseline wander and the ECG waveforms. All the above-mentioned characteristics demand a more comprehensive approach that works for a wider range of applications and avoids distorting the main ECG waves when removing the baseline drift.

Digital filters are commonly employed method to eliminate baseline wander. Cut-off frequency and phase response characteristics are two main factors considered in the majority of these designs. The use of linear phase filters prevents the issue of phase distortion [2]. For finite impulse response (FIR) filters, it is rather straightforward to achieve linear phase response directly. Feed-forward and feed-back technologies such as infinite impulse response (IIR) filters can also provide minimum phase distortion [3]. In all of these methods, the cut-off frequency should be chosen so that the information in the ECG signals remains undistorted while the baseline wander is removed, which results in a trade-off. Usually, the cut-off frequency is set according to the slowest detected (or assumed) heart rate. However, if there are ectopic beats in the ECG signal, it is even more difficult to find this particular frequency. It is a prevalent phenomenon that the overlap between the baseline wander and low frequency components of the ECG compromises the accuracy of the extracted features.

Time-variant filters are designed to increase flexibility in the adjustment and control of the cut-off frequency. In such methods, the cut-off frequency of the filter is controlled by the low frequency characteristics of the ECG signal [4]. Cubic spline curve fitting [5], linear spline curve fitting [6], and nonlinear spline curve fitting [7] belong to another family of filters that remove the baseline wander but often require some reference points. For instance, the linear spline curve fitting method [5] forms a subsignal of the ECG for a single cardiac cycle starting 60 ms before the P-wave and ending 60 ms after the T-wave and fits a first order polynomial to this sub-signal after subtracting the mean of sub-signal. Multirate system wavelet transform has also been utilized for the ECG baseline wander removal. The approach using wavelet adaptive filter (WAF) [8] consists of two steps. First, a wavelet transform decomposes the ECG signal into seven frequency bands. The second step is an adaptive filter that uses the signal of the seventh lowest frequency band as the primary input and a constant as a reference unit for filtering. Another multi-rate system, empirical mode decomposition (EMD) [9], has also been adopted to eliminate the baseline wander. Compared with the wavelet technique that uses some predefined basis functions to represent a signal, EMD relies on a fully data-driven mechanism; that is, EMD does not require any a-priori known basis.

Adaptive filters as a cascade structure [10] have also been used for this application. The first step of this approach uses an adaptive notch filter to eliminate the DC component of the ECG. The second step forms a comb filter assuming that the signal is an event-related signal. Blind source separation (BSS), in particular independent component analysis (ICA)

[11–13], is another choice to remove the baseline wander. As a specific type of BSS method, ICA has been extensively used in biomedical signals [14–16], such as the ECG and the EEG. It has been used as an effective method to decompose multichannel signals into fundamental components. As many more applications of ICA are being recognized, newer variations of ICA are being introduced. Standard ICA [17] (sICA) is a technique that is used to estimate source signals when several mixtures of signals are available. Both the source signals and the mixing process are unknown, and the sources are estimated only on the assumption that they are statistically independent. Comparing the formulation of the standard ICA, convolutive ICA (fICA) deems that the finite impulse response is closely associated with the mixing process, and the mixing process can be considered as a weighted and delayed mixture of sources [18, 19]. Fast and robust fixed-point ICA [20] is produced based on the idea that it is feasible to use contrast function to approximate negentropy. Through a fixed-point algorithm, the contrast function is maximized to extract latent sources with high speed. Temporally constrained ICA [21, 22] is a more flexible model to separate latent sources. By using prior knowledge or additional constraints, the targeted latent source is extracted. Moreover, there are many other forms of ICA for different applications such as topographic independent component analysis [23] and spatial and temporal independent component analysis [24].

In summary, the traditional methods are limited in either frequency delineation or reference choice, and the case of BBS in applications mentioned previously does not give sufficient evidence in noise removal. Based on these points of view, in the proposed method, a unified method utilizing an adaptive notch filter and BSS is used for baseline drift removal. Specifically, multichannel signals are constructed using a single-channel signal, and ICA is applied to the ECG. The main contributions of our work lie in combining the capabilities of adaptive filters and BSS, expanding the capabilities of the independent components for this application by customizing the ICA method towards the removal of the ECG baseline wander. Furthermore, the factors affecting the performance of the separation process are explored and improved in this paper.

The rest of the paper is organized as follows. The overall structure of the proposed method is illustrated in Section 2. The adaptive notch filter, as employed in the paper, is described in Section 3. The concepts and formulation of the ICA, the fast and robust fixed-point ICA, and the customized form are introduced in Section 4. Section 5 introduces the process of detecting the components that cause the baseline wander and verifies this process. This section also explores the factors that affect the separation of the results. Finally, Section 6 concludes the paper.

2. Method

Figure 1 shows the framework of the proposed method. As it can be seen in Figure 1, the first step of the proposed method is an adaptive notch filter, designed to form subsignals of the ECG, as described later. Next, as shown in Figure 1,

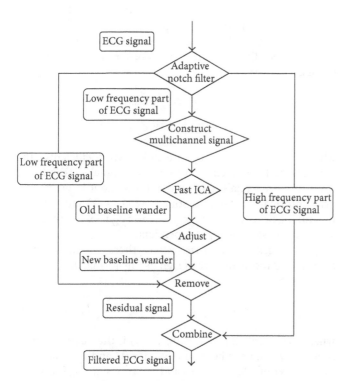

FIGURE 1: Schematic diagram of proposed method.

the proposed method utilizes ICA to remove the baseline drift. Considering the noisy nature of the typical raw ECG signal, in this study, subsignals in low frequencies of the ECG are formed and these filtered signals are, then, formed by an adaptive notch filter, then used as the input to the ICA algorithm. Moreover, with regard to the inputs fed to the ICA algorithm, in this study, only a single-channel ECG signal is available. Therefore, knowing that ICA requires multichannel signals to process as its input, in order to use ICA to remove baseline wander, one needs to build multichannel signals from the single-channel ECG. In order to address this issue in the proposed method, a systematic process was created in which delayed versions of the ECG are stacked to form the multi-channel signal. In addition, as shown in Figure 1, the independent component formed by the ICA as the output, which is originally labeled as the baseline wander, needs to be further adjusted to form a better estimate of the baseline wander. This is due to the fact that, while one of the components resembles the baseline drift, it is unlikely that any of the original components detected by the ICA is "purely" the baseline wander.

The specific steps shown in Figure 1 are further described below.

(a) Form sub-signals of ECG using an adaptive notch filter: as shown in Figure 1, the adaptive notch filter [25, 26] is designed and customized to form the sub-signal. The reason for using the adaptive notch filter is its flexibility as well as its relatively superior performance compared with other filters. As mentioned above, applying the ICA algorithm on a sub-signal of the ECG has the advantage of reducing the errors

coming from multi-channel signals in estimating the baseline wander.

(b) Construct multi-channel signals: applying ICA requires that the signals are multi-channel ones. However, in many ECG processing applications only the single-channel ECG signal is available and/or processed. The proposed method applies the methodology in [11] to construct multi-channel signals by delaying the single-channel signal. In our study, the multi-channel signals are constructed using sixty signals, which are delayed 10 sample points (~83 ms) of the original signal in succession.

(c) Adjust the baseline wander extracted by ICA: the baseline wander extracted by ICA is an approximation of the true baseline wander because (1) there will be some errors in the resulting component due to the fact that the estimation process used in the ICA (in particular in the first few attempts) may be nonoptimal; (2) in the ICA analysis there may be more than one maximum in the estimation function and, therefore, the true baseline wander may not be located accurately; (3) the constructed multi-channel signals cannot convey all information about the baseline wander and, as such, the proposed process may alleviate the issues associated with the non-optimal construction of multi-channel signals. The 10-sample shift of the signals provides large enough variations between the multisignal component to alleviate the issues concerning dependencies for ICA processing.

3. Adaptive Notch Filter

The adaptive notch filter [26] is based on the same theoretical foundations as adaptive noise cancellation [25]. There are two inputs in the structure of the adaptive noise cancelling. One is the primary input, containing the signal and the noise and the other one is the reference input, which is the reference signal related to the noise in the primary input. Using least mean square (LMS) criterion, the reference signal is gradually approached to the noise in the primary input. When the stability is achieved, the output is acquired through subtracting the reference input from the primary input. This type of filter can deal with inputs that are deterministic or stochastic, stationary or time-variant. If the inputs are stationary stochastic, the solution of the adaptive noise cancelling approaches closely Wiener filter [25]. As to the adaptive notch filter, the reference signal is the signal with one- or multifixed frequencies, which are treated as the frequencies to be excluded.

The advantages of adaptive notch filters lie in the following aspects: (1) if the frequency of the interference is not precisely known or the interference drifts in the frequency, the exact excluded frequency could be measured/adapted during the filtering process; (2) the filter is tunable since the null point moves with the reference frequencies; (3) the adaptive notch filter can be made very sharp at the reference frequency; (4) through adjusting the parameters, the adaptive notch filter can be considered as a time-invariant filter by

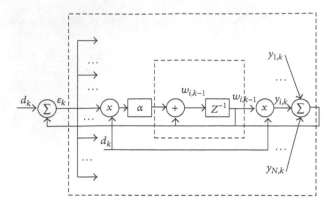

FIGURE 2: The diagram of adaptive noise cancelling.

lessening the influence of the time-varying components. The inference of adaptive notch filter is described in [25, 26]. The diagram of adaptive noise cancelling is shown in Figure 2. The system is an N-stage tapped delay line (TDL). The weight of the filter is updated according to the following equations:

$$y_k = w_k^T x_k,$$

$$\varepsilon_k = d_k - y_k, \tag{1}$$

$$w_{k+1} = w_k + \partial \varepsilon_k x_k,$$

where x is the reference input, d is the desired response, y is the output of the filter, w is the weight of the filter, ∂ is the adaptation constant, and k is the time index. As described in [26], the response from $E(z)$ to $Y(z)$ includes two parts. In practical applications, it is feasible to make the time-varying component to be insignificant ($\beta/N \approx 0$) by changing the values of N and setting β as follows:

$$\beta = \frac{\sin(N w_r T)}{\sin(w_r T)}, \tag{2}$$

where w_r is the frequency of the interference. If the reference input is considered to be the following form:

$$x = C \cos(w_r T + \theta), \tag{3}$$

the transfer function of adaptive notch filter can be expressed as follows:

$$H(z) = \frac{z^2 - 2z \cos(w_r T) + 1}{z^2 - 2(1 - N\partial C^2/4) z \cos(w_r T) + (1 - N\partial C^2/2)}. \tag{4}$$

Therefore, the parameter N can be set to the fixed value as described above. It can be seen that the above-mentioned filter is very flexible and can be adjusted using the adaption constants ∂ and C to provide the desired bandwidth and depth of a suitable notch filter.

4. Independent Component Analysis

After applying the notch filter, the main step used is ICA. First, the "standard" ICA is described. ICA can be briefly explained using a simple example of separating two source signals $s_1(t)$ and $s_2(t)$ that were mixed by an unknown linear process. Two different linear mixtures, $x_1(t)$ and $x_2(t)$, are given as follows:

$$x_1(t) = c_{11}s_1 + c_{12}s_2,$$

$$x_2(t) = c_{21}s_1 + c_{22}s_2, \tag{5}$$

where c_{11}, c_{12}, c_{21}, and c_{22} are unknown coefficients. The objective of the problem is to recover the signal $s_1(t)$ and $s_2(t)$ from mixture signals $x_1(t)$ and $x_2(t)$ without knowing any prior information about the source signals $s_1(t)$ and $s_2(t)$ and the mixing process (i.e., c_{11}, c_{12}, c_{21}, and c_{22}), except that $s_1(t)$ and $s_2(t)$ are statistically independent.

In the generalized case, where there are more latent sources and more mixture of signals, the formal definition of ICA is as follows:

$$x_i(t) = c_{i1}s_1 + c_{i2}s_2 + \cdots + c_{in}s_n, \quad i \in [1, n], \tag{6}$$

where $s_i(t)$ is called latent source, $x_i(t)$ is the mixture signal, c_{ij} is the mixing coefficient between $x_i(t)$ and $s_j(t)$, and n is the number of latent sources and mixture signals. The above formulation can be expressed as the following matrix form:

$$X = C_{n \times n} \cdot S, \tag{7}$$

where X is the matrix of mixture signals, in which each column is one mixture signal; S is the matrix of latent signals, in which each column is one latent signal; and $C_{n \times n}$ is the matrix for mixing coefficients.

The feasibility of solving the ICA problem lies in the condition that the latent sources are independent of each other. According to the Central Limit Theorem, the distribution of a sum of independent random variables approaches a Gaussian distribution. This implies that the solution of ICA can be achieved when distribution diverges from Gaussianity. The deviation from Gaussianity can be determined using measures such as Negentropy.

Negentropy is one measure of non-gaussianity defined based on the concept of entropy, which is the fundamental concept of information theory. Entropy, E, as a measure of information in random variables is defined for a discrete random variable y as follows:

$$E(y) = -\sum_i P(y = c_i) \log P(y = c_i), \tag{8}$$

where c_i is the possible values of Y and $P(Y = c_i)$ means the probability when the value of Y is c_i. For a continuous random variable y, entropy E is defined as the following equation:

$$E(y) = -\int f(y) \log(f(y)) \, dy, \tag{9}$$

where f is the probability distribution function. Negentropy, J, is then defined as follows:

$$J(y) = E(y_{\text{gauss}}) - E(y), \tag{10}$$

where y_{gauss} is a Gaussian random variable with the same covariance matrix as y. A fundamental conclusion in information theory is that a Gaussian variable has the largest entropy among all random variables of equal variance. Hence, negentropy is always nonnegative, and it is zero only if Y has a Gaussian distribution.

The exact calculation of negentropy requires an accurate estimation of the probability distribution function, which may be computationally costly or data intensive. Therefore, it is often preferred to find simple approximations of negentropy. Simple approximations of negentropy have been introduced [27], which are based on the maximum entropy principle. In general, the following family of approximations is the most commonly used group:

$$J(y) = \sum_{i=1}^{p} k_i [E(G_i(y)) - E(G(v))]^2, \qquad (11)$$

where k_i are constants and v is a gaussian random variable with zero mean and unit variance. Often, the value of p and k_i can be set to one. Therefore, the above formulation becomes as follows:

$$J(y) = [E(G(y)) - E(G(v))]^2. \qquad (12)$$

The following formulations of G functions have proved very useful in practical applications:

$$G_1(y) = \frac{1}{a_1} \log \cosh(a_1 y), \qquad g_1(y) = \tanh(a_1 y),$$

$$G_2(y) = -\frac{1}{a_2} \exp\left(-\frac{a_2 y^2}{2}\right), \qquad g_2(y) = y \exp\left(-\frac{a_2 y^2}{2}\right),$$

$$G_3(y) = \frac{1}{4} y^4, \qquad g_3(y) = y^3,$$

$$\qquad (13)$$

where $1 \le a_1 \le 2$, $a_2 \approx 1$, and g is the first derivative of the function G.

Before applying the main processing operations of the ICA, it is often necessary to perform some preprocessing. Usually, the two different operations are conducted: centering and whitening. Centering requires that the random variable y is a zero-mean random variable, and it is performed by subtracting its mean vector. Whitening will make the random variable uncorrelated and set their variances equal to unity by using the eigenvalue decomposition of their covariance matrix:

$$E\{yy^T\} = DVD^T, \qquad (14)$$

where D is the orthogonal matrix of eigenvectors and V is the diagonal matrix of eigenvalues. Now, assuming that z is a new random variable after whitening, consider the following:

$$z = DV^{-1/2}D^T y. \qquad (15)$$

Whitening makes the problem change from estimating mixing matrix to estimating a new one $\widetilde{C}$:

$$z = DV^{1/2}D^T Cs = \widetilde{C}s. \qquad (16)$$

Among several improvements of ICA, fast and fixed-point independent component analysis [20], as a direct extension of the standard ICA, was developed for calculating latent sources with high speed. The basic rule of fast and fixed-point independent component analysis is to find a direction, which can maximize non-Gaussianity of $w^T x$. Non-Gaussianity is decided according to the approximation of nongaussianity as mentioned above. The following is the basic description of the algorithm.

(a) Initialize a weight vector w in one direction.

(b) Change the weight vector according to the following criteria: $w' = E\{xg(w^T x)\} - E\{g'(w^T x)\}w$, and normalize the weight vector as $w = w'/\|w'\|$.

(c) If the weights have not converged, go back to step (b),

where w is the weight vector to calculate latent source $s = w^T x$ and convergence means that the old weight vector and the new weight vector are in the same direction.

In this study, the fast and fixed-point independent component analysis [20] is used as the implementation of ICA block shown in Figure 1.

5. Results

An ECG dataset of human volunteer undergoing lower body negative pressure (LBNP) [28] as a surrogate of hemorrhage was employed to verify the effectiveness of removing baseline wander. This data set was created under Institutional Review Board approval. The LBNP dataset consisted of a total of 91 subjects. Each subject had a single vector lead ECG recording collected at the sampling rate of 500 Hz. The baseline wander in ECG signals demonstrated significant level of variations in the amplitude over the course of the LBNP experiment. During LBNP, subjects are exposed to increasing negative pressure to their lower bodies. This causes a redistribution of blood volume to the lower extremities and abdomen causing a decrease in blood pressure and cardiac output and resulting in an increased respiratory rate.

The results of the proposed method are compared with a reference method, called robust locally weighted regression [29], which is often treated as one of the most robust and commonly used methods to remove baseline drift. The robust locally weighted regression method employs two techniques: the local fitting of polynomials and an adaptation of iterated weighted least squares to remove the baseline drift.

5.1. Results of Adaptive Notch Filter. One objective of the proposed system is the removal of unwanted frequencies around 0 Hz as well as 60 Hz. As the frequencies around zero are excluded, the filter acts as a high-pass filter. In order to lessen the influence of the time-varying components, one needs to first set a suitable parameter N to obtain a desirable level of time-varying component, β/N. Figure 3 shows the value of the time-varying component β/N for different values of N.

Figure 3 indicates that the value of N determines the degree at which the time varying component influences

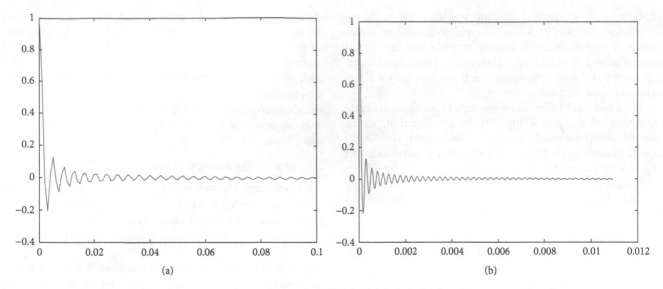

FIGURE 3: The resulting value of β/N (a) $N = 256$; (b) $N = 4096$.

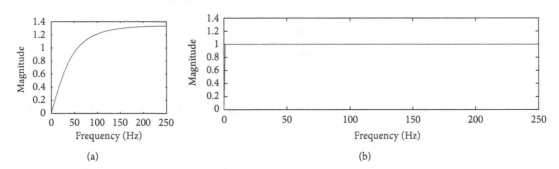

FIGURE 4: Transfer function for two choices of adaptive notch filters (a) $C = 1$; (b) $C = 0.01$.

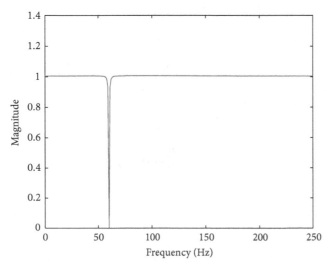

FIGURE 5: Transfer function of the adaptive notch filter around 60 Hz.

the filter. In general, with the increase in the value of N, this influence decreases gradually. In this study, the value of N was set to 10,000. The parameter ∂ identifies whether or not the

adaptation converges [25]. The value of ∂ should be greater than 0 but less than the reciprocal of the largest eigenvalue, λ, of the matrix R, which is defined as the correlation matrix of signal [25]. In this study, the value of ∂ was set to 0.0001. The bandwidth of the filter can be approximated using the following equation [26]:

$$\text{BW} = \frac{N \partial C^2}{2T} \ \ (\text{rad/s}). \tag{17}$$

Figure 4 shows the transfer function of the resulting adaptive notch filter, and, as expected, this filter acts as a high-pass filter. Note that the value of C provides yet another degree of freedom for this filter design process, and, hence, Figure 4 presents the transfer function for two different filters formed using two different values of C, each resulting in a very different bandwidth. A main advantage of the adaptive notch filter used here is that changing the values of parameters N, ∂, and C can provide a wide spectrum of desired filters with diverse shapes of transfer function.

Adaptive notch filter for frequencies around 60 Hz is designed similarly. The parameter N was to 2048, ∂ to 0.001, and C to 0.1. Figure 5 depicts the transfer function of the resulting adaptive notch filter.

TABLE 1: Experimental results of removing the baseline wander.

Subject	Shift/elevation	Error$_1$	Error$_2$
1	290/0	2.0996	0.7847
2	250/1	28.1832	2.7037
3	300/4	193.9524	3.4495
4	300/1	24.3905	1.0727
5	300/3	89.1358	3.6282
6	290/2	17.9017	1.1614
7	300/1	28.955	1.0623
8	200/0	107.7542	13.4439
9	300/2	203.8138	4.0846
10	290/2	81.7942	2.2818
11	290/2	256.3747	8.7264
12	300/2	41.0977	2.4223
13	260/1	44.2238	2.279
14	260/2	101.7592	2.3317
15	310/2	700.1481	101.429
16	290/1	12.7575	1.3522
17	290/1	45.6429	2.6412
18	310/0	36.8833	11.8224
19	290/1	9.1224	1.88
20	290/2	181.3923	23.0193
21	300/2	25.4492	2.6421
22	370/4	252.4353	8.5616
23	260/2	304.7066	7.4637
24	290/1	116.9048	3.77
25	300/1	16.3922	1.05
26	290/0	3.4748	0.6671
27	300/2	144.4347	1.8579
28	290/0	23.9724	2.1641
29	290/1	14.5089	0.2205
30	290/1	155.3859	3.6707
31	300/1	50.6959	2.6757
32	300/1	27.2665	1.101
33	300/1	56.7045	1.999
34	290/2	324.4399	10.0313
35	300/1	42.6266	0.8791
36	290/2	539.7357	31.3238
37	290/1	19.8874	0.8131
38	290/1	14.3623	2.6499
39	260/1	8.8582	6.4787
40	300/4	135.0286	3.0056
41	290/1	29.5551	2.7541
42	300/1	43.3923	3.0052
43	290/0	51.0465	6.9241
44	290/0	31.9213	5.4646
45	290/1	9.7597	1.3328
46	270/1	22.7897	1.3598
47	290/2	93.5265	1.899
48	290/0	8.7422	1.5607
49	350/6	892.829	74.3034
50	300/3	209.4986	6.3436

TABLE 1: Continued.

Subject	Shift/elevation	Error$_1$	Error$_2$
51	300/3	60.5121	2.6645
52	290/1	3.7123	0.9486
53	290/4	247.2271	5.138
54	250/1	32.0128	2.8609
55	310/0	20.1471	1.336
56	310/0	5.2858	4.0839
57	290/0	7.1664	0.9526
58	300/1	35.4656	0.8932
59	290/1	10.9895	0.8653
60	300/3	115.7327	4.8387
61	300/1	26.7803	0.7141
62	290/2	9.3222	2.8809
63	290/1	16.9436	0.9469
64	300/0	27.7014	1.7794
65	290/1	55.1891	4.9226
66	310/6	620.3234	8.0999
67	400/2	23.6969	0.5595
68	290/2	36.63757	1.4766
69	290/2	241.5044	11.7279
70	290/1	5.5229	0.3386
71	290/2	173.1734	7.0318
72	300/2	77.4627	3.2468

5.2. Experimental Results and Problems Analysis. The results of both methods, that is, the proposed and the reference methods, are examined and compared in all 91 subjects. A unified "span" value, described in the reference method [29], which is designed to assess the quality of the methods in removing the baseline wander, is calculated for all cases. This value for all experimental results was 1500, which is the level identifying a very high quality of baseline removal.

The 91 cases, based on the closeness of the results of the two methods, are divided into two groups. The details of the results are shown for 72 out of 91 subjects in Table 1; for these subjects the proposed algorithm achieves almost identical results as the reference method. The results of the remaining 19 subjects, which will be discussed separately, show that the proposed method cannot be able to remove the baseline drift optimally.

In Table 1, "shift" and "elevation" are the values for adjustments to the original independent component (baseline wander) to form the new baseline wander in the horizontal and vertical directions; "error$_1$" represents the difference between the old baseline wander (sig$_1$) before shift and the baseline wander (sig) from the reference method calculated as follows:

$$error_1 = \frac{(sig_1 - sig)^2}{n}, \qquad (18)$$

where n is the number of sample points in the baseline wander, and finally "error$_2$" represents the difference between

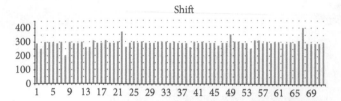

FIGURE 6: Value of "shift" that adjusts the old baseline wander to form the new one for all 72 subjects.

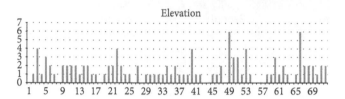

FIGURE 7: Value of "elevation" that adjust the old baseline wander to form the new one for all 72 subjects.

the new baseline wander (sig_2) and the baseline wander (sig) from the reference method calculated as follows:

$$error_2 = \frac{(sig_2 - sig)^2}{n}. \tag{19}$$

As it can be seen in Table 1, for all cases $error_2$ is significantly smaller than $error_1$ which shows the impact of that method in "purifying" the baseline wander and creating a better estimate of the drift. In order to better assess the performance of the proposed method in removing the baseline wander, more analyses are conducted on the results.

Figures 6 and 7 show the shift and elevation for all 72 subjects. As can be seen, both of these variables are almost the same for all subjects and do not change across different subjects (x-axis) or vary in a small scope. This observation illustrates the reason to adjust the parameters between the old baseline wander and the new baseline wander.

Figure 8 shows the error reduction in 72 subjects after adjusting shift and elevation value. It can be seen that in all of these cases the errors decrease significantly after adjusting the baseline wander compared with the baseline wander. The average percentage of error reduction Aver E reaches up to 90.13%. The formulation of the average percentage of error reduction is shown in the following:

$$percentage\,(i) = \frac{(error_1 - error_2)}{error_1}, \quad i \in [1,n],$$
$$Aver\,E = \sum_{i=1}^{i=n} percentage\,(i), \tag{20}$$

where i is the index of subject and n is the total number of subjects.

Sample signals before baseline removal and after baseline removal with the proposed method as well as the reference method are shown in Figure 9. As shown in Figure 9, the results of the two methods in all above-mentioned 72 subjects

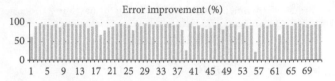

FIGURE 8: Improved percentages of error after adjustment.

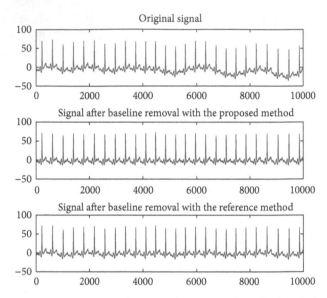

FIGURE 9: Comparison between the proposed method and the reference method.

are very similar. In addition, as it can be seen, both methods are very effective in removing the baseline drift.

However, as mentioned above, on the ECG of the remaining 19 subjects, the results of the proposed method and the reference method are not as similar; that is, the value of $error_2$ (which shows the difference between the two methods) is significant. This is because in these signals the inherent pattern observed from ECG is highly distorted hence leading to spurious estimations. As mentioned before, we have visually inspected all 91 cases. By examining the signals for these 19 cases, it was discovered that the high value of $error_2$ does not seem to come from the inability of the proposed method to remove the baseline wander. In such case, the possible reason and improvement are discussed in the following part.

As a comparison between the proposed method and reference method, some such sample results are shown in Figure 10. In these cases, due to the presence of significantly stronger baseline drifts, the reference method seems not to be eliminating almost all the baseline drift. The reason for this might lie in the fact that the reference method relies heavily on the parameters set that may work very well for some ECG signals but not for others. As shown in Figure 10, our proposed method shows more effective performance in removing the baseline around times such as 4700, 5500, 7500, and 9500. Another major advantage is that the proposed

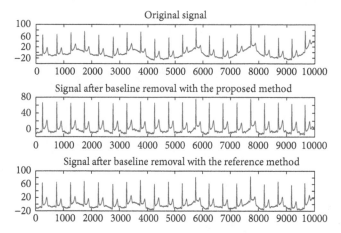

FIGURE 10: Comparison of the proposed method to the reference method.

method is computationally faster than the reference method while achieving the same quality of results.

5.3. Further Experimental Analysis of Method. As mentioned above, in the experiment, multi-channel signals are constructed through a single-channel signal. The multi-channel signals are constructed using sixty signals, which are 10 sample point delayed successions of the original signal. By observation, the number of the constructed signals greatly impacts the success of finding the true baseline wander. Moreover, the degree of delay has a close relationship with the smoothness of the baseline wander. Experimentally, it can be considered that more channels and smaller delayed signals may achieve better results, meaning that the constructed multi-channel signals may convey enough information in order to accurately extract the baseline wander.

In addition, as discussed above, the LBNP dataset shows a significant level of variations in the baseline drift. Therefore, in further analysis of the method, the sub-signals were segmented to verify whether the slow changes in the trend of the baseline wander affect the results of the proposed method in separating the baseline wander. The sub-signals were chosen to be only 10,000 sample points long from the beginning of the original signal in LBNP dataset. Experimental results showed that the slow changing trend of the baseline wander did not affect the performance of the proposed method in extracting the baseline wander. In other words, the baseline drift with slow changing trends can also be successfully extracted using the proposed method.

6. Conclusion

While using the blind source separation paradigm, the ECG baseline wander or drift may be removed. The present paper demonstrates a hierarchical method utilizing ICA to significantly improve the performance of this process and achieve improved performance. Compared with the existing methods, the proposed method has the following advantages. (1) The proposed method provides more flexibility with

regard to parameter estimation and selection. (2) When following the steps proposed for adjustment of ICA process, the fundamental assumption of baseline noise coming from an independent source can be further verified, which supports the validity of using the method for ECG baseline removal. Such an assumption, verified by additional experimental results, would present a chance to remove other types of noise. (3) The filtering process proposed for forming the multi-channel signals provides a highly flexible method to form the input to ICA.

References

[1] L. T. Sheffield, A. Berson, D. Bragg-Remschel et al., "Recommendations for standard of instrumentation and practice in the use of ambulatory electrocardiography," *Circulation*, vol. 71, no. 3, pp. 626A–636A, 1985.

[2] J. A. van Alsté, W. van Eck, and O. E. Herrmann, "ECG baseline wander reduction using linear phase filters," *Computers and Biomedical Research*, vol. 19, no. 5, pp. 417–427, 1986.

[3] L. P. Harting, N. M. Fedotov, and C. H. Slump, "On baseline drift suppressing in ECG-recordings," in *Proceedings of the IEEE Benelux Signal Processing Symposium*, pp. 133–136, 2004.

[4] L. Sornmo, "Time-varying digital filtering of ECG baseline wander," *Medical and Biological Engineering and Computing*, vol. 31, no. 5, pp. 503–508, 1993.

[5] C. R. Meyer and H. N. Keiser, "Electrocardiogram baseline noise estimation and removal using cubic splines and state-space computation techniques," *Computers and Biomedical Research*, vol. 10, no. 5, pp. 459–470, 1977.

[6] C. Papaloukas, D. I. Fotiadis, A. P. Liavas, A. Likas, and L. K. Michalis, "A knowledge-based technique for automated detection of ischaemic episodes in long duration electrocardiograms," *Medical and Biological Engineering and Computing*, vol. 39, no. 1, pp. 105–112, 2001.

[7] V. S. Chouhan and S. S. Mehta, "Total removal of baseline drift from ECG signal," in *Proceedings of International Conference on Computing: Theory and Applications (ICCTA '07)*, pp. 512–515, March 2007.

[8] K. L. Park, K. J. Lee, and H. R. Yoon, "Application of a wavelet adaptive filter to minimise distortion of the ST-segment," *Medical and Biological Engineering and Computing*, vol. 36, no. 5, pp. 581–586, 1998.

[9] M. Blanco-Velasco, B. Weng, and K. E. Barner, "ECG signal denoising and baseline wander correction based on the empirical mode decomposition," *Computers in Biology and Medicine*, vol. 38, no. 1, pp. 1–13, 2008.

[10] J. Raimon, P. Laguna, N. V. Thakor, and P. Caminal, "Adaptive baseline wander removal in the ECG: comparative analysis with cubic spline technique," in *Proceeding of Computers in Cardiology*, pp. 143–146, October 1992.

[11] Z. Barati and A. Ayatollahi, "Baseline wandering removal by using independent component analysis to single-channel ECG data," in *Proceedings of International Conference on Biomedical and Pharmaceutical Engineering (ICBPE '06)*, pp. 152–156, December 2006.

[12] M. P. S. Chawla, H. K. Verma, and V. Kumar, "Artifacts and noise removal in electrocardiograms using independent component analysis," *International Journal of Cardiology*, vol. 129, no. 2, pp. 278–281, 2008.

[13] M. P. S. Chawla, H. K. Verma, and V. Kumar, "Independent component analysis: a novel technique for removal of artifacts and baseline wander in ECG," in *Proceedings of the 3rd National Control Instrumentation System Conference*, pp. 14–18, 2006.

[14] M. Keralapura, M. Pourfathi, and B. Sirkeci-Mergen, "Impact of contrast functions in Fast-ICA on twin ECG separation," *IAENG International Journal of Computer Science*, vol. 38, no. 1, pp. 38–47, 2011.

[15] K. Arfanakis, D. Cordes, V. M. Haughton, C. H. Moritz, M. A. Quigley, and M. E. Meyerand, "Combining independent component analysis and correlation analysis to probe interregional connectivity in fMRI task activation datasets," *Magnetic Resonance Imaging*, vol. 18, no. 8, pp. 921–930, 2000.

[16] Y. Ye, Z. L. Zhang, J. Zeng, and L. Peng, "A fast and adaptive ICA algorithm with its application to fetal electrocardiogram extraction," *Applied Mathematics and Computation*, vol. 205, no. 2, pp. 799–806, 2008.

[17] A. Hyvärinen and E. Oja, "Independent component analysis: algorithms and applications," *Neural Networks*, vol. 13, no. 4-5, pp. 411–430, 2000.

[18] M. Milanesi, N. Vanello, V. Positano et al., "Frequency domain approach to blind source separation in ECG monitoring by wearable system," in *Proceedings of Computers in Cardiology*, pp. 767–770, September 2005.

[19] M. Milanesi, N. Vanello, V. Positano, M. F. Santarelli, and L. Landini, "Separation and identification of biomedical signals based on frequency domain independent component analysis," *WSEAS Transactions on Systems*, vol. 4, no. 10, pp. 1752–1761, 2005.

[20] A. Hyvarinen, "Fast and robust fixed-point algorithms for independent component analysis," *IEEE Transactions on Neural Networks*, vol. 10, no. 3, pp. 626–634, 1999.

[21] C. J. James and O. J. Gibson, "Temporally constrained ICA: an application to artifact rejection in electromagnetic brain signal analysis," *IEEE Transactions on Biomedical Engineering*, vol. 50, no. 9, pp. 1108–1116, 2003.

[22] J. Lee, K. L. Park, and K. J. Lee, "Temporally constrained ICA-based foetal ECG separation," *Electronics Letters*, vol. 41, no. 21, pp. 1158–1160, 2005.

[23] A. Hyvärinen, P. O. Hoyer, and M. Inki, "Topographic independent component analysis," *Neural Computation*, vol. 13, no. 7, pp. 1527–1558, 2001.

[24] V. D. Calhoun, T. Adali, G. D. Pearlson, and J. J. Pekar, "Spatial and temporal independent component analysis of functional MRI data containing a pair of task-related waveforms," *Human Brain Mapping*, vol. 13, no. 1, pp. 43–53, 2001.

[25] B. Widrow, J. R. Glover, J. M. McCool et al., "Adaptive noise cancelling: principles and applications," *Proceedings of the IEEE*, vol. 63, no. 12, pp. 1692–1716, 1975.

[26] J. R. Glover, "Adaptive noise canceling applied to sinusoidal interferences," *IEEE Transactions on Acoustics, Speech, and Signal Processing*, vol. 25, no. 6, pp. 484–491, 1977.

[27] A. Hyvarinen, "New approximations of differential entropy for independent component analysis and projection pursuit," in *Advances in Neural Information Processing Systems*, vol. 10, pp. 273–279, 1998.

[28] S. Y. Ji, A. Belle, K. R. Ward et al., "Heart rate variability analysis during central hypovolemia using wavelet transformation," *Journal of Clinical Monitoring and Computing*, pp. 1–14, 2013.

[29] W. S. Cleveland, "Robust locally weighted regression and smoothing scatterplots," *Journal of the American Statistical Assocaition*, vol. 74, pp. 829–836, 1979.

16

A Learning-Based Approach for Biomedical Word Sense Disambiguation

Hisham Al-Mubaid and Sandeep Gungu

University of Houston-Clear Lake, Houston, TX 77058, USA

Correspondence should be addressed to Hisham Al-Mubaid, hisham@uhcl.edu

Academic Editor: Massimo Cafaro

In the biomedical domain, word sense ambiguity is a widely spread problem with bioinformatics research effort devoted to it being not commensurate and allowing for more development. This paper presents and evaluates a learning-based approach for sense disambiguation within the biomedical domain. The main limitation with supervised methods is the need for a corpus of manually disambiguated instances of the ambiguous words. However, the advances in automatic text annotation and tagging techniques with the help of the plethora of knowledge sources like ontologies and text literature in the biomedical domain will help lessen this limitation. The proposed method utilizes the interaction model (mutual information) between the context words and the senses of the target word to induce reliable learning models for sense disambiguation. The method has been evaluated with the benchmark dataset NLM-WSD with various settings and in biomedical entity species disambiguation. The evaluation results showed that the approach is very competitive and outperforms recently reported results of other published techniques.

1. Introduction

Word sense disambiguation is the task of determining the correct sense of a given word in a given context. In the general language domain, and within natural language processing (NLP), the word sense disambiguation (WSD) problem has been studied and investigated extensively over the past few decades [1, 2]. In the biomedical domain, on the other hand, WSD is more widely spread in the biological and medical texts and sometimes with more severe consequences. The amount of WSD research in the biomedical domain is not proportional to the extent of the problem. As an example, in the biomedical texts, the term *"blood pressure"* has three possible senses according to the Unified Medical Language System (UMLS) [3] as follows: *organism function*, *diagnostic procedure*, and *laboratory or test result*. Thus, if this term *blood pressure* is found in a medical text, the reader has to manually judge and determines which one of these three senses is intended in that text. Word sense disambiguation contributes in many important applications including the text mining, information extraction, and information retrieval systems [1, 2, 4]. It is also considered a key component in most intelligent knowledge discovery and text mining applications.

The main classes of approaches of word sense disambiguation include supervised methods and unsupervised methods. The supervised methods rely on training and learning phases that require a dataset or corpus containing manually disambiguated instances to be used to train the system [5, 6]. The unsupervised methods, on the other hand, are based on knowledge sources like ontology, for example, from UMLS, or text corpora [2, 4, 7, 8]. Our approach in this paper is a supervised approach. In this paper, we present and evaluate a supervised method for biomedical word sense disambiguation. The method is based on machine learning and uses some feature selection techniques in constructing feature vectors for the words to be disambiguated. We conducted the evaluation using the NLM-WSD benchmark corpus and species disambiguation dataset. The evaluation results proved the competitiveness of the proposed approach as it outperforms some recently published techniques including supervised techniques.

2. Related Work

In the biomedical domain, the applications of text mining and machine learning techniques were quite successful and encouraging [6]. Most of the methods for biomedical entity name recognition, classification, or disambiguation can be roughly divided into three categories: (i) supervised and machine-learning-based techniques, (ii) statistical and corpus-based techniques, and (iii) syntactic and rule-based techniques [9–11]. Moreover, the bioinformatics literature shows that biomedical WSD has been a quite active area of research with a number of approaches proposed and applied to biomedical data [1, 2, 4, 8, 12, 13].

Agirre et al. proposed a graph-based WSD technique which is considered unsupervised but relies on UMLS [2]. The concepts of UMLS are represented as a graph, and WSD is done using personalized page rank algorithm [2].

In another related research, Jimeno-Yepes and Aronson [4] presented a review and evaluation of four WSD approaches that rely on UMLS as the source for knowledge for disambiguation. In [1], Stevenson et al. use supervised learners with linguistic features extracted from the context of the word in combination with MeSH terms for disambiguation.

The UMLS has been used, by Humphrey et al., as a knowledge source for assigning the correct sense for a given word [13]. They used journal descriptor indexing of the abstract containing the term to assign a semantic type from UMLS metathesaurus [3, 13].

In bioinformatics and computational biology, there are quite a few tasks similar to WSD like biomedical term disambiguation, gene protein name disambiguation, and disambiguating species for biomedical named entities [9–11]. The task of biomedical named entity disambiguation or classification is an augmentation of the well-known task of biomedical named entity recognition (NER). In NER, biomedical entity names, for example, gene names, are recognized and extracted from the text. In the biomedical named entity disambiguation, the extracted entity names (e.g., gene product names) will be applied onto a process such that each occurrence should be disambiguated as either *gene* name or *protein* name as the same name can refer to a gene or protein. For example, the biomedical entity name *SBP2* can be a *gene* name or a *protein* name depending on the context [10, 11]. Furthermore, in species disambiguation, the term *c-myc* is a gene, but it can be either in a human gene (*homo sapiens*) or mouse gene (*mus musculus*) depending on the context [9–11, 14–16].

In [9], Wang et al. devised a rule based system to disambiguate biomedical entity names, like gene products, based on species. In that approach [9], some parsing techniques are used and syntactic parse tree with paths between words to determine if there exists a path between species word and the entity name. They employed and examined several parsers in the task including *C&C*, *Enju*, *Minipar*, and *Stanford-Genia* [9, 15, 16].

3. A Method for WSD

A word sense disambiguation method is an algorithm that assigns the most accurate sense to a given word in a given context. Our method is a supervised method requiring a training corpus that contains manually disambiguated instances of the ambiguous words. The method is based on a word classification and disambiguation technique that we have proposed in a preliminary work [17]. In the previous work, [17], we introduced a method for term disambiguation and evaluated it with biomedical terms to disambiguate *gene* and *protein* names in medical texts.

The method relies on representing the instances of the word to be disambiguated, w_x, as a *feature vector*, and the components of this vector are neighborhood context words in the training instances. In the context of the target word, w_x, we select the words with the high *discriminating* capabilities as the components of the vectors. As a supervised technique, this method consists of two stages *learning* (or *training*) stage and a *testing* (or *application*) stage. The trained models (*classifiers*) produced from the learning phase will then be used to disambiguate unseen and unlabeled examples in the testing phase. That is, during the learning phase, the constructed feature vectors of the training instances will be used as labeled examples to train classifiers. The classifier will be then used to disambiguate unseen and unlabeled examples in the application phase. One of the main strength of this method is that the features are selected for learning and classification.

Feature Selection. The features selected from the training examples have great impact on the effectiveness of the machine learning technique. Extensive research efforts have been devoted to feature selection in machine learning research [18–21]. The labeled training instances will be used to extract the word features for the feature vectors.

Suppose the word w_x has two senses s_1, s_2, let the set C_1 be the set of w_x instances labeled with s_1, and suppose C_2 contains instances of w_x labeled with sense s_2. So, each instance of w_x labeled with sense s_1 or s_2 (i.e., in the set C_1 or in the set C_2) can be viewed as

$$p_n \cdots p_3 p_2 p_1 < w_x; \qquad s_i > f_1 f_2 f_3 \cdots f_n, \qquad (1)$$

where the words $p_1, p_2, \ldots, p_n$ and $f_1, f_2, \ldots, f_n$ are the context words surrounding this instance, and n is the *window size*. Next, we collect all the context words p_i and f_i of all instances in C_1 and C_2 in one set W (s.t. $W = \{w_1, w_2, \ldots, w_m\}$). Each context word $w_i \in W$ may occur in the contexts of instances labeled with s_1 or with s_2 or combination and in any distribution. We want to determine that, if we see a context word w_q in an ambiguous instance/example, to what extent this occurrence of w_q suggests that this example belongs to C_1 or to C_2. Thus, we use as features those context words w_i that can highly discriminate between C_1 and C_2. For that, we use feature selection techniques such as *mutual information* (MI) [19, 20] as follows. For each context word $w_i \in W$ in the labeled training examples, we compute four values a, b, c, and d as follows:

a = number of occurrences of w_i in C_1,

b = number of occurrences of w_i in C_2,

c = number of examples of C_1 that do not contain w_i,

d = number of examples of C_2 that do not contain w_i.

Therefore, the *mutual information* (MI) can be defined as

$$MI = \frac{N * a}{(a+b) * (a+c)}, \quad (2)$$

and N is the total number of training examples. MI is a well-known concept in information theory and statistical learning. MI is a measure of interaction and common information between two variables [22]. In this work, we adapted MI to represent the interaction between the context words w_i and the class label based on the values a through d as defined above. We utilized the training corpus of the labeled instances of the word to be disambiguated to compile the list of all context words ($W = \{w_1, w_2, \ldots, w_m\}$) as explained above; all instances of one sense are under one class label. We notice that if the context word, w_i, is mostly occurring in class C_1 (or mostly in C_2), then the MI indicates this as shown in (2). Thus, MI can be used as a means to estimate the amount of information interaction between a context work and a class label. So, MI is used to select the context words with the highest discriminating capability between C_1 and C_2. For simplicity, and without loss of generality, we assume that we have two senses (two class labels). Moreover, following the same intuitive reasoning of mutual information, MI, we define another method, M2, for selecting the words as features to be included in the feature vectors as follows:

$$M2 = \frac{a+d}{b+c}. \quad (3)$$

In the following example, assume that the target word w_x has 10 instances already labeled with one of two senses as shown in Table 1. Class C_1 are the instances of w_x with the first sense, while C_2 are the instances of w_x instances in the second sense. Each instance is shown with its context words within certain window size. The target word w_x is shown in bold face. In this example, $N = 10$ is the total number of training examples. The values of a, b, c, d for w_p are (4,1,1,4), respectively. That is, w_p has 4 occurrences in C_1 and one instance in C_2, and so on. The values of a, b, c, d for w_q are (3, 2, 2, 3), respectively. As we can see, w_p is more highly related with the class C_1 than w_q, and so it has more discriminating power than w_q, and this is quantified by their MI values. MI values for w_p and w_q are 1.8 and 1.2, respectively.

Then, MI (or M2) value is computed for all context words $w_i \in W$. Then, the context words w_i are ordered based on their MI values, and the top k words w_i with highest MI values are selected as features. In this research, we experimented with k values of 100, 200, and 300. With $k = 100$, for example, each training example will be represented by a vector of 100 entries such that the first entry represent the context word w_i with the highest MI value, and the second entry represents the context word with the second highest MI value and so on.

Then, for a given training example, the feature vector entry is set to $+MI$ (or $-MI$) if the corresponding feature (*context word*) occurs (does not occur) in that training example and set to $-MI$ otherwise. Table 2 shows the top 10 context words with the ten highest MI values for

TABLE 1: An example of a training corpus of 10 instances of an ambiguous word w_x where 5 instances are in the first sense listed under class label C_1 and 5 instances of the second sense listed under class C_2. The context word w_p has 4 and 1 occurrences in Class C_1 and C_2, respectively, while w_q has 3 and 2 occurrences in C_1 and C_2, respectively.

C_1	C_2
$\cdots w_p \cdots \mathbf{w_x} \cdots w_q \cdots$	$\cdots w_p \cdots \mathbf{w_x} \cdots$
$\cdots w_p \cdots \mathbf{w_x} \cdots w_q \cdots$	$\cdots w_q \cdots \mathbf{w_x} \cdots$
$\cdots w_p \cdots \mathbf{w_x} \cdots$	$\cdots w_q \cdots \mathbf{w_x} \cdots$
$\cdots w_p \cdots \mathbf{w_x} \cdots$	$\cdots \mathbf{w_x} \cdots$
$\cdots w_q \cdots \mathbf{w_x} \cdots$	$\cdots \mathbf{w_x} \cdots$

TABLE 2: Context words with the top MI values for the ambiguous word "*cold*".

Context words w_i
Import
Understand
Ischemia
Reperfus
Respons
Stor
Arteri
Attempt
Repress
Quantit

the ambiguous word "*cold*" in the NLM-WSD benchmark corpus explained in Section 3. These 10 words will be used to compose the feature vectors for training or testing examples of the terms to be disambiguated. For example, a simple feature vector of size 5 can be as follows:

$$\begin{bmatrix} 1.23 & -1.21 & 0.95 & 0.92 & -0.88 \end{bmatrix}. \quad (4)$$

This feature vector represents an instance that has the first, third, and fourth context words available in its context, and 1.23 is the MI value of the context word with the highest MI.

The Learning Phase. From the labeled training examples of the word, we build the feature vectors using the top context words selected by MI or M2 as features. After that, we use the support vector machine (SVM) [23] as the learner to train the classifier using the training vectors. SVM has been shown as one of the most successful and efficient machine learning algorithms and is well founded theoretically and experimentally [7, 17, 18, 23]. The applications of SVM are abound; in particular, in NLP domain like text categorization, relation extraction, named entity recognition, SVM proved to be the best performer. We use *SVM-light* (http://svmlight.joachims.org/) implementation with the default parameters and with the Radial Basis Function (RBF) kernel.

The Disambiguation Step. In the testing step, we want to disambiguate an instance w_q of the word w. We construct a feature vector V_q for the instance w_q the same way as in the learning step. The induced learning model (classifier) from the learning step will be employed to classify it (assign w_q) to one of the two senses.

4. Evaluation and Experiments

4.1. Biomedical WSD (NLM-WSD)

Dataset. We used the benchmark dataset NLM-WSD for biomedical word sense disambiguation [24]. This dataset was created as a unified and benchmark set of ambiguous medical terms that have been reviewed and disambiguated by reviewers from the field. Most of the previous work on biomedical WSD uses this dataset [1, 2, 4]. The NLM-WSD corpus contains 50 ambiguous terms with 100 instances for each term for a total of 5000 examples. Each example is basically a *Medline* abstract containing one or more occurrences of the ambiguous word. The instances of these ambiguous terms were disambiguated by 11 annotators who assigned a sense for each instance [24]. The assigned senses are semantic types from UMLS. When the annotators did not assign any sense for an instance, then that instance is tagged with "*none*". Only one term "*association*" with all of its 100 instances were annotated *none* and so dropped from the testing.

Text Preprocessing. On this benchmark corpus, we have carried out some text preprocessing steps.

  (i) Converting all words to *lowercase*.

  (ii) Removing *stopwords*: removing all common function words like "*is*" "*the*" "*in*",... and so forth.

  (iii) Performing word *stemming* using *Porter* stemming algorithm [25].

Moreover, unlike other previous work, words with less than 3 or more than 50 characters are not ignored currently (unless dropped by the stopword removal step). Also words with parentheses or square brackets are not ignored and part of speech is not used.

After the text preprocessing is completed, for each word we convert the instances into numeric feature vectors. Then, we use SVM for training and testing with 5-fold cross validation 5FCV such that 80% of the instances are used for training and the remaining 20% are used for testing, and this is repeated five times by changing the training-testing portions of the data. The accuracy is taken as the mean accuracy of the five folds and the accuracy is computed as

$$\text{Accuracy} = \frac{\text{no. of instances with correct assigned senses}}{\text{total no. of tested instances}}. \tag{5}$$

We also use the *baseline* method which is the most frequent sense (mfs) for each word.

Experiments. Initially, we evaluated our WSD method with all the 49 words (excluding *association* as mentioned previously) such that, a word is included in the evaluation only if it has at least two or more senses with each sense having at least two instances annotated with it. This lead, to a total of 31 words tested in this evaluation, and 18 words were dropped because they do not have at least two instances annotated for each one of two senses. For example, the word "*depression*" has two senses: *mental or behavioral dysfunction* and *functional concept*. Out of the 100 instances of *depression*, 85 instances are tagged with the first sense, and remaining 15 instances are tagged with "*None*" (i.e., no instances tagged with a second sense), and so it was excluded in this evaluation. Likewise, the word "*discharge*" was not tested as it has only one instance tagged with the first sense, 74 instances tagged with the second sense, and 25 instances tagged with *None*. We used $k = 200$, and the *window* size is 5. The accuracy results of this first evaluation (EV1) are shown in Table 4. The detailed results of this evaluation are included in Table 5.

In the second evaluation (EV2) and third evaluation (EV3), we changed the parameter and the word/features selection formula. In EV2, we set $k = 300$, and window size is still 5. In EV3, we kept $k = 300$, window = 5, and changed the word/feature selection formula to M2 defined in (3). Table 5 contains the results of EV2 and EV3. To judge on performance of our method and compare our results with similar techniques, we included several reported results from three recent publications from 2008 to 2010 [1, 2, 4] with our results in Table 6 under the same experimental settings.

4.2. Species Disambiguation. In biomedical text, named entities, like gene name, are used the same way irrespective of the species of the entity. As a result, it will be difficult to extract relevant medical information automatically from texts using information extraction system. In biomedical named entity species disambiguation, for a given entity name, for example, *c-myc*, we want to disambiguate this entity name, *c-myc*, based on the species (e.g., *human* versus *mouse*) [9]. In one instance, *c-myc* might refer to a human gene, while in another instance it refers to a mouse gene.

For example, in Table 3, the biomedical entity name BCL-2 (*a protein name*) in the first text (no. 1) is human while in the second one is a mouse protein. We examined our system on this task of species disambiguation. We obtained the data from the project of Wang et al. [9]. From their data, we tested the biomedical entity names that occur in at least two species with at least 3 occurrences in each species. This enables us to use two instances for training and one for testing and repeat it three times. If the entity has 5 or more occurrences in one species, we repeat five times using 5FCV as in Section 4.1. We extracted and tested our system on a total 465 instances of entity names with an average of 8 instances per species for each entity name. In the original dataset (gold standard), 90% of the terms have all their instances occurring in only one species [9] and so cannot be tested in our system. Our system requires that each term should have instances in two or more species with at least 3 occurrences in each species. The results of Wang et al. are shown in Table 7, whereas the

TABLE 3: A sample text from species disambiguation.

Homosapiens (human)	Mus Musculus (mouse)
(No. 1) Significantly, Diva lacks critical residues in the conserved BH3 region that mediate the interaction between BH3-containing proapoptotic Bcl-2 homologues and their prosurvival binding partners. Consistent with this, Diva did not bind to cellular Bcl-2 family members including Bcl-2, Bcl-XL, Bcl-w, Mcl-1, and A1/Bfl-1	(No. 2) The BCL-2 family has various pairs of antagonist and agonist proteins that regulate apoptosis. Whether their function is interdependent is uncertain. Using a genetic approach to address this question, we utilized gain- and loss-of-function models of Bcl-2 and Bax and found that apoptosis and thymic hypoplasia characteristic of Bcl-2-deficient mice are largely absent in mice also deficient in Bax

TABLE 4: Accuracy results of the first evaluation, EV1, where each sense has to have at least two instances tagged with it.

	Accuracy
Fold 1	0.912
Fold 2	0.931
Fold 3	0.917
Fold 4	0.897
Fold 5	0.862
Average	**0.903**

TABLE 5: Detailed accuracy results of three evaluations EV1, EV2, and EV3.

Word	Baseline (mfs)	EV1	EV2	EV3
Adjustment	0.67	0.99	0.96	0.93
Blood_Pressure	0.54	0.98	0.80	0.83
Cold	0.91	0.94	0.92	0.95
Condition	0.98	0.95	0.95	0.95
Culture	0.89	0.87	0.96	0.94
Degree	0.97	0.93	0.93	0.93
Evaluation	0.50	0.98	0.82	0.85
Extraction	0.94	0.94	0.93	0.94
Failure	0.86	0.83	0.83	0.83
Fat	0.97	0.93	0.93	0.93
Ganglion	0.93	0.93	0.91	0.93
Glucose	0.91	0.90	0.90	0.93
Growth	0.63	0.92	1.00	0.96
Immune Suppression	0.59	0.98	0.88	0.87
Implantation	0.83	0.91	0.96	0.87
Japanese	0.92	0.92	0.97	0.92
Lead	0.93	0.84	0.84	0.84
Man	0.63	0.98	0.90	0.92
Mosaic	0.54	0.99	0.77	0.87
Nutrition	0.51	0.94	0.70	0.88
Pathology	0.86	0.79	0.96	0.92
Radiation	0.62	0.83	0.93	0.89
Reduction	0.82	0.63	0.63	0.63
Repair	0.76	0.92	0.91	0.96
Sex	0.80	0.94	0.97	0.88
Support	0.80	0.67	0.67	0.67
Surgery	0.98	0.95	0.95	0.95
Ultrasound	0.84	0.93	0.93	0.91
Variation	0.80	0.86	0.94	0.89
Weight	0.55	0.83	0.57	0.85
White	0.54	1.00	0.69	0.77
Mean Accuracy	**0.775**	**0.903**	**0.87**	**0.88**

results of our proposed system are shown in Table 8 in terms of precision, recall, and F1.

5. Discussion and Conclusion

The main weakness of the supervised and machine-learning-based methods for WSD is their dependency on the annotated training text which includes manually disambiguated instances of the ambiguous word [2, 17]. However, over the time, the increasing volumes of text and literature in very high rates and the new algorithms and techniques for text annotation and concept mapping will alleviate this problem. Moreover, the advances in ontology development and integration in the biomedical domain will facilitate even more the process of automatic text annotation.

In this paper, we reported a machine learning approach for biomedical WSD. The approach was evaluated with a benchmark dataset, NLM-WSD, to facilitate the comparison with the results of previous work. The average accuracy results of our method, compared to some recent reported results (Table 6), are promising and proving that our method outperforms those recently reported methods. Table 6 contains the results for 11 methods: baseline method (mfs), our method (last column), and 9 other methods from recent work published in 2008 to 2010 (from [1, 2, 4]). The average accuracy of our method is the highest (90.3%), and the closest one is NB (86.0%).

Our method also outperforms all 10 other methods in 12 out of 31 words followed by NB which outperforms the rest in 7 words.

Stevenson et al. in their paper [1] report extensive accuracy results of their method (we call it *Stevenson-2008*) along with four other methods including Joshi-2005 and McInnes-2007, with various combinations of words from

NLM-WSD corpus used for testing. For example, Joshi-2005 tested their system on 28 words (out of the whole set 50 words) and other techniques used 22 words, 15 words, or the whole set [1]. In Table 6, the results of the three methods

TABLE 6: Comparison of our results with the best reported results from recent reported techniques.

Word	Baseline (mfs)	Stevenson et al. [1]			Previous Results Agirre et al. [2]			Jimeno-Yepes and Aronson [4]			Our method (EV1)
		Joshi-2005	McInnes 2007	Stevenson-2008	Single	Subset	Full	NB	CombSW	CombV	
Adjustment	67	71	70	74		33.3	35.5	76.3	69	53.9	99
Blood pressure	54	53	46	46	53.0	50	48	57.0	38	44	98
Cold	91	90	89	88	32.6	26.3	28.4	92.6	39	79	94
Condition	98	—	89	89	95.7	39.1	48.9	97.8	78	69	95
Culture	89	—	94	95		33	77	93.0	100	54	87
Degree	97	89	79	95		95.4	93.8	96.9	88	82	93
Evaluation	50	69	73	81	59	54	50	78.0	52	50	98
Extraction	94	84	86	85		23	27.6	94.3	98	86	94
Failure	86	—	73	67		27.6	72.4	86.2	86	100	83
Fat	97	84	77	84	56.2	63	95.9	97.3	91	84	93
Ganglion	93	—	94	96	66	77	64	95.0	88	86	93
Glucose	91	—	90	91	91	91	90	91.0	78	39	90
Growth	63	71	69	68	37	37	37	73.0	55	66	92
Immune suppression	59	80	75	80	64	59	62	79.0	60	65	98
Implantation	83	94	92	93	75	84.7	84.7	98.0	94	97	91
Japanese	92	77	76	75	70.9	70.9	64.6	92.4	63	94	92
Lead	93	89	90	94	93.1	93.1	93.1	93.1	83	86	84
Man	63	89	80	90	61.5	34.8	44.6	87.0	65	42	98
Mosaic	54	87	75	87		60.8	66	82.5	84	72	99
Nutrition	51	52	49	54		33.7	32.6	55.1	45	43	94
Pathology	86	85	84	85		34.3	28.3	85.9	76	83	79
Radiation	62	82	81	84	58.2	53.1	53.1	83.7	76	76	82
Reduction	82	91	92	89	36.4	54.5	54.5	81.8	100	82	63
Repair	76	87	93	88	63.2	72.1	76.5	95.6	87	88	92
Sex	80	88	87	87	84	85	85	84.0	60	53	94
Support	80	—	91	89	80	80	80	80.0	100	90	67
Surgery	98	—	94	97	95.9	97	97	98.0	43	96	95
Ultrasound	84	92	85	90	84	84	83	85.0	81	83	93
Variation	80	—	91	95	85	80	75	91.0	65	86	86
Weight	55	83	79	81	56.6	56.6	56.6	84.9	66	68	83
White	54	79	74	76	68.9	67.8	63.3	81.1	57	58	100
Average	**77.5**	**81.1**	**81.2**	**83.6**	**68.8**	**59.7**	**63.5**	**86.0**	**73.1**	**72.7**	**90.3**

(Joshi-2005, McInnes-2007, and Stevenson-2008) are taken from Stevenson et al. [1]. These three methods are supervised methods and used various machine learning algorithm and wide sets of features. For example, Stevenson-2008 used linguistic features, CUI's, MeSH terms, and combination of these features. They employed three learners VSM (vector space model), Naïve Bayes (NB), and SVM. The results included in Table 6 are their best results with VSM and (linguistic + MeSH) features [1]. The method of Joshi-2005 uses five supervised learning methods and collocation features, while McInnes-2007 uses NB [1].

Our evaluation is done on 31 words (*as explained in Section 3*). We obtained the results of the other methods on these 31 words from the references shown in Table 6 to allow for direct comparison. The best result reported in their paper is 87.8% using all words with VSM model and for McInnes 85.3% also with the whole set [1]. The best result of Stevensons-2008 for subsets was 85.1% using a subset of 22 words defined by Stevenson et al. [1].

The results of the three methods (single, subset, full) in Table 6 are taken directly from Agirre et al. [2]. As shown in Table 6, the average accuracy of these three methods (68.8%, 59.7%, and 63.5%) on the 31 words is significantly lower than our method (90.3%) and also the average accuracy of their method on the whole set (65.9%, 63.0%, and 65.9%); we note that their method is unsupervised and does not

TABLE 7: The averaged evaluation results from Wang et al. [9].

	Micro-avg.			Macro-avg.		
	Precision	Recall	F1	Precision	Recall	F1
RULE-MAJORITY	72.2	62.39	66.94	27.77	46.67	29.32
RULE-SP	74.09	64.03	68.69	29.77	53.81	32.2
RULE-SPSENT	72.94	63.03	67.63	30.22	54.76	32.93
C&C	73.82	63.79	68.44	30.51	53.59	33.43
ENJU	72.98	63.06	67.66	31.35	55	34.61
ENJU-Genia	73	63.08	67.68	30.11	53.42	32.97
Minipar	73.02	63.1	67.69	30.19	53.56	33.1
Stanford	73.67	63.66	68.3	31.17	56.35	34.35
Stanford-Genia	73.48	63.5	68.13	30.61	55.61	33.78
ML	82.69	82.69	82.69	27.01	27.84	27.37
RELATION	75.24	63.99	69.16	31.97	55.61	34.8
HYBRID	83.8	83.8	83.8	57.56	49.72	49.9

TABLE 8: Precision, recall, and F1 results of our method on the fivefold in the species disambiguation experiments.

	Micro-avg		
	Precision	Recall	F1
Fold 1	81.86	92.78	87.0
Fold 2	82.08	94.77	88.0
Fold 3	82.95	97.31	89.6
Fold 4	84.12	98.70	90.8
Fold 5	81.25	85.83	83.5
Average	82.45	93.88	87.8
Total instances tested: 465			

require tagged instances [2]. In another work, Jimeno Yepes and Aronson evaluate four unsupervised methods on the whole NLM-WSD set [4] as well as NB and combination of the four methods. The accuracy of the four methods ranges from 58.3% to 88.3% (NB) on the whole set, and NB was found to be the best performer followed by *CombSW* (76.3%) [4]. The average accuracy results of NB and two combinations (NB, CombSW, and CombV) on our 31 word-subset are 86%, 73.1%, and 72.1% respectively which are lower than our results, see Table 6.

When we applied our system onto the species disambiguation task, the results are also encouraging as shown in Table 8. The evaluation results of our method compare very well with those reported in [9] as shown in Table 7. From their results (Table 7), we notice that the best overall performance was obtained with the ML method (machine learning) with *precision*, *recall*, and *F1* values being equal at 82.69. Our results as shown in Table 8 are not directly comparable with those in Table 7 due to the difference in the size of test set. However, we can see that our method's performance is reasonably well standing in terms of precision, recall, and F1. The main strength of this method is in using MI values as weights encoded in the feature vectors. These weights enable the learner to induce quite

reliable models for sense disambiguation. As the components of the vectors, +MI and −MI, are the common information between context word and class labels, the induced learners are finely calibrated towards the disambiguation task.

All the results showed that the technique is fairly successful and effective in the disambiguation task. Thus, more research work should be exerted to carry out further improvements on the performance of this technique. In future work of this research, we plan to investigate the possibility of disambiguating entity names when all instances of that entity are occurring in one species. Currently, our method is supervised and required annotated instances in both classes to be able to test new samples.

References

[1] M. Stevenson, Y. Guo, R. Gaizauskas, and D. Martinez, "Knowledge sources for word sense disambiguation of biomedical text," in *Proceedings of the Workshop on Current Trends in Biomedical Natural Language Processing (BioNLP '08)*, pp. 80–87, 2008.

[2] E. Agirre, A. Soroa, and M. Stevenson, "Graph-based word sense disambiguation of biomedical documents," *Bioinformatics*, vol. 26, no. 22, Article ID btq555, pp. 2889–2896, 2010.

[3] B. L. Humphreys, D. A. B. Lindberg, H. M. Schoolman, and G. O. Barnett, "The unified medical language system: an informatics research collaboration," *Journal of the American Medical Informatics Association*, vol. 5, no. 1, pp. 1–11, 1998.

[4] A. J. Jimeno-Yepes and A. R. Aronson, "Knowledge-based biomedical word sense disambiguation: comparison of approaches," *BMC Bioinformatics*, vol. 11, article 569, 2010.

[5] J. W. Son and S. B. Park, "Learning word sense disambiguation in biomedical text with difference between training and test distributions," in *Proceedings of the 3rd ACM International Workshop on Data and Text Mining in Bioinformatics (DTM-BIO '09)*, pp. 59–66, November 2009.

[6] H. Xu, M. Markatou, R. Dimova, H. Liu, and C. Friedman, "Machine learning and word sense disambiguation in the biomedical domain: design and evaluation issues," *BMC Bioinformatics*, vol. 7, article 334, 2006.

[7] H. Al-Mubaid and C. Ping, "Biomedical term disambiguation: an application to gene-protein name disambiguation," in *Proceedings of the 3rd International Conference on Information Technology: New Generations (ITNG '06)*, pp. 606–612, Las Vegas, Nev, USA, April 2006.

[8] G. K. Savova, A. R. Coden, I. L. Sominsky et al., "Word sense disambiguation across two domains: biomedical literature and clinical notes," *Journal of Biomedical Informatics*, vol. 41, no. 6, pp. 1088–1100, 2008.

[9] X. Wang, J. Tsujii, and S. Ananiadou, "Disambiguating the species of biomedical named entities using natural language parsers," *Bioinformatics*, vol. 26, no. 5, Article ID btq002, pp. 661–667, 2010.

[10] P. Chen and H. Al-Mubaid, "Context-based term disambiguation in biomedical literature," in *Proceedings of the 19th International Florida Artificial Intelligence Research Society Conference (FLAIRS '06)*, pp. 62–67, Orlando, Fla, USA, May 2006.

[11] H. Al-Mubaid, "Context-based technique for biomedical term classification," in *Proceedings of the IEEE Congress on Evolutionary Computation (CEC '06)*, pp. 5726–5733, Vancouver, Canada, July 2006.

[12] M. Stevenson et al., "Disambiguation of biomedical text using a variety of knowledge sources," *BMC Bioinformatics*, vol. 9, supplement 11, article S7, 2008.

[13] S. M. Humphrey, W. J. Rogers, H. Kilicoglu, D. Demner-Fushman, and T. C. Rindflesch, "Word sense disambiguation by selecting the best semantic type based on journal descriptor indexing: preliminary experiment," *Journal of the American Society for Information Science and Technology*, vol. 57, no. 1, pp. 96–113, 2006.

[14] M. Stevenson, E. Agirre, and A. Soroa, "Exploiting domain information for Word Sense Disambiguation of medical documents," *Journal of the American Medical Informatics Association*. In press.

[15] Y. Miyao and J. Tsujii, "Feature forest models for probabilistic HPSG parsing," *Computational Linguistics*, vol. 34, no. 1, pp. 35–80, 2008.

[16] Y. Miyao, K. Sagae, R. Sætre, T. Matsuzaki, and J. Tsujii, "Evaluating contributions of natural language parsers to protein-protein interaction extraction," *Bioinformatics*, vol. 25, no. 3, pp. 394–400, 2009.

[17] P. Chen and H. Al-Mubaid, "Context-based term disambiguation in biomedical literature," in *Proceedings of the 19th International Florida Artificial Intelligence Research Society Conference (FLAIRS '06)*, pp. 62–67, Orlando, Fla, USA, May 2006.

[18] G. Forman, "An Extensive Empirical study of feature selection metrics for text classification," *Journal of Machine Learning Research*, vol. 3, pp. 1289–1305, 2003.

[19] L. Galavotti, F. Sebastiani, and M. Simi, "Experiments on the use of feature selection and negative evidence in automated text categorization," in *Proceedings of the 4th European Conference on Research and Advanced Technology for Digital Libraries*, 2000.

[20] Y. Yang and J. P. Pedersen, "A comparative study on feature selection in text categorization," in *Proceedings of the 4th International Conference on Machine Learning and Computing*, 1997.

[21] Z. Zheng and R. Srihari, "Optimally combining positive and negative feature for text categorization," in *Proceedings of the Workshop on Learning from Imbalanced Data Sets II (ICML '03)*, 2003.

[22] C. D. Manning and H. Schutze, *Foundations of Statistical Natural Language Processing*, The MIT Press, 1999.

[23] T. Joachims, "Text categorization with support vector machines: learning with many relevant features," in *Proceedings of the 10th European Conference on Machine Learning*, 1998.

[24] M. Weeber, J. Mork, and A. Aronson, "Developing a test collection for biomedical word sense disambiguation," in *Proceedings of the Symposium American Medical Informatics Association (AMIA '01)*, 2001.

[25] M. F. Porter, "An algorithm for suffix stripping," *Program*, vol. 14, pp. 130–137, 1980.

17

Functional Implications of Local DNA Structures in Regulatory Motifs

Qian Xiang

School of Information Science and Technology, Sun Yat-Sen University, Guangzhou 510275, China

Correspondence should be addressed to Qian Xiang; xiangqiangz@gmail.com

Academic Editors: H.-W. Chang, Y.-H. Cheng, Y. Liu, and C.-H. Yang

The three-dimensional structure of DNA has been proposed to be a major determinant for functional transcription factors (TFs) and DNA interaction. Here, we use hydroxyl radical cleavage pattern as a measure of local DNA structure. We compared the conservation between DNA sequence and structure in terms of information content and attempted to assess the functional implications of DNA structures in regulatory motifs. We used statistical methods to evaluate the structural divergence of substituting a single position within a binding site and applied them to a collection of putative regulatory motifs. The following are our major observations: (i) we observed more information in structural alignment than in the corresponding sequence alignment for most of the transcriptional factors; (ii) for each TF, majority of positions have more information in the structural alignment as compared to the sequence alignment; (iii) we further defined a DNA structural divergence score (SD score) for each wild-type and mutant pair that is distinguished by single-base mutation. The SD score for benign mutations is significantly lower than that of switch mutations. This indicates structural conservation is also important for TFBS to be functional and DNA structures will provide previously unappreciated information for TF to realize the binding specificity.

1. Introduction

Gene expression is regulated mainly through specific interaction of transcription factors (TFs) with gene promoter elements. Although a large amount of various TF binding sites (TFBS) have been characterized through targeted low-throughput experiments or high throughput methods, such as chromatin immunoprecipitation coupled to sequencing (ChIP-seq) and protein binding microarray (PBM) assays [1, 2], there is no distinct nucleotide sequence which is shared by all recognized TFBS and most TFs may interact with many diverse sequences. The specificity of TF bindings is commonly represented by position weight matrices (PWMs), the components of which give the probabilities of finding each nucleotide at each binding site position [3].

While nucleotide sequence might be the key determinant for functional TF-DNA interaction, local DNA structure is also important as shape readout is one of the main recognition modes that are used by a large class of TFs when they scan the genome for regulatory interaction [4]. Although the DNA structure is somehow dependent on nucleotide sequence, similar sequence does not guarantee similar structure and vice versa. Divergent DNA sequences can share a similar local structure. Conversely, similar DNA sequences can adopt distinct local structures [5–7]. There is strong evidence that TFBS with different nucleotide order can also be recognized by the same TF and many TFs are capable to interact with diverse types of DNA sequences [1]. These observations indicate that although these TFBS are different on nucleotides sequence, they may be similar in structure and perform similar biological functions.

Here we ask whether there are some particular local structures, which are associated with the binding site of TFs. To address this question, we use hydroxyl radical cleavage pattern as proxy for the local structure of each TFBS [5]. We show here that there are DNA structural elements that are highly enriched in TFBS and these structural elements are not predictable on the basis of DNA sequence information alone. Our results suggest that DNA structures will provide previously unappreciated information for TF to realize the binding specificity and consideration of local DNA structure as well as nucleotide sequence will be important to understanding the regulatory interaction of TF-DNA.

2. Materials and Methods

2.1. Data Sets Used for This Work. Yeast genome sequences are downloaded from the website of http://www.yeastgenome .org/. The PWMs for 114 yeast TFs are derived from in vitro experiments in the literature [8], which denote the inherent sequence affinities of TF. The golden-standard set for true TFBS sites are achieved from file p005_c3.gff downloaded from [9]. Only 89 TFs with at least 10 annotated TF binding sites will be analyzed further.

2.2. DNA Structural Profile and Divergence Score (SD Score). Hydroxyl radical is a nearly ideal chemical probe for mapping genomic DNA structure. Here, all possible single-base substitutions for each putative TFBS were generated. We use the proposed algorithm in [5, 6] to predict the hydroxyl radical cleavage pattern for each wild type and mutant, respectively. The cleavage pattern for each sequence provides a measure of local DNA structure and is regarded as the DNA structural profile. The pairwise Euclidean distance for putative TFBS i between the DNA structural profiles for the wild-type $W_i = [w_{i1}, \ldots w_{iN}]$ and mutant $M_i = [m_{i1}, \ldots m_{iN}]$ pair is defined as

$$d_E(i) = \sqrt{\sum_{j=1}^{N} \left(w_{ij} - m_{ij}\right)^2}, \tag{1}$$

where N is the length of TFBS. For the convenience of the comparisons among different TFBS, Euclidean distances are divided by their motif lengths, respectively:

$$\text{SD-score} = \frac{1}{N}\sqrt{\sum_{j=1}^{N} \left(w_{ij} - m_{ij}\right)^2}. \tag{2}$$

Therefore the DNA structural divergence score (SD score) is defined as the normalized Euclidean distance.

2.3. Calculation of DNA Structure and Sequence Conservation. We measure the conservation in DNA structure and sequence in terms of information content, which is defined in the same way as in [6, 10]:

$$R(l) = \frac{E_{\max} - H(l)}{E_{\max}}, \tag{3}$$

where $E_{\max}$ is the maximum amount of uncertainty possible at any given position (in bits), and $H(l)$ is the uncertainty at position l based on the observed binding sites. The decrease in uncertainty represents the total information content at the position after the binding site alignment [10]. In order to compare the conservation between sequence and structure directly, information was divided by their maximum possible entropies, respectively, so that $R(l)$ represents the amount of normalized information content present at position l [6].

2.4. Enrichment Analysis. All of the wild-type and mutant pairs are classified into three datasets denoted as benign mutations, switch mutations, and loss mutations. We adopted the same definition of three scenarios in [11] to classify single-base mutations in TF binding sites: (i) Benign mutation—the mutant sequence is also recognized by the same TF and the substitution is expected to have a very mild effect on DNA structure. (ii) Switch mutation—the mutant sequence is no longer recognized by the original TF, but it is recognized by an alternative TF. (iii) Loss—the mutant binding site is no longer recognized by any TF.

Enrichment of lower SD score in benign mutation pairs and higher SD score in switch mutation pairs were evaluated in a simple and elegant way introduced by [12]. First, all pairs with possible single-base substitutions to the putative TFBS were exhaustively enumerated and serve as background control. The DNA structural profiles were calculated and compared for each pair. Next, the Euclidean distance between pairwise structural profiles was computed and defines the DNA structural divergence scores, which are divided into different bins. The fraction of benign or switch mutation pairs in each bin was calculated as T. The fraction of background control pairs in each bin was also calculated as B. The enrichment score is then defined as

$$E\_\text{score} = \frac{T}{B}. \tag{4}$$

By this scheme, no relation between mutation types and SD score will have an enrichment of 1. Correlation between mutation types and SD score will have value $\gg 1$, while those mutation types that show significant anticorrelation with respect to SD score will have a value $\ll 1$. In order to determine the distribution of the enrichment score under the null hypothesis of no enrichment, the same amount of pairs as those of benign mutations or switch mutations are randomly sampled from the background dataset by 1,000 times and significance P value was evaluated by hypergeometric tail probability.

3. Results and Discussion

3.1. Many DNA Structural Patterns in Motif Having Less Sequence Similarity. As a first step towards establishing a general scheme to find hydroxyl radical cleavage patterns that are shared by a set of binding sites of transcription factors, we examined the DNA consensus structural pattern of the yeast Asparagine-rich Zinc-Finger factor AZF1 as an example, which is the glucose-dependent positive regulator of CLN3 transcription in *S. cerevisiae* genome [13]. TF binding sites with different sequence composition can have similar cleavage patterns. For example, Greenbaum et al. showed that common structural motifs were detected in a large collection of DHSs that are found in the ENCODE regions of human genome [6]. Inspired by this work, we here ask whether similar structural motif exists for TF binding sites. Using the same methodology as mentioned in [6], the range of predicted continuous-value hydroxyl radical cleavage intensity is divided into 50 bins. The probabilities of finding each discretized intensity level at each binding

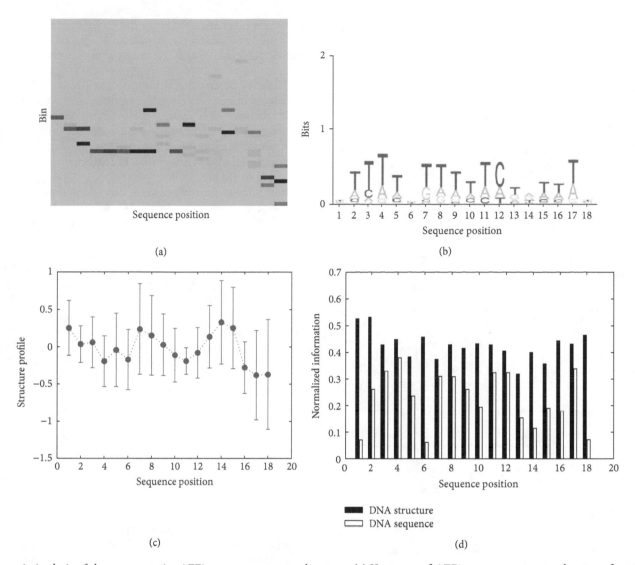

FIGURE 1: Analysis of the representative AZF1 consensus structural pattern. (a) Heat map of AZF1 consensus structural pattern found in putative TFBS. (b) Sequence logos of AZF1 found in putative TFBS. (c) Mean and standard deviation of predicted hydroxyl radical cleavage patterns. (d) Conservation of structure versus sequence in AZF1.

site position are calculated and represented as a position frequency matrix.

The representative structural motif is depicted as heat map in Figure 1(a). Here, x-axis represents sequence position in the TFBS and y-axis represents cleavage value bins. Green cells in the heat map indicate that no cleavage values for bin Y at position X are present, whereas red cells indicate a large proportion of the cleavage values in that bin. Obviously, each column would be uniformly colored if cleavage values were randomly distributed. For comparison, the corresponding sequence alignment among all the TF binding sites is also examined and shown in Figure 1(b). We found little similarity between nucleotide patterns and structural patterns.

To further investigate the above point, we plotted the mean predicted hydroxyl radical cleavage pattern values along with their corresponding standard deviation for each position of AZF1 in Figure 1(c). The mean cleavage intensity at any given position closely mirrors what is indicated in

the heat map. Moreover, we also calculated the similarity for both sequence and structure of AZF1 in terms of information content. More specifically, we calculate the maximum entropy minus the observed entropy at each position of the alignment, normalized by the maximum entropy. Entropy is a measure of degeneracy or uncertainty. Information is a measure of the decrease of uncertainty. Therefore, an alignment with higher information content is more conserved [6]. According to the result of AZF1 shown in Figure 1(d), it is obvious that the structural alignment contained more information than the corresponding sequence alignment in all positions.

Encouraged by our ability to predict the consensus structural pattern within TF binding sites, we attempted to generalize these procedures in order to find universal DNA structural properties for various transcriptional factors. Towards this end, we compiled a collection of 5587 putative TF binding sites which are likely to be functional TFBS in *S. cerevisiae* genome [9]. We next exploited the motifs dataset in order to

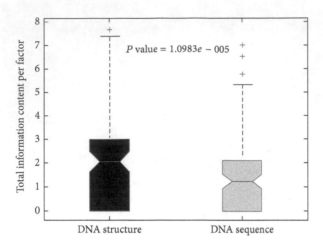

FIGURE 2: Total information content per factor in structure versus sequence.

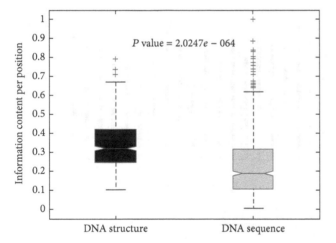

FIGURE 3: Information content per position in structure versus sequence.

generate the DNA consensus structural patterns and compare the conservation between sequence and structure in terms of information content. We calculated the total information content of the cleavage pattern alignment for each TF along with the corresponding information content of the nucleotide sequence alignment.

As indicated in Figure 2, the structural alignment contained significantly more information than the corresponding nucleotide sequence alignment for most of the transcriptional factors (P-value $< 1.1 \times 10^{-5}$, two-sample Kolmogorov-Smirnov test). It suggests that DNA structures are more conserved than DNA sequences for most of the TFBS.

Furthermore, we compared the conservation between sequence and structure by the information content per position. The results in Figure 3 show that majority of positions have more information in the structural alignment as compared to the sequence alignment (P-value $< 2.1 \times 10^{-64}$, two-sample Kolmogorov-Smirnov test). The higher information content observed in the structure compared with that in the sequence is suggestive that conservation in sequence can only

partly explain conservation in the DNA structure. Most of the additional conservation can be attributed to structural functional regulatory of TF binding sites.

3.2. Effect of Binding Site Substitution on DNA Structure. We next want to quantify the effect of binding site variation on DNA structure. For each of the collected 5587 putative TF binding sites, we exhaustively enumerated all possible single-base substitutions and measured the similarity between profiles for all wild-type and mutant sequence pairs that differ only by a single substitution.

Similarly as those three scenarios which were defined in [11], we can distinguish all pairs of sequences which differ by a single substitution into three types. Among all of the 133885 unique wild-type and mutant pairs which are generated by single-base substitutions for all of the collected 5587 putative TFBS, the substitutions in 4959 pairs, which do not change the original TF-DNA interaction relationship, are regarded as benign mutations. On the other hand, there are 1706 pairs whose original motif and the substituted sequence are both members of the TFBS dataset, but they are recognized by different TFs. We consider these mutations as switch mutations. All the other 127220 pairs are loss mutations where the substitutions result in a sequence that is no longer in the collected TFBS dataset. Overall the analysis revealed that it is apparent that the majority (95%) of single nucleotide substitutions result in loss of functional binding site.

Here we define DNA structural divergence score (SD score) for each mutation as the normalized Euclidean distance between two structural profiles. Extreme DNA structural divergence can be attributed to several possible factors, such as DNA sequence substitution, chromosomal structure, or positive selection for DNA local structure. Thus we sought to determine the potential sources accounting for the observed divergence between DNA structures for single-base substitution pairs. Parker et al. have showed that single-base substitutions have a wide range of effect to DNA structure from minor to drastic [7]. Inspired by their work, we here ask whether there is an enrichment of small SD score that exists for benign mutations compared to the background distribution.

We then collected a total of 133885 pairs with single-base substitutions to serve as a background control. We divided DNA SD score into different bins and computed the enrichment scores for benign mutations in each bin. The enrichment score is the fraction of benign mutations in each bin, divided by the fraction of all mutations in the same bin. To determine the distribution of the enrichment score under the null hypothesis of no enrichment, we generated 1,000 data sets with 4,959 randomly sampled mutations. Figure 4 clearly shows that loci with extremely small DNA SD score (<0.1) were significantly enriched for benign mutations (P-value < 0.0001, hypergeometric tail probability).

Similarly, we also studied the situation for switch mutations by generating another 1,000 datasets with 1706 randomly sampled mutations. On the contrary, the results in Figure 5 indicated that loci with extremely large DNA SD score (>0.4) were significantly enriched for switch mutations (P-value ≈ 0, hypergeometric tail probability). All these

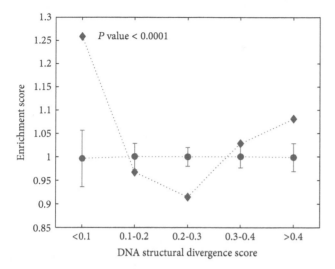

FIGURE 4: Benign mutations show extremly low DNA structural divergence.

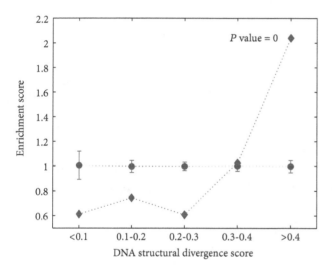

FIGURE 5: Switch mutations show extremely large DNA structural divergence.

findings clearly indicate that DNA structural conservation is important for TFBS to be functional and the DNA structural patterns change a lot between different TFs.

4. Conclusions

The binding nature of transcription factor to specific locations in the genome is one of the most important features for gene regulation in cells but remains poorly understood. We here showed that the predicted hydroxyl radical cleavage pattern can be successfully used to provide putative DNA structural profiles for each TFBS. The comparison results

clearly demonstrated that higher information content at the structure level was observed than that at the sequence level for most of the TFs and in the majority of positions. Moreover, we compared the DNA structural profiles between wild-type and mutant motifs and assessed how drastically each type of substitution affected DNA structures. The statistically analysis indicated that not all effects of mutation are equal: for example, benign mutations are less likely to change the DNA structures, compared to switch mutations. We therefore speculate that some of the functional information in the TFBS is conferred by DNA structure as well as nucleotide sequence. One future implication of these findings is that it may point the way to improved accuracy in the prediction of the functional regulatory interactions. Our results may also provide aid to distinguish which mutation in promoter elements is more likely to cause abnormal transcription by affecting the DNA structure.

Acknowledgments

This research is supported by Natural Science Foundation of China (Grant No. 61003141). The author gives special thanks to Professor Xianhua, Dai, and Dr. Zhiming, Dai, for helpful discussions on the project.

References

[1] D. Schmidt, M. D. Wilson, B. Ballester et al., "Five-vertebrate ChIP-seq reveals the evolutionary dynamics of transcription factor binding," *Science*, vol. 328, no. 5981, pp. 1036–1040, 2010.

[2] C. Zhu, K. J. R. P. Byers, R. P. McCord et al., "High-resolution DNA-binding specificity analysis of yeast transcription factors," *Genome Research*, vol. 19, no. 4, pp. 556–566, 2009.

[3] G. D. Stormo, "DNA binding sites: representation and discovery," *Bioinformatics*, vol. 16, no. 1, pp. 16–23, 2000.

[4] M. Maienschein-Cline, A. R. Dinner, W. S. Hlavacek, and F. Mu, "Improved predictions of transcription factor binding sites using physicochemical features of DNA," *Nucleic Acids Research*, vol. 40, no. 22, p. e175, 2012.

[5] J. A. Greenbaum, B. Pang, and T. D. Tullius, "Construction of a genome-scale structural map at single-nucleotide resolution," *Genome Research*, vol. 17, no. 6, pp. 947–953, 2007.

[6] J. A. Greenbaum, S. C. J. Parker, and T. D. Tullius, "Detection of DNA structural motifs in functional genomic elements," *Genome Research*, vol. 17, no. 6, pp. 940–946, 2007.

[7] S. C. J. Parker, L. Hansen, H. O. Abaan, T. D. Tullius, and E. H. Margulies, "Local DNA topography correlates with functional noncoding regions of the human genome," *Science*, vol. 324, no. 5925, pp. 389–392, 2009.

[8] G. Badis, E. T. Chan, H. van Bakel et al., "A library of yeast transcription factor motifs reveals a widespread function for Rsc3 in targeting nucleosome exclusion at promoters," *Molecular Cell*, vol. 32, no. 6, pp. 878–887, 2008.

[9] K. D. MacIsaac, T. Wang, D. B. Gordon, D. K. Gifford, G. D. Stormo, and E. Fraenkel, "An improved map of conserved regulatory sites for Saccharomyces cerevisiae," *BMC Bioinformatics*, vol. 7, article 113, 2006.

[10] T. D. Schneider and R. M. Stephens, "Sequence logos: a new way to display consensus sequences," *Nucleic Acids Research*, vol. 18, no. 20, pp. 6097–6100, 1990.

[11] L. Michal, O. Mizrahi-Man, and Y. Pilpel, "Functional characterization of variations on regulatory motifs," *PLoS Genetics*, vol. 4, no. 3, Article ID e1000018, 2008.

[12] J. Li, Y. Liu, X. Xin et al., "Evidence for positive selection on a number of microRNA regulatory interactions during recent human evolution," *PLoS Genetics*, vol. 8, no. 3, Article ID e1002578, 2012.

[13] M. G. Slattery, D. Liko, and W. Heideman, "The function and properties of the Azf1 transcriptional regulator change with growth conditions in Saccharomyces cerevisiae," *Eukaryotic Cell*, vol. 5, no. 2, pp. 313–320, 2006.

18

Robust Microarray Meta-Analysis Identifies Differentially Expressed Genes for Clinical Prediction

John H. Phan,[1] Andrew N. Young,[2] and May D. Wang[1]

[1] Department of Biomedical Engineering, Georgia Institute of Technology and Emory University, 313 Ferst Drive,
Atlanta, GA 30332, USA
[2] Department of Pathology and Laboratory Medicine, Emory University School of Medicine, Grady Health System,
Grady Memorial Hospital, Atlanta, GA 30303, USA

Correspondence should be addressed to May D. Wang, maywang@bme.gatech.edu

Academic Editors: N. S. T. Hirata, M. A. Kon, and K. Najarian

Combining multiple microarray datasets increases sample size and leads to improved reproducibility in identification of informative genes and subsequent clinical prediction. Although microarrays have increased the rate of genomic data collection, sample size is still a major issue when identifying informative genetic biomarkers. Because of this, feature selection methods often suffer from false discoveries, resulting in poorly performing predictive models. We develop a simple meta-analysis-based feature selection method that captures the knowledge in each individual dataset and combines the results using a simple rank average. In a comprehensive study that measures robustness in terms of clinical application (i.e., breast, renal, and pancreatic cancer), microarray platform heterogeneity, and classifier (i.e., logistic regression, diagonal LDA, and linear SVM), we compare the rank average meta-analysis method to five other meta-analysis methods. Results indicate that rank average meta-analysis consistently performs well compared to five other meta-analysis methods.

1. Introduction

We develop a simple, yet robust meta-analysis-based feature selection (FS) method for microarrays that ranks genes by differential expression within several independent datasets, then combines the ranks using a simple average to produce a final list of rank-ordered genes. Such meta-analysis methods can increase the power of microarray data analysis by increasing sample size [1]. The subsequent improvement to differentially expressed gene (DEG) detection, or to FS is essential for downstream clinical applications. Many of these applications, such as disease diagnosis and disease subtyping, are predictive in nature and are important for guiding therapy. However, DEG detection can be difficult due to technical and biological noise or due to small sample sizes relative to large feature sizes [2]. These properties are typical of many microarray datasets. Despite small sample sizes, the number of gene expression datasets available to the research community has grown [3]. Thus, it is important to develop methods that can use all available knowledge

by simultaneously analyzing several microarray datasets of similar clinical focus. However, combining high-throughput gene expression datasets can be difficult due to technological variability. Differences in microarray platform [4] or normalization and preprocessing methods [5] affect the comparability of gene expression values. Laboratory batch effects can also affect reproducibility [6]. Numerous studies have proposed novel strategies to remove batch effects [7]. However, in some cases, batch effect correction can have undesirable consequences [8]. In light of these challenges, several studies have proposed novel methods for meta-analysis of multiple microarray datasets.

Existing microarray meta-analysis methods either combine separate statistics for each gene expression dataset or aggregate samples into a single large dataset to estimate global gene expression. The study by Park et al. used analysis of variance to identify unwanted effects (e.g., the effect of different laboratories) and modeled these effects to detect DEGs [9]. Choi et al. used a similar approach to compute an "effect size" quantity, representing a measure of precision for

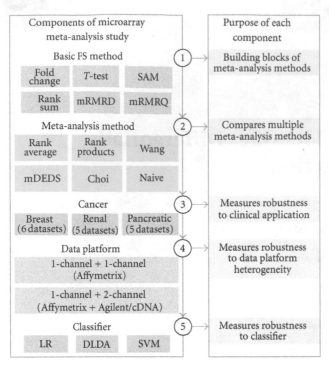

FIGURE 1: Study design diagram. We compare the predictive performance of meta-analysis-based feature selection (FS) methods by designing a study that considers five components: (1) basic FS methods that are the building blocks of some of the meta-analysis methods, (2) meta-analysis-based FS methods, (3) clinical application, (4) microarray data platform, and (5) classifier (logistic regression, diagonal LDA and linear SVM). Since the "best" meta-analysis-based FS method may be dataset- or application-specific, assessing performance over a wide variety of factors enables an evaluation of the method's robustness.

each study, and used this "effect size" to directly compare and combine microarray datasets [10]. Wang et al. combined the fold change of genes between classes from three microarray datasets and weighted each dataset by its variance such that datasets with higher variance contribute less to the final statistic [11]. Yoon et al. conducted a large-scale study of gene expression by examining the variation of genes across multiple microarray datasets, regardless of the clinical focus [12]. Breitling and Herzyk ranked fold changes between all interclass pairs of samples and computed the product of all ranks for each gene [13]. More recently, Campain and Yang reviewed several meta-analysis methods and assessed their performance using both classification accuracy and synthetic data [14]. Research has shifted towards methods that consider multiple FS methods, reflecting the fact that no single FS method performs well for all datasets [15]. Although several meta-analysis methods exist, except for the study by Campain and Yang, the literature rarely compares these methods in a comprehensive manner.

We develop the rank average method, a simple meta-analysis-based FS method, for identifying DEGs from multiple microarray datasets and design a study (Figure 1) to compare rank average to five other meta-analysis-based FS methods. We focus on the predictive ability of genes

emerging from meta-analysis and show that rank average meta-analysis is robust with respect to three factors. These three factors are (1) clinical application (i.e., breast, renal, and pancreatic cancer diagnosis or subtyping), (2) data platform heterogeneity (i.e., combining different microarray platforms), and (3) classifier. Using a comprehensive factorial analysis, we rate each meta-analysis-based FS method relative to its peers. In terms of identifying genetic features with reproducible predictive performance and in terms of robustness to multiple factors, results indicate that rank average meta-analysis performs consistently well in comparison to five other meta-analysis-based FS methods.

2. Methods

2.1. Microarray Datasets. We use six breast cancer, five renal cancer, and five pancreatic cancer gene expression datasets (Table 1) to compare meta-analysis-based FS methods. Each renal cancer dataset examines patient samples from several subtypes of tumors: clear cell (CC), oncocytoma (ONC), chromophobe (CHR), and papillary (PAP). We are interested in identifying genes differentially expressed between the CC subtype and all other subtypes, that is, CC versus ONC/CHR/PAP. These renal cancer datasets share a similar clinical focus. However, they are heterogeneous in terms of microarray platform [16–21]. Similarly, the breast cancer datasets are heterogeneous in both platform and clinical focus [22–26]. Although patient samples from each dataset have undergone different treatment for breast cancer and have been extracted at different stages of the disease, each sample is labeled as either estrogen receptor positive (ER+) or negative (ER−). Thus, we assess the performance of classifiers that predict the estrogen receptor status. The pancreatic cancer datasets also include a variety of platforms and clinical focuses [27–31]. We identify genes to discriminate pancreatic cancer versus noncancer patient samples. These datasets contain different numbers of probes (or probesets in the case of Affymetrix datasets) due to differences in microarray platform. Within each dataset group, we reduce the number of probes in each dataset to a common shared set based on probe sequence similarity.

2.2. Rank Average Meta-Analysis. The meta-analysis-based FS method proposed in this paper ranks genes individually in each dataset and computes the average rank of each gene. Gene rank order is determined by a measure of differential expression (which can be any of a number of basic FS methods such as fold change or t-test) and we assume that this rank order is invariant to batch effects. Using the average rank of a gene across several datasets to obtain the final multidataset rank order, we can infer (1) the relative strength of that gene in differentiating the patient samples of interest and (2) the consistency of the gene's differential expression across multiple studies.

The remainder of this section uses the following mathematical notation. K is the total number of datasets, M is the total number of genes in each dataset, and N_k is the number of samples in dataset k, where $k = 1 \cdots K$ and N is the total

TABLE 1: Microarray datasets.

(a) Breast cancer estrogen receptor status

Dataset	ER+	ER−	Platform	No. of probes
MDACC Train	80	50	Affy HG-U133A	22283
MDACC Test	60	40	Affy HG-U133A	22283
Miller	213	34	Affy HG-U133A	22283
Sotiriou	72	24	Affy HG-U133A	22283
Minn	57	42	Affy HG-U133A	22283
Van't Veer	226	69	Agilent 2-Color	24496

Common probes: 8953.

(b) Renal cancer subtype

Dataset	CC	Other	Platform	No. of probes
Schuetz	13	12	Affy HG-Focus	8793
Jones	32	29	Affy HG-U133A	22283
Kort	10	30	Affy HG-U133+2.0	54675
Yusenko	26	27	Affy HG-U133+2.0	54675
Higgins	26	9	cDNA 2-Color	22689

Common probes: 946.

(c) Pancreatic cancer diagnosis

Dataset	Normal	Cancer	Platform	No. of probes
Badea	39	39	Affy HG-U133+2.0	54675
Ishikawa	25	24	Affy HG-U133A/B	44928
Pei	16	36	Affy HG-U133+2.0	54675
Pilarsky	18	27	Affy HG-U133A/B	44928
Iacobuzio-Donahue	5	17	cDNA 2-Color	43910

Common probes: 4530.

number of samples in all datasets. We denote a gene i in dataset k as a vector

$$\overline{g}_{i,k} = \left(x_1^{i,k}, x_2^{i,k}, \ldots, x_{N_k}^{i,k}\right), \tag{1}$$

where $x_j^{i,k}$ is the expression value of gene i of sample j in dataset k. In the case of sample aggregation (i.e., the naive method of meta-analysis), we denote a gene i across all datasets with

$$\overline{g}_{i,\bullet} = \left(\left(x_1^{i,1}, x_2^{i,1}, \ldots, x_{N_1}^{i,1}\right), \left(x_1^{i,2}, x_2^{i,2}, \ldots, x_{N_2}^{i,2}\right), \ldots, \right.$$
$$\left. \left(x_1^{i,K}, x_2^{i,K}, \ldots, x_{N_K}^{i,K}\right)\right). \tag{2}$$

Using this notation, we can define a function, $r_{i,k,\vartheta} = R_\vartheta(\overline{g}_{i,k})$, to compute the rank, $r_{i,k,\vartheta}$, of a gene, $\overline{g}_{i,k}$, using a ranking algorithm denoted by ϑ. A smaller rank indicates a greater degree of differential expression. In the case of sample aggregation, the ranking function takes the form $r_{i,\bullet,\vartheta} = R_\vartheta(\overline{g}_{i,\bullet})$. The average rank, $\overline{r}_i$, of a gene i across all datasets, weighted by number of samples in each dataset, N_k, is

$$\overline{r}_i = \frac{1}{N} \sum_{k=1}^{K} N_k R_{\vartheta_k}\left(\overline{g}_{i,k}\right). \tag{3}$$

Weighting gives preference to ranks from datasets with larger sample sizes.

We consider several basic FS, or gene ranking, methods as follows: fold change (FC), t-test (T), significance analysis of microarrays (SAM) [32], rank-sum (RS), minimum redundancy maximum relevance using the difference formulation (mRMRD), and mRMR using the quotient formulation (mRMRQ) [33]. We explicitly define the rank algorithm for the kth dataset as

$$\vartheta_k \in \{FC, T, SAM, RS, mRMRD, mRMRQ\}. \tag{4}$$

For each dataset and each basic FS method, we use three-fold cross-validation to compute an estimate of classification performance (measured using AUC) averaged over 20 feature sizes (ranging from the top single feature to the top twenty features). We then choose the basic FS method, ϑ_k, with highest estimated classification performance for each dataset. Because each basic FS method makes different assumptions about DEGs and the correctness of these assumptions varies from dataset to dataset, allowing a different basic FS method for each dataset can improve performance.

2.3. Predictive Performance. We use classification performance to assess meta-analysis-based FS methods with the assumption that improved FS leads to higher prediction performance when classifying samples from an independent

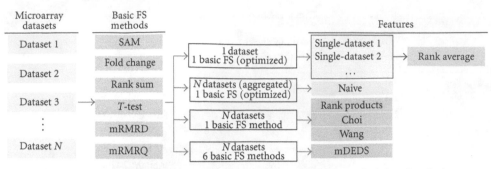

(a) Selecting features from multiple microarray datasets using six meta-analysis-based methods

Homogeneous data

1,2	1,2	1,3	1,3	1,4	1,4	2,3	2,3	2,4	2,4	3,4	3,4	
1	2	1	3	1	4	2	3	2	4	3	4	
						X	X	X	X	X	X	1
		X	X	X	X					X	X	2
X	X			X	X			X	X			3
X	X	X	X			X	X					4

Feature selection datasets

Training datasets

Validation datasets

Heterogeneous data

1,5	2,5	3,5	4,5	
1	2	3	4	
	X	X	X	1
X		X	X	2
X	X		X	3
X	X	X		4

(b) Example of dataset permutations for evaluating meta-analysis predictive performance

FIGURE 2: Procedure for comparing the predictive performance of six microarray meta-analysis-based FS methods. (a) Features are selected from microarray datasets using the rank average meta-analysis method (pink box), several other meta-analysis methods (orange boxes: mDEDS, rank products, Choi, and Wang), and a naive method (blue box) that aggregates samples into a larger dataset. Rank average meta-analysis chooses a single feature selection (FS) method from among several basic FS methods (SAM, fold change, rank sum, t-test, mRMRD, and mRMRQ) for each individual dataset that optimizes prediction performance (via cross-validation) over the top 20 features. A simple weighted average of gene ranks from all individual datasets produces the final set of rank average meta-analysis features. The rank products, Choi, and Wang methods use one basic FS method to select features from multiple datasets while the mDEDS method uses all six basic FS methods. (b) Features are selected from two or more datasets from each group to build a classifier (pink boxes), which is trained with samples from only one dataset (yellow boxes). The performance of the classifier is assessed using independent datasets (datasets not used for training or feature selection, green boxes). The predictive performance of a microarray meta-analysis-based FS method is an average over all permutations of training and validation datasets (blue boxes). In the example, datasets 1–4 consist of one-channel Affymetrix arrays while dataset 5 (in the case of heterogeneous data) consists of two-channel arrays.

dataset. We assess prediction performance using independent training and testing datasets because of the small sample size of some of the datasets and because we want to reflect clinical scenarios in which predictive models would likely be derived from data collected from a separate batch of patients. We compare our proposed rank average meta-analysis method to other meta-analysis methods including: (1) the rank products method [13], (2) the mDEDS method [14], (3) Choi et al.'s method of interstudy variability [10], (4) Wang et al.'s method of weighting differential expression by variance [11], and (5) a naive method that aggregates samples from multiple datasets. The rank products, mDEDS, Choi, and Wang methods can be applied to multiple datasets as well as to single datasets. For each method and each dataset group, we compute single-dataset performance, combined homogeneous-dataset performance (from two to four datasets combined), and combined heterogeneous-dataset performance (Figure 2(a)).

Classification performance depends on both feature selection and number of samples available for training. We are interested in performance gains due to meta-analysis-based FS alone. We isolate this performance gain by training classifiers with samples from a single dataset only, while allowing the features used for training to come from multiple datasets. Thus, any improvement (or degradation) in classification performance of a meta-analysis-based FS method in comparison to the baseline single-dataset FS is due to features selected rather than to increases in training sample size. We assess classification performance using a separate validation dataset and permute the datasets such that each individual dataset in each dataset group—renal, breast, and pancreatic cancer—is used at least once for validation. Moreover, for each permutation, we use 100 iterations of bootstrap sampling from the training datasets to estimate classification performance. Figure 2(b) is an example of the permutations possible with a five-dataset group (datasets 1–4 are the same platform while dataset 5 is a different platform), in which the prediction performance of two-dataset combination is assessed. This procedure can be expanded to handle three-dataset, four-dataset, or higher combinations for FS.

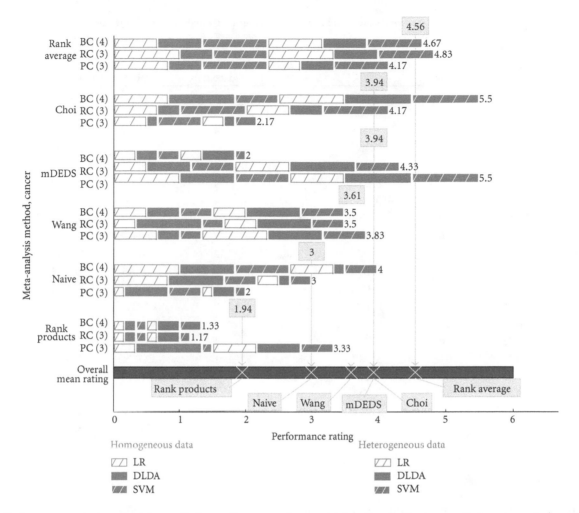

FIGURE 3: Rating meta-analysis methods by prediction performance when combining all available datasets. Each meta-analysis method (rank average, rank products, Wang, mDEDS, Choi, and naive) is rated relative to its peers. We assess performance rating across three factors: (1) clinical application (breast cancer: BC, renal cancer: RC, and pancreatic cancer: PC), (2) data platform heterogeneity (homogeneous: orange, heterogeneous: blue), and (3) classifier (logistic regression: LR, diagonal LDA: DLDA and linear SVM). For each combination of factors, the rating of each meta-analysis method is represented by an additive bar. Methods with higher absolute prediction performance receive higher ratings (and longer bars). When considering absolute prediction performance, rank average, with a mean overall rating of 4.56, performs consistently well compared to its peers.

The procedure for measuring predictive performance of heterogeneous-dataset combination is slightly different. Each dataset group contains several one-channel Affymetrix datasets and one two-channel dataset (either cDNA or Agilent). Gene expression values of the two-channel datasets are computed as log ratios, resulting in different dynamic ranges compared to the one-channel datasets. We assess the robustness of each meta-analysis-based FS method to heterogeneous data platforms by first determining the performance of the method when combining only Affymetrix data (Figure 2(b), homogeneous data), then comparing to results obtained when combining a mixture of Affymetrix and two-channel arrays (Figure 2(b), Heterogeneous Data). For example, we compute heterogeneous combination performance by combining one or more Affymetrix datasets to the two-channel dataset, then training a classifier using one of the Affymetrix datasets, and testing samples from

an independent dataset (again Affymetrix). Thus, not only should a good meta-analysis-based FS method perform well with respect to single dataset FS, but also the method should exhibit minimal performance degradation, if any, when combining heterogeneous data platforms.

3. Results

3.1. Robustness of Rank Average Meta-Analysis. We rate each meta-analysis method by absolute prediction performance (Figure 3). Based on this criterion, we find that rank average meta-analysis, with the highest overall mean rating of 4.56, performs consistently well compared to five other meta-analysis methods including the mDEDS, rank products, Choi, Wang, and naive methods. This analysis answers the question: which meta-analysis-based FS method consistently exhibits the largest prediction performance when combining

Table 2: Differentially expressed genes identified from rank average meta-analysis of multiple microarray datasets.

Breast cancer			Renal cancer			Pancreatic cancer		
Gene symbol	Weighted average rank	Top 20 in # of datasets	Gene symbol	Weighted average rank	Top 20 in # of datasets	Gene symbol	Weighted average rank	Top 20 in # of datasets
ESR1	0.20	6	LOX	13.65	4	S100P	31.42	2
NAT1	33.99	3	COL5A2	16.86	3	LAMC2	51.44	2
DNALI1	48.46	1	ADFP	19.08	4	PHLDA2	201.93	1
SCUBE2	69.27	1	SCNN1A	19.25	2	S100A2	233.07	0
TFF1	76.74	1	LOXL2	21.37	3	MSLN	234.39	1
MYB	82.17	0	ELTD1	27.17	4	WFDC2	236.00	1
CYP2B7P1	86.93	1	PPARGC1A	30.73	1	ITGB6	238.13	0
PDZK1	98.81	0	IFITM1	31.19	2	HK2	239.87	2
PADI2	114.44	0	RALGPS1	37.17	2	R88990*	244.34	0
DNAJC12	123.83	0	VWF	37.85	2	ANO1	252.57	1
TSPAN1	126.87	0	CD70	41.65	0	MXRA5	261.28	0
CDH3	127.46	1	ARHGDIB	42.60	1	PLEK2	264.09	0
XBP1	134.70	0	P4HA1	48.91	2	CDC2	279.79	2
KRT18	136.35	0	BST2	50.56	2	VCAN	285.59	0
EEF1A2	138.25	0	F2R	52.22	1	FERMT1	286.92	1
SLC16A6	140.73	1	SPARC	52.86	1	MCOLN3	309.32	0
ACADSB	142.55	1	LDB2	56.29	2	TNFRSF21	315.68	1
SRD5A1	159.99	1	GJA1	58.54	0	KYNU	324.78	0
CHAD	164.19	0	PLAG1	60.29	1	TACC3	333.27	0
P4HTM	165.08	1	DSG2	68.03	1	TMC5	336.72	0

* Gene symbol not available, using accession number instead.

all available datasets? We assign a rating to each meta-analysis method for every combination of three factors that include (1) clinical application or dataset group, (2) data platform heterogeneity (combining similar or different microarray platforms), and (3) classifiers (logistic regression: LR, diagonal linear discriminant: DLDA, and linear SVM). Ratings for each meta-analysis method are relative to its peers, with higher ratings indicating better prediction performance under the same combination of factors. In Figure 3, bars are proportional to performance ratings. Using pancreatic cancer (PC) as an example, the rank average meta-analysis method has a rating of five (corresponding to a predictive performance AUC of 81.5, See Supplemental Table S1 available online at doi:10.1100/2012/989637) when analyzing homogeneous datasets and when using the logistic regression classifier. This means that its absolute prediction performance is higher than that of four other meta-analysis methods compared under the same conditions (i.e., homogeneous data, logistic regression classifier). The results illustrated in Figure 3 and obtained through a comprehensive analysis of three factors suggest that, relative to its peers, rank average meta-analysis is robust when considering absolute prediction performance.

3.2. Rank Average Identifies Biologically Sensible Genes. For each dataset group, we combine all available microarray datasets and use the rank average meta-analysis method

to identify DEGs. Assessing DEG detection performance by examining the genes is difficult unless we know, via validation, whether or not these genes are truly differentially expressed. However, because of the sheer number of genes in high-throughput datasets, the validation process is often time and resource intensive. Despite this, we examine the top ranked genes from each dataset group to verify that the rank average meta-analysis method is identifying genes that are biologically sensible.

Table 2 lists the top 20 genes selected from meta-analysis of each of the three dataset groups: six breast cancer, five renal cancer, and five pancreatic cancer datasets. We optimize the FS method for each individual dataset using three-fold cross validation and the diagonal LDA classifier. The optimal FS method for each dataset differs. We compare ER+ and ER− samples for each breast cancer dataset and find, not surprisingly, that the ESR1 gene (estrogen receptor) is the top ranked gene for all but one dataset. Accordingly, the weighted average rank of ESR1 places it at the top of the combined list. Among the other genes in the list, NAT1 [34], DNALI1, SCUBE2 [35], and TFF1 [36] have been implicated in breast cancer. Although the individual dataset ranks of these genes vary from low to relatively high ranks (e.g., 200 to 300), it is the consistency of selecting these genes from multiple datasets that places them at the top of the combined list. In Table 2, we include the number of individual datasets in which the gene is ranked in the top 20.

TABLE 3: Properties of six microarray meta-analysis methods.

	Rank average	mDEDS	Rank products	Choi	Wang	Naive (control)
Basic FS methods considered	FC, T, SAM, RS, mRMRQ/D	FC, T, SAM, RS, mRMRQ/D	FC[1]	T[2]	FC[3]	FC, T, SAM, RS, mRMRQ/D
Chooses data-specific basic FS method(s)	*Yes*	No	No	No	No	*Yes*
Rank-Based	*Yes*	No	*Yes*	No	No	No

[1]Fold change between all interclass pairs of samples. [2]Most similar to a t-statistic, but includes an estimate of interstudy variation. [3]Computes a variance-weighted average of fold change. FC: Fold Change, T = t-statistic (t-test), SAM: significance analysis of microarrays, RS: rank sum test, mRMRQ/D: minimum redundancy, maximum relevance with quotient/difference.

We compare the renal cancer clear cell subtype to three other subtypes (i.e., chromophobe, oncocytoma, and papillary) to identify DEGs. The top gene we identify is LOX, which is an oncogene implicated in clear cell renal cancer [37]. The ADFP gene, ranked at #3 in the combined list, is especially interesting because it may be a potential urinary biomarker for detecting renal cancer [38]. ADFP is ranked favorably in all but the Higgins dataset, in which it is ranked at number 75.

The rank average meta-analysis method identifies S100P as the top pancreatic cancer gene, which has been implicated in several studies [39, 40]. The S100P gene has a relatively favorable ranking in the Pilarsky and Pei datasets and moderate to un-favorable rankings in the other datasets, indicating that analysis of individual datasets may not readily identify the gene. Another example, LAMC2, is ranked favorably in the Ishikawa and Pei datasets, but relatively higher in the other datasets. Overall, LAMC2 is ranked second in the combined results and is, according the to literature, a purported pancreatic cancer gene [41]. Weighted average ranks for the pancreatic cancer results increase quickly compared to the breast and renal cancer results, indicating increased heterogeneity among the ranks of the individual datasets. One explanation for this is the slight difference in dataset subtype comparisons. For example, one of the datasets, Ishikawa, extracted RNA samples from pancreatic juice rather than from solid tumors.

The degree of differential expression (and consequently, the rank) of a gene can vary significantly from dataset to dataset. Combining DEG detection results by averaging ranks across datasets reduces variability and improves statistical confidence. Analysis of a single microarray dataset may result in errors during DEG detection—for example, false positives and false negatives (genes that should be differentially expressed, but not favorably ranked). In general, these errors can be reduced by increasing sample size. Combining microarray datasets by averaging ranks effectively increases sample size while enabling robust analysis of heterogeneous data.

4. Discussion

In order to understand the differences in performance among the six meta-analysis-based FS methods, we identify and list the differences and similarities in Table 3. We focus on three properties: (a) basic FS methods forming the basis of meta-analysis, (b) the manner in which these basic FS methods are chosen and applied to individual microarray datasets, and (c) the use of ranks.

Among the five meta-analysis methods (not including the naive control method) rank average and mDEDS are the only methods that consider multiple basic FS methods—for example, fold change, t-statistic, SAM, and rank sum—for detecting DEGs (Table 3, row 1). The rank products, Choi and Wang methods use modified forms of basic FS methods. Moreover, rank average is the only method that chooses one basic FS method for each dataset to maximize prediction performance (Table 3, row 2). In contrast, mDEDS uses all of the available basic FS methods for each dataset. Finally, rank average and rank products are the only meta-analysis methods that are rank-based (Table 3, row 3).

Among the basic FS methods, no method can be considered the best because of the data-dependent nature of microarray analysis. Thus, rank average and mDEDS benefit by considering multiple basic FS methods. However, some basic FS methods can produce erroneous results when inappropriately applied (e.g., using a t-statistic with gene expression data that is not normally distributed). Rank average meta-analysis further benefits from selecting a single basic FS that optimizes prediction performance. On the other hand, the performance of mDEDS meta-analysis can degrade if it includes a basic FS method that is incompatible with the data. Likewise, the performance of rank products can degrade when the fold change FS method is not appropriate for the data. The Choi and Wang methods may also suffer from this problem. However, they seem to perform fairly well when applied to the datasets in this study (see Figure 3). Finally, rank-based meta-analysis methods that consider multiple basic FS methods allow a fair comparison among the basic FS methods. In light of these results, for microarray meta-analysis, we recommend (1) to use rank-based methods, (2) to consider a wide variety of basic FS methods, and (3) to optimize the FS method for each individual dataset based on application-specific criteria (e.g., prediction performance for diagnostic applications).

Despite the benefits summarized in Table 3, rank average meta-analysis and the evaluation criteria presented in this study are not without limitations. The limitations of this study include (1) the scope of data and classifiers considered, (2) the criterion for measuring performance of a meta-analysis method, and (3) normalization and pre-processing of gene expression data. First, the results of this study may be dataset-specific. Although we have strived to provide a wide range of scenarios to allow adequate assessment of these meta-analysis methods, results may differ when applied to other dataset groups. Second, we use prediction AUC as the performance criterion. However, microarray-based clinical prediction is only one possible application. Other applications may need to identify genes based on biological relevance [15]. It is unclear which meta-analysis methods would perform well in such applications. The rank average meta-analysis method benefits from choosing a basic FS method for each individual dataset that optimizes (via cross-validation) prediction performance. Thus, there is a potential bias in the performance of rank average meta-analysis. On the other hand, the ability to choose basic FS methods that perform well for a particular application, such as prediction, could be considered a favorable property of rank average meta-analysis. Finally, it is possible that normalization of gene expression datasets (e.g., quantile normalization) can improve the performance of meta-analysis by reducing batch effect. Specifically, removal of batch effects (1) can improve prediction performance when training and testing are applied to independent, heterogeneous datasets and (2) can improve the performance of simple meta-analysis methods that aggregate samples from multiple heterogeneous datasets. However, we do not consider any batch-effect normalization procedures in this study.

5. Conclusions

In order to address the sample-size problem in gene expression analysis as well as the need for accurate solutions for clinical prediction problems, we proposed the rank average meta-analysis-based FS method. Rank average meta-analysis identifies differentially expressed genes from multiple microarray datasets. We used a comprehensive study of multiple factors and found that rank average performs consistently well compared to five other meta-analysis methods in terms of prediction performance. This comprehensive study enabled us to measure the robustness of rank average to three factors that are often encountered in clinical prediction applications. These factors include clinical application (e.g., breast, renal, and pancreatic cancer), microarray data platform heterogeneity, and classifier model (logistic regression, diagonal LDA, and SVM). Rank average meta-analysis, performs well because it selects dataset-specific basic FS methods and then averages the ranks across all individual datasets to produce a final robust gene ranking. In comparison to five other meta-analysis methods the rank average method is not always the best method for some factor combinations. However, it is consistently among the best performing in terms of its ability to identify predictive genes. Although we presented results from analysis of microarray gene expression data, the proposed methods may be generalized for other bioinformatics problems that require feature selection.

Acknowledgments

This work was supported in part by Grants from National Institutes of Health (Bioengineering Research Partnership R01CA108468, Center for Cancer Nanotechnology Excellence U54CA119338); Georgia Cancer Coalition (Distinguished Cancer Scholar Award to M. D. Wang); Hewlett Packard; and Microsoft Research. The funding sources listed here have supported this multiyear investigation of microarray meta-analysis for clinical prediction, including covering the stipends and salaries of multiple coauthors, computing hardware and software licenses, travel expenses to technical meetings to present this work, and publication expenses.

References

[1] K. M. Lin, J. Kang, H. Shin, and J. Lee, "A cube framework for incorporating inter-gene information into biological data mining," *International Journal of Data Mining and Bioinformatics*, vol. 3, no. 1, pp. 3–22, 2009.

[2] J. H. Phan, R. A. Moffitt, T. H. Stokes et al., "Convergence of biomarkers, bioinformatics and nanotechnology for individualized cancer treatment," *Trends in Biotechnology*, vol. 27, no. 6, pp. 350–358, 2009.

[3] D. B. Allison, X. Cui, G. P. Page, and M. Sabripour, "Microarray data analysis: from disarray to consolidation and consensus," *Nature Reviews Genetics*, vol. 7, no. 1, pp. 55–65, 2006.

[4] L. Shi, W. Tong, H. Fang et al., "Cross-platform comparability of microarray technology: intra-platform consistency and appropriate data analysis procedures are essential," *BMC Bioinformatics*, vol. 6, no. 2, article S12, 2005.

[5] B. M. Bolstad, R. A. Irizarry, M. Åstrand, and T. P. Speed, "A comparison of normalization methods for high density oligonucleotide array data based on variance and bias," *Bioinformatics*, vol. 19, no. 2, pp. 185–193, 2003.

[6] P. Stafford and M. Brun, "Three methods for optimization of cross-laboratory and cross-platform microarray expression data," *Nucleic Acids Research*, vol. 35, no. 10, article e72, 2007.

[7] W. E. Johnson, C. Li, and A. Rabinovic, "Adjusting batch effects in microarray expression data using empirical Bayes methods," *Biostatistics*, vol. 8, no. 1, pp. 118–127, 2007.

[8] L. Lusa, L. M. McShane, J. F. Reid et al., "Challenges in projecting clustering results across gene expression-profiling datasets," *Journal of the National Cancer Institute*, vol. 99, no. 22, pp. 1715–1723, 2007.

[9] T. Park, S. G. Yi, Y. K. Shin, and S. Y. Lee, "Combining multiple microarrays in the presence of controlling variables," *Bioinformatics*, vol. 22, no. 14, pp. 1682–1689, 2006.

[10] J. K. Choi, U. Yu, S. Kim, and O. J. Yoo, "Combining multiple microarray studies and modeling interstudy variation," *Bioinformatics*, vol. 19, no. 1, pp. i84–i90, 2003.

[11] J. Wang, K. R. Coombes, W. E. Highsmith, M. J. Keating, and L. V. Abruzzo, "Differences in gene expression between B-cell chronic lymphocytic leukemia and normal B cells: a meta-analysis of three microarray studies," *Bioinformatics*, vol. 20, no. 17, pp. 3166–3178, 2004.

[12] S. Yoon, Y. Yang, J. Choi, and J. Seong, "Large scale data mining approach for gene-specific standardization of microarray gene expression data," *Bioinformatics*, vol. 22, no. 23, pp. 2898–2904, 2006.

[13] R. Breitling and P. Herzyk, "Rank-based methods as a nonparametric alternative of the T-statistic for the analysis of biological microarray data," *Journal of Bioinformatics and Computational Biology*, vol. 3, no. 5, pp. 1171–1189, 2005.

[14] A. Campain and Y. H. Yang, "Comparison study of microarray meta-analysis methods," *BMC Bioinformatics*, vol. 11, article 408, 2010.

[15] J. H. Phan, Q. Yin-Goen, A. N. Young, and M. D. Wang, "Improving the efficiency of biomarker identification using biological knowledge," *Pacific Symposium on Biocomputing*, pp. 427–438, 2009.

[16] A. N. Schuetz, Q. Yin-Goen, M. B. Amin et al., "Molecular classification of renal tumors by gene expression profiling," *Journal of Molecular Diagnostics*, vol. 7, no. 2, pp. 206–218, 2005.

[17] J. Jones, H. Otu, D. Spentzos et al., "Gene signatures of progression and metastasis in renal cell cancer," *Clinical Cancer Research*, vol. 11, no. 16, pp. 5730–5739, 2005.

[18] E. J. Kort, L. Farber, M. Tretiakova et al., "The E2F3-oncomir-1 axis is activated in Wilms' tumor," *Cancer Research*, vol. 68, no. 11, pp. 4034–4038, 2008.

[19] M. V. Yusenko, R. P. Kuiper, T. Boethe et al., "High-resolution DNA copy number and gene expression analyses distinguish chromophobe renal cell carcinomas and renal oncocytomas," *BMC Cancer*, vol. 9, article 152, 2009.

[20] M. V. Yusenko, D. Zubakov, and G. Kovacs, "Gene expression profiling of chromophobe renal cell carcinomas and renal oncocytomas by Affymetrix GeneChip using pooled and individual tumours," *International Journal of Biological Sciences*, vol. 5, no. 6, pp. 517–527, 2009.

[21] J. P. T. Higgins, R. Shinghal, H. Gill et al., "Gene expression patterns in renal cell carcinoma assessed by complementary DNA microarray," *American Journal of Pathology*, vol. 162, no. 3, pp. 925–932, 2003.

[22] L. Shi, G. Campbell, W. D. Jones et al., "The MicroArray Quality Control (MAQC)-II study of common practices for the development and validation of microarray-based predictive models," *Nature Biotechnology*, vol. 28, no. 8, pp. 827–838, 2010.

[23] L. D. Miller, J. Smeds, J. George et al., "An expression signature for p53 status in human breast cancer predicts mutation status, transcriptional effects, and patient survival," *Proceedings of the National Academy of Sciences of the United States of America*, vol. 102, no. 38, pp. 13550–13555, 2005.

[24] C. Sotiriou, C. Wirapati, S. Loi et al., "Gene expression profiling in breast cancer: understanding the molecular basis of histologic grade to improve prognosis," *Journal of the National Cancer Institute*, vol. 98, no. 4, pp. 262–272, 2006.

[25] A. J. Minn, G. P. Gupta, P. M. Siegel et al., "Genes that mediate breast cancer metastasis to lung," *Nature*, vol. 436, no. 7050, pp. 518–524, 2005.

[26] M. J. van de Vijver, Y. D. He, L. J. van 't Veer et al., "A gene-expression signature as a predictor of survival in breast cancer," *The New England Journal of Medicine*, vol. 347, no. 25, pp. 1999–2009, 2002.

[27] L. Badea, V. Herlea, S. O. Dima, T. Dumitrascu, and I. Popescu, "Combined gene expression analysis of whole-tissue and microdissected pancreatic ductal adenocarcinoma identifies genes specifically overexpressed in tumor epithelia," *Hepato-Gastroenterology*, vol. 55, no. 88, pp. 2016–2027, 2008.

[28] H. Pei, L. Li, B. L. Fridley et al., "FKBP51 affects cancer cell response to chemotherapy by negatively regulating Akt," *Cancer Cell*, vol. 16, no. 3, pp. 259–266, 2009.

[29] M. Ishikawa, K. Yoshida, Y. Yamashita et al., "Experimental trial for diagnosis of pancreatic ductal carcinoma based on gene expression profiles of pancreatic ductal cells," *Cancer Science*, vol. 96, no. 7, pp. 387–393, 2005.

[30] C. Pilarsky, O. Ammerpohl, B. Sipos et al., "Activation of Wnt signalling in stroma from pancreatic cancer identified by gene expression profiling," *Journal of Cellular and Molecular Medicine*, vol. 12, no. 6B, pp. 2823–2835, 2008.

[31] C. A. Iacobuzio-Donahue, A. Maitra, M. Olsen et al., "Exploration of global gene expression patterns in pancreatic adenocarcinoma using cDNA microarrays," *American Journal of Pathology*, vol. 162, no. 4, pp. 1151–1162, 2003.

[32] V. G. Tusher, R. Tibshirani, and G. Chu, "Significance analysis of microarrays applied to the ionizing radiation response," *Proceedings of the National Academy of Sciences of the United States of America*, vol. 98, no. 9, pp. 5116–5121, 2001.

[33] C. Ding and H. Peng, "Minimum redundancy feature selection from microarray gene expression data," *Journal of Bioinformatics and Computational Biology*, vol. 3, no. 2, pp. 185–205, 2005.

[34] I. Bièche, I. Girault, E. Urbain, S. Tozlu, and R. Lidereau, "Relationship between intratumoral expression of genes coding for xenobiotic-metabolizing enzymes and benefit from adjuvant tamoxifen in estrogen receptor alpha-positive postmenopausal breast carcinoma," *Breast Cancer Research*, vol. 6, no. 3, pp. R252–R263, 2004.

[35] T. Z. Parris, A. Danielsson, S. Nemes et al., "Clinical implications of gene dosage and gene expression patterns in diploid breast carcinoma," *Clinical Cancer Research*, vol. 16, no. 15, pp. 3860–3874, 2010.

[36] S. J. Prest, F. E. May, and B. R. Westley, "The estrogen-regulated protein, TFF1, stimulates migration of human breast cancer cells," *The FASEB Journal*, vol. 16, no. 6, pp. 592–594, 2002.

[37] H. Liu, A. R. Brannon, A. R. Reddy et al., "Identifying mRNA targets of microRNA dysregulated in cancer: with application to clear cell Renal Cell Carcinoma," *BMC Systems Biology*, vol. 4, article 51, 2010.

[38] J. J. Morrissey, A. N. London, J. Luo, and E. D. Kharasch, "Urinary biomarkers for the early diagnosis of kidney cancer," *Mayo Clinic Proceedings*, vol. 85, no. 5, pp. 413–421, 2010.

[39] T. Arumugam, D. M. Simeone, K. Van Golen, and C. D. Logsdon, "S100P promotes pancreatic cancer growth, survival, and invasion," *Clinical Cancer Research*, vol. 11, no. 15, pp. 5356–5364, 2005.

[40] H. J. Whiteman, M. E. Weeks, S. E. Dowen et al., "The role of S100P in the invasion of pancreatic cancer cells is mediated through cytoskeletal changes and regulation of cathepsin D," *Cancer Research*, vol. 67, no. 18, pp. 8633–8642, 2007.

[41] M. Katayama, A. Funakoshi, T. Sumii, N. Sanzen, and K. Sekiguchi, "Laminin γ2-chain fragment circulating level increases in patients with metastatic pancreatic ductal cell adenocarcinomas," *Cancer Letters*, vol. 225, no. 1, pp. 167–176, 2005.

19

Tumor Necrosis Factor-α as a Diagnostic Marker for Neonatal Sepsis: A Meta-Analysis

Bokun Lv,[1,2] **Jie Huang,**[1] **Haining Yuan,**[1,2] **Wenying Yan,**[3] **Guang Hu,**[2] **and Jian Wang**[1]

[1] *Systems Sepsis Team, Soochow University Affiliated Children's Hospital, Suzhou 215003, China*
[2] *Center for Systems Biology, Soochow University, Suzhou 215006, China*
[3] *Suzhou Zhengxing Translational Biomedical Informatics Ltd., Taicang 215400, China*

Correspondence should be addressed to Jian Wang; wangjian_sdfey@sina.com

Academic Editors: B. Shen, J. Wang, and J. Wang

Neonatal sepsis (NS) is an important cause of mortality in newborns and life-threatening disorder in infants. The meta-analysis was performed to investigate the diagnosis value of tumor necrosis factor-α (TNF-α) test in NS. Our collectible studies were searched from PUBMED, EMBASE, and the Cochrane Library between March 1994 and August 2013. Accordingly, 347 studies were collected totally, in which 15 articles and 23 trials were selected to study the NS in our meta-analysis. The TNF-α test showed moderate accuracy of the diagnosis of NS both in early-onset neonatal sepsis (sensitivity = 0.66, specificity = 0.76, $Q^* = 0.74$) and in late-onset neonatal sepsis (sensitivity = 0.68, specificity = 0.89, $Q^* = 0.87$). We also found the northern hemisphere group in the test has higher sensitivity (0.84) and specificity (0.83). A diagnostic OR analysis found that the study population may be the major reason for the heterogeneity. Accordingly, we suggest that TNF-α is also a valuable marker in the diagnosis of NS.

1. Introduction

Neonatal sepsis (NS), as one of the major causes, leads to neonatal mortality and morbidity, especially in neonates born preterm [1]. Early diagnosis and management of the newborn infant with NS play key roles in preventing severe and life-threatening complications [2]. During the first hours of life, reliable infection markers are absent in NS. Therefore, neonatologists often begin early antibiotic treatment in newborn infants with risk factors for infection, exposing many neonates to unnecessary treatments. Due to the limitation of the treatment strategy in early diagnosis of sepsis, the isolation of causative organisms from microbiological cultures takes up to 72 h, which cannot be used to identify most infected infants [3].

Procalcitonin (PCT), a 116-amino acid peptide considered as a precursor in calcium homeostasis, has been proved to be a valuable marker for distinguishing sepsis from other noninfectious disease [4, 5]. C-reactive protein (CRP), another biomarker, is a protein discovered in the blood and whose levels will rise after inflammation [6–8]. To date, CRP and PCT have been proposed for inclusion as two mostly used

diagnostic markers in the international definition of sepsis [9, 10]. Recently, many studies have found that some new markers also play important roles in the diagnosis of neonatal sepsis. However, the systematic research and comparison of these biomarkers for diagnosing NS are limited. For example, we have investigated the diagnosis value of serum amyloid A (SAA) in NS [11]. Here, we continue to evaluate the value of the tumor necrosis factor-α (TNF-α), by considering it as a useful marker. TNF-α is a cytokine involved in systemic inflammation, which belongs to a member of a group of cytokines that stimulate the acute phase reaction [12].

Thus, the objective of this meta-analysis was to investigate the value of TNF-α for detecting NS. Although a lot of works indicate that both PCT and CRP are two superior markers for diagnosis of sepsis and infection, we suggest here the TNF-α is also a promising marker in NS. A deeper meta-analysis of these studies is thus currently needed.

2. Methods

2.1. Studies Retrieval and Selection. In order to perform a systematic analysis of the available evidence on the efficacy of

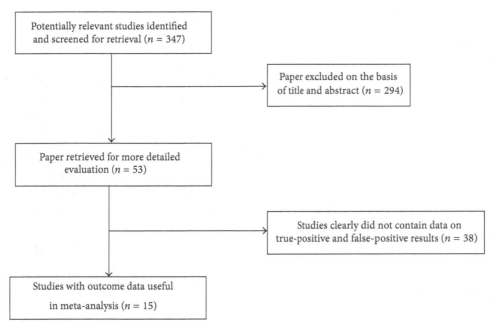

FIGURE 1: Summary of study assessment and inclusion in the meta-analysis of studies involving diagnosis of neonatal sepsis using a TNF-α test.

TNF-α in NS [13], the common approach of literature search was performed in PUBMED, EMBASE, and the Cochrane Library for relevant citations from March 1994 to August 2013. The search terms used were "TNF-α," "neonatal," "neonate," "sepsis," "infant," "newborn," and "tumor necrosis factors-α". The reference lists of all known primary and review articles were also searched. No language restriction was used, so that we have examined the references of known articles to fully retrieve the data.

If an article does not include enough data for calculating sensitivity and specificity (2 × 2 table), we asked the corresponding author to provide us with necessary data. If there was no response from the corresponding author, a reminder was sent after one week. If we still cannot achieve the data after this process, the study was excluded from meta-analysis. The selection of articles was performed by two investigators independently to ensure the high accuracy.

2.2. Data Extraction. Data collected from the studies included the first author, publication year, diagnostic cut-off point and time, test methods, and sensitivity and specificity data. So the numbers of true-positive, false-positive, false-negative, and true-negative results were extracted for each study. Accuracy data was extracted to construct 2 × 2 table at a specific time. We have requested the information from the authors, if no enough data on the criteria was found in the studies.

2.3. Statistical Analysis. We used Meta-Disc 1.4 software and Review Manager 5.0 to perform the statistical analysis [14]. Diagnoses were grouped into two groups according to the time of TNF-α test for diagnosis of NS. One group is the time points of TNF-α measurement for the diagnosis of early-onset neonatal sepsis (EONS), which were 0–72 h of age;

the other group is the time points of TNF-α measurement for the diagnosis of late-onset neonatal sepsis (LONS), in which the age of neonates is older than 72 h. We calculated the sensitivity, specificity, diagnostic odds ratio (OR), and corresponding 95% confidence intervals (CI) from each study. We also gained the pooled sensitivity, specificity, and diagnosis OR from each group.

The diagnostic OR expresses how much greater the odds of having sepsis are for newborns who have a positive test result, relatively to newborns who have a negative result [15]. For the estimates of diagnostic OR, heterogeneity was assessed by using the Cochrane Q statistic. Normally, I^2 lies between 0% and 100%. If $I^2 < 50\%$, then there is a lot of homogeneity among studies in meta-analysis; whereas $I^2 > 50\%$ shows there is more heterogeneity among studies. A value of 0% indicates no observed heterogeneity, and larger values show increasing heterogeneity [16]. We explored the reasons for heterogeneity by carrying out the subgroup analysis and examined characteristics of included studies.

In order to summarize these results, we constructed summary receiver operator characteristic (SROC) curves, which showed the relationship between sensitivity and the false positives (1-specificity). Q^* values was received from the SROC curves. Meanwhile, the area under the (SROC) curves was also calculated from the SROC curves, which have been proposed as a way to assess diagnostic data in the context of a meta-analysis [17].

3. Results

3.1. Study Selection. The literature search was completed in August 2013. We found 347 potentially relevant restudies, but only 15 articles met our inclusion criteria. Figure 1 shows

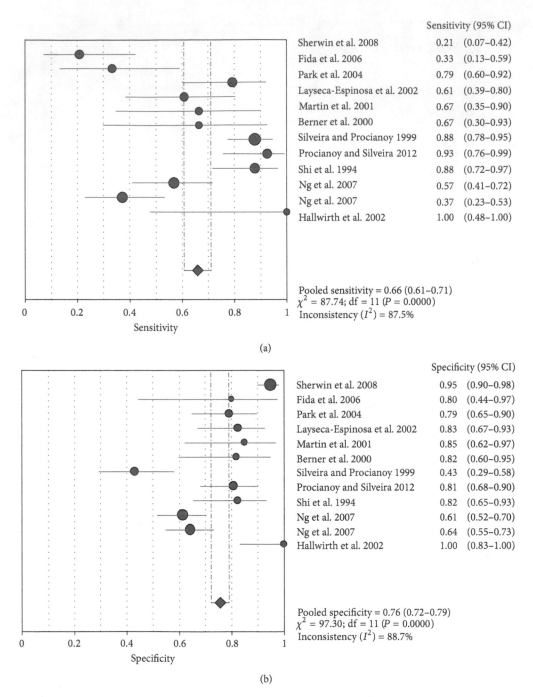

Sensitivity (95% CI)

Sherwin et al. 2008	0.21	(0.07–0.42)
Fida et al. 2006	0.33	(0.13–0.59)
Park et al. 2004	0.79	(0.60–0.92)
Layseca-Espinosa et al. 2002	0.61	(0.39–0.80)
Martin et al. 2001	0.67	(0.35–0.90)
Berner et al. 2000	0.67	(0.30–0.93)
Silveira and Procianoy 1999	0.88	(0.78–0.95)
Procianoy and Silveira 2012	0.93	(0.76–0.99)
Shi et al. 1994	0.88	(0.72–0.97)
Ng et al. 2007	0.57	(0.41–0.72)
Ng et al. 2007	0.37	(0.23–0.53)
Hallwirth et al. 2002	1.00	(0.48–1.00)

Pooled sensitivity = 0.66 (0.61–0.71)
$\chi^2 = 87.74$; df = 11 ($P = 0.0000$)
Inconsistency (I^2) = 87.5%

(a)

Specificity (95% CI)

Sherwin et al. 2008	0.95	(0.90–0.98)
Fida et al. 2006	0.80	(0.44–0.97)
Park et al. 2004	0.79	(0.65–0.90)
Layseca-Espinosa et al. 2002	0.83	(0.67–0.93)
Martin et al. 2001	0.85	(0.62–0.97)
Berner et al. 2000	0.82	(0.60–0.95)
Silveira and Procianoy 1999	0.43	(0.29–0.58)
Procianoy and Silveira 2012	0.81	(0.68–0.90)
Shi et al. 1994	0.82	(0.65–0.93)
Ng et al. 2007	0.61	(0.52–0.70)
Ng et al. 2007	0.64	(0.55–0.73)
Hallwirth et al. 2002	1.00	(0.83–1.00)

Pooled specificity = 0.76 (0.72–0.79)
$\chi^2 = 97.30$; df = 11 ($P = 0.0000$)
Inconsistency (I^2) = 88.7%

(b)

FIGURE 2: Forest plot for sensitivity and specificity of the TNF-α test to diagnose neonatal sepsis at the EONS.

the chart of literature search. Detailed information for each included study is presented in Table 1.

3.2. Accuracy of the TNF-α Test in the Diagnosis of Proven Early-Onset Neonatal Sepsis. Eleven articles and twelve trials were included to estimate the use of the TNF-α test in the diagnosis of proven early-onset neonatal sepsis (EONS). EONS was defined as the clinical sepsis in the 0–72 h after delivery, met the inclusion criteria in [18–27].

In these trials, we can get the TP, TN, FP, FN, sensitivity, specificity, DOR, PPV, and NPV from the articles.

The sensitivity ranged from 20.8% to 100% and pooled sensitivity is 66.1% (95% CI 60.7%–70.1%), specificity ranged from 43.1% to 100% and pooled specificity is 75.6% (95% CI 72.2%–78.9%), and the detailed forest map is shown in Figure 2. We calculated the significant heterogeneity among studies (sensitivity, $I^2 = 87.5\%$; specificity, $I^2 = 88.7\%$); it indicated that patient selection or other relevant factors might be responsible for heterogeneity.

The value of DOR of TNF-α was 7.43 (95% CI 3.47–15.90), as shown in Figure 3. In these articles, we calculated the significant heterogeneity ($I^2 = 77.9\%$). The SROC curve for

TABLE 1: Characteristics of studies included in the meta-analysis of the diagnosis of neonatal sepsis using a TNF-α test.

Study	Study population	Patients (n)	Sepsis diagnosis	Cut-off (pg/mL)	Time	Country
Hotoura et al. 2012 [1]	Cases: newborns with suspected sepsis Control: infection-free infants	82	Culture; clinical	30	LONS	Greece
Hotoura et al. 2012 [1]	Cases: newborns with suspected sepsis Control: infection-free infants	82	Culture; clinical	15	LONS	Greece
Sherwin et al. 2008 [28]	Cases: NICU newborns with suspected sepsis Control: neonates without sepsis	164	Culture; clinical	180	EONS	New Zealand
Sherwin et al. 2008 [28]	Cases: NICU newborns with suspected sepsis Control: neonates without sepsis	164	Culture; clinical	70	LONS	New Zealand
Sherwin et al. 2008 [28]	Cases: NICU newborns with suspected sepsis Control: neonates without sepsis	164	Culture; clinical	180	LONS	New Zealand
Kocabaş et al. 2007 [14]	Cases: neonates with a suspected clinical sepsis Control: healthy neonates without infectious	55	Culture; clinical	7.5	LONS	Turkey
Fida et al. 2006 [18]	Cases: neonates with clinical or proven or possible infected sepsis Control: disease without infection	28	Culture; clinical	29.86	EONS	Saudi Arabia
Park et al. 2004 [19]	Cases: newborns with suspected sepsis Control: neonates without sepsis	77	Culture; clinical	41	EONS	Korea
Layseca-Espinosa et al. 2002 [20]	Cases: neonates with clinical or proven sepsis Control: disease without infection	63	Culture; clinical	0.18	EONS	Spain
Martin et al. 2001 [21]	Cases: newborns with suspected sepsis Control: neonates without sepsis	32	Culture; clinical	20	EONS	Sweden
Berner et al. 2000 [22]	Cases: newborns with suspected sepsis Control: neonates without sepsis	31	Culture; clinical	48	EONS	Germany
Silveira and Procianoy 1999 [23]	Cases: newborn infants with clinical sepsis or probably infected with clinical sepsis Control: neonates without sepsis	117	Culture; clinical	12	EONS	Brazil
Ng et al. 1997 [29]	Cases: VLBW infants with suspected clinical sepsis Control: noninfected newborns	101	Culture; clinical	17	LONS	Hong Kong

TABLE 1: Continued.

Study	Study population	Patients (n)	Sepsis diagnosis	Cut-off (pg/mL)	Time	Country
Ng et al. 1997 [29]	Cases:VLBW infants with suspected clinical sepsis Control: noninfected newborns	101	Culture; clinical	17	LONS	Hong Kong
Ng et al. 1997 [29]	Cases: VLBW infants with suspected clinical sepsis Control: noninfected newborns	101	Culture; clinical	17	LONS	Hong Kong
Hotoura et al. 2011 [30]	Cases: full-term neonates with suspected or documented infection Control: infection-free infants	95	Culture; clinical	30	LONS	Greece
Hotoura et al. 2011 [30]	Cases: full-term neonates with suspected or documented infection Control: infection-free infants	95	Culture; clinical	15	LONS	Greece
Hallwirth et al. 2002 [24]	Cases: neonates with sepsis Control: neonates without sepsis	25	Culture; clinical	20000	LONS	Austria
Procianoy and Silveira 2012 [25]	Cases: very low birth weight infants with clinical sepsis Control: neonates without sepsis	84	Culture; clinical	30	EONS	Brazil
Shi et al. 1994 [26]	Cases: neonates with sepsis Control: neonates without sepsis	67	Culture; clinical	267.2	EONS	CHINA
Ng et al. 2007 [27]	Cases: very low birth weight infants with suspected sepsis Control: neonates without sepsis	155	Culture; clinical	0.6	EONS	Hong Kong
Ng et al. 2007 [27]	Cases: very low birth weight infants with suspected sepsis Control: neonates without sepsis	155	Culture; clinical	0.6	EONS	Hong Kong
Hallwirth et al. 2002 [24]	Cases: neonates with sepsis Control: neonates without sepsis	25	Culture; clinical	20000	EONS	Austria

TNF-α markers was plotted in Figure 4; the AUC was 0.81 with the standard error being 0.04. The pooled diagnostic accuracy (Q^*) of 0.7430 with the standard error was 0.04.

3.3. Accuracy of the TNF-α Test in the Diagnosis of Proven Late-Onset Neonatal Sepsis. Six articles and eleven trials were included to estimate the use of the TNF-α test in the diagnosis of proven late-onset neonatal sepsis (LONS). LONS was defined as the clinical sepsis 72 h after birth, met the inclusion criteria in [1, 14, 24, 28–30].

In these trials, we can also get much information from the articles. The sensitivity ranged from 23.1% to 100% and pooled sensitivity is 68.0% (95% CI 62.8%–72.8%), specificity ranged from 73.2% to 100% and pooled specificity is 88.5% (95% CI 85.9% 90.7%), and the detailed forest map is

shown in Figure 5. We calculated the significant heterogeneity among studies (sensitivity, I^2 = 91.9%; specificity, I^2 = 87.5%), which indicated that patient selection or other relevant factors might be responsible for heterogeneity.

The value of DOR of TNF-α was 37.44 (95% CI 19.07–73.48), as shown in Figure 6. In these articles, we calculated the significant heterogeneity (I^2 = 41.6%). The SROC curves for TNF-α markers were plotted in Figure 7; the AUC was 0.93 with the standard error being 0.017. The pooled diagnostic accuracy (Q^*) of 0.8696 with the standard error was 0.02.

3.4. Intensive Study of the TNF-α Test in the Diagnosis of Proven Late Onset Neonatal Sepsis. In the LONS study, study

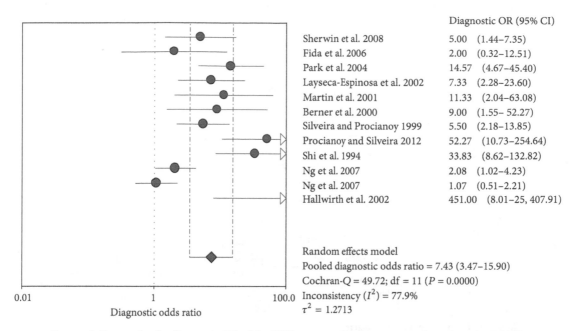

	Diagnostic OR (95% CI)
Sherwin et al. 2008	5.00 (1.44–7.35)
Fida et al. 2006	2.00 (0.32–12.51)
Park et al. 2004	14.57 (4.67–45.40)
Layseca-Espinosa et al. 2002	7.33 (2.28–23.60)
Martin et al. 2001	11.33 (2.04–63.08)
Berner et al. 2000	9.00 (1.55– 52.27)
Silveira and Procianoy 1999	5.50 (2.18–13.85)
Procianoy and Silveira 2012	52.27 (10.73–254.64)
Shi et al. 1994	33.83 (8.62–132.82)
Ng et al. 2007	2.08 (1.02–4.23)
Ng et al. 2007	1.07 (0.51–2.21)
Hallwirth et al. 2002	451.00 (8.01–25, 407.91)

Random effects model
Pooled diagnostic odds ratio = 7.43 (3.47–15.90)
Cochran-Q = 49.72; df = 11 (P = 0.0000)
Inconsistency (I^2) = 77.9%
τ^2 = 1.2713

FIGURE 3: Forest plot for diagnostic OR of the TNF-α test to diagnose neonatal sepsis at the EONS.

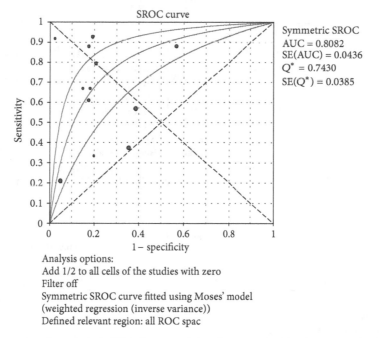

Symmetric SROC
AUC = 0.8082
SE(AUC) = 0.0436
Q^* = 0.7430
SE(Q^*) = 0.0385

Analysis options:
Add 1/2 to all cells of the studies with zero
Filter off
Symmetric SROC curve fitted using Moses' model
(weighted regression (inverse variance))
Defined relevant region: all ROC spac

FIGURE 4: Summary receiver operating characteristic (SROC) curve of the TNF-α test for the diagnosis of early-onset neonatal sepsis. Each point represents one study in the SROC curve.

populations come from different countries, but in general they can be further divided into two regions: the northern hemisphere and the southern hemisphere.

Eight trials were included to estimate the use of the TNF-α test in the northern hemisphere at the diagnosis of proven late-onset neonatal sepsis [1, 14, 29, 30]. In these trials, sensitivity ranged from 61.4% to 100% and pooled sensitivity is 84.0% (95% CI 78.8%–88.4%), specificity ranged from 68.8% to 96.6% and pooled specificity is 83.3% (95% CI 79.6%–86.6%), and the detailed forest maps are shown in

Figure 8. We calculated the significant heterogeneity among studies (sensitivity, I^2 = 77.4%; specificity, I^2 = 76.3%), which indicated that patient selection or other relevant factors might be responsible for heterogeneity.

The value of DOR of TNF-α test in the northern hemisphere at the diagnosis of proven late-onset neonatal sepsis was 44.94 (95% CI 20.71–97.50), as shown in Figure 9. In these articles, we calculated the significant heterogeneity (I^2 = 47.1%). The SROC curves for TNF-α markers were plotted in Figure 10; the AUC was 0.93 with the standard error

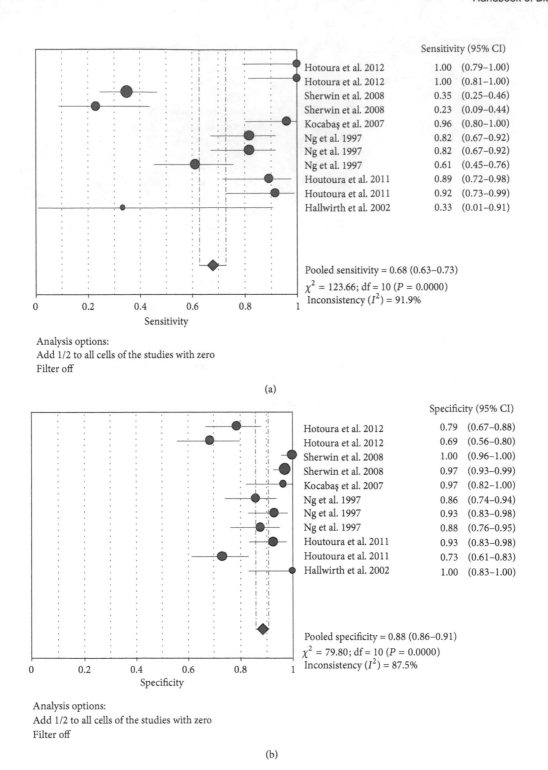

Sensitivity (95% CI)

	Sensitivity	(95% CI)
Hotoura et al. 2012	1.00	(0.79–1.00)
Hotoura et al. 2012	1.00	(0.81–1.00)
Sherwin et al. 2008	0.35	(0.25–0.46)
Sherwin et al. 2008	0.23	(0.09–0.44)
Kocabaş et al. 2007	0.96	(0.80–1.00)
Ng et al. 1997	0.82	(0.67–0.92)
Ng et al. 1997	0.82	(0.67–0.92)
Ng et al. 1997	0.61	(0.45–0.76)
Houtoura et al. 2011	0.89	(0.72–0.98)
Houtoura et al. 2011	0.92	(0.73–0.99)
Hallwirth et al. 2002	0.33	(0.01–0.91)

Pooled sensitivity = 0.68 (0.63–0.73)
$\chi^2 = 123.66$; df = 10 ($P = 0.0000$)
Inconsistency (I^2) = 91.9%

0   0.2   0.4   0.6   0.8   1
Sensitivity

Analysis options:
Add 1/2 to all cells of the studies with zero
Filter off

(a)

Specificity (95% CI)

	Specificity	(95% CI)
Hotoura et al. 2012	0.79	(0.67–0.88)
Hotoura et al. 2012	0.69	(0.56–0.80)
Sherwin et al. 2008	1.00	(0.96–1.00)
Sherwin et al. 2008	0.97	(0.93–0.99)
Kocabaş et al. 2007	0.97	(0.82–1.00)
Ng et al. 1997	0.86	(0.74–0.94)
Ng et al. 1997	0.93	(0.83–0.98)
Ng et al. 1997	0.88	(0.76–0.95)
Houtoura et al. 2011	0.93	(0.83–0.98)
Houtoura et al. 2011	0.73	(0.61–0.83)
Hallwirth et al. 2002	1.00	(0.83–1.00)

Pooled specificity = 0.88 (0.86–0.91)
$\chi^2 = 79.80$; df = 10 ($P = 0.0000$)
Inconsistency (I^2) = 87.5%

0   0.2   0.4   0.6   0.8   1
Specificity

Analysis options:
Add 1/2 to all cells of the studies with zero
Filter off

(b)

FIGURE 5: Forest plot for sensitivity and specificity of the TNF-α test to diagnose neonatal sepsis at the LONS.

being 0.017. The pooled diagnostic accuracy (Q^*) of 0.8710 with the standard error was 0.02.

Three trials were included to estimate the use of the TNF-α test in the southern hemisphere at the diagnosis of proven late-onset neonatal sepsis [24, 28]. In these trials, sensitivity ranged from 23.1% to 35% and pooled sensitivity is 32.1% (95% CI 23.5%–41.7%), specificity ranged from 97.1% to 100% and pooled specificity is 98.3% (95% CI 95.8%–99.5%), and

the detailed forest map is shown in Figure 11. We calculated the significant heterogeneity among studies (sensitivity, $I^2 = 0$%; specificity, $I^2 = 56.0$%), which indicated that patient selection or other relevant factors might be responsible for heterogeneity.

The value of DOR of TNF-α test in the northern hemisphere at the diagnosis of proven late-onset neonatal sepsis was 20.88 (95% CI 3.84–113.49), as shown in Figure 12. In

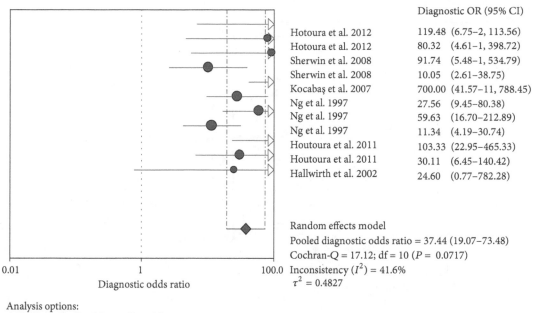

	Diagnostic OR (95% CI)
Hotoura et al. 2012	119.48 (6.75–2, 113.56)
Hotoura et al. 2012	80.32 (4.61–1, 398.72)
Sherwin et al. 2008	91.74 (5.48–1, 534.79)
Sherwin et al. 2008	10.05 (2.61–38.75)
Kocabaş et al. 2007	700.00 (41.57–11, 788.45)
Ng et al. 1997	27.56 (9.45–80.38)
Ng et al. 1997	59.63 (16.70–212.89)
Ng et al. 1997	11.34 (4.19–30.74)
Houtoura et al. 2011	103.33 (22.95–465.33)
Houtoura et al. 2011	30.11 (6.45–140.42)
Hallwirth et al. 2002	24.60 (0.77–782.28)

Random effects model
Pooled diagnostic odds ratio = 37.44 (19.07–73.48)
Cochran-Q = 17.12; df = 10 (P = 0.0717)
Inconsistency (I^2) = 41.6%
τ^2 = 0.4827

Analysis options:
Add 1/2 to all cells of the studies with zero
Filter off

FIGURE 6: Forest plot for diagnostic OR of the TNF-α test to diagnose neonatal sepsis at the LONS.

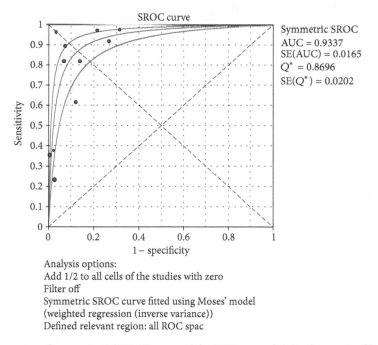

Symmetric SROC
AUC = 0.9337
SE(AUC) = 0.0165
Q^* = 0.8696
SE(Q^*) = 0.0202

Analysis options:
Add 1/2 to all cells of the studies with zero
Filter off
Symmetric SROC curve fitted using Moses' model
(weighted regression (inverse variance))
Defined relevant region: all ROC spac

FIGURE 7: Summary receiver operating characteristic (SROC) curve of the TNF-α test for the diagnosis of late-onset neonatal sepsis. Each point represents one study in the SROC curve.

these articles, we calculated the significant heterogeneity (I^2 = 35.5%). The SROC curves for TNF-α markers were plotted in Figure 13; the AUC was 0.0468 with the standard error being 0.224. The pooled diagnostic accuracy (Q^*) of 0.1052 with the standard error was 0.309.

3.5. Comparison of the Diagnostic Accuracy of Markers for Neonatal Sepsis. In LONS, PCT and CRP have been proven to be useful markers for the diagnosis of NS [3, 9, 31]. In order to

show the value of diagnosis of the TNF-α test for NS in LONS, we compared TNF-α with PCT and CRP in LONS. Six articles and eleven trials were used to evaluate the diagnosis of TNF-α. Compared with 55% (95% CI 45%–65%) for the CRP test and 72% (95% CI 63%–81%) for the PCT test [14], the pooled sensitivity for the TNF-α test was 68% (95% CI 63%–73%).

The pooled specificity for the TNF-α was slightly higher than for the CRP and PCT test (88.5% (95% CI 86%–91%) versus 85% (95% CI 81%–88%) versus 77% (95% CI 72%–81%)).

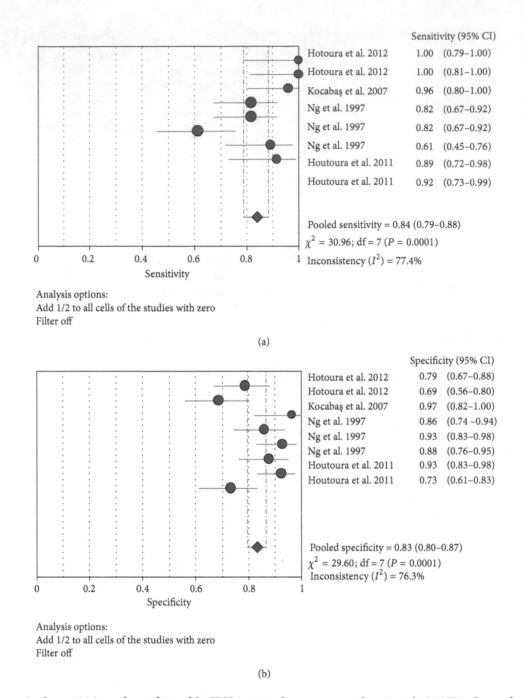

FIGURE 8: Forest plot for sensitivity and specificity of the TNF-α test to diagnose neonatal sepsis at the LONS in the northern hemisphere.

Furthermore, the pooled diagnostic OR for the TNF-α was higher than CRP and PCT (37.4 (95% CI 19.1–73.5) versus 8.6 (95% CI 3.5–21.0) versus 11.6 (95% CI 5.2–26.0)). The Q^* value was slightly higher for the TNF-α than CRP and PCT (0.87 versus 0.75 versus 0.77). In SROC curve the TNF-α's AUC is almost equal to CRP (0.93 versus 0.96). As many articles reported that PCT and CRP are good markers, the TNF-α is also a good marker for the diagnosis of NS in LONS.

3.6. *Analysis of Heterogeneity.* Heterogeneity is very critical in a meta-analysis, so we should try to explore the reason

for the heterogeneity. Generally speaking, variations include several influence factors, for instance the cut-off value, study population, inject antibodies, and so forth.

Firstly, we consider the cut-off value. In our study, many data are so large, so we suppose that this is the possible reason for the heterogeneity. We excluded two studies of [24, 28] whose cut-off values were relatively large. But the I^2 (heterogeneity test) almost does not change (41.7% versus 41.6%). So the cut off value is not the reason for the heterogeneity. Secondly, we consider the study population. The I^2 is reduced from 41.6% to 0% when two studies of

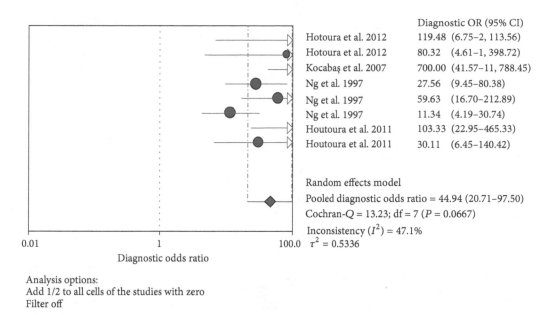

	Diagnostic OR (95% CI)
Hotoura et al. 2012	119.48 (6.75–2, 113.56)
Hotoura et al. 2012	80.32 (4.61–1, 398.72)
Kocabaş et al. 2007	700.00 (41.57–11, 788.45)
Ng et al. 1997	27.56 (9.45–80.38)
Ng et al. 1997	59.63 (16.70–212.89)
Ng et al. 1997	11.34 (4.19–30.74)
Houtoura et al. 2011	103.33 (22.95–465.33)
Houtoura et al. 2011	30.11 (6.45–140.42)

Random effects model
Pooled diagnostic odds ratio = 44.94 (20.71–97.50)
Cochran-Q = 13.23; df = 7 (P = 0.0667)
Inconsistency (I^2) = 47.1%
τ^2 = 0.5336

Analysis options:
Add 1/2 to all cells of the studies with zero
Filter off

FIGURE 9: Forest plot for diagnostic OR of the TNF-α test to diagnose neonatal sepsis at the LONS in the northern hemisphere.

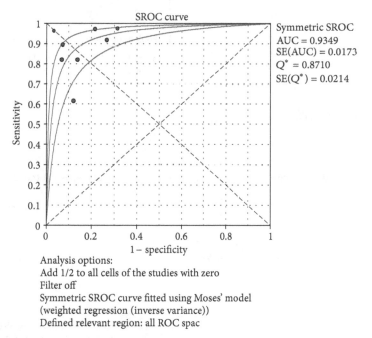

Symmetric SROC
AUC = 0.9349
SE(AUC) = 0.0173
Q^* = 0.8710
SE(Q^*) = 0.0214

Analysis options:
Add 1/2 to all cells of the studies with zero
Filter off
Symmetric SROC curve fitted using Moses' model
(weighted regression (inverse variance))
Defined relevant region: all ROC spac

FIGURE 10: Summary receiver operating characteristic (SROC) curve of the TNF-α test for the diagnosis of late-onset neonatal sepsis in the northern hemisphere. Each point represents one study in the SROC curve.

[28, 29] were excluded from the meta-analysis. Their study population is different from others. So the study population may be the major reason for the heterogeneity.

3.7. Publication Bias. The publication bias is difficult to avoid in meta-analysis [32]. In each study, we often choose favorable results and give up negative results; many "blindness" of test results was never reported. The limit of current available data may bias our conclusion.

4. Discussion

NS is one of the most common diseases and life-threating disorder in neonate, and thus it can bring the high mortality and morbidity in infants. So the identification of biomarkers is very important to improve the diagnosis of NS. The clinical signs are nonspecific and laboratory indicators including blood culture are not reliable [33]. The sensitivities of markers are not always so high [34]. So it is necessary to find a good marker for NS.

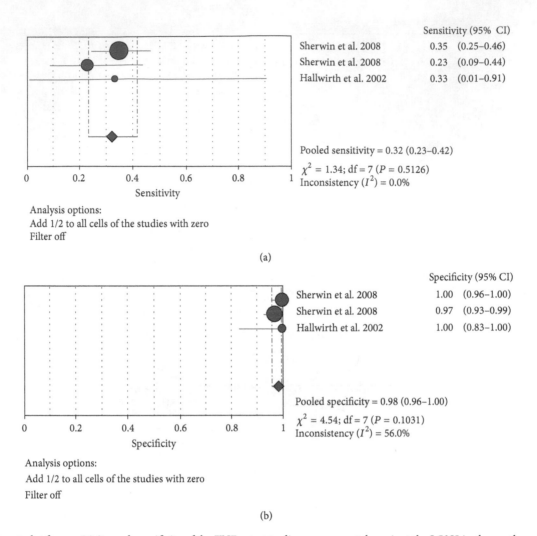

(a)

(b)

FIGURE 11: Forest plot for sensitivity and specificity of the TNF-α test to diagnose neonatal sepsis at the LONS in the southern hemisphere.

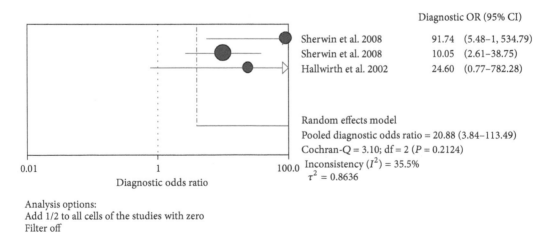

FIGURE 12: Forest plot for diagnostic OR of the TNF-α test to diagnose neonatal sepsis at the LONS in the southern hemisphere.

It is well known that an excellent marker should have high sensitivity and specificity. In our meta-analysis, the TNF-α tests' sensitivity is 0.66 for the diagnosis of early-onset neonatal sepsis, and the specificity is 0.46 and the Q^* is 0.74. At the late-onset neonatal sepsis, the TNF-α test's sensitivity is 0.68, whereas the specificity is 0.89 and the Q^* is 0.87. In particular, TNF-α shows a higher accuracy for the diagnosis of NS in LONS. Therefore, we have further analyzed the regional issues in LONS. To this end, we have classified studies into two groups, that is, northern hemisphere

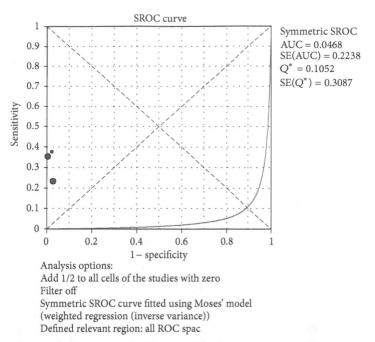

FIGURE 13: Summary receiver operating characteristic (SROC) curve of the TNF-α test for the diagnosis of late-onset neonatal sepsis in the southern hemisphere. Each point represents one study in the SROC curve.

group [1, 14, 29, 30] and southern hemisphere group [24, 28]. Our analysis found that the northern hemisphere group has higher sensitivity and specificity (sensitivity = 84%, specificity = 83%). The results show that the TNF-α has appropriate accuracy for the diagnosis of NS and thus is a good biomarker for the diagnosis of NS.

CRP is an excellent marker and has been applied in clinic [10]. The sensitivity of CRP is 30%–97%, and the specificity ranged from 75% to 100% [35]. In our meta-analysis, TNF-α' sensitivity ranged from 23.1% to 100%, and specificity ranged from 73.2% to 100%. The study from TNF-α is similar to CRP, so the TNF-α is a useful marker in the diagnosis of NS. In addition, PCT is more excellent marker which has better accuracy than CRP for the diagnosis of NS [3]. In our meta-analysis, the pooled sensitivity of TNF-α is slightly lower than that of the PCT test in EONS (66.1% versus 74%), the pooled specificity also in such (76% versus 86%). But in LONS, the pooled specificity of TNF-α is higher than that of the PCT test (89% versus 77%), although the pooled sensitivity is slightly lower than PCT (68% versus 72%). Generally speaking, the data of TNF-α and PCT is greater than CRP. This result again shows that TNF-α is good marker in the diagnosis of NS.

In conclusion, TNF-α shows the moderate accuracy in the diagnosis of NS, both in EONS and LONS. If we test the accuracy of TNF-α by further dividing data into two regions, the study in northern hemisphere shows a better result. Because of the relatively few testing data, the experiments results need to be further studied and the clinical validation is also needed.

Conflict of Interests

The authors declare that there is no conflict of interests regarding the publication of this paper.

Authors' Contribution

Bokun Lv and Jie Huang equally contributed to this work.

Acknowledgments

This work was supported by the National Natural Science Foundation of China Grants (81272143 and 21203131), the Natural Science Foundation of Jiangsu Province (K200509), the Natural Science Foundation of the Jiangsu Higher Education Institutions of China (12KJB180014), Jiangsu Innovation Team Grant LJ201141, and Program of Innovative and Entrepreneurial Talent.

References

[1] E. Hotoura, V. Giapros, A. Kostoula, P. Spyrou, and S. Andronikou, "Pre-inflammatory mediators and lymphocyte subpopulations in preterm neonates with sepsis," Inflammation, vol. 35, no. 3, pp. 1094–1101, 2012.

[2] U. K. Mishra, S. E. Jacobs, L. W. Doyle, and S. M. Garland, "Newer approaches to the diagnosis of early onset neonatal sepsis," Archives of Disease in Childhood, vol. 91, no. 3, pp. F208–F212, 2006.

[3] Z. Yu, J. Liu, Q. Sun, Y. Qiu, S. Han, and X. Guo, "The accuracy of the procalcitonin test for the diagnosis of neonatal sepsis: a meta-analysis," Scandinavian Journal of Infectious Diseases, vol. 42, no. 10, pp. 723–733, 2010.

[4] B. Uzzan, R. Cohen, P. Nicolas, M. Cucherat, and G.-Y. Perret, "Procalcitonin as a diagnostic test for sepsis in critically ill adults and after surgery or trauma: a systematic review and meta-analysis," Critical Care Medicine, vol. 34, no. 7, pp. 1996–2003, 2006.

[5] B. Müller, M. Christ-Crain, E. S. Nylen, R. Snider, and K. L. Becker, "Limits to the use of the procalcitonin level as a diagnostic marker," *Clinical Infectious Diseases*, vol. 39, no. 12, pp. 1867–1868, 2004.

[6] E. Bilavsky, H. Yarden-Bilavsky, S. Ashkenazi, and J. Amir, "C-reactive protein as a marker of serious bacterial infections in hospitalized febrile infants," *Acta Paediatrica*, vol. 98, no. 11, pp. 1776–1780, 2009.

[7] A. Kordek, M. Hałasa, and W. Podraza, "Early detection of an early onset infection in the neonate based on measurements of procalcitonin and C-reactive protein concentrations in cord blood," *Clinical Chemistry and Laboratory Medicine*, vol. 46, no. 8, pp. 1143–1148, 2008.

[8] L. Simon, F. Gauvin, D. K. Amre, P. Saint-Louis, and J. Lacroix, "Serum procalcitonin and C-reactive protein levels as markers of bacterial infection: a systematic review and meta-analysis," *Clinical Infectious Diseases*, vol. 39, no. 2, pp. 206–217, 2004.

[9] J. P. S. Caldas, S. T. M. Marba, M. H. S. L. Blotta, R. Calil, S. S. Morais, and R. T. D. Oliveira, "Accuracy of white blood cell count, C-reactive protein, interleukin-6 and tumor necrosis factor alpha for diagnosing late neonatal sepsis," *Jornal de Pediatria*, vol. 84, no. 6, pp. 536–542, 2008.

[10] M. M. Levy, M. P. Fink, J. C. Marshall et al., "2001 SCCM/ESICM/ACCP/ATS/SIS international sepsis definitions conference," *Intensive Care Medicine*, vol. 29, no. 4, pp. 530–538, 2003.

[11] H. Yuan, J. Huang, B. Lv et al., "Diagnosis value of the serum amyloid a test in neonatal sepsis: a meta-analysis," *BioMed Research International*, vol. 2013, Article ID 520294, 9 pages, 2013.

[12] L. P. Francesconi, K. M. Cereser, R. Mascarenhas, L. Stertz, C. S. Gama, and P. Belmonte-de-Abreu, "Increased annexin-V and decreased TNF-alpha serum levels in chronic-medicated patients with schizophrenia," *Neuroscience Letters*, vol. 502, no. 3, pp. 143–146, 2011.

[13] W. M. Bernardo, F. T. Aires, R. M. Carneiro, F. P. Sá, V. E. Rullo, and D. A. Burns, "Effectiveness of probiotics in the prophylaxis of necrotizing enterocolitis in preterm neonates: a systematic review and meta-analysis," *Jornal de Pediatria*, vol. 89, no. 1, pp. 18–24, 2013.

[14] E. Kocabaş, A. Sarikçioğlu, N. Aksaray, G. Seydaoğlu, Y. Seyhun, and A. Yaman, "Role of procalcitonin, C-reactive protein, interleukin-6, interleukin-8 and tumor necrosis factor-α in the diagnosis of neonatal sepsis," *Turkish Journal of Pediatrics*, vol. 49, no. 1, pp. 7–20, 2007.

[15] A. S. Glas, J. G. Lijmer, M. H. Prins, G. J. Bonsel, and P. M. M. Bossuyt, "The diagnostic odds ratio: a single indicator of test performance," *Journal of Clinical Epidemiology*, vol. 56, no. 11, pp. 1129–1135, 2003.

[16] J. P. T. Higgins, S. G. Thompson, J. J. Deeks, and D. G. Altman, "Measuring inconsistency in meta-analyses," *British Medical Journal*, vol. 327, no. 7414, pp. 557–560, 2003.

[17] S. D. Walter, "Properties of the Summary Receiver Operating Characteristic (SROC) curve for diagnostic test data," *Statistics in Medicine*, vol. 21, no. 9, pp. 1237–1256, 2002.

[18] N. M. Fida, J. A. Al-Mughales, and M. F. Fadellah, "Serum concentrations of interleukin-1 alpha, interleukin-6 and tumor necrosis factor-alpha in neonatal sepsis and meningitis," *Saudi Medical Journal*, vol. 27, no. 10, pp. 1508–1514, 2006.

[19] K. H. Park, B. H. Yoon, S.-S. Shim, J. K. Jun, and H. C. Syn, "Amniotic fluid tumor necrosis factor-alpha is a marker for the prediction of early-onset neonatal sepsis in preterm labor," *Gynecologic and Obstetric Investigation*, vol. 58, no. 2, pp. 84–90, 2004.

[20] E. Layseca-Espinosa, L. F. Pérez-González, A. Torres-Montes et al., "Expression of CD64 as a potential marker of neonatal sepsis," *Pediatric Allergy and Immunology*, vol. 13, no. 5, pp. 319–327, 2002.

[21] H. Martin, B. Olander, and M. Norman, "Reactive hyperemia and interleukin 6, interleukin 8, and tumor necrosis factor-alpha in the diagnosis of early-onset neonatal sepsis," *Pediatrics*, vol. 108, no. 4, p. E61, 2001.

[22] R. Berner, B. Tüxen, A. Clad, J. Forster, and M. Brandis, "Elevated gene expression of interleukin-8 in cord blood is a sensitive marker for neonatal infection," *European Journal of Pediatrics*, vol. 159, no. 3, pp. 205–210, 2000.

[23] R. C. Silveira and R. S. Procianoy, "Evaluation of interleukin-6, tumour necrosis factor-α and interleukin-1β for early diagnosis of neonatal sepsis," *Acta Paediatrica*, vol. 88, no. 6, pp. 647–650, 1999.

[24] U. Hallwirth, G. Pomberger, D. Zaknun et al., "Monocyte phagocytosis as a reliable parameter for predicting early-onset sepsis in very low birthweight infants," *Early Human Development*, vol. 67, no. 1-2, pp. 1–9, 2002.

[25] R. S. Procianoy and R. C. Silveira, "Association between high cytokine levels with white matter injury in preterm infants with sepsis," *Pediatric Critical Care Medicine*, vol. 13, no. 2, pp. 183–187, 2012.

[26] Y. Shi, C. Shen, J. Wang, H. Li, S. Qin, and R. Liu, "Role of tumor necrosis factor in neonatal sepsis," *Chinese Medical Sciences Journal*, vol. 9, no. 1, pp. 45–48, 1994.

[27] P. C. Ng, K. Li, K. M. Chui et al., "IP-10 is an early diagnostic marker for identification of late-onset bacterial infection in preterm infants," *Pediatric Research*, vol. 61, no. 1, pp. 93–98, 2007.

[28] C. Sherwin, R. Broadbent, S. Young et al., "Utility of interleukin-12 and interleukin-10 in comparison with other cytokines and acute-phase reactants in the diagnosis of neonatal sepsis," *American Journal of Perinatology*, vol. 25, no. 10, pp. 629–636, 2008.

[29] P. C. Ng, S. H. Cheng, K. M. Chui et al., "Diagnosis of late onset neonatal sepsis with cytokines, adhesion molecule, and C-reactive protein in preterm very low birthweight infants," *Archives of Disease in Childhood*, vol. 77, no. 3, pp. F221–F227, 1997.

[30] E. Hotoura, V. Giapros, A. Kostoula, P. Spirou, and S. Andronikou, "Tracking changes of lymphocyte subsets and pre-inflammatory mediators in full-term neonates with suspected or documented infection," *Scandinavian Journal of Immunology*, vol. 73, no. 3, pp. 250–255, 2011.

[31] B. S. Naher, M. A. Mannan, K. Noor, and M. Shahiddullah, "Role of serum procalcitonin and C-reactive protein in the diagnosis of neonatal sepsis," *Bangladesh Medical Research Council Bulletin*, vol. 37, no. 2, pp. 40–46, 2011.

[32] T. B. Knudsen, T. B. Kristiansen, L. Simon et al., "Issues pertaining to data extraction and classification and publication bias in meta-analysis of the diagnostic accuracy of markers for bacterial infection," *Clinical Infectious Diseases*, vol. 40, no. 9, pp. 1372–1374, 2005.

[33] J. S. Gerdes, "Diagnosis and management of bacterial infections in the neonate," *Pediatric Clinics of North America*, vol. 51, no. 4, pp. 939–959, 2004.

[34] C. Chiesa, A. Panero, J. F. Osborn, A. F. Simonetti, and L. Pacifico, "Diagnosis of neonatal sepsis: a clinical and laboratory challenge," *Clinical Chemistry*, vol. 50, no. 2, pp. 279–287, 2004.

[35] T. Chan and F. Gu, "Early diagnosis of sepsis using serum biomarkers," *Expert Review of Molecular Diagnostics*, vol. 11, no. 5, pp. 487–496, 2011.

20

A Comparative Analysis of Synonymous Codon Usage Bias Pattern in Human Albumin Superfamily

Hoda Mirsafian,[1] Adiratna Mat Ripen,[2] Aarti Singh,[1] Phaik Hwan Teo,[1] Amir Feisal Merican,[1,3] and Saharuddin Bin Mohamad[1,3]

[1] Institute of Biological Sciences, Faculty of Science, University of Malaya, 50603 Kuala Lumpur, Malaysia
[2] Allergy and Immunology Research Centre, Institute for Medical Research, Jalan Pahang, Kuala Lumpur, Malaysia
[3] Crystal, Institute of Biological Sciences, Faculty of Science, University of Malaya, 50603 Kuala Lumpur, Malaysia

Correspondence should be addressed to Saharuddin Bin Mohamad; saharuddin@um.edu.my

Academic Editors: Y. Lai, S. Ma, and Z. Su

Synonymous codon usage bias is an inevitable phenomenon in organismic taxa across the three domains of life. Though the frequency of codon usage is not equal across species and within genome in the same species, the phenomenon is non random and is tissue-specific. Several factors such as GC content, nucleotide distribution, protein hydropathy, protein secondary structure, and translational selection are reported to contribute to codon usage preference. The synonymous codon usage patterns can be helpful in revealing the expression pattern of genes as well as the evolutionary relationship between the sequences. In this study, synonymous codon usage bias patterns were determined for the evolutionarily close proteins of albumin superfamily, namely, albumin, α-fetoprotein, afamin, and vitamin D-binding protein. Our study demonstrated that the genes of the four albumin superfamily members have low GC content and high values of effective number of codons (ENC) suggesting high expressivity of these genes and less bias in codon usage preferences. This study also provided evidence that the albumin superfamily members are not subjected to mutational selection pressure.

1. Introduction

Amino acids, the monomeric unit of proteins, are encoded by triplet of nucleotides called codons. Most of the amino acids have alternative codons which are known as synonymous codons. The frequencies with which these synonymous codons are used are unequal [1], some codons being used preferentially than others. Furthermore, Plotkin et al. [2] reported that codon usage is tissue-specific. The phenomenon of codon usage bias, which can be interpreted as an outcome of either mutational bias or translational selection, is an essential feature of most genomes across all the three domains of life [3]. The patterns of codon usage within the mammalian genomes are markedly different from other taxa. In mammals, the codon usage bias is found to be influenced by the variation in isochores (GC content) or variation in tRNA pool of the cell [4, 5]. The differences in codon usage or the variation in tRNA abundance can elicit varied responses to the environmental changes, in terms of regulation of translation mechanism and cell phenotype [6]. Urrutia and Hurst [7] reported that, in humans, the codon usage bias is positively related to gene expression but is inversely related to the rate of synonymous substitution. Several factors contribute to synonymous codon usage bias such as gene expression level, protein hydropathy, protein secondary structure, and translational selection [8–11]. Information on the synonymous codon usage pattern can provide significant insights pertaining to the prediction, classification, and molecular evolution of genes and design of highly expressed genes and cloning vectors [12]. It may be useful in better understanding of host-pathogen interactions as information on synonymous codon usages can reveal about the host-pathogen coevolution and adaptation of pathogens to specific hosts [13].

The evolutionarily close proteins of albumin superfamily are comprised of albumin (ALB), α-fetoprotein (AFP), vitamin D-binding protein (VDBP), and afamin (AFM). In human, the genes encoding these proteins are mapped to chromosome 4. These proteins are synthesized primarily and predominantly in liver but the expression pattern varies temporally. One common functional property amongst all the members of albumin superfamily is their tendency to serve as transporters to various cellular components, metabolites, and so forth. ALB, an abundant serum protein of MW of ~66 KDa, binds and transports a variety of ligands such as steroids, fatty acids, bilirubin, lysolecithin, prostaglandins, thyroid hormones, and drugs. In addition to this, ALB is known to be involved in various cellular functions including oxygen-free radicals scavenging, anticoagulation, and maintenance of physiological pH and oncotic pressure of the plasma [14]. AFP (MW ~67 KDa), a serum glycoprotein which is expressed at high levels by fetal liver and visceral yolk sac [15, 16], is critical for the female fertility rather than embryonic development [17]. VDBP or Gc globulin (MW ~58 KDa) is synthesized by various tissues, namely, liver, kidneys, gonads, and fat, and also by neutrophils [18]. Apart from binding and transporting vitamin D sterols, VDBP's physiological functions include scavenging of G-actin [19], macrophage activation [20], and enhancement of chemotactic activity of C5a and C5a des-Arg molecules [21, 22]. AFM or α-albumin (MW ~87 KDa) is synthesized by liver and brain capillary endothelial cells. It mediates the transport of α-tocopherol across the blood-brain barrier [23].

The members of albumin superfamily have been found to act as markers in various disease states in humans. AFP in maternal serum is an indicative of Down's syndrome and neural tube defects in the fetus [24, 25]. AFP levels are elevated in patients with high risk for hepatocellular carcinoma. In some patients, an increase in AFP levels manifests liver metastasis with gastric cancer and the condition is termed as α-fetoprotein producing gastric cancer (AFPGC) [26, 27]. VDBP may serve as a biomarker for vascular injury as predicted by proteomic identification [28]. AFM may act as a potential adjunct marker to cancer antigen 125 (CA125) for the diagnosis of ovarian cancer [29]. A vast array of research has been done on the members of albumin superfamily; however, so far, studies related to the usage of synonymous codon and the factors influencing the codon usage in this gene family have not been done. In this study, we applied bioinformatics approaches to elucidate the pattern of synonymous codon usage bias and its consequences on the expression level of genes in the albumin superfamily.

2. Materials and Methods

2.1. Sequences. The mRNA reference sequences of human serum albumin (ALB), afamin (AFM), α-fetoprotein (AFP), and vitamin D-binding protein (VDBP) in FASTA format were retrieved from GenBank of the National Center for Biotechnology Information (NCBI) (http://www.ncbi.nlm.nih.gov/genbank/). Open Reading Frame (ORF) of the mRNA sequences of human albumin superfamily was obtained by using ExPASy Translate tool (http://web.expasy.org/translate/).

2.2. Hydrophobicity Analysis. Grand average of hydrophobicity score (Gravy score) was calculated to quantify the general average hydrophobicity for the translated gene product found in albumin superfamily. It was calculated as the arithmetic mean of the sum of the hydrophobic indices of each amino acid as shown in

$$\frac{1}{N}\sum_{i=1}^{N} K_i, \tag{1}$$

where N corresponds to the number of amino acids, while K_i represents hydrophobic index of amino acid. The Gravy score of a protein can be either negative or positive depending on the frequency of amino acids with distinct properties. Negative Gravy score implies that the protein is hydrophilic and is soluble in water. In contrast, protein with positive Gravy is considered as hydrophobic and is water soluble [30].

2.3. Codon Usage Analysis. The nucleotide distribution for albumin superfamily was analyzed using ExPASy ProtParam tool (http://web.expasy.org/protparam/). The quantities of individual nucleotide (A, T, G, and C) were determined and used to sum up the AT and GC content for each protein in the albumin superfamily.

2.4. Rare Codon (RC) Analysis. Rare codon (RC) is considered as low-usage codon in the genome such as synonymous codon or stop codon [31]. The RC analysis was performed using the GenScript web server (http://www.genscript.com/cgi-bin/tools/rare_codon_analysis/) to examine the number of highest-usage and lowest-usage codons in the human albumin superfamily.

2.5. Indices of Codon Usage Deviation. Indices of codon usage deviation were calculated using CodonW (J Peden, version 1.4.2 http://codonw.sourceforge.net/) [32] to measure deviation between the observed codon usage and expected codon usage. Based on that, two internal measures were applied including identification of GC variation and third nucleotide preference in codon [33, 34]. These were obtained by calculating the number of GC nucleotides and number of G or C nucleotides at the third position of synonymous codon (GC_3), except the start and termination codons. In addition, the expected effective number of codons (ENC) for each albumin superfamily protein was calculated. ENC is the measure of codon usage affected only by the GC_3 as a consequence of mutation pressure and genetic drift. The ENC was calculated according to [35]

$$\text{ENC} = 2 + s + \frac{29}{s^2 + (1-s)^2}, \tag{2}$$

where s corresponds to the GC_3 value ranging from 0 to 100%.

2.6. Relative Synonymous Codon Usage (RSCU). Relative synonymous codon usage (RSCU) was calculated in order to examine the frequency of each synonymous codon that encoded the same amino acid without confounding effect

TABLE 1: Genomic information of the reference sequences, grand average hydrophobicity score, ENCs, GC content, and GC$_3$ of human albumin superfamily members.

	Human albumin superfamily			
	Albumin (ALB)	Afamin (AFM)	Alpha-fetoprotein (AFP)	Vitamin D-binding protein (VDBP)
GenBank accession number	NM_000477.5	NM_001133.2	NM_001134.1	NM_000583.3
Gene length (bp)	2264	1997	2032	2024
Grand average of hydrophobicity score (Gravy score)	−0.354	−0.248	−0.388	−0.336
GC content	42.95	42.02	39.28	44.63
Effective number of codons (ENC)	53.91	51.65	54.78	56.62
GC$_3$	38.00	37.10	37.30	42.80

on the composition of amino acid. The index was calculated as follows [36]:

$$\text{RSCU}_{ij} = \frac{X_{ij}}{(1/n_i) \sum_{j=1}^{n_i} X_{ij}}, \tag{3}$$

where X_{ij} is the amount of jth codon to represent the ith amino acid that can be encoded by n_i synonymous codons.

3. Results and Discussion

Genomic information of mRNA sequences of the four members of human albumin superfamilyis shown in Table 1. The mRNA sequences of albumin superfamily were translated into protein sequences using the ExPASy Translate Tool. Only the ORF with no intermediate stop codon was selected for codon usage analysis. The similarity of nucleotide and amino acid sequences of the albumin superfamily members is summarized in Figure 1. The results showed that ALB and AFP are more closely related compared to AFM and VDBP. AFP and VDBP have almost similar gene length of 2032 bp and 2024 bp, respectively. ALB possesses the longest (2264 bp), while AFM has the shortest gene length (1997 bp). Moreover, human ALB and AFP possessed exactly the same length of ORF (1830 bp), while AFM (1800 bp) has similar length of the ORF compared to that of ALB and AFP. VDBP (1425 bp) has the shortest length of ORF within the albumin superfamily. The similarity pattern of ORF among ALB, AFM, and AFP indicated that they may carry out similar biological functions, especially AFM, since its function is not well-known.

The solubility of protein for the members of the albumin superfamily was assessed through Gravy score (Table 1). All the family members are found to have negative Gravy score, suggesting that these proteins are water soluble. This is in accordancewith the biological role of these proteins as serum transporters.

The nucleotide distribution of albumin superfamily is shown in Table 2. The members of this superfamily exhibit low GC content (<44.63%). ALB and AFP shows similar nucleotide distribution pattern implying that they share similarity in their structures and biological functions. There is a close relationship between the nucleotide composition

TABLE 2: Nucleotide distribution of human albumin superfamily members.

	ALB (%)	AFP (%)	AFM (%)	VDBP (%)
A	30.4 (556)	32.6 (596)	32.8 (591)	29.9 (426)
T	26.7 (488)	25.4 (465)	27.9 (502)	25.5 (363)
G	23.0 (421)	21.7 (397)	20.1 (361)	21.4 (305)
C	19.9 (365)	20.3 (372)	19.2 (346)	23.2 (331)
AT	57.049	57.978	60.722	55.368
GC	42.951	42.022	39.278	44.632

The values in parenthesis represent the number of individual nucleotides in the genes of human albumin superfamily members.

and gene function [37]. AFM has the highest AT content, whereas VDBP has the lowest AT content. Although AFM and VDBP are grouped in the same superfamily, they show differential nucleotide composition suggesting variation in their biological functions compared to the other members of albumin superfamily.

Rare codon analysis was carried out using the GenScript web server as described in Materials and Methods. A graph of codon frequency distribution was plotted to identify the quantities of rare codons present in each albumin superfamily protein (Figure 2). Frequency of codon usage with a value of 100 indicates that the codons are highly used for a given amino acid. Conversely, the frequency of codon usage with a value of less than 30 is determined as low-frequency codon, which is likely to affect the expression efficiency. Percentages of low-frequency codon present in protein ALB, AFM, AFP, and VDBP are 4%, 3%, 4%, and 4%, respectively. This result suggested that members of the albumin superfamily contain a significantly small number of rare codons that may reduce translational efficiency of the genes.

Indices of codon usage deviation are used to determine the differences between the observed and expected codon usage. The results for the effective number of codon (ENC), GC content, and G or C nucleotides at the third position of synonymous codon are summarized in Table 1. The effective number of codons (ENC) for each member of human albumin superfamily was calculated in order to examine the pattern of synonymous codon usage independent of the gene length. The ENC value ranges from 20 to 61, in which value

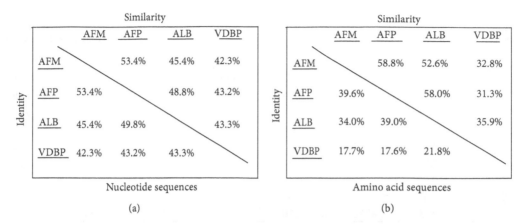

FIGURE 1: Comparison of percent similarity and identity of nucleotide sequences and amino acid sequences of human albumin superfamily members.

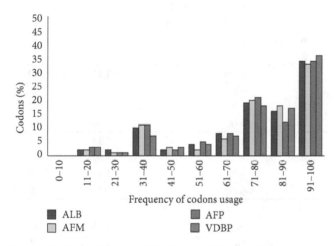

FIGURE 2: Codon frequency distribution of human albumin superfamily members.

of 20 indicates extreme bias toward the usage of one codon, while value of 61 represents equal usage of the synonymous codons [35, 38]. Result from this analysis revealed that the ENC value of albumin superfamily varies from 51.65 to 56.62. The overall ENC value of albumin superfamily is greater than 50. The high ENC value suggested that the synonymous codons of albumin superfamily were equally used and hence displayed less biased synonymous codon usage.

The GC content of albumin superfamily is given in Table 1. GC content may affect the thermostability, bendability, and the ability of DNA helix transition from B to Z form. GC content can be related to the ability of coding region to be in an open chromatin state, leading to active transcription [39]. It is evident that all the members of albumin superfamily genes have low GC content, indicating that these family members are highly expressed. Furthermore, it has been reported that highly transcribed genes may have low mutation rates because they are subjected to DNA repair [40]. However, within the albumin superfamily, VDBP contains the highest GC content indicating that it has the lowest expressivity level.

GC content at the third position of codons (GC_3) is a putative indicator of the extent of base composition bias. Table 1 revealed that the albumin superfamily has low GC_3 values ranging from 37.1% to 42.8%. The albumin superfamily has low GC_3 value because the majority of genes in this superfamily are located in AT-rich region. Genes in AT-rich regions within the genome would prefer to use A or T ending codon. The low usage of codons ending with G or C signifies less GC codon usage bias in albumin superfamily. In other words, it proved the homogeneity of synonymous codon usage pattern in albumin superfamily.

The synonymous codon bias usage of each albumin superfamily protein was computed and tabulated in Table 3. The most preferentially used codon for a given amino acid is highlighted in red. Asn of AFP and His, Cys, and Arg of VDBP have equal usage of the synonymous codons. The variation of relative synonymous codon usage (RSCU) values not only indicated the different frequency of occurrence of each codon for a given amino acid in different albumin superfamily protein but also revealed the preference of either A + U or G + C codon usage as listed in Table 3. The results of RSCU analysis (Table 3) are summarized in Table 4. Preferential codon usage in albumin superfamily indicates that the codons with A or U at the third position are more preferred compared to G or C ending codons. Table 4 also shows that the total score of A + U and G + C codon usage in the proteins of albumin superfamily is not equal to 20. It is because some amino acid residues are encoded in equal frequencies by both A or U and G or C ending codons and hence are excluded from the analysis. The tendency of albumin superfamily to use high A + U and low G + C indicated that the mutational bias does not play a significant role in synonymous codon usage.

4. Conclusions

The members of albumin superfamily, namely, ALB, AFP, AFM, and VDBP, exhibit sequence and structural similarities. The proteins possess three homologous folding domains as a result of conserved pattern of cysteine residues in

TABLE 3: Relative synonymous codon usage in human albumin superfamily members. The value in bold indicates the codons used with high frequency.

Amino acid	Codons	RSCU[1]	Number	RSCU[2]	Number	RSCU[3]	Number	RSCU[4]	Number
Phe	UUU	**1.43**	25	**1.06**	17	**1.30**	28	**1.16**	11
	UUC	0.57	10	0.94	15	0.70	15	0.84	8
Leu	UUA	0.94	10	1.00	10	**1.20**	11	0.53	5
	UUG	1.13	12	1.10	11	0.87	8	0.63	6
	CUU	**1.78**	19	0.90	9	**1.20**	11	1.16	11
	CUC	0.66	7	0.40	4	0.98	9	0.95	9
	CUA	0.38	4	0.90	9	0.65	6	1.05	10
	CUG	1.13	12	**1.70**	17	1.09	10	**1.68**	16
Ile	AUU	**1.33**	4	**1.32**	15	1.07	10	**1.13**	3
	AUC	**1.33**	4	0.71	8	0.75	7	**1.13**	3
	AUA	0.33	1	0.97	11	**1.18**	11	0.75	2
Val	GUU	1.12	12	**1.47**	11	**1.44**	13	0.89	6
	GUC	0.65	7	0.80	6	0.67	6	**1.19**	8
	GUA	0.74	8	0.80	6	0.67	6	1.04	7
	GUG	**1.49**	16	0.93	7	1.22	11	0.89	6
Ser	UCU	0.64	3	1.26	8	**2.06**	12	1.43	10
	UCC	**1.50**	7	0.47	3	0.86	5	1.29	9
	UCA	1.29	6	**1.58**	10	1.03	6	**1.71**	12
	UCG	0.64	3	0.47	3	0.00	0	0.00	0
Pro	CCU	**1.67**	10	**1.71**	9	**1.71**	12	1.38	9
	CCC	1.00	6	0.76	4	0.71	5	0.92	6
	CCA	1.17	7	1.52	8	1.57	11	**1.54**	10
	CCG	0.17	1	0.00	0	0.00	0	0.15	1
Thr	ACU	0.97	7	**1.78**	16	1.18	10	1.25	10
	ACC	1.24	9	0.67	6	0.82	7	**1.38**	11
	ACA	**1.52**	11	1.33	12	**1.53**	13	1.13	9
	ACG	0.28	2	0.22	2	0.47	4	0.25	2
Ala	GCU	**1.90**	30	1.20	15	**1.57**	11	**1.82**	15
	GCC	0.89	14	0.88	11	0.71	5	1.09	9
	GCA	1.08	17	**1.68**	21	1.29	9	0.85	7
	GCG	0.13	2	0.24	3	0.43	3	0.24	2
Tyr	UAU	**1.37**	13	**1.06**	9	**1.06**	9	**1.13**	9
	UAC	0.63	6	0.94	8	0.94	8	0.88	7
His	CAU	**1.38**	11	**1.63**	13	**1.23**	8	**1.00**	4
	CAC	0.63	5	0.38	3	0.77	5	**1.00**	4
Gln	CAA	**1.10**	11	**1.15**	23	**1.26**	17	**1.33**	8
	CAG	0.90	9	0.85	17	0.74	10	0.67	4
Asn	AAU	**1.29**	11	**1.00**	10	**1.03**	17	**1.33**	12
	AAC	0.71	6	**1.00**	10	0.97	16	0.67	6
Lys	AAA	**1.33**	40	**1.29**	33	**1.33**	28	0.93	20
	AAG	0.67	20	0.71	18	0.67	14	**1.07**	23
Asp	GAU	**1.39**	25	**1.27**	21	**1.30**	15	**1.23**	16
	GAC	0.61	11	0.73	12	0.70	8	0.77	10
Glu	GAA	**1.23**	38	**1.24**	34	**1.36**	40	**1.26**	27
	GAG	0.77	24	0.76	21	0.64	19	0.74	16
Cys	UGU	0.86	15	**1.06**	18	0.81	13	**1.00**	14
	UGC	**1.14**	20	0.94	16	**1.19**	19	**1.00**	14

TABLE 3: Continued.

Amino acid	Codons	RSCU[1]	Number	RSCU[2]	Number	RSCU[3]	Number	RSCU[4]	Number
Arg	CGU	**0.67**	3	**0.50**	2	**0.55**	2	0.00	0
	CGC	0.22	1	0.25	1	0.27	1	0.00	0
	CGA	**0.67**	3	**0.50**	2	**0.55**	2	**0.92**	2
	CGG	0.44	2	0.25	1	0.00	0	0.46	1
Ser	AGU	**1.29**	6	**1.54**	9	0.79	5	**0.86**	6
	AGC	0.64	3	0.51	3	**1.42**	9	0.71	5
Arg	AGA	**2.89**	13	**2.75**	11	**3.27**	12	**2.31**	5
	AGG	1.11	5	1.75	7	1.36	5	**2.31**	5
Gly	GGU	0.92	3	0.75	3	0.62	4	0.29	1
	GGC	0.92	3	0.75	3	0.77	5	**1.43**	5
	GGA	**1.85**	6	**1.50**	6	**2.00**	13	**1.43**	5
	GGG	0.31	1	**1.50**	4	0.62	4	0.86	3

RSCU[1]: RSCU values for ALB; RSCU[2]: RSCU values for AFP; RSCU[3]: RSCU values for AFM; RSCU[4]: RSCU values for DBP.

TABLE 4: A + U and G + C preferential codon usage of human albumin superfamily members.

	A + U	G + C
ALB	17	3
AFP	17	1
AFM	18	2
VDBP	11	4

the members of albumin superfamily [41, 42]. Our study on codon usage bias in the members of the albumin gene family revealed that they are also similar in terms of their low GC content, low GC_3, and high ENC values. In addition, they are not having a bias in the usage of synonymous codons and are highly expressible genes. Furthermore, low GC and GC_3 values revealed that mutational bias and translational selection do not play a significant role in shaping the codon usage pattern in the albumin superfamily.

Conflict of Interests

The authors declare that there is no conflict of interests regarding the publication of this paper.

Acknowledgments

The authors would like to thank Director General of Ministry of Health, Malaysia, for granting permission to publish this paper. This research is cosupported by the High Impact Research Grant UM-MOHE UM.C/625/1/HIR/MOHE/30 from the Ministry of Higher Education, Malaysia, and University of Malaya Research Grant (UMRG), Grant no. RP004C-BAFR.

References

[1] J. L. Bennetzen and B. D. Hall, "Codon selection in yeast," *Journal of Biological Chemistry*, vol. 257, no. 6, pp. 3026–3031, 1982.

[2] J. B. Plotkin, H. Robins, and A. J. Levine, "Tissue-specific codon usage and the expression of human genes," *Proceedings of the National Academy of Sciences of the United States of America*, vol. 101, no. 34, pp. 12588–12591, 2004.

[3] L. Duret, "Evolution of synonymous codon usage in metazoans," *Current Opinion in Genetics and Development*, vol. 12, no. 6, pp. 640–649, 2002.

[4] G. Bernardi, B. Olofsson, and J. Filipski, "The mosaic genome of warm-blooded vertebrates," *Science*, vol. 228, no. 4702, pp. 953–958, 1985.

[5] K. A. Dittmar, J. M. Goodenbour, and T. Pan, "Tissue-specific differences in human transfer RNA expression," *PLoS Genetics*, vol. 2, no. 12, pp. 2107–2115, 2006.

[6] H. S. Najafabadi, H. Goodarzi, and R. Salavati, "Universal function-specificity of codon usage," *Nucleic Acids Research*, vol. 37, no. 21, Article ID gkp792, pp. 7014–7023, 2009.

[7] A. O. Urrutia and L. D. Hurst, "Codon usage bias covaries with expression breadth and the rate of synonymous evolution in humans, but this is not evidence for selection," *Genetics*, vol. 159, no. 3, pp. 1191–1199, 2001.

[8] S. K. Gupta and T. C. Ghosh, "Gene expressivity is the main factor in dictating the codon usage variation among the genes in *Pseudomonas aeruginosa*," *Gene*, vol. 273, no. 1, pp. 63–70, 2001.

[9] Q. Liu, "Analysis of codon usage pattern in the radioresistant bacterium *Deinococcus radiodurans*," *BioSystems*, vol. 85, no. 2, pp. 99–106, 2006.

[10] G. D'Onofrio, T. C. Ghosh, and G. Bernardi, "The base composition of the human genes is correlated with the secondary structures of the encoded proteins," *Gene*, vol. 300, no. 1-2, pp. 179–187, 2002.

[11] H. Naya, H. Romero, N. Carels, A. Zavala, and H. Musto, "Translational selection shapes codon usage in the GC-rich genome of *Chlamydomonas reinhardtii*," *FEBS Letters*, vol. 501, no. 1-3, pp. 127–130, 2001.

[12] X.-S. Liu, Y.-G. Zhang, Y.-Z. Fang, and Y.-L. Wang, "Patterns and influencing factor of synonymous codon usage in porcine circovirus," *Virology Journal*, vol. 9, article 68, pp. 1–9, 2012.

[13] A. Pandit and S. Sinha, "Differential trends in the codon usage patterns in HIV-1 genes," *PLoS ONE*, vol. 6, no. 12, Article ID e28889, 2011.

[14] J. P. Nicholson, M. R. Wolmarans, and G. R. Park, "The role of albumin in critical illness," *British Journal of Anaesthesia*, vol. 85, no. 4, pp. 599–610, 2000.

[15] R. R. Meehan, D. P. Barlow, R. E. Hill, B. L. Hogan, and N. D. Hastie, "Pattern of serum protein gene expression in mouse visceral yolk sac and foetal liver," *The EMBO Journal*, vol. 3, no. 8, pp. 1881–1885, 1984.

[16] M. A. Dziadek and G. K. Andrews, "Tissue specificity of alpha-fetoprotein messenger RNA expression during mouse embryogenesis," *The EMBO Journal*, vol. 2, no. 4, pp. 549–554, 1983.

[17] P. Gabant, L. Forrester, J. Nichols et al., "Alpha-fetoprotein, the major fetal serum protein, is not essential for embryonic development but is required for female fertility," *Proceedings of the National Academy of Sciences of the United States of America*, vol. 99, no. 20, pp. 12865–12870, 2002.

[18] L. Chishimba, D. R. Thickett, R. A. Stockley, and A. M. Wood, "The vitamin D axis in the lung: a key role for vitamin D-binding protein," *Thorax*, vol. 65, no. 5, pp. 456–462, 2010.

[19] L. R. Otterbein, C. Cosio, P. Graceffa, and R. Dominguez, "Crystal structures of the vitamin D-binding protein and its complex with actin: structural basis of the actin-scavenger system," *Proceedings of the National Academy of Sciences of the United States of America*, vol. 99, no. 12, pp. 8003–8008, 2002.

[20] S. B. Mohamad, H. Nagasawa, Y. Uto, and H. Hori, "Preparation of Gc protein-derived macrophage activating factor (GcMAF) and its structural characterization and biological activities," *Anticancer Research*, vol. 22, no. 6, pp. 4297–4300, 2002.

[21] R. R. Kew and R. O. Webster, "Gc-globulin (vitamin D-binding protein) enhances the neutrophil chemotactic activity of C5a and C5a des Arg," *Journal of Clinical Investigation*, vol. 82, no. 1, pp. 364–369, 1988.

[22] S. J. DiMartino, A. B. Shah, G. Trujillo, and R. R. Kew, "Elastase controls the binding of the vitamin D-binding protein (Gc-Globulin) to neutrophils: a potential role in the regulation of C5a co-chemotactic activity," *Journal of Immunology*, vol. 166, no. 4, pp. 2688–2694, 2001.

[23] I. Kratzer, E. Bernhart, A. Wintersperger et al., "Afamin is synthesized by cerebrovascular endothelial cells and mediates α-tocopherol transport across an in vitro model of the blood-brain barrier," *Journal of Neurochemistry*, vol. 108, no. 3, pp. 707–718, 2009.

[24] M. J. Seller, "Alphafetoprotein in midtrimester Down's syndrome fetal serum," *Journal of Medical Genetics*, vol. 27, no. 4, pp. 240–243, 1990.

[25] J. H. Brock, "Alphafetoprotein and neural tube defects," *Journal of Clinical Pathology*, vol. 29, no. 10, pp. 157–164, 1976.

[26] S. Hirajima, S. Komatsu, D. Ichikawa et al., "Liver metastasis is the only independent prognostic factor in AFP-producing gastric cancer," *World Journal of Gastroenterology*, vol. 19, no. 36, pp. 6055–6061, 2013.

[27] X.-D. Li, C.-P. Wu, M. Ji et al., "characteristic analysis of a-fetoprotein-producing gastric carcinoma in China," *World Journal of Surgical Oncology*, vol. 11, no. 246, 2013.

[28] N. F. Huang, K. Kurpinski, Q. Fang, R. J. Lee, and S. Li, "Proteomic identification of biomarkers of vascular injury," *The American Journal of Translational Research*, vol. 3, no. 2, pp. 139–148, 2011.

[29] H. Dieplinger, D. P. Ankerst, A. Burges et al., "Afamin and apolipoprotein A-IV: novel protein markers for ovarian cancer," *Cancer Epidemiology Biomarkers and Prevention*, vol. 18, no. 4, pp. 1127–1133, 2009.

[30] J. Kyte and R. F. Doolittle, "A simple method for displaying the hydropathic character of a protein," *Journal of Molecular Biology*, vol. 157, no. 1, pp. 105–132, 1982.

[31] T. Ikemura, "Correlation between the abundance of Escherichia coli transfer RNAs and the occurrence of the respective codons in its protein genes: a proposal for a synonymous codon choice that is optimal for the *E. coli* translational system," *Journal of Molecular Biology*, vol. 151, no. 3, pp. 389–409, 1981.

[32] J. F. Peden, *Analysis of Codon Usage*, University of Nottingham, 2000.

[33] J. A. Novembre, "Accounting for background nucleotide composition when measuring codon usage bias," *Molecular Biology and Evolution*, vol. 19, no. 8, pp. 1390–1394, 2002.

[34] J. M. Comeron and M. Aguadé, "An evaluation of measures of synonymous codon usage bias," *Journal of Molecular Evolution*, vol. 47, no. 3, pp. 268–274, 1998.

[35] F. Wright, "The 'effective number of codons' used in a gene," *Gene*, vol. 87, no. 1, pp. 23–29, 1990.

[36] M. Nei and S. Kumar, *Molecular Evolution and Phylogenetics*, Oxford University Press, New York, NY, USA, 2000.

[37] J. A. L. Garcia, A. Fernández-Guerra, and E. O. Casamayor, "A close relationship between primary nucleotides sequence structure and the composition of functional genes in the genome of prokaryotes," *Molecular Phylogenetics and Evolution*, vol. 61, no. 3, pp. 650–658, 2011.

[38] A. Fuglsang, "The effective number of codons," *Biochemical and Biophysical Research Communications*, vol. 317, no. 3, pp. 957–964, 2004.

[39] A. E. Vinogradov, "DNA helix: the importance of being GC-rich," *Nucleic Acids Research*, vol. 31, no. 7, pp. 1838–1844, 2003.

[40] O. G. Berg and M. Martelius, "Synonymous substitution-rate constants in *Escherichia coli* and *Salmonella typhimurium* and their relationship to gene expression and selection pressure," *Journal of Molecular Evolution*, vol. 41, no. 4, pp. 449–456, 1995.

[41] H. S. Lichenstein, D. E. Lyons, M. M. Wurfel et al., "Afamin is a new member of the albumin, α-fetoprotein, and vitamin D-binding protein gene family," *Journal of Biological Chemistry*, vol. 269, no. 27, pp. 18149–18154, 1994.

[42] H. Nishio and A. Dugaiczyk, "Complete structure of the human α-albumin gene, a new member of the serum albumin multigene family," *Proceedings of the National Academy of Sciences of the United States of America*, vol. 93, no. 15, pp. 7557–7561, 1996.

21

A Neural-Network-Based Approach to White Blood Cell Classification

Mu-Chun Su,[1] Chun-Yen Cheng,[1] and Pa-Chun Wang[2]

[1] *Department of Computer Science & Information Engineering, National Central University, Jhongli 32001, Taiwan*
[2] *General Hospital, Taipei 10656, Taiwan*

Correspondence should be addressed to Mu-Chun Su; muchun@csie.ncu.edu.tw

Academic Editors: C.-C. Liu and C. H. Yeang

This paper presents a new white blood cell classification system for the recognition of five types of white blood cells. We propose a new segmentation algorithm for the segmentation of white blood cells from smear images. The core idea of the proposed segmentation algorithm is to find a discriminating region of white blood cells on the HSI color space. Pixels with color lying in the discriminating region described by an ellipsoidal region will be regarded as the nucleus and granule of cytoplasm of a white blood cell. Then, through a further morphological process, we can segment a white blood cell from a smear image. Three kinds of features (i.e., geometrical features, color features, and LDP-based texture features) are extracted from the segmented cell. These features are fed into three different kinds of neural networks to recognize the types of the white blood cells. To test the effectiveness of the proposed white blood cell classification system, a total of 450 white blood cells images were used. The highest overall correct recognition rate could reach 99.11% correct. Simulation results showed that the proposed white blood cell classification system was very competitive to some existing systems.

1. Introduction

The microscopic inspection of blood smears provides diagnostic information concerning patients' health status. The inspection results of the differential blood count reveal a wide range of important hematic pathologies. For example, the presence of infections, leukemia, and some particular kinds of cancers can be diagnosed based on the results of the classification and the count of white blood cells. The traditional method for the differential blood count is performed by experienced operators. They use a microscope and count the percentage of the occurrence of each type of cell counted within an area of interest in smears. Obviously, this manual counting process is very tedious and slow. In addition, the cell classification and counting accuracy may depend on the capabilities and experiences of the operators. Therefore, the necessity of an automated differential counting system becomes inevitable.

There are two kinds of techniques to implement an automated differential counting system. While the first and the dominant technique is based on the flow cytometry, the other technique is based on image processing. There are many commercially available systems which adopt the flow cytometry technique for counting cells. The flow-cytometry-based systems have an advantage (i.e., they can offer high throughput), but they suffer from one drawback (i.e., they cannot produce the images of the blood samples for further chance of verification in case some abnormal conditions were detected). Recently, several different approaches to implement an image-processing-based white blood cell recognition system have been proposed [1–11].

White blood cells can be categorized into several classes according to the morphology of their contours and their nuclei. The classification of white blood cells usually involves the following three stages: (1) the segmentation of a white blood cell from a smear image, (2) the extraction of effective features, and (3) the design of a classifier. For example, Young adopted four features and the minimum distance classifier for classifying 5 types of cells [4]. Sheikh et al. used wavelet transform coefficients and artificial neural networks for recognizing the white blood cell, the red blood cells, and platelets [8]. Bikhet et al. selected 10 features and adopted the minimum-distance classifier for constructing an automatic classification system which achieved the rate of 91% correct classification for a database consisting of 71 white blood cells [6]. Piuri and Scotti proposed an automatic detection and classification system based on 23 morphological features and a neural classifier [7]. A classification system based on eigen-cell and parametric features was proposed in [5]. A system which achieved a classification rate of 77% for classifying bone marrow white blood cells was reported in [9]. Nilufar et al. proposed a classification system based on joint histogram-based features and a support vector machine [10]. Osowski et al. presented the application of a genetic algorithm and a support vector machine to the recognition of bone marrow blood cells [11]. Rezatofighi et al. adopted morphological features and textural features extracted by local binary pattern (LBP) and then trained two types of neural networks for classification [1]. Tabrizi et al. adopted principal component analysis for features selection and used a learning vector quantization neural network for classifying 5 types of white blood cells [2]. Ghosh et al. fed four statistical significant features to Naïve Bayes classifier for classifying five types of white blood cells with 83.2% overall accuracy [3]. Each approach has its own considerations for adopting what kinds of features and classifier.

To a certain extent, the performance of an automatic white blood cell classification system depends on a good segmentation algorithm for segmenting white blood cells from their background. There are many different approaches (e.g., clustering [8], thresholding [5, 6, 10], morphological operator [11, 12], Gram-Schmidt orthogonalization method [1], edge detection [13], region growing [14], watershed [15], colors [16–18], and support vector machine (SVM) [19]) to segment white blood cells from the background. Each approach has its advantages and disadvantages. For example, the conventional color-based methods and the thresholding method are simple but are not able to accurately segment the white blood cells from the background. Some approaches (e.g., the SVM method and the region growing method) can provide reasonably accurate segmentation results, but they are either costly to be implemented or require high computational resources. A review on some of the general segmentation methods can be found in [20]. While some color-based segmentation methods (e.g., [17]) were directly conducted on the RGB color space, some approaches (e.g., [16, 18]) adopted the HSI color space (especially on the S component). In general, the S-component-based methods outperformed the RGB-based methods. In [16], the accuracy performance varied from 98.0% to 99.54% for the acute myeloid leukemia type and from 94.24% to 99.13 for the acute lymphocytic leukemia type.

In this paper, we propose a new approach to implementing an automatic white blood cell classification system. First of all, we try to identify the color characteristics of the pixels of the nucleus and granule of cytoplasm of white blood cells in the HSI color space. Based on the found discriminating region and a morphological process, we can segment a white blood cell from a smear image. In the

following, we extract three kinds of features (i.e., geometrical features, color features, and LDP-based texture features) from the segmented cell region. These features are fed into three different neural networks for classifying five types of the white blood cells. The proposed system will be introduced in Section 2. The experimental results are given in Section 3. Finally, Section 4 concludes the paper.

2. The Proposed Automatic White Blood Cell Classification System

The proposed automatic white blood cell classification system involves the following three stages: (1) the segmentation of a white blood cell, (2) the extraction of effective features, and (3) the design of a classifier.

2.1. Stage 1. The Segmentation. In this paper, we propose a new color-based approach to segment five types of white blood cells from their background. This new color-based method is based on the idea of constructing a discriminating region for the scatter plot of pixels belonging to white blood cells. Via checking whether a pixel lies inside the discriminating region, white blood cells can be effectively segmented from the background. The database of the white blood cells used in this paper was downloaded from the CellaVision Competency Software Databases which contain slides stained with either a May Grünwald Giemsa (MGG) or a Wright staining protocol [21]. Figure 1(a) shows a sample of the images. First of all, an expert was asked to manually segment the white blood cells from the background to provide ground truth information. We then collected a set of pixels belonging to white blood cells. Figure 1(b) shows the scatter plot of these collected pixels on the HSI color space. Obviously, most of these pixels are clustered inside a rotated ellipsoid. We can use the principal component analysis (PCA) method to find the principal axes of these pixels on the original HSI space and then use the principal axes information to rotate the ellipsoid to be parallel to the new coordinate system as shown in Figure 1(c). Finally, the discriminating region for white blood cell pixels can be described by the following equations:

$$
\begin{bmatrix} H' \\ S' \\ I' \end{bmatrix} = R \begin{bmatrix} H \\ S \\ I \end{bmatrix} = \begin{bmatrix} R_{11} & R_{12} & R_{13} \\ R_{21} & R_{22} & R_{23} \\ R_{31} & R_{32} & R_{33} \end{bmatrix} \begin{bmatrix} H \\ S \\ I \end{bmatrix}
$$
$$
\frac{\left(H' - C_H\right)^2}{r_H^2} + \frac{\left(S' - C_S\right)^2}{r_S^2} + \frac{\left(I' - C_I\right)^2}{r_I^2} \leq 1, \tag{1}
$$

where the matrix R is a 3×3 rotation matrix, the vector (H', S', I') is the rotated version of the original color vector (H, S, I), the parameter (C_H, C_S, C_I) is the rotated ellipsoid center, and the parameters r_H, r_S, and r_I are the three semiprincipal axes of length. The appropriate values of the rotation matrix, the three semiprincipal axes, and the center may vary with the stain used to generate the blood cell images.

We may then use the ellipsoidal equations defined in (1) to verify whether a pixel belongs to a white blood cell. If the HSI information of a pixel satisfies (1), then it will be claimed to be

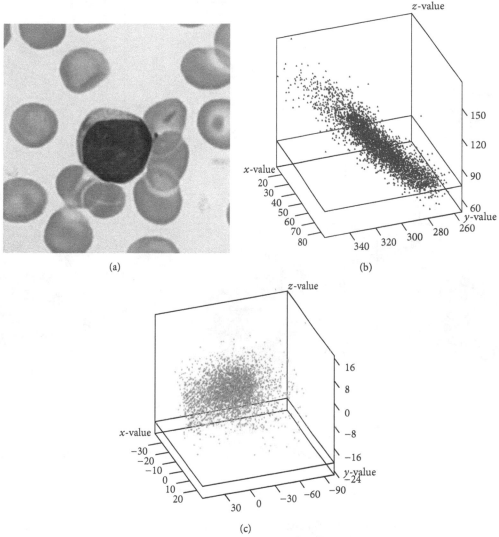

FIGURE 1: Blood cell images. (a) The original image. (b) The scatter plot of the collected pixels of the white blood cells in the *HSI* color space. (c) The scatter plot rotated to a new coordinate system.

a white blood cell pixel. Some detected cells images are shown in Figure 2(a). Obviously, the segmented white blood cells are broken and noisy; therefore, we still need to adopt some morphological operators (e.g., dilation, closing, and a 7×7 median filter) to remove unwanted small noisy regions and fill holes in the detected cell region as shown in Figure 2(b).

2.2. Stage 2. Feature Extraction. The feature extraction plays an important role in the performance of an automatic white blood cell classification system. Most of the existing methods adopt the following features such as geometrical features (e.g., area, radius, perimeter, convex area, major axis length, compactness, and orientation), textural features (e.g., momentum, contrast, entropy, and kewness), and color features (e.g., color distribution and histogram). For example, Piuri and Scotti greatly depended on the geometrical features [7]. Tabrizi et al. adopted both geometrical features and textural features [2]. Osowski et al. integrated all those three kinds of features to form 164 features for their classifiers [11].

In this paper, three kinds of features are extracted for classification. The first kind of features is the geometrical features consisting of the area feature, Area, the length feature, $\text{Length}_{\text{var}}$, and the compactness feature, Comp. The area feature, Area, is the amount of pixels which belong to the segmented cell region. As for the last two features, $\text{Length}_{\text{var}}$ and the compactness, Comp, are computed as follows:

(1) $\text{Length}_{\text{var}}$:

$$\text{Length}_{\text{var}} = \frac{1}{N_b} \sum_{i=1}^{N_b} \left(\text{length}_i - \overline{\text{length}} \right)^2, \qquad (2)$$

where length_i represents the length between the ith pixel on the cell boundary and the cell center. The parameter $\overline{\text{length}}$ represents the mean of those lengths. And

(2) Comp:

$$\text{Comp} = \frac{\text{the perimeter of the cell}^2}{\text{the area of the cell}}. \qquad (3)$$

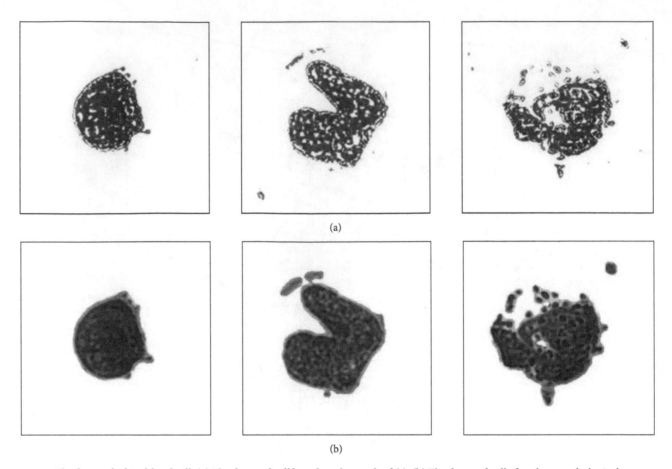

FIGURE 2: The detected white blood cell. (a) The detected cell based on the result of (1). (b) The detected cell after the morphological operators.

The color features, Hue$_{var}$, Saturation$_{var}$, and Intensity$_{var}$, are the three variances of the hue, saturation, and intensity components of the pixels belonging to the white cell.

As for the textural features, there are different ways to compute textural features. For example, Osowski et al. computed the angular second momentum, contrast, entropy, and so forth [11]. Rezatofighi et al. introduced the textural features extracted by local binary pattern (LBP) and cooccurrence matrix [1]. They found that the performance of the cooccurrence matrix-based features had better performance in comparison with the LBP-based features; however, the computational time for computing the cooccurrence matrix-based features was significantly higher than the time required by the computations of the LBP-based features.

Based on the aforementioned discussions, we proposed the use of the local-directional-pattern- (LDP-) based features to make a tradeoff between the computational time and the performance. The LBP operator, a gray-scale invariant texture primitive, was originally proposed by Ojala et al. [22]. Later on, the local-directional-pattern- (LDP) was proposed to overcome the disadvantages of LBP (e.g., nonmonotonic illumination variation and random noise). The LDP is an eight bit binary code and is obtained by computing the relative edge response value of a pixel in all eight directions at each pixel position [23].

In our system, we were interested at the three most prominent directions in order to generate the LDP. Figures 3(a)-3(b) illustrate an example of transforming a 3×3 windowed image into a LDP code. We then use the LDP operator to transform a gray image to a LDP labeled image where the value of each pixel is the computed LDP code corresponding to the pixel at the same position at the original gray image as shown in Figure 3(b). In the following, we can use a so-called "LDP histogram" with 218 bins (i.e., from 00000111($= 7$) to 11100000($=224$)) to represent this LDP labeled image as shown in Figure 3(c). The LDP histogram represents the relative frequency of occurrence of the various LDP codes in the LDP labeled image. Figure 3(d) shows the average LDP histogram computed from 60 cell images consisting of 5 types of white blood cell images. We found that bins, 19, 25, 35, 38, 49, 50, 70, 76, 98, 100, 137, 140, 145, and 196, are the 14 bins with the 14 largest values which are larger than a threshold, 400. These 14 bins accounted for a very large proportion of the relative frequency of occurrences. Therefore, we decided to use a reduced histogram with those 14 especially important bins to represent a LDP labeled image as shown in Figure 3(e).

In total, we have extracted 20 features for the classification purpose, Area, Length$_{var}$, Comp, Hue$_{var}$, Saturation$_{var}$, Intensity$_{var}$, LDP$_{19}$, LDP$_{25}$, LDP$_{35}$, LDP$_{38}$, LDP$_{49}$, LDP$_{50}$,

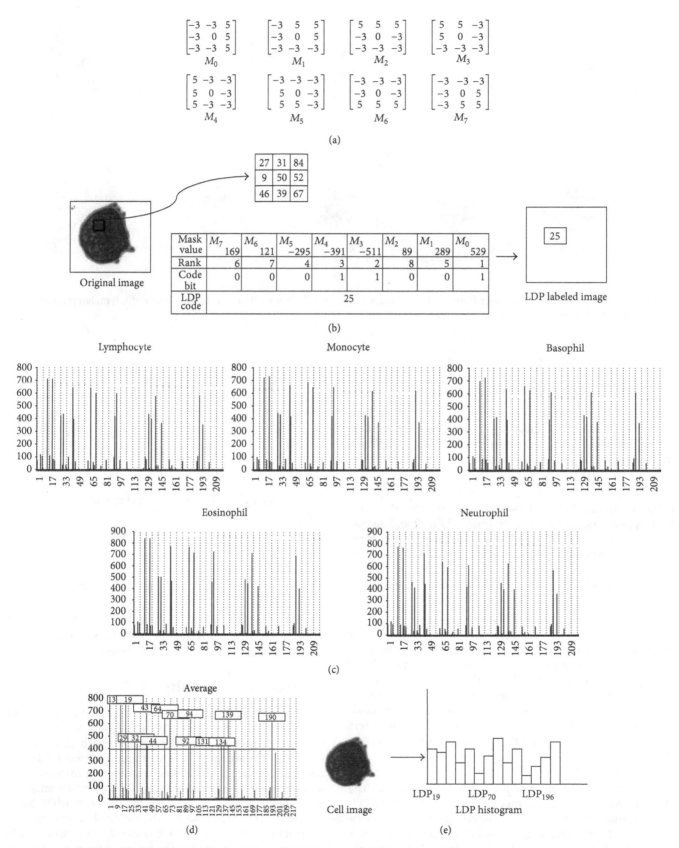

FIGURE 3: LDP-based features. (a) The Kirsch edge masks used for detecting the 8 directions. (b) The LDP code. (c) The LDP histograms with 218 bins. (d) The average LDP histogram. (e) The reduced LDP histogram with 14 bins for representing the cell image.

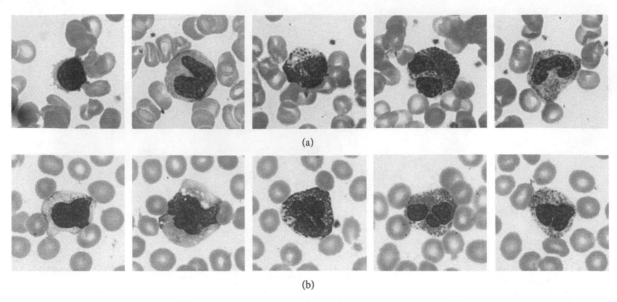

(a)

(b)

FIGURE 4: Samples of white cell images from the CellaVision Competency Software Databases. From left to right, lymphocyte, monocyte, eosinophil, basophil, and neutrophil. (a) Data set 1. (b) Data set 2.

LDP_{70}, LDP_{76}, LDP_{98}, LDP_{100}, LDP_{137}, LDP_{140}, LDP_{145}, and LDP_{196}.

2.3. Stage 3. Classification. After the set of features have been extracted, we proceed to the design of classifiers. Three different kinds of neural-network-based classifiers were employed in the design of classifiers.

2.3.1. The Multilayer Perceptron. Multilayer perceptrons (MLPs), one of the most popular neural networks, have been applied successfully to solve many difficult and diverse problems by using the well-known backpropagation algorithm to train them [24]. The performance of a trained MLP depends on its architecture, initial weights, and the number of training epochs. From many simulations, an MLP with the architecture $20 \times 12 \times 10 \times 5$ was constructed.

2.3.2. The Support Vector Machine. The support vector machine (SVM) is another widely adopted neural network [24]. It is a linear machine with powerful learning ability and good generalization capability. The design of a successful SVM classifier involves the choice of the so-called kernel functions. In our system, we employed the use of the radial-basis functions (RBFs). The number of RBFs and their centers are automatically set by the number of support vectors and their values.

2.3.3. Hyperrectangular Composite Neural Networks. The class of hyperrectangular composite neural networks (HRC-NNs), a kind of hybrid networks developed by our previous work [25–28], integrates the paradigms of neural networks with the rule-based approach. The values of the synaptic weights of a trained HRCNN can be interpreted as a set of crisp If-Then rules. In addition, a specially designed training algorithm can achieve 100% correct recognition rate for the

training set [25–28]. The mathematical description of a two-layer HRCNN with J hidden nodes is given as follows:

$$\text{Out}(\underline{x}) = f\left(\sum_{j=1}^{J} \text{Out}_j(\underline{x}) - \eta\right),$$

$$\text{Out}_j(\underline{x}) = f\left(\text{net}_j(\underline{x})\right),$$

$$\text{net}_j(\underline{x}) = \sum_{i=1}^{n} f\left(\left(M_{ji} - x_i\right)\left(x_i - m_{ji}\right)\right) - n, \quad (4)$$

$$f(y) = \begin{cases} 1 & \text{if } y \geq 0 \\ 0 & \text{if } y < 0, \end{cases}$$

where M_{ji} and $m_{ji} \in \mathfrak{R}$ are adjustable synaptic weights of the jth hidden node, $\underline{x} = (x_1, \ldots, x_n)^T$ is an input pattern, n is the dimensionality of input variables, η is a small positive real number, and $\text{Out}(\underline{x}) : \mathfrak{R}^n \to \{0, 1\}$ is the output function of a two-layer HRCNN with J hidden nodes.

3. Experimental Results

The database of the white blood cells used in the experiments was downloaded from the CellaVision Competency Software Databases which contain slides stained with either a May Grünwald Giemsa or a Wright staining protocol [21]. The databases contain 9-10 slides each having approximately 100 white blood cell images and a large RBC overview image for RBC characterization. There are five types of white blood cells (e.g., lymphocyte, monocyte, eosinophil, basophil, and neutrophil). There were 450 white blood cell images used in our experiments. These 450 images came from two different data sets. The difference between these two data sets was the colorant used to stain cells. Figure 4 shows some examples from the two data sets. The color of the white blood cells

TABLE 1: The number of cell images for each kind of white cells.

	Lymphocyte	Monocyte	Basophil	Eosinophil	Neutrophil	Total
Set 1	12	12	12	12	12	60
Set 2	83	31	2	5	269	390
Total	95	43	14	17	281	450

TABLE 2: The segmentation results.

Data set	1		2	
Cell type	Sensitivity	Specificity	Sensitivity	Specificity
Lymphocyte	0.995	0.994	1.000	0.986
Monocyte	0.997	0.988	0.999	0.983
Basophil	0.970	0.992	0.999	0.970
Eosinophil	0.794	0.994	0.867	0.993
Neutrophil	0.990	0.990	1.000	0.978
Average	0.949	0.992	0.973	0.982

which came from data set 2 looks more near purple than the cells from data set 1. Table 1 tabulates the number of cell images for each type of white cells.

3.1. Experiment One: The Cell Segmentation. In this experiment, we would like to test the performance of the proposed segmentation algorithm introduced in the first stage of the proposed automatic white blood cell classification system. Since the preparation of staining procedure and blood concentration of individual may result in the inconsistency of color in cell images, we constructed one discriminate region of white blood cell tones particularly suitable for each data set. The two discriminating regions were constructed based on 500 and 800 pixels which were randomly selected from the images from the two data sets, respectively. The found discriminating region for each data set was given as follows: for data set 1,

$$\begin{bmatrix} H' \\ S' \\ I' \end{bmatrix} = \begin{bmatrix} -0.6590 & 0.3518 & -0.7135 \\ 0.7527 & 0.5438 & 0.3711 \\ -0.2574 & 0.7620 & 0.5943 \end{bmatrix} \begin{bmatrix} H \\ S \\ I \end{bmatrix}$$

$$\frac{(H'-6.042)^2}{52.645^2} + \frac{(S'-2.916)^2}{17.274^2} + \frac{(I'-0.252)^2}{11.154^2} \le 1; \quad (5)$$

for data set 2,

$$\begin{bmatrix} H' \\ S' \\ I' \end{bmatrix} = \begin{bmatrix} -0.3683 & 0.5550 & -0.7459 \\ 0.8238 & 0.5667 & 0.0149 \\ -0.4309 & 0.6090 & 0.6659 \end{bmatrix} \begin{bmatrix} H \\ S \\ I \end{bmatrix}$$

$$\frac{(H'+16.433)^2}{56.761^2} + \frac{(S'+0.0512)^2}{40.027^2} + \frac{(I'+8.735)^2}{21.894^2} \le 1. \quad (6)$$

TABLE 3: The classification results of the three neural-network-based classifiers.

Classifier	Training set	Testing set	Overall
MLP	99.67%	98.01%	99.11%
SVM	100.0%	92.72%	97.55%
HRCNN	100.0%	66.90%	88.89%

The evaluation of the proposed segmentation algorithm was based on the computations of the sensitivity and specificity rates:

$$\begin{aligned} \text{sensitivity} = &\text{ number of true positives} \\ &\times (\text{number of true positives} \\ &+ \text{number of false negatives})^{-1}, \\ \text{specificity} = &\text{ number of true negatives} \\ &\times (\text{number of true negatives} \\ &+ \text{number of false positives})^{-1}. \end{aligned} \quad (7)$$

While the sensitivity rate relates to the test's ability to identify positive results (i.e., white blood cell pixels), the specificity rate relates to the test's ability to identify negative results (i.e., background pixels). Table 2 tabulates the segmentation results. For the four types, lymphocyte, monocyte, eosinophil, and neutrophil, the sensitivity and specificity rates were all above 0.97. It indicated that the segmentation results were good. As for the basophil type, the specificity rate was still high (i.e., 0.993), but the sensitivity rate was only 0.794 (for data set 1) and 0.867 (for data set 2). It indicated that the basophil type was a little undersegmented. We found that the low sensitivity may be due to the large amount of red granules in a basophil. The segmentation performance was not 100% correct; however, the classification performance could be high if the most important regions of the cells were correctly segmented. The classification performance was validated at the second experiment.

3.2. Experiment Two: The Classification Comparisons. The 450 images were split into a training set consisting of 299 images and a testing set consisting of 151 images. The classification results for these three types of classifiers were tabulated in Table 3 based on the average of the classification rates of all classes. While the SVM and the HRCNN could achieve 100% correct rate for the training set, the MLP could reach the highest rate for the testing data set. The MLP outperformed the other two classifiers based on the comparisons of the overall correct rate.

TABLE 4: The comparisons of the classification rates among different classification systems.

Method	Number of types	Segmentation	Classifier	Overall rate	Number of images
Ours	5	Discriminating region	MLP	99.11%	450
Ours	5	Discriminating region	SVM	97.55%	450
Ours	5	Discriminating region	HRCNN	88.89%	450
Rezatofighi et al. [1]	5	Gram-Schmidt orthogonalization and snake	SVM	86.10%	400
Tabrizi et al. [2]	5	Gram-Schmidt orthogonalization and snake	LVQ	94.10%	400
Ghosh et al. [3]	5	Watershed	Bayes classifier	83.2%	150
Young [4]	5	Histogram threshold	Distance classifier	92.46%	199
Yampri et al. [5]	5	Automatic thresholding and adaptive contour	Minimized error	96.0%	100
Bikhet et al. [6]	5	Entropy threshold and iterative threshold	Distance classifier	90.14%	71
Piuri and Scotti [7]	5	Opening and Canny edge detector	KNN, FF-NN, and RBF	92%~82%	113

The comparisons of our proposed white cell recognition system with other white cell classification systems were shown in Table 4. Those existing systems constructed their own databases instead of using a public database as we did. The rightest column shows the number of images used in their experiments. Among these systems, we used the largest amount of images to evaluate the proposed system. In addition, based on the comparisons of the overall rate, our proposed system incorporated with a trained MLP achieved the highest correct rate.

Most of the systems shown in Table 4 did not mention the information about the computational time. While Rezatofighi et al. [1] reported that it took 16 minutes for the differential counting of 100 white cells with the image size 720 × 576 on a Pentium-4 PC at 3.2 GHz with 1 GB RAM, our system took 0.88 seconds (from segmentation to classification) to classify a cell image with the size 360 × 360 on a Pentium-4 PC at 2.6 GHz with 2 GB RAM.

4. Conclusions

In this paper, we proposed a new segmentation algorithm for segmenting a white cell from a smear image. This segmentation algorithm is based on finding a discriminating region of white blood cell tones in the *HSI* color space. The found discriminating region can be described by a 3D ellipsoid. Then we proposed the use of 20 features consisting of 3 geometrical features, 3 color features, and 14 LDP features. Finally, three different neural-network-based classifiers were adopted for classifying white blood cells into one of the five types. Compared to other systems tabulated in Table 4, our proposed system incorporated with a trained MLP could reach the highest performance. The performance was evaluated on a public database.

Conflict of Interests

The authors declare that there is no conflict of interests regarding the publication of this paper.

Acknowledgments

This paper was partly supported by the National Science Council, Taiwan, under NSC 101-2221-E-008-124-MY3, 101-2911-I-008-001, the CGH-NCU Joint Research Foundation Project no. 102 NCU-CGH A4, and the LSH-NCU Joint Research Foundation Project no. 102- NCU-LSH-102-A-018.

References

[1] S. H. Rezatofighi, K. Khaksari, and H. Soltanian-Zadeh, "Automatic recognition of five types of white blood cells in peripheral blood," in *Proceedings of the International Conference of Image Analysis and Recognition*, vol. 6112, pp. 161–172, 2010.

[2] P. R. Tabrizi, S. H. Rezatofighi, and M. J. Yazdanpanah, "Using PCA and LVQ neural network for automatic recognition of five types of white blood cells," in *Proceedings of the 32nd Annual International Conference of the IEEE Engineering in Medicine and Biology Society (EMBC '10)*, pp. 5593–5596, September 2010.

[3] M. Ghosh, D. Das, S. Mandal et al., "Statistical pattern analysis of white blood cell nuclei morphometry," in *Proceedings of the IEEE Students' Technology Symposium (TechSym '10)*, pp. 59–66, April 2010.

[4] I. T. Young, "The classification of white blood cells," *IEEE Transactions on Biomedical Engineering*, vol. 19, no. 4, pp. 291–298, 1972.

[5] P. Yampri, C. Pintavirooj, S. Daochai, and S. Teartulakarn, "White blood cell classification based on the combination of eigen cell and parametric feature detection," in *Proceedings of the 1st IEEE Conference on Industrial Electronics and Applications (ICIEA '06)*, pp. 1–4, May 2006.

[6] S. F. Bikhet, A. M. Darwish, H. A. Tolba, and S. I. Shaheen, "Segmentation and classification of white blood cells," in *Proceedings of the IEEE Interntional Conference on Acoustics, Speech, and Signal Processing*, vol. 4, pp. 2259–2261, June 2000.

[7] V. Piuri and F. Scotti, "Morphological classification of blood leucocytes by microscope images," in *Proceedings of the IEEE International Conference on Computational Intelligence for Measurement Systems and Applications (CIMSA '04)*, pp. 103–108, July 2004.

[8] H. Sheikh, B. Zhu, and E. M. Tzanakou, "Blood cell identification using neural networks," in *Proceedings of the IEEE*

22nd Annual Northeast Bioengineering Conference, pp. 119–120, March 1996.

[9] N. T. Umpon and S. Dhompongsa, "Morphological granulometric features of nucleus in automatic bone marrow white blood cell classification," *IEEE Transactions on Information Technology in Biomedicine*, vol. 11, no. 3, pp. 353–359, 2007.

[10] S. Nilufar, N. Ray, and H. Zhang, "Automatic blood cell classification based on joint histogram based feature and Bhattacharya Kernel," in *Proceedings of the 42nd Asilomar Conference on Signals, Systems and Computers (ASILOMAR '08)*, pp. 1915–1918, October 2008.

[11] S. Osowski, R. Siroic, T. Markiewicz, and K. Siwek, "Application of support vector machine and genetic algorithm for improved blood cell recognition," *IEEE Transactions on Instrumentation and Measurement*, vol. 58, no. 7, pp. 2159–2168, 2009.

[12] C. Di Rubeto, A. Dempster, S. Khan, and B. Jarra, "Segmentation of blood images using morphological operators," in *Proceedings of the 15th International Conference on Pattern Recognition*, pp. 397–400, 2000.

[13] I. Cseke, "A fast segmentation scheme for white blood cell images," in *Proceedings of the 11th IAPR International Conference on Pattern Recognition, Conference C: Image, Speech and Signal Analysis*, pp. 530–533, 1992.

[14] J. M. Chassery and C. Garbay, "An iterative segmentation method based on contextual color and shape criterion," *IEEE Transactions on Pattern Analysis and Machine Intelligence*, vol. 6, no. 6, pp. 794–800, 1984.

[15] K. Jiang, Q. M. Liao, and S. Y. Dai, "A novel white blood cell segmentation scheme using scale-space filtering and watershed clustering," in *Proceedings of the 2nd International Conference on Machine Learning and Cybernetics*, vol. 5, pp. 2820–2825, November 2003.

[16] N. Hazlyna and M. Y. Mashor, "Segmentation technique for acute leukemia blood cells images using saturation component and moving l-mean clustering procedures," *International Journal of Electrical, Electronic Engineering and Technology*, vol. 1, pp. 23–35, 2011.

[17] J. Wu, P. Zeng, Y. Zhou, and C. Oliver, "A novel color image segmentation method and its application to white blood cell image analysis," in *Proceedings of the 8th International Conference on Signal Processing (ICSP '06)*, vol. 2, pp. 245–248, 2006.

[18] A. N. A. Salihah, M. Y. Mashor, N. H. Harun, A. A. Abdullah, and H. Rosline, "Improving colour image segmentation on acute myelogenous leukaemia images using contrast enhancement techniques," in *Proceedings of the IEEE EMBS Conference on Biomedical Engineering and Sciences (IECBES '10)*, pp. 246–251, December 2010.

[19] N. Guo, L. Zeng, and Q. Wu, "A method based on multispectral imaging technique for white blood cell segmentation," *Computers in Biology and Medicine*, vol. 37, no. 1, pp. 70–76, 2007.

[20] R. Adollah, M. Y. Mashor, N. F. Mohd Nasir, H. Rosline, H. Mahsin, and H. Adilah, "Blood cell image segmentation: a review," in *Proceedings of the 4th Kuala Lumpur International Conference on Biomedical Engineering (Biomed '08)*, pp. 141–144, June 2008.

[21] CellaVision Inc., 2011, http://www.cellavision.com/.

[22] T. Ojala, M. Pietikäinen, and T. Mäenpää, "Multiresolution gray-scale and rotation invariant texture classification with local binary patterns," *IEEE Transactions on Pattern Analysis and Machine Intelligence*, vol. 24, no. 7, pp. 971–987, 2002.

[23] T. Jabid, H. Kabir, and O. Chaei, "Local Directional Pattern (LDP) for face recognition," in *Proceedings of the International Conference on Consumer Electronics (ICCE '10)*, pp. 329–330, January 2010.

[24] S. Haykin, *Neural Networks: A Comprehensive Foundation*, Prentice Hall, New York, NY, USA, 2nd edition, 1999.

[25] M. C. Su, "Use of neural networks as medical diagnosis expert systems," *Computers in Biology and Medicine*, vol. 24, no. 6, pp. 419–429, 1994.

[26] M. C. Su, C. T. Hsieh, and C. Chin, "A neuro-fuzzy approach to speech recognition without time alignment," *Fuzzy Sets and Systems*, vol. 98, no. 1, pp. 33–41, 1998.

[27] M. C. Su, "Neural-network-based fuzzy model and its application to transient stability prediction in power systems," *IEEE Transactions on Systems, Man and Cybernetics C*, vol. 29, no. 1, pp. 149–157, 1999.

[28] J. H. Chen, M. C. Su, C. Y. Chen, F. H. Hsu, and C. C. Wu, "Application of neural networks for detecting erroneous tax reports from construction companies," *Automation in Construction*, vol. 20, no. 7, pp. 935–939, 2011.

22

Genome-Wide Characterisation of Gene Expression in Rice Leaf Blades at 25°C and 30°C

Zhi-guo E,[1] Lei Wang,[1] Ryan Qin,[2] Haihong Shen,[3] and Jianhua Zhou[4]

[1] China National Rice Research Institute, No. 359, Tiyuchang Road, Hangzhou 310006, China
[2] iBioinfo Group, Lexington, MA 02421, USA
[3] School of Life Science, Gwangju Institute of Science and Technology, Gwangju 500-712, Republic of Korea
[4] Nantong University, Nantong 226001, China

Correspondence should be addressed to Jianhua Zhou; jianhua55@msn.com

Academic Editors: B. Shen, J. Wang, and J. Wang

Rice growth is greatly affected by temperature. To examine how temperature influences gene expression in rice on a genome-wide basis, we utilised recently compiled next-generation sequencing datasets and characterised a number of RNA-sequence transcriptome samples in rice seedling leaf blades at 25°C and 30°C. Our analysis indicated that 50.4% of all genes in the rice genome (28,296/56,143) were expressed in rice samples grown at 25°C, whereas slightly fewer genes (50.2%; 28,189/56,143) were expressed in rice leaf blades grown at 30°C. Among the genes that were expressed, approximately 3% were highly expressed, whereas approximately 65% had low levels of expression. Further examination demonstrated that 821 genes had a twofold or higher increase in expression and that 553 genes had a twofold or greater decrease in expression at 25°C. Gene ontology (GO) and Kyoto Encyclopedia of Genes and Genomes (KEGG) analyses suggested that the ribosome pathway and multiple metabolic pathways were upregulated at 25°C. Based on these results, we deduced that gene expression at both transcriptional and translational levels was stimulated at 25°C, perhaps in response to a suboptimal temperature condition. Finally, we observed that temperature markedly regulates several super-families of transcription factors, including bZIP, MYB, and WRKY.

1. Introduction

Rice (*Oryza sativa* L.) includes two major subspecies, *indica* and *japonica*. Owing to its importance in food security, extensive studies utilising genetic manipulation, improved cultivation and crossing of subspecies have been conducted in rice during recent decades to improve quality and yield. Like all other plants, rice constantly experiences environmental changes and hostile abiotic stress conditions, such as drought, cold, pollution due to heavy metals and salinity, in addition to biotic stresses, such as viral infection. To minimise abiotic and/or biotic stress-induced damage, plants have developed adaptations and stress tolerance during evolution through the regulation of gene expression and changes in cellular processes. Two major pathways, abscisic acid (ABA)-dependent and ABA-independent pathways, have been extensively studied in plants in response to biotic and/or abiotic stresses [1–3]. ABA is a hormone produced during metabolic reactions.

In response to abiotic stress, the ABA-dependent pathway induces the expression of many stress-related genes by regulating the activities of transcription factors. Among many transcription factors, several super-families, including basic leucine zipper (bZIP) [4–6], MYB [7, 8], and WRKY [9–11], have been shown to play critical roles in the regulation of stress response genes in rice.

bZIP proteins include a family of transcriptional regulators that are exclusively present in eukaryotes. Furthermore, they characteristically harbour a bZIP domain composed of two structural features: a DNA-binding basic region and the leucine-zipper dimerisation region. They have been shown to regulate diverse plant-specific phenomena, including seed maturation and germination, flower induction and development, photomorphogenesis and stress and hormone signalling. There are approximately 90 bZIP transcription factor-encoding genes in the rice genome [5].

The *MYB* gene family includes at least 155 members that have been identified by a genome-wide analysis and represents one of the richest groups of transcription factors in rice. MYB proteins are characterised by a highly conserved MYB DNA-binding domain and can be classified into four major groups, 1R-MYB, 2R-MYB, 3R-MYB, and 4R-MYB, on the basis of the number and position of MYB repeats. MYB transcription factors are involved in plant development, secondary metabolism, hormone signal transduction, disease resistance, and abiotic stress tolerance [12].

WRKY genes encode transcription factors with a WRKY domain that belongs to zinc-finger proteins. WRKY proteins contain one or two conserved WRKY domains, which are encoded by approximately 60 N-terminal amino acid residues with a WRKYGQ(K/E)K sequence, followed by a C2H2 or C2HC zinc-finger motif. An exhaustive search for *WRKY* genes using HMMER and a hidden Markov model resulted in the identification of 98 and 102 *WRKY* genes in *O. japonica* and *O. indica* rice, respectively. WRKY genes play important roles in disease resistance, responses to salicylic and jasmonic acid, seed development and germination, senescence, abiotic stress responses and ABA responses in rice [13].

Despite all this knowledge, the mechanisms that regulate gene expression in rice are not completely understood. To investigate how external factors, such as temperature, affect rice development and growth through the regulation of gene expression, we searched the available transcriptome databases. We identified two transcriptome RNA-sequence (RNA-Seq) datasets of high quality from rice seedling leaf blades leaf blades grown at 25°C or 30°C. We found that the expression of more than 1300 genes in rice showed a twofold or higher difference between leaf blades that were grown at 25°C compared with those grown at 30°C. Gene ontology (GO) and Kyoto Encyclopedia of Genes and Genomes (KEGG) analyses showed that transcription of many abiotic stress genes and genes involved in ribosome biogenesis were induced at 25°C, indicating that rice grown at 25°C has more active transcription and translation than rice grown at 30°C. Furthermore, we found that among the transcription factor super-families, bZIP, MYB, NAC, and WRKY were significantly regulated in rice at 25°C. Our studies provide useful information on the rice transcriptome in response to suboptimal temperatures.

2. Materials and Methods

2.1. Transcriptome Sequencing Datasets of Rice Seedling Leaf Blades. Two publicly available RNA-Seq datasets using deep-sequencing of rice seedling leaf blades were downloaded from Gene Expression Omnibus (GEO) under the accession number GSE42096 (http://www.ncbi.nlm.nih.gov/geo/query/acc.cgi?acc=GSE42096) and used for primary analyses. The leaf blades analysed were obtained from wild-type seedlings grown at 30°C or 25°C. For each dataset, RNA-Seq was conducted by paired-end approaches using an Illumina HiSeq 2000 instrument. The read length was 90 bp.

2.2. Sequencing Analysis. Sequence alignment between the transcriptome reads was conducted and reads were checked for quality and mapped to the reference genome sequences by Bowtie 2 using the parameters "end-to-end" and "very-sensitive". The reference genome, transcript annotation, and GO datasets were downloaded from MSU Rice Genome Annotation Project, release 7. The number of reads for a gene was designated as reads per kb per million total reads (RPKM) after normalisation to the number of mapped genome locations. KEGG gene classifications were downloaded from its database.

2.3. Statistical Analyses. To determine whether expression was differentially regulated under different temperatures (25°C versus 30°C), we conducted statistical analyses based on the fold-changes in gene expression by adding median counts as a pseudocount. Pathway analyses were based on the binomial probability of observing a number of gene changes in a given pathway. Differences were considered statistically significant when the *P* value was <0.05.

3. Results

3.1. RNA-Seq Datasets of the Transcriptome from Rice. To accurately determine rice gene expression profiles, we took advantage of recent advances in deep-sequencing technologies. Many RNA-Seq datasets of the transcriptome of rice and other plants are publicly available. Using these datasets, we identified transcriptome sequencing libraries of two rice samples in a single GEO dataset, GSE42096, generated by the Chinese Academy of Sciences and the National Centre for Plant Gene Research (http://www.ncbi.nlm.nih.gov/geo/query/acc.cgi?acc=GSE42096). Profiling of these transcriptome RNAs by high-throughput sequencing was conducted by both single-end and paired-end approaches using an Illumina HiSeq 2000 platform. Paired-end sequencing provided 90 basepairs (bp) per read from each end. RNA-Seq of the transcriptome for each sample generated approximately 25 million reads. Sequence analysis indicated that the datasets were of exceptionally high quality with very low background noise (Supplementary Figure 1 available online on http://dx.doi.org/10.1155/2014/917292).

3.2. Gene Expression in Rice at 25°C and 30°C. To characterize expressed transcripts, a reference genome dataset was required. We searched existing databases and found that the MSU Rice Genome Annotation Project on *O. sativa japonica*, released on 31st Oct 2011, is the most complete rice genome database available with more than 56,143 annotated genes, slightly more than the 55986 reported by Kawahara et al. [14]. Therefore, we used this database as our reference for analysing gene expression in the two leaf blade transcriptome datasets. We used Bowtie 2 to align and map the transcriptome reads to rice genome. On the basis of our analysis, we calculated the number of reads as reads per billion (RPB) for each mRNA in two samples. We normalised RPB by read per kbp and RPKM. We found that at 25°C there were 19,766 annotated genes with >1 RPKM read, whereas at 30°C

TABLE 1: Top ranked pathways that are regulated (1374 genes) at 25°C by GO analysis.

Rank	Pathway	Pathway annotation	Pathway size	Observed	Ratio	P value
1	Process: metabolic process	rice:GO:0008152	7390	391	0.05	$4.3E-52$
2	Process: response to stress	rice:GO:0006950	3620	241	0.07	$1.9E-46$
3	Process: response to abiotic stimulus	rice:GO:0009628	2195	177	0.08	$1.5E-44$
4	Process: cellular process	rice:GO:0009987	7325	365	0.05	$3.3E-42$
5	Function: catalytic activity	rice:GO:0003824	3688	227	0.06	$2.7E-38$
6	Component: membrane	rice:GO:0016020	3728	220	0.06	$2.1E-34$
7	Process: biosynthetic process	rice:GO:0009058	4673	250	0.05	$1.6E-32$
8	Process: response to endogenous stimulus	rice:GO:0009719	1490	118	0.08	$4.9E-29$
9	Component: cytosol	rice:GO:0005829	2289	151	0.07	$2.1E-28$
10	Process: response to biotic stimulus	rice:GO:0009607	1081	96	0.09	$1.9E-27$
11	Component: ribosome	rice:GO:0005840	481	61	0.13	$9.5E-26$
12	Function: structural molecule activity	rice:GO:0005198	518	63	0.12	$1.5E-25$

the number of genes that had at least 1 RPKM was 19,350. The distribution of expressed genes with different RPKM levels was similar between 25°C and 30°C (Supplementary Figure 2). Approximately 30 genes had extremely high expression levels (>1000 RPKM), 3% of annotated genes (550–600) were highly expressed (>100 RPKM) and more than 33% of expressed genes (6900) were expressed at only a modest level (10–100 RPKM). Of the genes that were expressed, 64% (12,000) had fewer than 9 RPKM, suggesting that most genes were expressed at a low level. Expression of the other 36,000 genes was not detectable.

3.3. Differential Gene Expression in Rice between 30°C and 25°C. We then compared the genes with varied expression in rice growing at 30°C and 25°C. We calculated ratios between the number of reads at 30°C and the number of reads at 25°C. As shown in Supplementary Figure 3, the left part of the histogram shows the number of genes with an increased expression at 25°C. We found that the expression of 257 genes was upregulated more than threefold in rice grown at 25°C, whereas expression of 173 genes was downregulated more than threefold at 25°C. Moreover, there were more genes that were upregulated (564) than downregulated (380) at 25°C, with expression level changes between twofold and threefold. Among approximately 2712 genes with a 1.5–2.0-fold change in expression, 1617 genes were upregulated and 1095 genes (1.5–2.0-fold) were downregulated. Our results indicate that more genes were upregulated at 25°C than at 30°C, suggesting that at 25°C, rice plants need to respond to a suboptimal lower temperature by altering gene transcription.

3.4. GO Analysis of Genes That Are Upregulated and Downregulated. To examine the mechanisms of the molecular and cellular responses to a suboptimal lower temperature of 25°C, we performed GO and KEGG analysis in genes of the rice transcriptome that had an twofold or higher change in expression between 25°C and 30°C. In total, we found that the expression of 821 genes was upregulated by twofold or higher at 25°C, whereas 553 genes showed downregulated expression at 25°C. Among the 1374 genes that were either

upregulated or downregulated, GO analysis indicated that 4 of the 10 top-ranked GO categories were stress related, with 17.54% of genes (241/1374) related to "response to stress" (ranked at no. 2 with $P = 1.88E - 46$), 12.88% of genes (177/1374) related to "response to abiotic stimulus" (ranked at no. 3 with $P = 1.55E - 44$), 8.59% of genes (118/1374) related to "response to endogenous stimulus" (ranked at no. 8 with $P = 4.90E - 29$) and 6.99% of genes (96/1374) related to "response to biotic stimulus" (ranked at no. 10 with $P = 1.91E - 27$), suggesting that 25°C could be considered as a cold-stress condition (Table 1). Other high-ranked GO categories included membrane processes (ranked no. 1) and metabolic processes and ribosome (ranked no. 11), indicating that metabolism and protein translation are perhaps also upregulated at 25°C.

3.5. KEGG Pathway Analysis of Upregulated and Downregulated Genes. To further characterise the pathways that are involved in temperature-induced stress responses, we performed KEGG pathway analysis. We observed that the expression of genes that are involved in ribosome biogenesis was significantly upregulated at 25°C, with an adjusted P value of $5.2E - 29$ (Table 2). In addition, 57 of the potential 362 transcripts that had been annotated in the ribosome pathway had a twofold or higher increase in expression at 25°C compared with 30°C. These upregulated transcripts represent 15.7% of the genes in the ribosome pathway. In contrast, none of the 362 transcripts showed decreased expression. Taken together, these results strongly suggested that both transcription and translation were more active at 25°C than 30°C. Other major pathways showing significant changes in expression on KEGG analysis included metabolic and biosynthesis pathways. Of note, P values for pathways that were upregulated were markedly more significant than pathways that were downregulated.

3.6. Expression Analysis of bZIP, WRKY and MYB Transcription Factors. The relative growth rate (RGR) in rice is influenced by temperature, with an optimal growth rate at 30°C [15]. Rice also has a stress response mechanism that

TABLE 2: Top ranked pathways that are regulated (1374 genes) at 25°C by KEGG analysis.

Rank	Pathway	Pathway annotation	Pathway size	Observed	Ratio	P value
1	Ribosome	rice:osa03010	362	57	0.16	$5.2E-29$
2	Metabolic pathways	rice:osa01100	1565	119	0.08	$1.0E-27$
3	Biosynthesis of secondary metabolites	rice:osa01110	745	65	0.09	$1.3E-18$
4	Starch and sucrose metabolism	rice:osa00500	130	20	0.15	$5.9E-11$
5	Alpha-Linolenic acid metabolism	rice:osa00592	34	9	0.26	$8.7E-08$
6	Glyoxylate and dicarboxylate metabolism	rice:osa00630	62	11	0.18	$2.6E-7$
7	Carbon fixation in photosynthetic organisms	rice:osa00710	85	12	0.14	$9.6E-07$
8	Diterpenoid biosynthesis	rice:osa00904	24	7	0.29	$1.2E-06$
9	Photosynthesis	rice:osa00195	148	15	0.10	$3.2E-06$
10	Plant hormone signal transduction	rice:osa04075	150	14	0.09	$1.6E-05$
11	Biosynthesis of unsaturated fatty acids	rice:osa01040	44	7	0.16	$8.0E-05$
12	Phenylpropanoid biosynthesis	rice:osa00940	94	9	0.10	$4.0E-04$

TABLE 3: Top ranked transcription factors that are regulated in rice by temperature.

Rank	Pathway	Pathway annotation	Pathway size	Observed	Ratio	P value
1	Rice transcription factor: WRKY	rice:TF:WRKY	107	15	0.14	$4.9E-08$
2	Rice transcription factor: NAC	rice:TF:NAC	124	12	0.096	$4.5E-05$
3	Rice transcription factor: AP2-EREBP	rice:TF:AP2-EREBP	169	14	0.082	$5.9E-05$
4	Rice transcription factor: orphans	rice:TF:orphans	85	9	0.105	0.00019
5	Rice transcription factor: bZIP	rice:TF:bZIP	95	9	0.095	0.00043
6	Rice transcription factor: MYB	rice:TF:MYB	128	10	0.078	0.00092
7	Rice transcription factor: tify	rice:TF:tify	21	4	0.190	0.00140
8	Rice transcription factor: MYB-related	rice:TF:MYB-related	100	7	0.07	0.00835
9	Rice transcription factor: C2H2	rice:TF:C2H2	104	7	0.067	0.01004
10	Rice transcription factor: pseudo ARR-B	rice:TF:pseudo_ARR-B	9	2	0.222	0.01811
11	Rice transcription factor: G2-like	rice:TF:G2-like	48	4	0.083	0.02342
12	Rice transcription factor: WRKY	rice:TF:WRKY	107	15	0.140	4.95634

is triggered in response to lower temperatures. As described above, transcription is more active at 25°C than at 30°C, indicating that gene expression is stimulated at 25°C. To characterise transcription factors that may be involved in the regulation of gene expression in rice growth at different temperatures and to understand how rice responds to the suboptimal temperature of 25°C, we analysed transcription factor families in rice (Supplementary Table S1), including the expression distribution patterns of the bZIP, MYB, WRKY, and HLH transcription factor super-families (Table 3, Supplementary Table S1 and Figure 1). Approximately 9.5% of bZIP (9/95), 14.1% of WRKY (15/107), 7.8% of MYB (12/128) and 3.5% of HLH (5/145) transcription factors had a twofold or higher change in expression. In contrast, a random calculation suggested that <2.57% (1374/56,143) of the genes should be upregulated or downregulated by twofold or more. Therefore, we conclude that expression of bZIP, WRKY, and MYB super-families was significantly regulated by temperature, with P values of $4.96E-08$ (WRKY), $4.3E-04$ (bZIP) and 0.008 (MYB) between 25°C and 30°C. These data are consistent with previous reports [16, 17] showing that these transcription factor super-families are upregulated or downregulated under colder or warmer temperatures. Other highly regulated transcription factor super-families include

NAC and AP2-EREBP. In contrast, other transcription factors such as bHLH and HB did not exhibit significant changes in expression.

4. Discussion

Like all plants, rice has to endure constant environmental changes. Among many factors, temperature has been shown to greatly influence rice growth. Rice can grow at a range of temperature, from as low as 12°C to as high as 40°C, but its optimal growth temperature is 30°C or warmer [15]. Unlike mammals, which have a constant body temperature, rice grows at temperatures that fluctuate daily between night and day. One of the mechanisms by which rice can adjust to temperature changes is through regulation of gene expression. Extensive studies have been conducted in rice to analyse the molecular basis of adaptation to both warmer temperatures and cold-stress conditions [3, 18–24]. However, global surveys of temperature-dependent changes in rice gene expression, particularly studies using next generation sequencing technology, are not extensive.

Because the rapid development and reduced cost of both next-generation sequencing and microarray technology, researchers have regularly deposited RNA-Seq datasets for

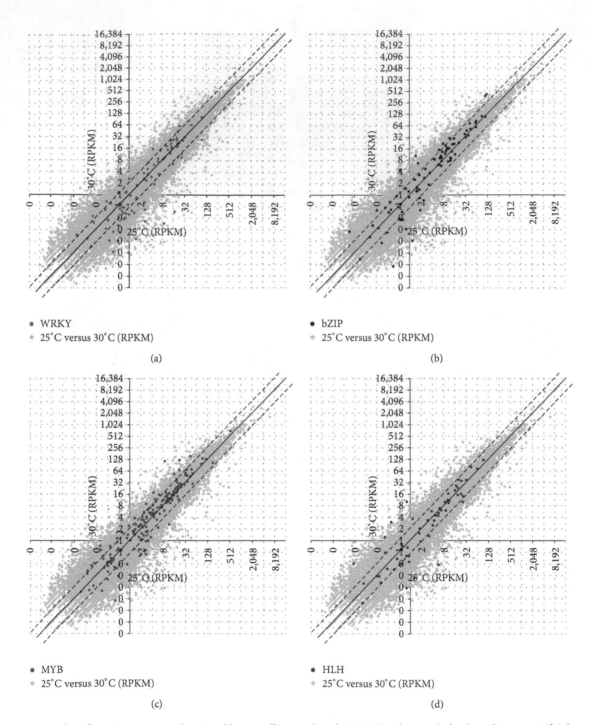

FIGURE 1: A scatter plot of gene expression values (per kb per million total reads, RPKM) in log2 scale for the 25°C versus 30°C datasets. Grey dots indicate each gene expressed in the two samples. Coloured dots indicate a specific group of genes. Two diagonal dashed lines indicate twofold changes (increases and decreases).

many organisms, including rice, in public domains. For example, several recent papers reported gene expression and splicing in rice using NGS and bioinformatics analysis [25–28]. To investigate how temperature may influence rice growth by affecting gene expression, we searched GEO databases (http://www.ncbi.nlm.nih.gov/geo/). We identified four sets of RNA-Seq transcriptome data from rice (GSE42096, GSE39307, GSE30490, and GSE27240) that were of a high quality. However, among these datasets, only four

samples in the GSE42096 dataset, which includes wild-type and TOG1 mutant rice leaf blades, were related to different temperatures (25°C and 30°C). Because mutant TOG1 has not yet been fully described in a public domain, we analysed only two wild-type rice leaf blade samples that grew at both 25°C and 30°C. We realised that the number of samples (two) was limited, but because the quality of these RNA-Seq datasets was exceptionally high, with more than 25 M reads each sample, we believe that our analysis will provide useful information on gene expression in rice to complement similar studies.

Gene expression is regulated at multiple levels. The most fundamental regulatory mechanisms that control the amount of proteins produced are transcription and translation. The cis-sequences in a gene, in particular the promoter, and transcription factors dictate how much RNA is transcribed from a gene, whereas ribosomes are directly related to the activities of protein translation. In our investigation, we demonstrated that the number of the genes that are expressed at 30°C (17,356) is similar to that at 25°C (17,966), indicating that it is necessary for only 1/3 of rice genes to be expressed to maintain growth under a given condition. Similarly, we observed that about 3% of genes were highly expressed at both 30°C and 25°C. The rest of the expressed genes had either a modest or a low expression level or no detectable expression.

However, the difference lies in the expression levels of specific genes between samples at 25°C and 30°C. We showed that 3986 genes had either increased or decreased expression levels of 1.50-fold or higher. Among these 3986 genes, 1374 had a twofold or higher increase (821) or decrease (553) when the temperature dropped from 30°C to 25°C, indicating perhaps that rice at 25°C has more active transcription. Consistent with this notion, by GO and KEGG analyses, we found that a significant number of genes in the ribosome pathways were upregulated at 25°C, suggesting that translation may be also more robust at 25°C. Considering previous reports that rice has a better growth rate at 30°C, or at least at temperatures warmer than 25°C [15], the more active transcription and translation at 25°C can be explained by the response of rice to a colder temperature. In fact, we observed in our GO analysis that 4 of the 12 top-ranked pathway categories were related to stress response. We deduced from our results that although 30°C is an optimal temperature for rice growth, transcription and translation for many genes are triggered at 25°C and this temperature (25°C) may be minimally sufficient to trigger the cold stress-response.

To further examine the molecular basis of the differential expression of rice genes between 25°C and 30°C, we examined rice transcription factor families (Figure 1, Table 3, Supplementary Table S1). In contrast to the WRKY super-family, bZIP and MYB transcription factor super-families had more downregulated than upregulated genes (1.5-fold cutoff) at 25°C. Although we were unable to draw definitive conclusions from this analysis, our results suggest that the WRKY super-family plays a positive role in the response to lower temperatures, whereas both bZIP and MYB super-families may have a negative impact on gene expression at 25°C, in agreement with a previous report that bZIP transcription factors, such as ZIP52, are negative regulators of cold stress [5]. In addition, we also showed that many transcription factors, including bHLH and HB, are not significantly regulated between 30°C and 25°C.

5. Conclusion

We concluded that only a small percentage of genes (3%) have a high expression level whereas more than 60% of genes have a very low expression level in rice. Both transcription and translation are more active at 25°C than at 30°C. Expression of bZIP, WRKY, and MYB is significantly regulated at 25°C.

Conflict of Interests

The authors declare that there is no conflict of interests regarding the publication of this article.

Acknowledgments

This research was supported by the special fund for Agro-Scientific Research in the Public Interest (201203029, 201203031), the Special Foundation for Basic Research and the Development of Central Level Scientific Research Institutes in China (2012RG006) (ZGE, LW), and the Priority Academic Program Development of Jiangsu Higher Education Institution (PAPD) (JZ).

References

[1] Y. Fujita, M. Fujita, K. Shinozaki, and K. Yamaguchi-Shinozaki, "ABA-mediated transcriptional regulation in response to osmotic stress in plants," Journal of Plant Research, vol. 124, no. 4, pp. 509–525, 2011.

[2] S. C. Lee and S. Luan, "ABA signal transduction at the crossroad of biotic and abiotic stress responses," Plant, Cell and Environment, vol. 35, no. 1, pp. 53–60, 2012.

[3] G. T. Huang, S. L. Ma, L. P. Bai et al., "Signal transduction during cold, salt, and drought stresses in plants," Molecular Biology Reports, vol. 39, no. 2, pp. 969–987, 2012.

[4] H. Takahashi, T. Kawakatsu, Y. Wakasa, S. Hayashi, and F. Takaiwa, "A rice transmembrane bZIP transcription factor, OsbZIP39, regulates the endoplasmic reticulum stress response," Plant and Cell Physiology, vol. 53, no. 1, pp. 144–153, 2012.

[5] C. Liu, Y. Wu, and X. Wang, "bZIP transcription factor OsbZIP52/RISBZ5: a potential negative regulator of cold and drought stress response in rice," Planta, vol. 235, no. 6, pp. 1157–1169, 2012.

[6] M. A. Hossain, Y. Lee, J. I. Cho et al., "The bZIP transcription factor OsABF1 is an ABA responsive element binding factor that enhances abiotic stress signaling in rice," Plant Molecular Biology, vol. 72, no. 4, pp. 557–566, 2010.

[7] X. Dai, Y. Xu, Q. Ma et al., "Overexpression of an R1R2R3 MYB gene, OsMYB3R-2, increases tolerance to freezing, drought, and salt stress in transgenic Arabidopsis," Plant Physiology, vol. 143, no. 4, pp. 1739–1751, 2007.

[8] L. Zhang, G. Zhao, J. Jia, X. Liu, and X. Kong, "Molecular characterization of 60 isolated wheat MYB genes and analysis of their expression during abiotic stress," Journal of Experimental Botany, vol. 63, no. 1, pp. 203–214, 2012.

[9] P. Agarwal, M. P. Reddy, and J. Chikara, "WRKY: its structure, evolutionary relationship, DNA-binding selectivity, role in stress tolerance and development of plants," Molecular Biology Reports, vol. 38, no. 6, pp. 3883–3896, 2011.

[10] H. Chen, Z. Lai, J. Shi, Y. Xiao, Z. Chen, and X. Xu, "Roles of arabidopsis WRKY18, WRKY40 and WRKY60 transcription factors in plant responses to abscisic acid and abiotic stress," BMC Plant Biology, vol. 10, article 281, 2010.

[11] R. Sharma, D. De Vleesschauwer, M. K. Sharma, and P. C. Ronald, "Recent advances in dissecting stress-regulatory crosstalk in rice," *Molecular Plant*, vol. 6, pp. 250–260, 2013.

[12] A. Nijhawan, M. Jain, A. K. Tyagi, and J. P. Khurana, "Genomic survey and gene expression analysis of the basic leucine zipper transcription factor family in rice," *Plant Physiology*, vol. 146, no. 2, pp. 333–350, 2008.

[13] C. A. Ross, Y. Liu, and Q. J. Shen, "The WRKY gene family in rice (*Oryza sativa*)," *Journal of Integrative Plant Biology*, vol. 49, no. 6, pp. 827–842, 2007.

[14] Y. Kawahara, M. de la Bastide, J. P. Hamilton et al., "Improvement of the *Oryza sativa* Nipponbare reference genome using next generation sequence and optical map data," *Rice*, vol. 6, article 4, 2013.

[15] T. Nagai and A. Makino, "Differences between rice and wheat in temperature responses of photosynthesis and plant growth," *Plant and Cell Physiology*, vol. 50, no. 4, pp. 744–755, 2009.

[16] Y. Xiang, N. Tang, H. Du, H. Ye, and L. Xiong, "Characterization of OsbZIP23 as a key player of the basic leucine zipper transcription factor family for conferring abscisic acid sensitivity and salinity and drought tolerance in rice," *Plant Physiology*, vol. 148, no. 4, pp. 1938–1952, 2008.

[17] N. Tang, H. Zhang, X. Li, J. Xiao, and L. Xiong, "Constitutive activation of transcription factor OsbZIP46 improves drought tolerance in rice," *Plant Physiology*, vol. 158, no. 4, pp. 1755–1768, 2012.

[18] Y. Cao, Q. Zhang, Y. Chen et al., "Identification of differential expression genes in leaves of rice (*Oryza sativa* L.) in response to heat stress by cDNA-AFLP analysis," *BioMed Research International*, vol. 2013, Article ID 576189, 11 pages, 2013.

[19] H. Chauhan, N. Khurana, P. Agarwal, and P. Khurana, "Heat shock factors in rice (*Oryza sativa* L.): genome-wide expression analysis during reproductive development and abiotic stress," *Molecular Genetics and Genomics*, vol. 286, no. 2, pp. 171–187, 2011.

[20] J. Zou, A. Liu, X. Chen et al., "Expression analysis of nine rice heat shock protein genes under abiotic stresses and ABA treatment," *Journal of Plant Physiology*, vol. 166, no. 8, pp. 851–861, 2009.

[21] D. Mittal, D. A. Madhyastha, and A. Grover, "Gene expression analysis in response to low and high temperature and oxidative stresses in rice: combination of stresses evokes different transcriptional changes as against stresses applied individually," *Plant Science*, vol. 197, pp. 102–113, 2012.

[22] D. Mittal, D. A. Madhyastha, and A. Grover, "Genome-wide transcriptional profiles during temperature and oxidative stress reveal coordinated expression patterns and overlapping regulons in rice," *PLoS ONE*, vol. 7, no. 7, Article ID e40899, 2012.

[23] R. B. Saad, D. Fabre, D. Mieulet et al., "Expression of the *Aeluropus littoralis AlSAP* gene in rice confers broad tolerance to abiotic stresses through maintenance of photosynthesis," *Plant, Cell and Environment*, vol. 35, no. 3, pp. 626–643, 2012.

[24] M. R. Park, K. Y. Yun, B. Mohanty et al., "Supra-optimal expression of the cold-regulated OsMyb4 transcription factor in transgenic rice changes the complexity of transcriptional network with major effects on stress tolerance and panicle development," *Plant, Cell and Environment*, vol. 33, no. 12, pp. 2209–2230, 2010.

[25] G. Zhang, G. Guo, X. Hu et al., "Deep RNA sequencing at single base-pair resolution reveals high complexity of the rice transcriptome," *Genome Research*, vol. 20, no. 5, pp. 646–654, 2010.

[26] T. Lu, G. Lu, D. Fan et al., "Function annotation of the rice transcriptome at single-nucleotide resolution by RNA-seq," *Genome Research*, vol. 20, no. 9, pp. 1238–1249, 2010.

[27] L. Gu and R. Guo, "Genome-wide detection and analysis of alternative splicing for nucleotide binding site-leucine-rich repeats sequences in rice," *Journal of Genetics and Genomics*, vol. 34, no. 3, pp. 247–257, 2007.

[28] B. B. Wang and V. Brendel, "Genomewide comparative analysis of alternative splicing in plants," *Proceedings of the National Academy of Sciences of the United States of America*, vol. 103, no. 18, pp. 7175–7180, 2006.

Permissions

The contributors of this book come from diverse backgrounds, making this book a truly international effort. This book will bring forth new frontiers with its revolutionizing research information and detailed analysis of the nascent developments around the world.

We would like to thank all the contributing authors for lending their expertise to make the book truly unique. They have played a crucial role in the development of this book. Without their invaluable contributions this book wouldn't have been possible. They have made vital efforts to compile up to date information on the varied aspects of this subject to make this book a valuable addition to the collection of many professionals and students.

This book was conceptualized with the vision of imparting up-to-date information and advanced data in this field. To ensure the same, a matchless editorial board was set up. Every individual on the board went through rigorous rounds of assessment to prove their worth. After which they invested a large part of their time researching and compiling the most relevant data for our readers. Conferences and sessions were held from time to time between the editorial board and the contributing authors to present the data in the most comprehensible form. The editorial team has worked tirelessly to provide valuable and valid information to help people across the globe.

Every chapter published in this book has been scrutinized by our experts. Their significance has been extensively debated. The topics covered herein carry significant findings which will fuel the growth of the discipline. They may even be implemented as practical applications or may be referred to as a beginning point for another development. Chapters in this book were first published by Hindawi Publishing Corporation; hereby published with permission under the Creative Commons Attribution License or equivalent.

The editorial board has been involved in producing this book since its inception. They have spent rigorous hours researching and exploring the diverse topics which have resulted in the successful publishing of this book. They have passed on their knowledge of decades through this book. To expedite this challenging task, the publisher supported the team at every step. A small team of assistant editors was also appointed to further simplify the editing procedure and attain best results for the readers.

Our editorial team has been hand-picked from every corner of the world. Their multi-ethnicity adds dynamic inputs to the discussions which result in innovative outcomes. These outcomes are then further discussed with the researchers and contributors who give their valuable feedback and opinion regarding the same. The feedback is then collaborated with the researches and they are edited in a comprehensive manner to aid the understanding of the subject.

Apart from the editorial board, the designing team has also invested a significant amount of their time in understanding the subject and creating the most relevant covers. They scrutinized every image to scout for the most suitable representation of the subject and create an appropriate cover for the book.

The publishing team has been involved in this book since its early stages. They were actively engaged in every process, be it collecting the data, connecting with the contributors or procuring relevant information. The team has been an ardent support to the editorial, designing and production team. Their endless efforts to recruit the best for this project, has resulted in the accomplishment of this book. They are a veteran in the field of academics and their pool of knowledge is as vast as their experience in printing. Their expertise and guidance has proved useful at every step. Their uncompromising quality standards have made this book an exceptional effort. Their encouragement from time to time has been an inspiration for everyone.

The publisher and the editorial board hope that this book will prove to be a valuable piece of knowledge for researchers, students, practitioners and scholars across the globe.

List of Contributors

Xinyang Deng
School of Computer and Information Science, Southwest University, Chongqing 400715, China

Qi Liu
School of Life Sciences and Biotechnology, Shanghai Jiao Tong University, Shanghai 200240, China
Department of Biomedical Informatics, Medical Center, Vanderbilt University, Nashville, TN 37235, USA

Yong Hu
Institute of Business Intelligence and Knowledge Discovery, Guangdong University of Foreign Studies,
Sun Yat-sen University, Guangzhou 510006, China

Yong Deng
School of Computer and Information Science, Southwest University, Chongqing 400715, China
School of Engineering, Vanderbilt University, Nashville, TN 37235, USA

Herng-Chia Chiu and Wen-Hsien Ho
Department of Healthcare Administration and Medical Informatics, Kaohsiung Medical University, 100 Shi-Chuan
1st Road, Kaohsiung 807, Taiwan

Te-Wei Ho
Bureau of Health Promotion, Department of Health, No. 2 Changqing St., Xinzhuang, New Taipei City 242, Taiwan

King-Teh Lee
Department of Healthcare Administration and Medical Informatics, Kaohsiung Medical University, 100 Shi-Chuan
1st Road, Kaohsiung 807, Taiwan
Department of Surgery, Kaohsiung Medical University Hospital, 100 Shi-Chuan 1st Road, Kaoshiung 807, Kaohsiung,
Taiwan

Hong-Yaw Chen
Yuan's Hospital, No. 162 Cheng Kung 1st Road, Kaohsiung 802, Kaohsiung, Taiwan

Hailin Chen
School of Information Science and Engineering, Central South University, Changsha 410083, China
Department of Computer Science and Technology, Hunan University of Humanities, Science and Technology, Loudi
417000, China

Zuping Zhang
School of Information Science and Engineering, Central South University, Changsha 410083, China

Yin-Fu Huang
Department of Computer Science and Information Engineering, National Yunlin University of Science and Technology,
123 University Road, Section 3, Douliu, Yunlin 640, Taiwan

Chia-Ming Wang
Graduate School of Engineering Science and Technology, National Yunlin University of Science and Technology,
123 University Road, Section 3, Douliu, Yunlin 640, Taiwan

Sing-Wu Liou
Supercomputing Research Center, National Chen Kung University, 1 University Road, Tainan, 70101, Taiwan

Matthias Dehmer
Institute for Bioinformatics and Translational Research, UMIT, 6060 Hall in Tyrol, Austria

Klaus R. Liedl
Faculty of Chemistry and Pharmacy, Leopold-Franzens-University Innsbruck, 6020 Innsbruck, Austria

Kanthida Kusonmano
Institute for Bioinformatics and Translational Research, UMIT, 6060 Hall in Tyrol, Austria
Faculty of Chemistry and Pharmacy, Leopold-Franzens-University Innsbruck, 6020 Innsbruck, Austria

Michael Netzer and Christian Baumgartner
Institute of Electrical and Biomedical Engineering, UMIT, 6060 Hall in Tyrol, Austria

Armin Graber
Institute for Bioinformatics and Translational Research, UMIT, 6060 Hall in Tyrol, Austria
Novartis Pharmaceuticals Corporation, Oncology Biomarkers and Imaging, One Health Plaza, East Hanover, NJ 07936, USA

Shu-Ying Chen
Department of Computer Science and Information Engineering, National Yunlin University of Science and Technology, 123 University Road, Section 3, Touliu, Yunlin 640, Taiwan

Qihua Tan
Research Unit of Human Genetics, Institute of Clinical Research, University of Southern Denmark, Sdr. Boulevard 29, 5000 Odense C, Denmark
Department of Clinical Genetics, Odense University Hospital, Sdr. Boulevard 29, 5000 Odense C, Denmark
Institute of Public Health, University of Southern Denmark, J. B. Winsløws Vej 9B, 5000 Odense C, Denmark

Mark Burton, Mads Thomassen and Torben A. Kruse
Research Unit of Human Genetics, Institute of Clinical Research, University of Southern Denmark, Sdr. Boulevard 29, 5000 Odense C, Denmark
Department of Clinical Genetics, Odense University Hospital, Sdr. Boulevard 29, 5000 Odense C, Denmark

Naomie Salim
Faculty of Computer Science and Information Systems, Universiti Tecknologi Malaysia, 81310 Skudai, Malaysia

Ali Ahmed
Faculty of Computer Science and Information Systems, Universiti Tecknologi Malaysia, 81310 Skudai, Malaysia
Faculty of Engineering, Karary University, Khartoum 12304, Sudan

Ammar Abdo
Faculty of Computer Science and Information Systems, Universiti Tecknologi Malaysia, 81310 Skudai, Malaysia
Department of Computer Science, Hodeidah University, Hodeidah, Yemen

Yeuntyng Lai, Morihiro Hayashida and Tatsuya Akutsu
Bioinformatics Center, Institute for Chemical Research, Kyoto University, Gokasho, Uji, Kyoto 611-0011, Japan

Marianthi Logotheti
Neuropsychiatric Research Laboratory, Department of Clinical Medicine, Örebro University, 701 82 Örebro, Sweden
Metabolic Engineering and Bioinformatics Program, Institute of Biology, Medicinal Chemistry and Biotechnology, National Hellenic Research Foundation, 48 Vassileos Constantinou Avenue, 11635 Athens, Greece
Laboratory of Biotechnology, School of Chemical Engineering, National Technical University of Athens, 15780 Athens, Greece

Nikolaos Venizelos
Neuropsychiatric Research Laboratory, Department of Clinical Medicine, Örebro University, 701 82 Örebro, Sweden

Olga Papadodima and Aristotelis Chatziioannou
Metabolic Engineering and Bioinformatics Program, Institute of Biology, Medicinal Chemistry and Biotechnology, National Hellenic Research Foundation, 48 Vassileos Constantinou Avenue, 11635 Athens, Greece

Fragiskos Kolisis
Laboratory of Biotechnology, School of Chemical Engineering, National Technical University of Athens, 15780 Athens, Greece

Yoko Ishino
Graduate School of Innovation & Technology Management, Yamaguchi University, 2-16-1 Tokiwadai, Ube, Yamaguchi 755-8611, Japan

Takanori Harada
Graduate School of Biomedical Sciences, Hiroshima University, 1-2-3 Kasumi, Minami-Ku, Hiroshima 734-8551, Japan

Taner Aruk
Scientific and Technological Research Council of Turkey (TUBITAK), 41470 Kocaeli, Turkey

Duran Ustek
Genetics Department, Institute for Experimental Medicine, Istanbul University, 34093 Istanbul, Turkey

Olcay Kursun
Computer Engineering Department, Istanbul University, 34320 Istanbul, Turkey

Zhifa Liu and Heping Zhang
Department of Biostatistics, Yale University School of Public Health, New Haven, CT 06520, USA

Xiaobo Guo
Department of Biostatistics, Yale University School of Public Health, New Haven, CT 06520, USA
Department of Statistical Science, School of Mathematics and Computational Science, Sun Yat-sen University, Guangzhou 510275, China

Yuan Jiang
Department of Statistics, Oregon State University, Corvallis, OR 97331, USA

Ashwin Belle and Kayvan Najarian
Department of Computer Science, Virginia Commonwealth University, Richmond, VA 23284, USA

Mark A. Kon
Department of Mathematics and Statistics, Boston University, Boston, MA 02215, USA

Yurong Luo, Ashwin Belle, Xuguang Qi, Michael Paul Pfaffenberger and Kayvan Najarian
Department of Computer Science, School of Engineering, Virginia Commonwealth University, 401West Main Street, Richmond, VA 23284, USA

Rosalyn H. Hargraves
Department of Electrical and Computer Engineering, School of Engineering, Virginia Commonwealth University, 401West Main Street, Richmond, VA 23284, USA

Ou Bai
Department of Biomedical Engineering, School of Engineering, Virginia Commonwealth University, 401West Main Street, Richmond, VA 23284, USA

Kevin R. Ward
Department of Emergency Medicine and Michigan Critical Injury and Illness Research Center, University of Michigan, Ann Arbor, MI 48109, USA

Hisham Al-Mubaid and Sandeep Gungu
University of Houston-Clear Lake, Houston, TX 77058, USA

Qian Xiang
School of Information Science and Technology, Sun Yat-Sen University, Guangzhou 510275, China

John H. Phan and May D.Wang
Department of Biomedical Engineering, Georgia Institute of Technology and Emory University, 313 Ferst Drive, Atlanta, GA 30332, USA

Andrew N. Young
Department of Pathology and Laboratory Medicine, Emory University School of Medicine, Grady Health System, Grady Memorial Hospital, Atlanta, GA 30303, USA

Bokun Lv and Haining Yuan
Systems Sepsis Team, Soochow University Affiliated Children's Hospital, Suzhou 215003, China
Center for Systems Biology, Soochow University, Suzhou 215006, China

Guang Hu
Center for Systems Biology, Soochow University, Suzhou 215006, China

JianWang and Jie Huang
Systems Sepsis Team, Soochow University Affiliated Children's Hospital, Suzhou 215003, China

Wenying Yan
Suzhou Zhengxing Translational Biomedical Informatics Ltd., Taicang 215400, China

Hoda Mirsafian, Aarti Singh and Phaik Hwan Teo
Institute of Biological Sciences, Faculty of Science, University of Malaya, 50603 Kuala Lumpur, Malaysia

Adiratna Mat Ripen
Allergy and Immunology Research Centre, Institute for Medical Research, Jalan Pahang, Kuala Lumpur, Malaysia

Amir Feisal Merican and Saharuddin Bin Mohamad
Institute of Biological Sciences, Faculty of Science, University of Malaya, 50603 Kuala Lumpur, Malaysia
Crystal, Institute of Biological Sciences, Faculty of Science, University of Malaya, 50603 Kuala Lumpur, Malaysia

Mu-Chun Su and Chun-Yen Cheng
Department of Computer Science & Information Engineering, National Central University, Jhongli 32001, Taiwan

Pa-Chun Wang
General Hospital, Taipei 10656, Taiwan

Zhi-guo E and Lei Wang
China National Rice Research Institute, No. 359, Tiyuchang Road, Hangzhou 310006, China

Ryan Qin
iBioinfo Group, Lexington, MA 02421, USA

Haihong Shen
School of Life Science, Gwangju Institute of Science and Technology, Gwangju 500-712, Republic of Korea

Jianhua Zhou
Nantong University, Nantong 226001, China